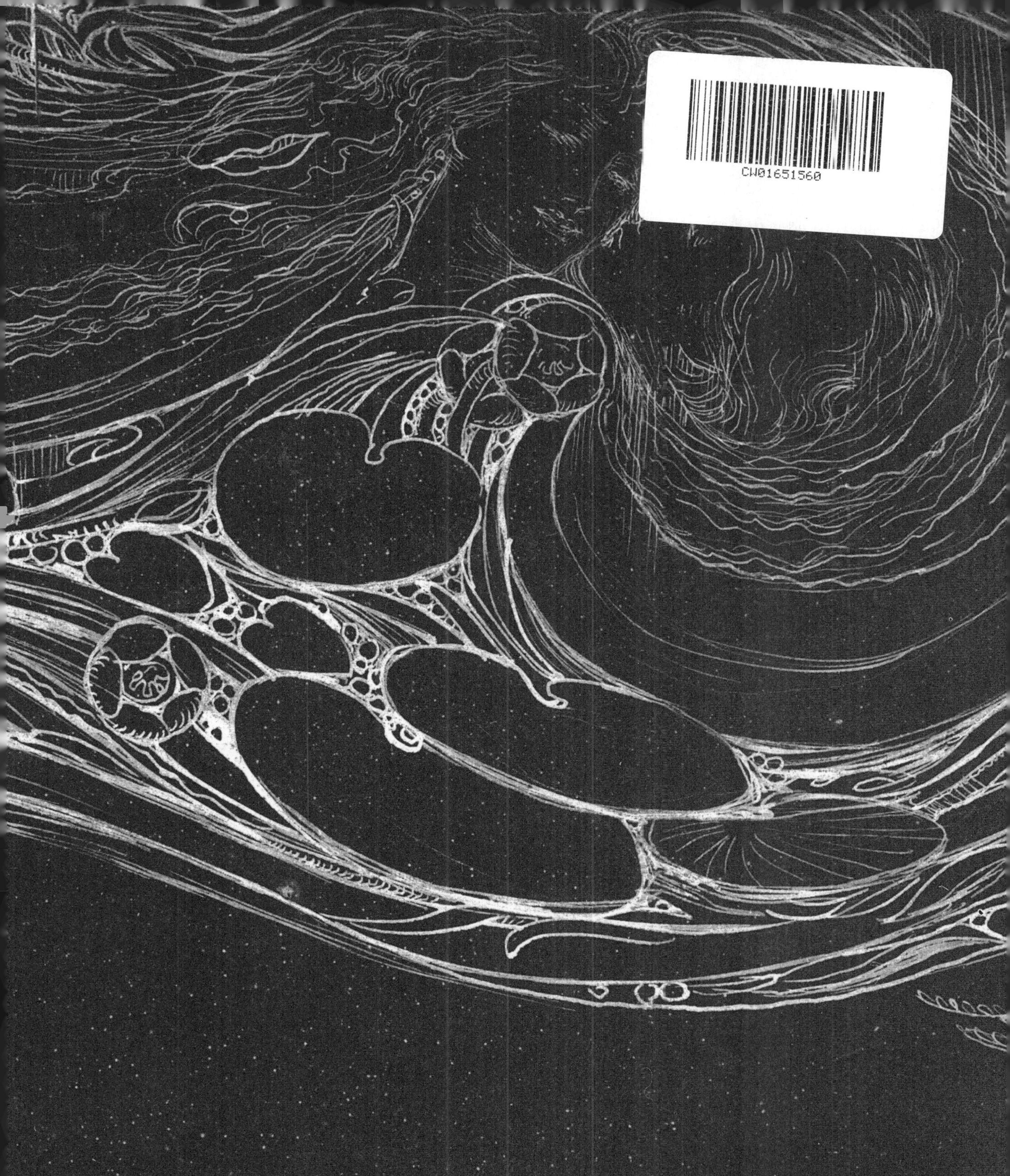

Christina Rossetti

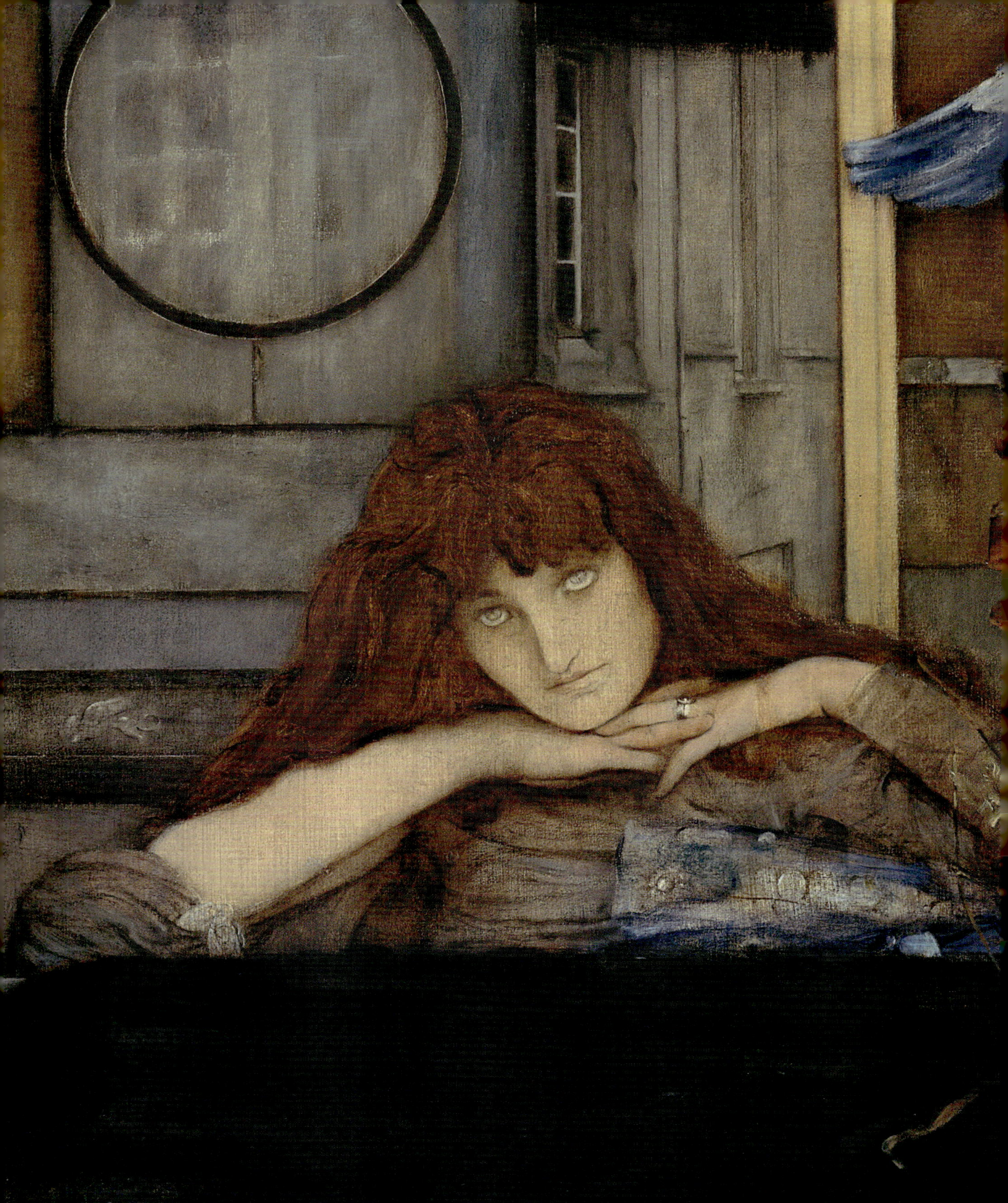

Yale University Press, New Haven and London

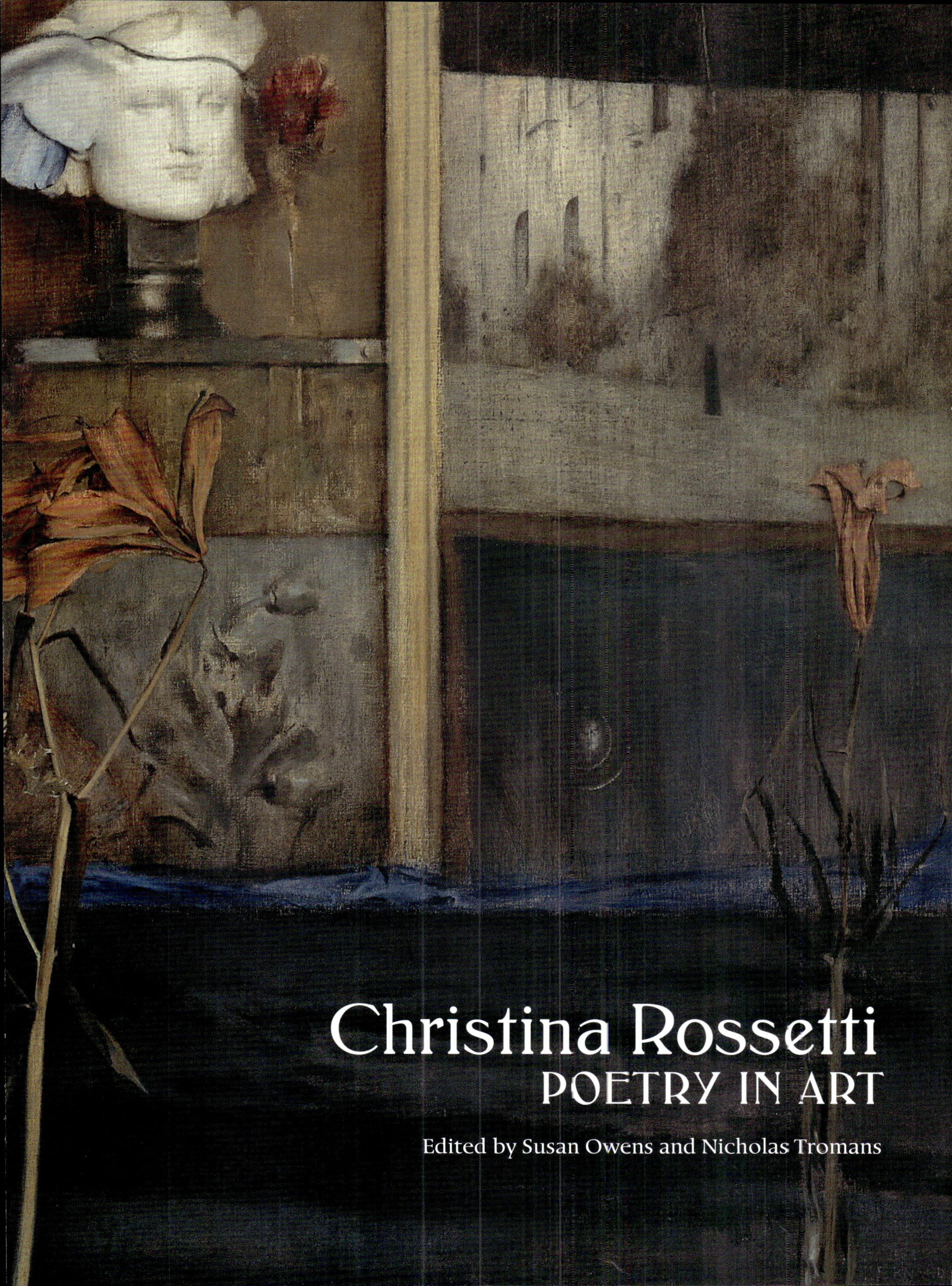

Christina Rossetti
POETRY IN ART

Edited by Susan Owens and Nicholas Tromans

First published by Yale University Press 2018
302 Temple Street, P. O. Box 209040, New Haven, CT 06520-9040
47 Bedford Square, London WC1B 3DP
yalebooks.com | yalebooks.co.uk

ISBN 978-0-300-234862 HB
Library of Congress Control Number: 2018942061

10 9 8 7 6 5 4 3 2 1
2022 2021 2020 2019 2018

Designed by Maggi Smith
Printed in China

MIX
Paper from responsible sources
FSC® C008047
FSC www.fsc.org

Front cover image: John Brett,
Portrait of Christina Rossetti, 1857,
oil on panel, 13.3 × 10.1 cm.
Private collection.

Back cover image: Dante Gabriel Rossetti,
'*"Miss Rossetti can point to work which could not easily be mended" (Times)*', 1862,
pen and wash on paper, 22 × 18 cm.
National Trust (Wightwick Manor).

Frontispiece: Fernand Khnopff,
I Lock My Door Upon Myself (Christina Georgina Rossetti), 1891,
oil on canvas, 72.7 × 141 cm.
Neue Pinakothek, Munich.

Overleaf: Julia Margaret Cameron,
The Minstrel Group, 1866,
albumen print from wet collodion glass negative, 34.5 × 28.5 cm.
Victoria and Albert Museum, London.

Contents

Acknowledgements

We should like to thank the Rossetti experts on whose scholarship we have sought to build, particularly Jan Marsh and Lorraine Janzen Kooistra. Special thanks are due to Stephen Calloway, whose collection has proved indispensable for our research.

The following have been generous with their help and expertise: Joanna Banham, Timothy Barringer, Ruth Brimacombe, Peter Brown, Susanna Brown, Dee Candlin, Briony Carlin, Rachael Chambers, Jane Cohen, Peter Cormack, Rodney Engen, Mark Evans, Peter Funnell, Sarah Grant, James Hamilton, Colin Harrison, Hannah Hawksworth, Ruth Hibbard, Mark Samuels Lasner, Anne Lyden, Cristina Meisner, Sarah Miller, Christopher Newall, Turlough O'Conor, Christiana Payne, Sarah Reynolds, Gill Saunders, Linda Schofield, Kim Sloan, Alison Smith, Angela Thirlwell, Michael Thompson, Simon Toll, Julian Treuherz, Marta Weiss and Catherine Whistler. We are particularly grateful to Tessa Kilgarriff for her painstaking work in researching and sourcing the illustrations for the book, as well as for compiling the Chronology.

We should like to offer our thanks to those at Yale University Press who have worked with us to create this book (Lydia Cooper, Clare Davis, Mark Eastment and Binita Naik); to Phoebe Colley who copy-edited the text; and to Maggi Smith for her elegant design.

Note on the text

All quotations of Rossetti's poetry are taken from *The Complete Poems*, edited by R. W. Crump, with notes and introduction by Betty S. Flowers (London: Penguin, 2005).

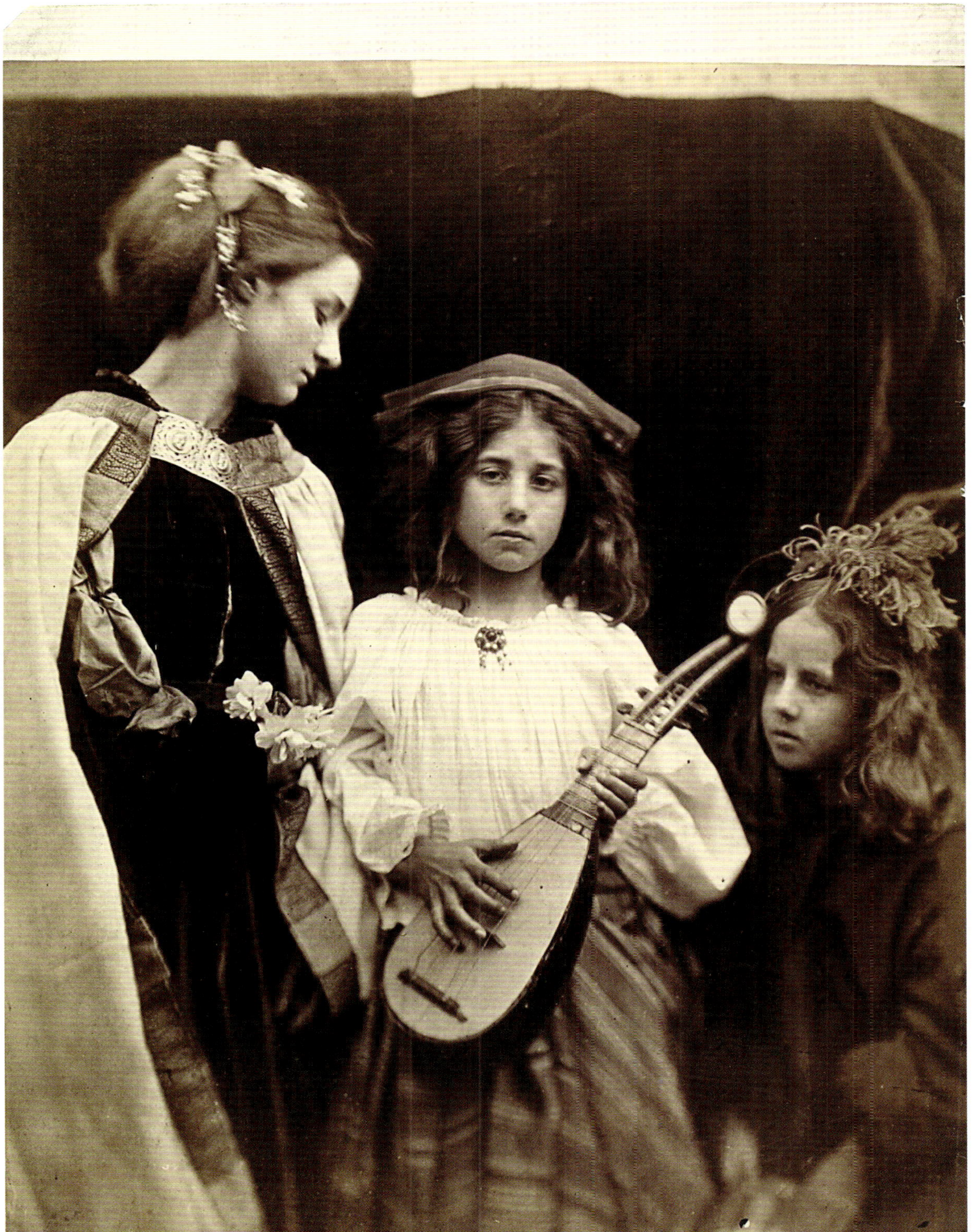
From Life
Study No 1.
Julia Margaret Cameron

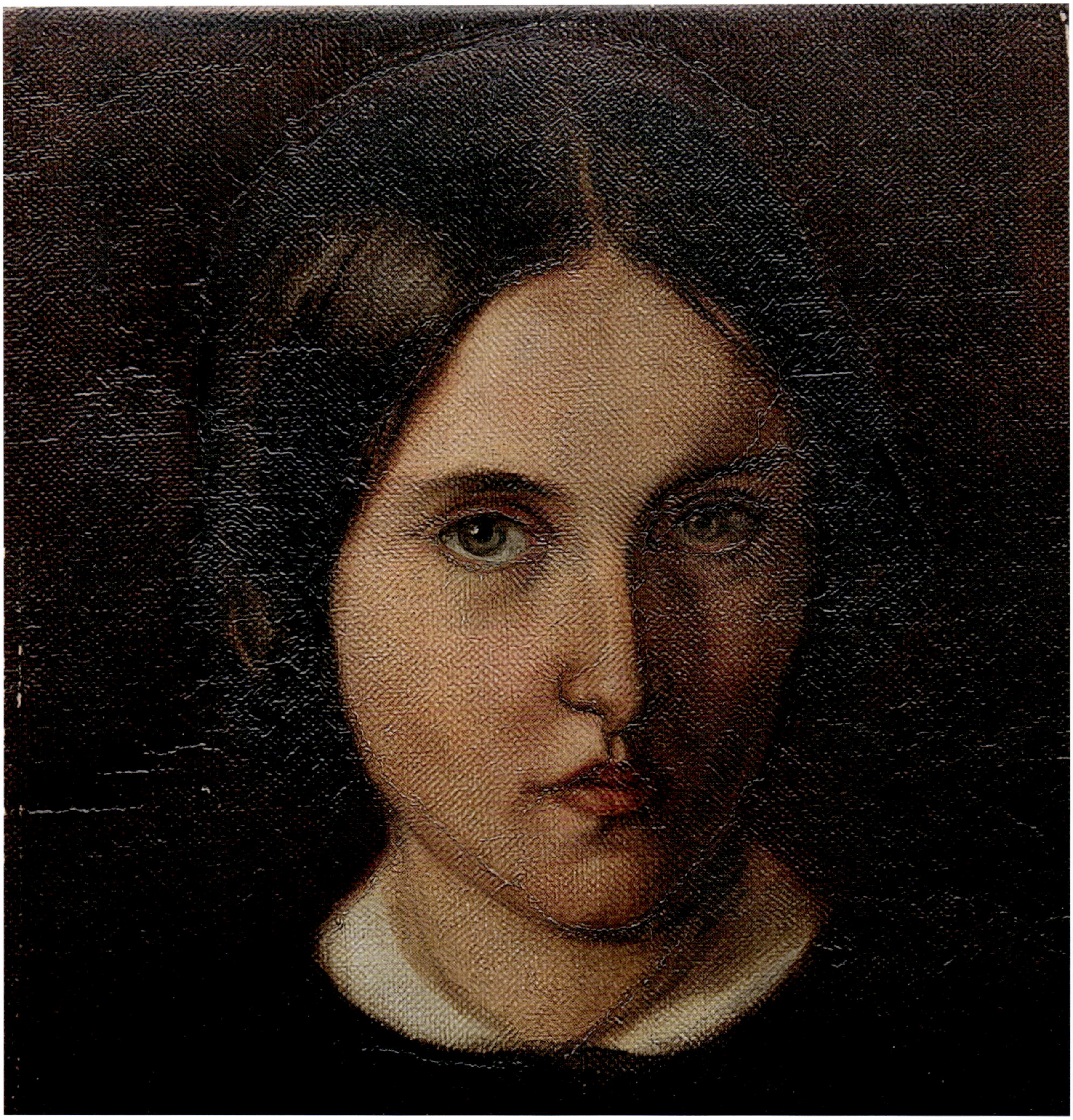

Introduction

SUSAN OWENS AND NICHOLAS TROMANS

CHRISTINA ROSSETTI is among the greatest of Victorian poets. Her colloquial style of address and musical clarity speak directly to us today, while her enigmatic words and striking imagery have inspired – perhaps even haunted – artists since her poetry first began to be published.

Pens and pencils were always at the ready when Rossetti and her three siblings were growing up. Their London home pulsated with art and literature; the children composed poems and stories, drew theatrical scenes and contributed to a family magazine.[1] This creative environment soon bore fruit: when Rossetti was just sixteen her proud maternal grandfather printed a selection of her poetry as a book, *Verses*; her brother Dante Gabriel drew an author portrait for her and sketched illustrations that were bound into one special copy. The following year, she was intimately involved with the ideas and the work of a new artistic avant-garde that challenged conventions and eventually reshaped British art: the Pre-Raphaelite Brotherhood (PRB), founded in 1848, of which her brothers Dante Gabriel and William Michael (figs 0.2 and 0.3) were members. The Pre-Raphaelites, who aimed to bring a new sincerity to art, placed literature at the heart of their movement: many of their subjects were drawn from literary sources, and indeed Gabriel was a poet as well as a painter. When the group drew up a list of their heroes – those they termed the 'Immortals' – it encompassed numerous writers, not only Dante, Chaucer, Spenser and Shakespeare but also recent and contemporary authors including Byron, Wordsworth, Keats, Shelley, Poe, Tennyson, Longfellow, Emerson and Thackeray. Some of Rossetti's early poems were published in the PRB's short-lived journal, *The Germ*. Of the poetry that emerged from within that circle, hers is now recognised as the most powerful.

Rossetti's involvement with the PRB's pictures went beyond expressing a keen interest in their progress and visiting exhibitions in which they were shown: she actively participated in the creation of

0.1 Dante Gabriel Rossetti, *Portrait of Christina Rossetti*, 1848, oil on canvas, 16.5 × 14.6 cm. Private collection.

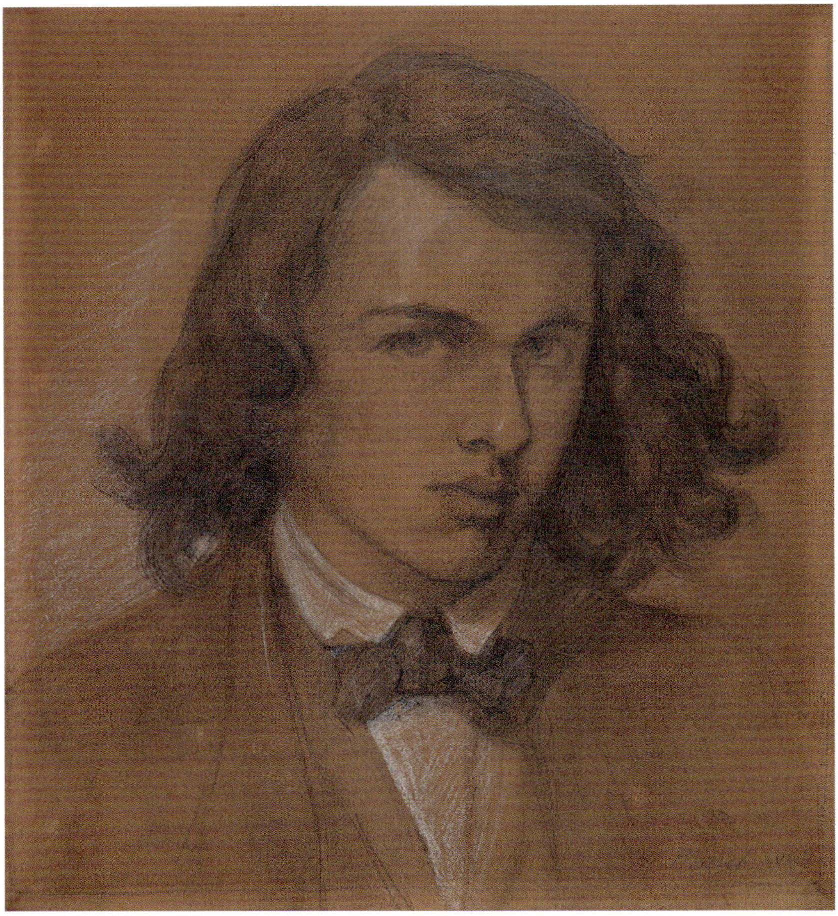

0.2 Dante Gabriel Rossetti,
Self-Portrait, 1847,
pencil and white chalk on paper,
20.7 × 16.8 cm.
National Portrait Gallery, London.

paintings by agreeing to model for members of the Brotherhood. As well as frequently sitting for her portrait (fig. 0.1), she posed for the figure of the Virgin Mary in two of Gabriel's earliest paintings and sat for the face of Christ in William Holman Hunt's painting *The Light of the World*. When Rossetti's work began to be published in periodicals, it was illustrated by John Everett Millais, another central member of the PRB, and by Frederick Sandys, a close associate. Her poetry collections *Goblin Market* and *The Prince's Progress* were published with designs by Gabriel, and her books for children, *Sing-Song* and *Speaking Likenesses*, were illustrated by Arthur Hughes, who had close connections to the PRB. Hughes was among the first artists to paint independent pictures inspired by the arresting imagery of Rossetti's verse and the emotions it evoked. Successive generations of artists were to co-opt her poetry to express their various themes. As a result, her pithy, enigmatic words are woven into many late-nineteenth-century paintings and drawings.

Rossetti even studied art herself. In 1851 and 1852 she attended the North London School of Drawing and Modelling (founded in 1850), where a friend of the Rossettis, Ford Madox Brown, was headmaster.

0.3 Christina Rossetti,
Portrait of William Michael Rossetti,
c.1853, pencil on paper, 17.9 × 12.8 cm.
The Cleveland Museum of Art,
Purchase from the J. H. Wade Fund.

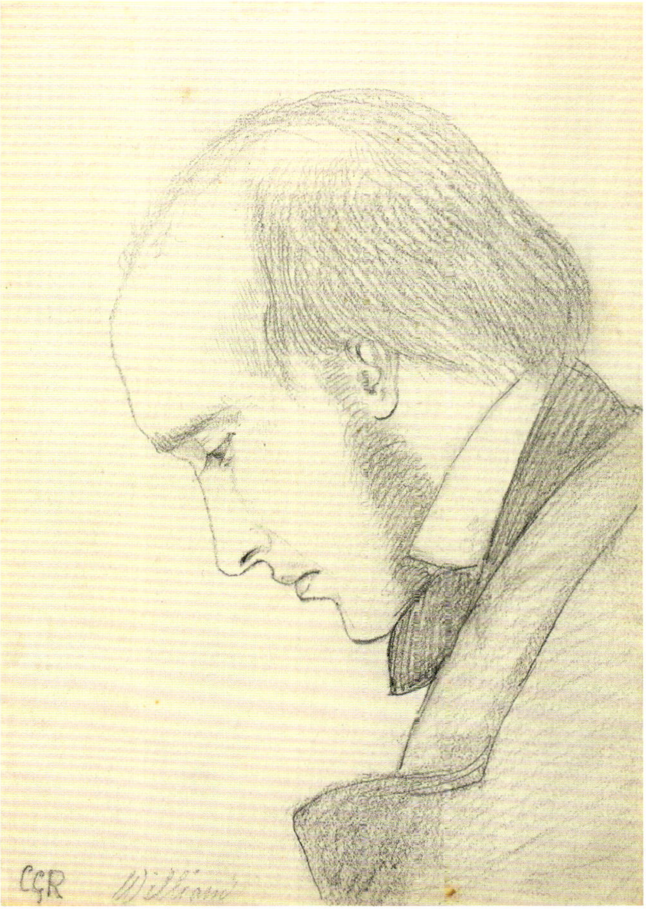

It was set up with the aim of training artisans, or 'art-workmen' as they were called, in the principles of design, and admitted women expressly in order to equip them with 'the means of obtaining an independent income'.[2] We can assume that Rossetti's aim in taking this step was to become sufficiently proficient to teach drawing, presumably at the day school she and her mother had opened in Arlington Street, near Camden Town, in 1851. Her attendance over a relatively long period – interrupted by her move to Frome, Somerset in 1853 to set up another small school – indicates a considerable degree of dedication to her craft, which certainly went a good way beyond that required by the sort of amateur drawing and watercolour painting her wealthier friends would have enjoyed. Another family friend, William Bell Scott – principal of the government school of design in Newcastle upon Tyne – was unimpressed by the standard of tuition at the North London School, recording how one day he visited the school and 'found Christina Rossetti among the pupils, who were all drawing ... wood-shavings picked up from a joiner's yard'.[3] An image of a class published in the *Illustrated London News* of January 1852, however, shows more varied objects for study. Plaster casts of classical sculpture, including a horse's head from the Elgin Marbles, stand on shelves alongside vases and urns, and bas-reliefs and examples of ornament hang on the walls (fig. 0.4). A teacher at a blackboard lectures on the principles determining the design of a gothic window. Above him, pinned-up plates from a textbook show the basic geometric shapes that govern more complex compositions, while to his left are three-dimensional models of these forms.[4] Rossetti, sitting among the other women on the balcony with her drawing-board on her knee, would have learned to copy these models as accurately as possible, beginning with the simplest of the examples and working up to more complex casts.

In Frome, although no longer able to carry on her tuition, Rossetti continued to practise diligently, asking William to buy paintbrushes and post them to her from London, and enthusiastically drawing portraits of her friends, her mother and her brothers. There is little evidence, however, that she continued drawing from observation with the same degree of dedication after her return to London in 1854 upon the abandonment of the day-school project. Instead, when she took up her pencils and watercolour brushes, she began increasingly to look inwards, consulting her imagination and making numerous small-scale emblematic drawings on manuscripts and in printed copies of her own works and those of others – even using the back of a calling card (fig. 0.5). These were created not with the thought of publication ('they are merely my own scratches and I cannot draw', she once hastily explained to a publisher), but for pleasure and for the interest of adding another dimension to a literary text.[5]

The artistic and literary wealth of Rossetti's family background; her involvement with the Pre-Raphaelite enterprise; her experience of her poetry being illustrated and of oil paintings being based on her words; her own art training and her long-standing practice of embellishing texts with images – all these factors combined to shape a creative life in which literature was the warp and visual art the weft.

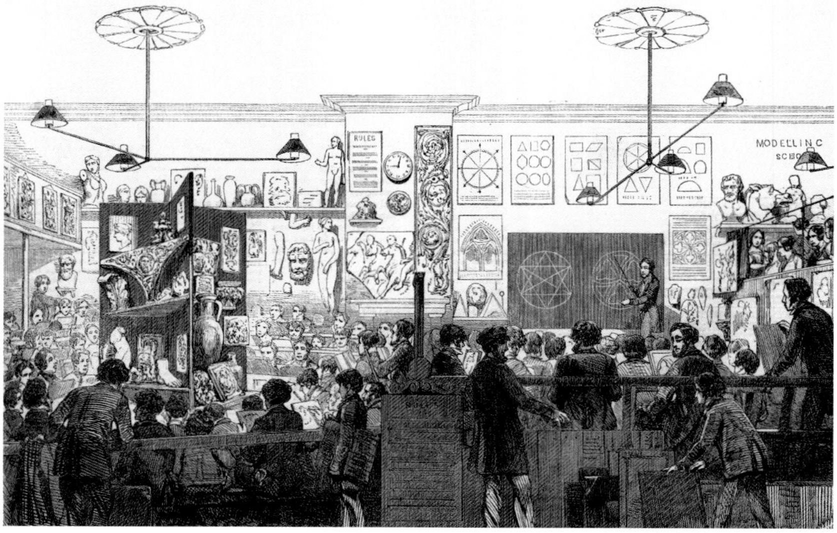

0.4 Anonymous engraver, *The North London School of Drawing and Modelling*, Camden Town, *Illustrated London News*, 17 January 1852, wood engraving.

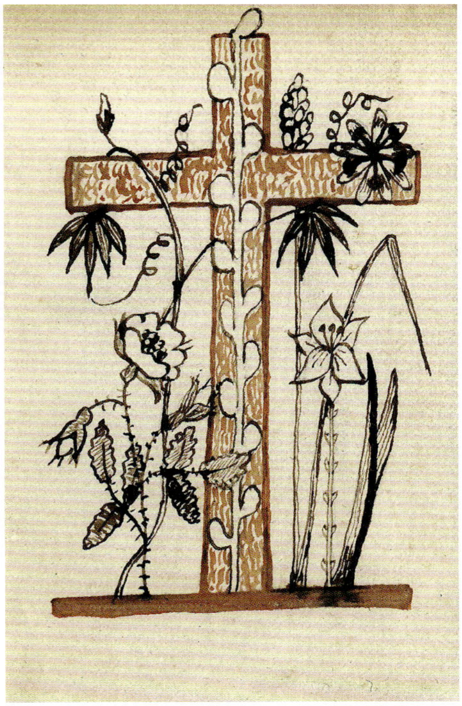

0.5 Christina Rossetti, *Cross and flowers drawn on the back of a calling card*, 1875, ink and watercolour on paper, 9.1 × 6.3 cm. Mark Samuels Lasner Collection, University of Delaware Library.

And yet Rossetti's attitude to visual art was not straightforward: she was aware of its limitations. The alteration in her approach to drawing when she was in her early twenties, a move away from observation and towards an imaginative inner vision, indicated a more general shift in attitude – or, perhaps, revealed a pre-existing attitude that her more comfortable circumstances, which no longer required her to teach children, allowed her to express. As a mature woman she valued intellectual depth and symbolism in art, and was critical of paintings that lacked these qualities. The role that visual art played in her later life is illustrated by the way she lived. While Gabriel filled Tudor House in Chelsea, his home for the last twenty years of his life, with an eclectic and ever-growing collection of paintings and other works of art, Christina's rooms were decorated very simply. The pictures on her walls – mostly family portraits – were those to which she responded emotionally, and which, to her, had profound meaning beyond their beauty. Her niece recalled that the 'few beautiful objects' she owned had been given to her by her brothers. Visiting Aunt Christina, one was more likely to be shown a preserved sea-mouse – a curiosity given to her by her great friend Charles Cayley – than a precious work of art.[6] Her creativity, we can infer, did not depend on a rich visual environment to flourish. Nor did it require a great deal of communion with nature – until she was in her mid-forties she could still claim never to have seen the dawn.[7] She was no Romantic. But then neither did she conform to the principles of Pre-Raphaelitism in any straightforward way. Although the extraordinary clarity of her images – a heart like a singing bird, water like a stone – lodges them firmly in our minds, these word-pictures have nothing to do with the central Pre-Raphaelite tenet of attention to the detail of natural form. Millais and Hunt might impress us with the hyper-realism of their landscapes, but when Rossetti evokes the natural world, it is in a symbolic way. She doesn't care about the species of singing bird – that would be beside the point. Her literary images are emblematic, in the same way as her illustrative drawings. In her poetry we get a sense of the visual world having been sifted and distilled for its symbolic value; it is the emotional resonance of her resulting imagery that creates such a powerful response in her readers' minds.

This book addresses the wide visual context of Rossetti's life and poetry – her complicated attitude to pictures (Chapter One); her evolving appearance in portraits and in Pre-Raphaelite compositions (Chapter Two); her own emblematic drawings (Chapter Three); the illustrators who mediated her verses (Chapter Four); and the wealth of independent pictures inspired by her poems (Chapter Five). In exploring Christina Rossetti through the prism of the visual arts, this book offers a new perspective on a poet whose intense vision continues to captivate us today.

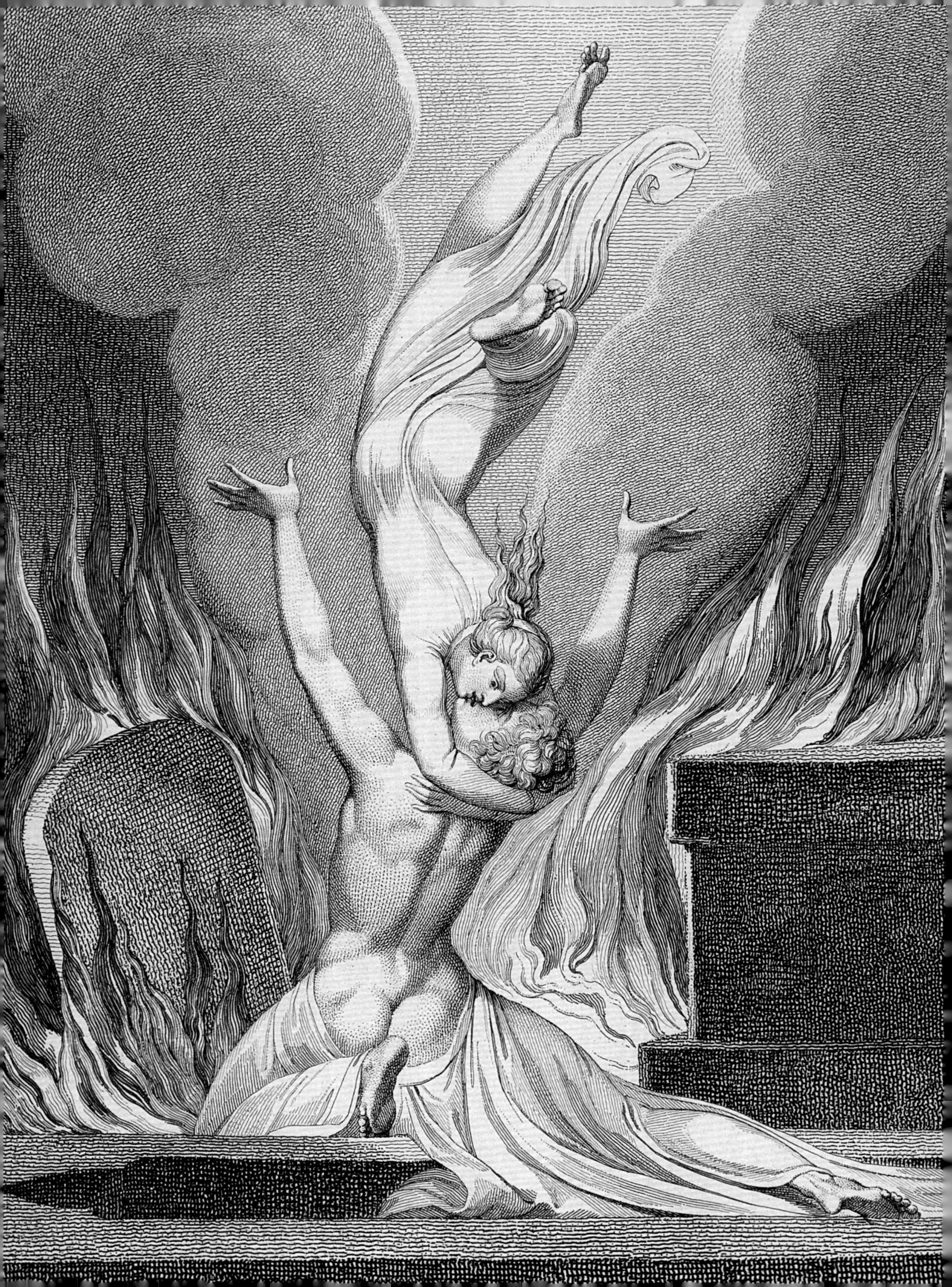

Pictures and prose and verse
Compose me

1 Christina Rossetti's Pictures

NICHOLAS TROMANS

THE HOUSE in which Christina Rossetti lived from 1876, and in which she died in 1894, still stands in Bloomsbury in central London. With its elaborate plaque commemorating the poet's residence, 30 Torrington Square is now a scruffily picturesque anomaly, its terrace a marooned Georgian survivor surrounded by various unlovely components of the University of London. The church where Rossetti worshipped, Christ Church, a few feet away on Woburn Square, was demolished in the 1970s, rendering homeless Edward Burne-Jones's painted memorial to the poet, completed by his faithful assistant T. M. Rooke in 1898 (figs 1.1 and 1.2).[1] Rather satisfyingly, however, in the context of this book's interest in pictures and their relationships to texts, almost next door to the poet's house now stands the Warburg Institute, headquarters of a recondite scholarly tradition of using images to interpret intellectual history.

Rossetti's first full-scale biographer Mackenzie Bell remembered her last home as plain and soot-encrusted, its standard architectural features 'inevitable', and the locale in general 'depressing'.[2] Bell says he felt the building, once entered, mysteriously captured the character of its famous inhabitant. Like her own best work, he wrote, it contained 'a quietude, a controlled and well-ordered sadness'. There was no dedicated library or study, and such books as there were did not dominate any of the interiors. Attributing any of the contents of the house as it was arranged during Rossetti's later years to the poet herself is not straightforward. She shared the house with her mother and her mother's two sisters, Charlotte and Eliza Polidori. Upon her mother's death in 1886, Christina inherited family portraits and other things bequeathed by her brother, the painter-poet Dante Gabriel Rossetti (known to the family as Gabriel). Her aunts died in 1890 and 1893, leaving her eventually, briefly, alone as custodian of what was in effect the family shrine. Following Christina's own death, her only surviving sibling, William Michael Rossetti, succeeded her in that role,

Detail of fig. 1.14

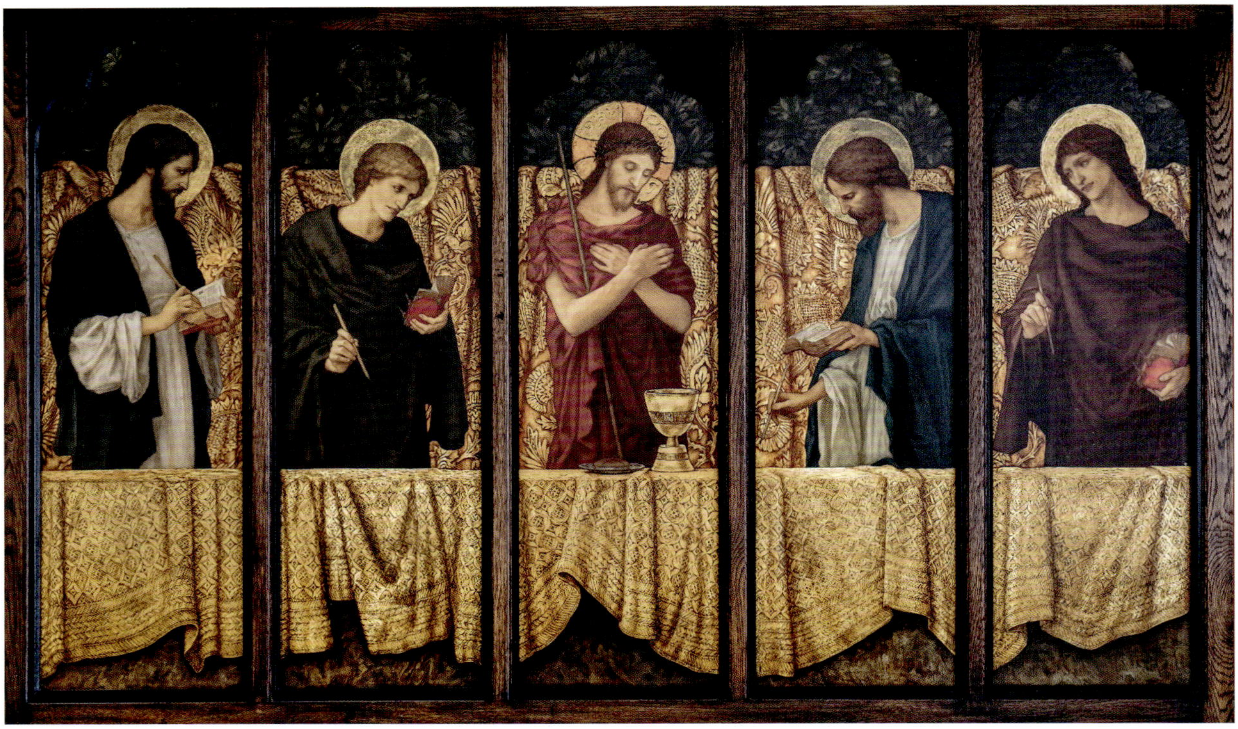

1.1 Above:
Thomas Matthews Rooke after a design by Edward Burne-Jones, *Memorial to Christina Rossetti*, 1897–8, oil on five panels, 116 × 196.4 cm. On loan to All Saints Church, Margaret Street, London.

1.2 Right:
Edward Burne-Jones, *Design for a Memorial to Christina Rossetti*, 1897, chalk and watercolour on paper, 33 × 49.5 cm. Private collection.

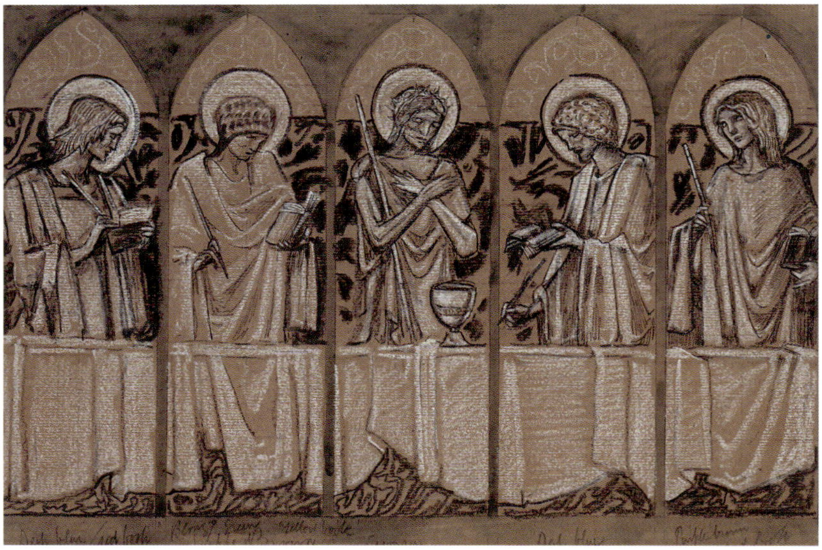

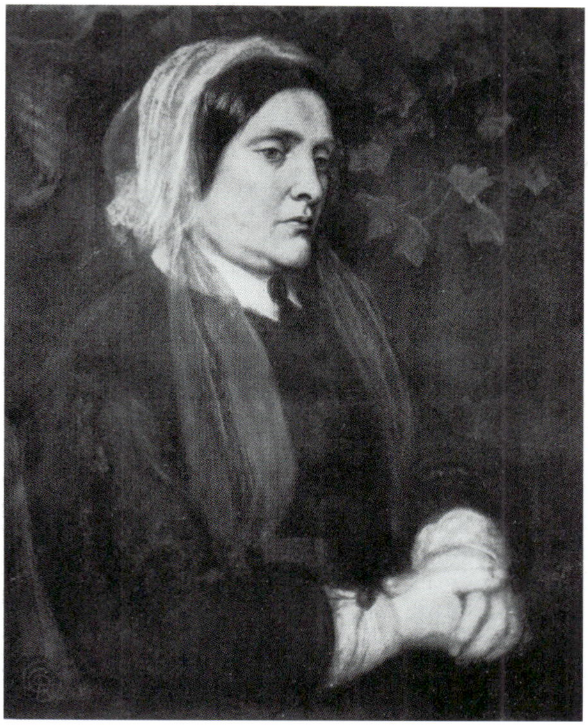 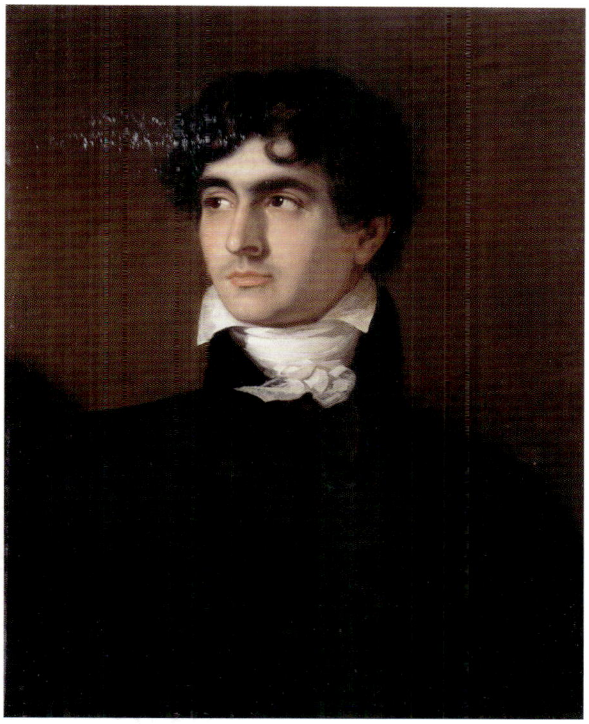

1.3 Above left:
Dante Gabriel Rossetti,
Portrait of Frances Rossetti, 1866,
oil on canvas, 187.2 × 161.3 cm.
Untraced, reproduced in *The Family Letters of Christina Georgina Rossetti*, ed. William Michael Rossetti (London: Brown, Langham & Co., 1900).
British Library, London.

1.4 Above right:
F. G. Gainsford,
John William Polidori, *c.*1816,
oil on canvas, 58.4 × 48 cm.
National Portrait Gallery, London.

becoming an industrious memorialist to his famous sister and brother, conscientiously sifting the family archives to feed a growing public fascination with this abundantly romantic Anglo-Italian Victorian clan.

In his 1898 biography, Bell takes the reader on a tour of the Torrington Square house as it was around the time of Rossetti's last years there.[3] The main sitting room, relatively cheerful and looking out over the square, was dominated by family portraits. In pride of place over the mantelpiece was Gabriel's portrait in oils of their mother (fig. 1.3), flanked by portraits of the artist himself and of William. Alongside these was the likeness of John Polidori (fig. 1.4): Byron's travelling physician, the Romantic reanimator of the vampire myth and brother to the elderly Polidori ladies (although his suicide as early as 1821 meant that neither Christina nor Gabriel had known him). Opposite, across the room, was Gabriel's magnificent large chalk portrait of Christina of 1866 (fig. 2.25). On the wall facing the window were photographs of his *Hamlet and Ophelia* and *Cassandra*, and between these a cheap reproduction of *The Good Shepherd* by Frederic Shields (fig. 1.5). Bell explains that Rossetti's couch was usually so placed that this print was in clear sight and that she held the image in high regard, telling him that 'That is the only representation of the subject I ever saw which brings to my mind at all adequately my conception of it'. She also told Bell, 'You see he does not treat sacred themes merely as an artist; they are part of his life'.[4] These phrases suggest a sensibility not easily charmed by pictures, certainly not ones showing Christian subjects. Being 'merely' an artist was not enough to succeed in making something meaningful, and Rossetti evidently held strong mental images of her own from which a departure might disappoint. Shields was a painter and designer from a working-class northern background, an admirer of Dante Gabriel Rossetti and of the Pre-Raphaelite mentor Ford Madox Brown, and one of the leading Victorian devotees of William Blake, who had died in 1827. His weird composites of Pre-Raphaelitism with a blousy late Baroque manner have not been greatly appreciated since his lifetime, any more than has his devout personality, which endeared him to the profoundly Christian poet. *The Good Shepherd* of which Rossetti was so fond showed Christ 'in His symbolical character, as a stately, tall, and handsome man' with his flock pressed close around.[5] This was not the sort of quasi-realistic image of Christ, to the pursuit of which many Victorian artists, including the Pre-Raphaelite William Holman Hunt, devoted so much effort: it was rather a conceptual or emblematic interpretation.

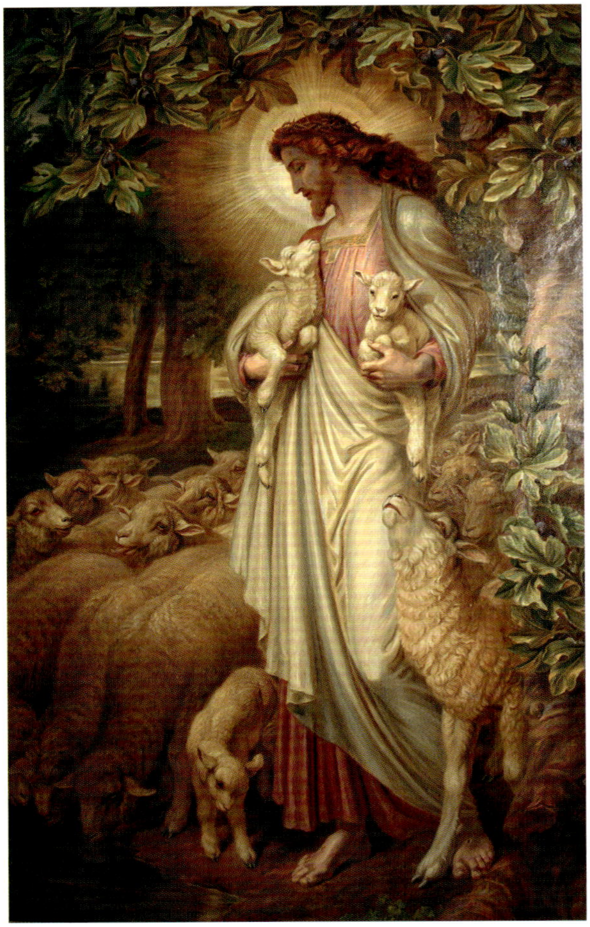

1.5 Frederic Shields, *The Good Shepherd*, undated, oil on canvas, 164 × 106 cm. Manchester Art Gallery.

The list of the contents of 30 Torrington Square – drawn up for probate following Rossetti's death – and William Michael Rossetti's later cataloguing of the family collections show that Christina owned many further modest works of art.[6] There were numerous portraits of the poet herself, including an early oil by her former fiancé James Collinson (fig. 2.9). Among the portraits by Gabriel were 'A very exact likeness of her at the age of thirty-four' (fig. 1.6) and the two imposing chalk drawings made by him when convalescing on the Kent coast in 1877 (figs 2.27 and 2.28). There were more portraits of the rest of the family, including a red chalk of Gabriel made by Christina herself in around 1850: now untraced, this was evidently part of her own efforts to add to the Rossetti family iconography.[7] There were gifts from artist friends including Barbara Bodichon, Alice Boyd and the still-life specialist Mary Harrison. Finally, there was a cluster of animal images, gifts that recognised the writer's penchant for anthropomorphic humour and weakness for furry creatures, such as an oil sketch of a rabbit warren by William Bell Scott and a tinted drawing of crocodiles by Ernest Griset. The latter was given by Gabriel in response to Christina's 1855 poem 'My Dream', describing a vision of a crocodile who, having eaten the other members of his bask, becomes remorseful at the approach of a 'wingèd vessel', 'white ... as an avenging ghost'.[8] The Christina Rossetti collection, if we should call it that, was largely created in a passive mode: others decided what would suit the walls of her home, and much that was listed as hers at the time of her death had only been so since her mother's belongings

1.6 Dante Gabriel Rossetti,
Portrait of Christina Rossetti,
20 May 1865,
pencil on paper.
Untraced.

'A very exact likeness of her at the age of thirty-four', reproduced in William Michael Rossetti, *Præraphaelite Diaries and Letters* (London: Hurst and Blackett, 1900). British Library, London.

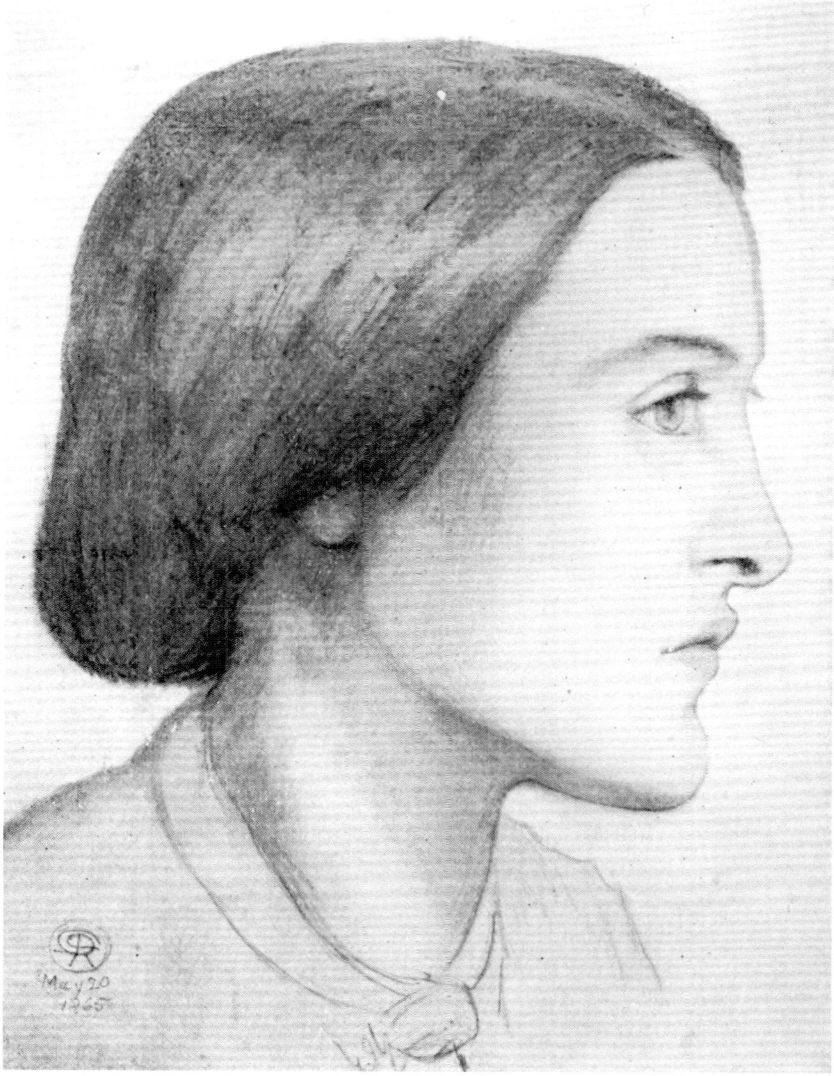

passed to her just eight years earlier. Her notorious determination to stamp upon pride wherever she found it in herself, and her restricted means (until the death of her mother when she herself was aged fifty-five), meant that accumulating valuable artworks was never likely to have been one of her ambitions.[9] But Rossetti certainly took some pleasure in the ways in which her pictures embodied ties to family and friends, to people, times and places she liked to remember. It was, in other words, a perfectly typical Victorian middle-class family collection of art, or at least would have been had the family in question not been the Rossettis. Once taken out of the context of the poet's home, most of her pictures had little value. In 1883, Rossetti sent some of the gifts from her artist friends to the loan exhibition mounted annually at St Jude's Church in Whitechapel for the benefit of East Enders, but they were evidently not eventually selected for display.[10] When the Torrington Square house and its contents were assessed early in 1895, following Rossetti's death in December 1894, all the pictures and drawings in the house were valued together at just £162. William Michael Rossetti queried this and, despite incurring further tax as the poet's legatee as a result, had this figure increased more than threefold.[11]

The problem with pictures

As Mackenzie Bell wrote, Rossetti's last home had grown, before her death, into a memorial to her aura. Seen in the larger context of the arc of her life – the early years of which, at least, were spent in close connection to the leading progressive tendencies within British art – the pictorial content of that house seems ruthlessly edited. Bell promotes the Symbolist notion that 'her inner vision was so keen that she was well-nigh independent of external sources'.[12] We get the sense that Rossetti had to work to reduce the images around her to this state of modesty, just as her poetry describes struggles to suppress, or transform, so much else:

> All others are outside myself;
> I lock my door and bar them out
> The turmoil, tedium, gad-about.
>
> I lock my door upon myself,
> And bar them out; but who shall wall
> Self from myself, most loathed of all?[13]

Renunciation led to the eventual triumph of the spirit, and abandoning the arts specifically might bring blissful rewards, as Rossetti suggested in one of her later devotional prose works, *Letter and Spirit: Notes on the Commandments* (1883):

> True, all our lives long we shall be bound to refrain our soul and keep it low: but what then? For the books we now forbear to read, we shall one day be endued with wisdom and knowledge. For the music we will not listen to, we shall join in the song of the redeemed. For the pictures from which we turn, we shall gaze unabashed on the Beatific Vision.[14]

Beatific vision meant looking directly upon God, something impossible during our earthly existence and unwise to mimic using art for fear of being guilty of idolatry. In another of her meditative prose works, *Seek and Find* (1879), Rossetti equates a Protestant suspicion of images with the Platonic theory of forms:

> [A]n artist may paint a lifelike picture, but he cannot endow it with life like his own; he may carve an admirable statue, but can never

compound a breathing fellow-man. Wise were those ancients who felt that all forms of beauty could be but partial expressions of beauty's very self: and who by clue of what they saw groped after Him they saw not. Beauty essential is the archetype of imparted beauty; Life essential, of imparted life; Goodness essential, of imparted goodness: but such objects, good, living, beautiful, as we now behold, are not that very Goodness, Life, Beauty, which (please God) we shall one day contemplate in beatific vision.[15]

Rossetti consistently implies a frustration with the nineteenth century's literalist theory of art, which so arrogantly claimed to be able to capture the truth about things. Of St Luke, the legendary founder of Christian art, Rossetti imagined that 'As a Painter he exercises self-restraint'.[16] Her sonnet 'In an Artist's Studio', composed in 1856 and usually assumed to relate to Gabriel's infatuation with Elizabeth Siddall, begins 'One face looks out from all his canvasses', and ends 'Not as she is, but as she fills his dream'.[17] Fresh from her 1865 tour of Northern Italy, Switzerland and Germany, reporting to her friend Anne Gilchrist, Rossetti dwelt on the landscapes she had seen: 'I don't say a word about art treasures, the truth being that I far prefer nature treasures'.[18] Yet she later confessed that even the magnificent appearance of the Alps, in full daylight, had saddened her ('Perhaps their sublimity impresses us like want of sympathy'), and that only when seen in a pinky sunset from indoors could she appreciate them.[19] 'I am deficient in the Turner faculty' she laments elsewhere, and suggests that it was dangerous for an artist to go travelling in search of picturesque reality: 'I have heard tell of a painter who sought far and wide for an atmosphere wherein to paint. At last he found an available atmosphere in Italy: and returning thither he worked? ... not so: he died.'[20]

If Rossetti mistrusted art, as understood as recording the visible world, then this surely is connected to the intense, even claustrophobic creative relationship she continued with her brother Gabriel from their childhood, and to her ambiguous membership of the Pre-Raphaelite circle. As early as about 1840, it is said, the sister's words were responded to by the brother's imagery.[21] In 1847, when their maternal grandfather had Christina's first book, *Verses*, privately printed, Gabriel made a series of illustrations to them, not reproduced in the book but surviving in a copy of it. The images come straight from the world of German Romanticism, and the only memorable one illustrates the full-on Gothic of 'The Ruined Cross', which tells of a young woman returning to die beneath a beloved monument of her childhood (fig. 1.7).[22] According to William Michael Rossetti, Gabriel's first completed oil painting was his

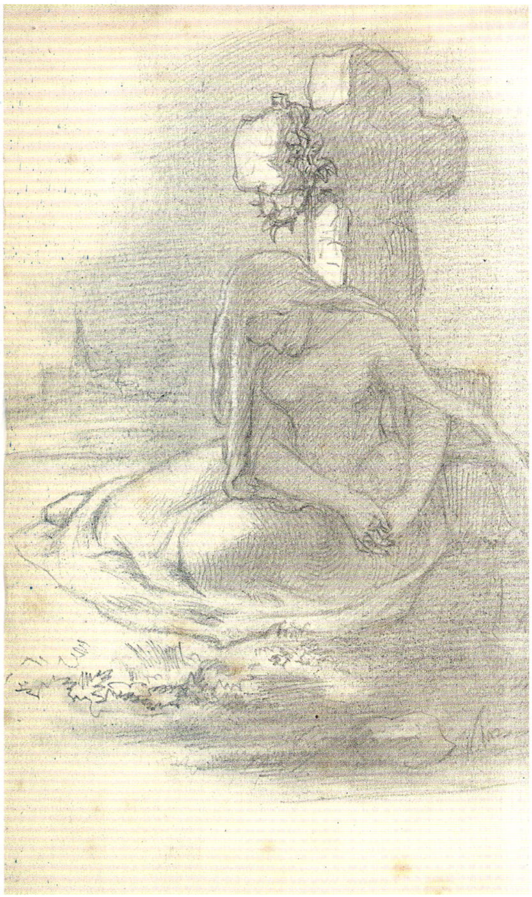

1.7 Dante Gabriel Rossetti, illustration to Christina Rossetti's poem 'The Ruined Cross', 1847, pencil on paper, bound into a copy of *Verses* (1847). Harry Ransom Center, The University of Texas at Austin.

1848 portrait of Christina (fig. 0.1) and his first subject-picture (and first exhibited painting to bear the initials of the Pre-Raphaelite Brotherhood) was *The Girlhood of Mary Virgin* (fig. 2.7) for which Christina was model.[23] The young poet was integral to her brother's identity as an artist, just as his guidance and artistic interpretation became central to her own public career. Jan Marsh, in her biography of Christina, has suggested that the four Rossetti children in some way 'shared out aspects of their father's career'.[24] Gabriele Rossetti was an Italian poet, scholar and political émigré, whose grand ambitions condemned him to the role of heroic failure. Perhaps the overwrought atmosphere of the Rossetti family home required the children in some way to rescue their father from himself, to themselves take up, as Marsh proposes, his unfinished work. Although Christina and Gabriel did not parcel things out over-tidily, both aspiring to be poet-artists to different degrees, we do sense that Christina had grown up assuming her brother to be the one in charge of pictures. Her successive homes accumulated a considerable collection of his portraits of her, and in later years she was as likely to circulate, as her 'authorised' representation, photographs of these as often as copies of the conventional studio *cartes-de-visite* that she also used. Gabriel helped to decide what she looked like (see Chapter Two).[25]

However often Rossetti found reason to object to paintings, she never, it seems, condemned one of her brother's, which were considered excessively sensual or decadent by plenty of others. Indeed she particularly admired some of Gabriel's most voluptuous pictures, especially two featuring his model Alexa Wilding, *Veronica Veronese* (1872) and *A Sea-Spell* (1877), writing of 'their glory of beauty' when shown at the memorial exhibition of his work over the winter of 1882–3.[26] Christina was perfectly able to see that a work such as *Lady Lilith* (fig. 1.8), Gabriel's modernised image of the myth of Eve's vampish alter ego, '*ought* surely to make her admirers recoil', but her tone here is ironic, recognising the impossibility, for herself at least, of rejecting the work of her brother.[27] That even his visual imagination needed to be kept in its place is implied, however, by Gabriel's complaint in a letter to Christina of 1853, when she was herself making a serious study of art, that she would not accept his offer of tuition: 'I am afraid you find art interfere[s] with the legitimate exercise of anguish', he wrote, with more than a hint of frustration.[28]

A Pre-Raphaelite poet?

In April 1849, in a letter to her brother William, Rossetti, again with irony, claims a small favour by rights of 'my double sisterhood', recognising her close attachment to the Pre-Raphaelite Brotherhood, which was established the previous year by her brothers and five friends including John Everett Millais and William Holman Hunt.[29] Her engagement to one of the Brothers, the painter James Collinson, lasted (on and off) from October 1848 to May or June 1850. She also contributed to *The Germ*, the short-lived PRB journal of 1850. Although

1.8 Dante Gabriel Rossetti, *Lady Lilith*, 1866–68, 1872–3, oil on canvas, 96.5 × 85 cm. Delaware Art Museum, Samuel and Mary R. Bancroft Memorial, 1935.

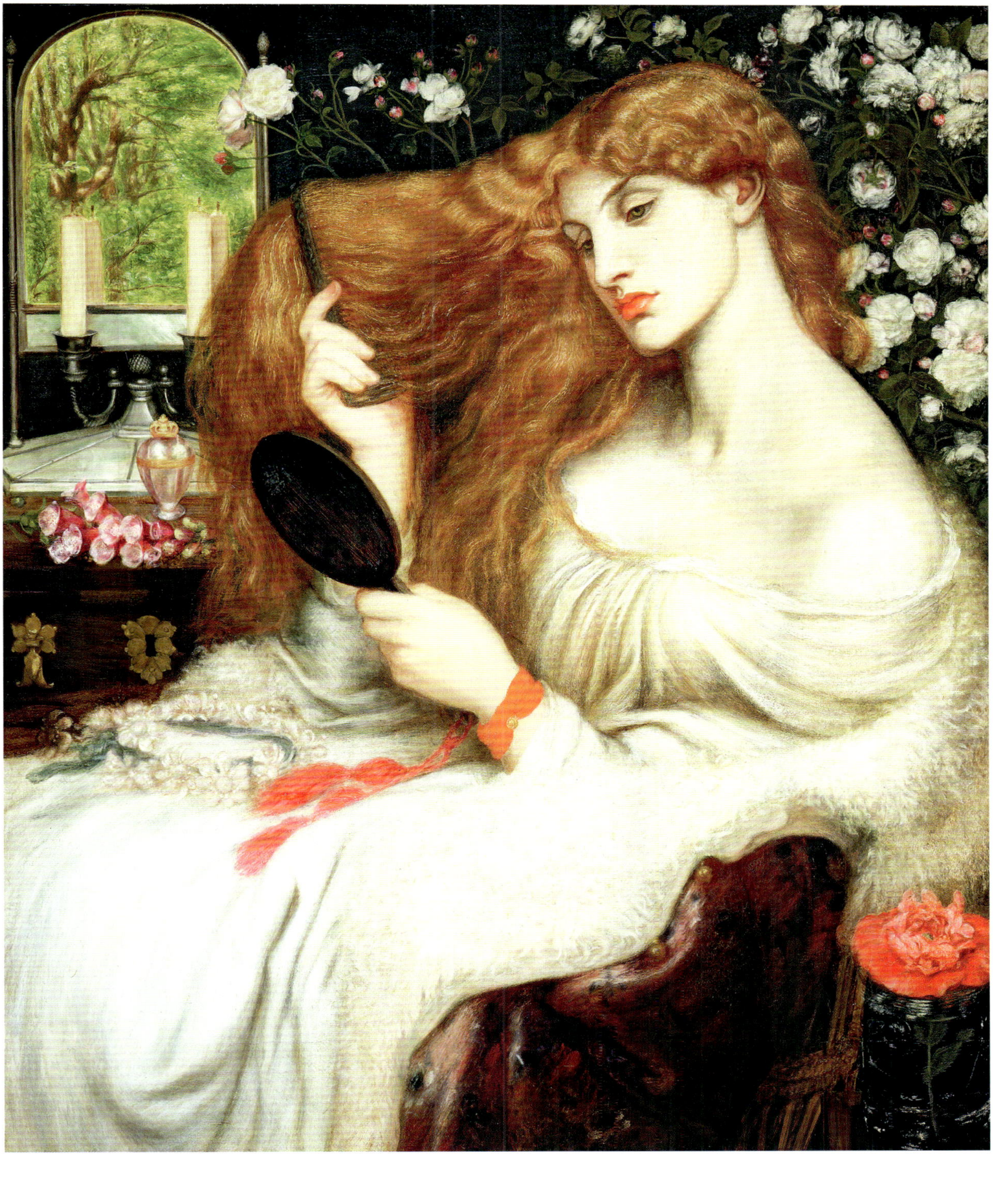

her poems printed there were credited to 'Ellen Alleyn', a pseudonym invented by Gabriel, and although she was just nineteen when the four numbers of *The Germ* appeared, these contributions mark the first publication of a selection of work in which we hear the poet's mature voice. That voice takes seriously the Pre-Raphaelite urge to recover a medieval spirituality, lyrical but severely unworldly. The Pre-Raphaelite aesthetic, as set out in 1848, allowed Christianity a central and yet still precarious place, a paradox personified by the diversity of religious opinion among the Rossetti siblings. Jesus topped the famous PRB 'List of Immortals' (otherwise largely staffed by writers and artists), and yet Dante Gabriel Rossetti introduced that personalised pantheon with the declaration that 'the following list of Immortals constitutes the whole of our Creed, and there exists no other Immortality than what is centred in their names and in the names of their contemporaries'. This was a deliberately outrageous replacing of the afterlife with cultural immortality, an act which, as the literary scholar Isobel Armstrong stresses, the (unconventionally) religious Holman Hunt had to work hard to explain away when writing up his own history of the Brotherhood many years later.[30] If we follow the idea of the Rossetti siblings dividing up their father's intellectual legacy between them, then it seems to have been now, during the first years of the PRB, that the brothers resumed his radical commitments while the sisters continued his scholarly and religious passions. Gabriele Rossetti had renounced his native Catholic identity to become, by the end of his life, a fiercely anticlerical freethinker. His daughters became, respectively, the most distinguished religious poet of the Victorian period, and, in Maria's case, an Anglican nun, then a very novel profession indeed. By 1848–50, Christina Rossetti's Christian poetry already sat uneasily alongside works such as her brother's *The Girlhood of Mary Virgin* and *Ecce Ancilla Domini!* (*The Annunciation*) (figs 2.7 and 2.10), paintings *about* the legends of the Mother of God but scarcely painted *for* her. Compare such earnest lines as these from Christina's 'Sweet Death' in the third number of *The Germ*:

> And youth and beauty die.
> So be it, O my God, Thou God of truth:
> Better than beauty and than youth
> Are Saints and Angels, a glad company;
> And Thou, O Lord, our Rest and Ease,
> Are better far than these.
> Why should we shrink from our full harvest? why
> Prefer to glean with Ruth? [31]

The second number of the journal included Rossetti's 'A Testimony' – a reprise on the opening of Ecclesiastes, 'vanity of vanities; all is vanity'. It appears immediately following an essay by Ford Madox Brown offering advice on how to paint your first picture, in the manner of a 1970s fanzine explaining how to form your own band. It may read now as a pretty straightforward boiling down of modern academic

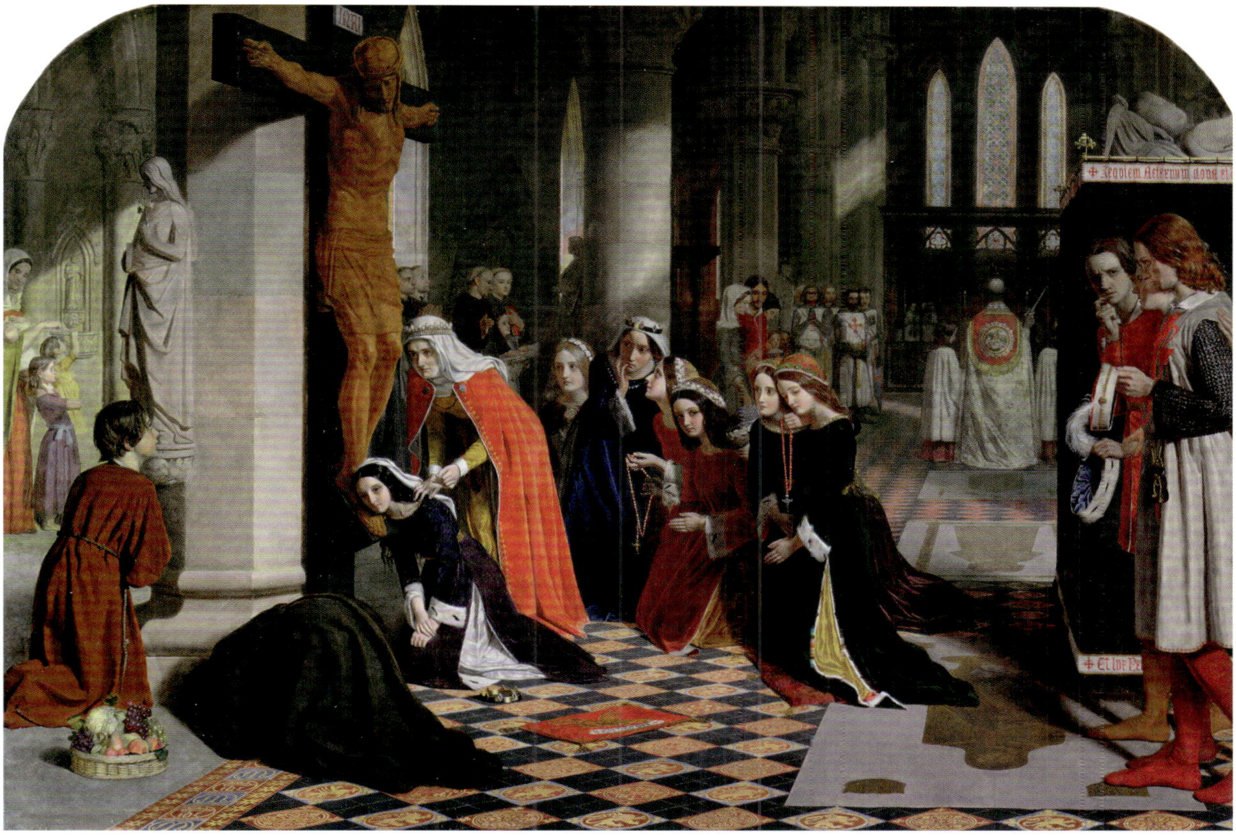

1.9 James Collinson, *An Incident in the Life of Saint Elizabeth of Hungary*, 1850, oil on canvas, 121 × 181.6 cm. Johannesburg Art Gallery.

method, tempered by Brown's impatient bluntness, but Rossetti owned to William that 'Mr Brown's article rather alarms me'.[32] The cause for this reaction was probably Brown's do-it-yourself emphasis, recommending artists to not use professional models but rather to invite 'any friend he may have of an artistic or poetic temperament' to act out the story being represented.[33] This is precisely how the early PRB operated, with Christina of course herself sitting for the Virgin in two of her brother's early paintings. Being made to see herself in this role of clubbable, impromptu actress, personating a holy figure, may have been uncomfortable. Nevertheless, it was not long after this – in 1851 – that Rossetti enrolled for classes at the newly established North London School of Drawing and Modelling in Camden Town, where Brown taught. Although her contact with the master was slight, Brown recalled that 'I had the honour of teaching the poet Christina Rossetti there for a few nights. She bid fair [to] draw as well as her brother had she continued', which is perhaps as flattering to his own capacity as a teacher as it is to Rossetti's innate artistic talent.[34]

Opening the second number of *The Germ* was 'The Child Jesus', a poem by James Collinson with an accompanying etching by the artist showing the infant Christ adored by his fellow children. The poem imagines various prefigurations of the Passion during the youth of Jesus

– such as his painting a cross on a lamb – in the typological mode later to be so ambitiously taken up by Holman Hunt. Collinson and Rossetti clearly stand out among the contributors to *The Germ* as enthusiastic explorers of Christian themes. There was also, as the Romantic history of the PRB has made familiar, a tortured aspect to these explorations, for Collinson had converted to Catholicism only to revert to the Church of England when the first move made him unacceptable to Christina, whom he had asked to marry him. His un-conversion lasted until the apparently low-key engagement was dropped in 1850 – around the time of the demise of *The Germ* – soon after which Collinson returned to the Catholic Church and resigned from the PRB, fearing the Brotherhood risked exposing the saints to ridicule.[35] He proceeded however with his own ambitious and very Pre-Raphaelite scene from the life of the medieval Saint Elizabeth of Hungary, which was exhibited in London in 1851 (fig. 1.9). Collinson clearly intended it as a challenge to the text that is usually identified as its inspiration, Charles Kingsley's 1848 verse drama, *The Saint's Tragedy*. Kingsley, a Christian Socialist and ferocious anti-Catholic, sought to show how Catholic qualifications for sainthood (death), or indeed membership of the clergy (celibacy), were inhuman and could only lead to sin and tragedy. The pious princess Elizabeth refuses to wear her crown in church in the presence of Christ's crown of thorns: this is the subject of Collinson's painting. But her instinctive humility is perverted by the ecclesiastical and aristocratic hierarchy, whose determination to make her into a saint destroys her. Kingsley's Introduction to *The Saint's Tragedy* openly avows the anti-'Romish' and indeed anti-feudal intention of his book, and scorns the recent *Life* of the saint published by the French Catholic writer, the Comte de Montalembert, in which several of the miracles later attributed to Elizabeth are retained.[36] Yet Rossetti transcribed portions of Montalembert's life for her fiancé to help him in his project, and eagerly asked William for news of the progress of the picture after their separation.[37] She also, in 1852, composed a sonnet on the same subject, which imagines Elizabeth more in the Catholic tradition of mystic visionary and martyr than according to Kingsley's characterisation of a good woman crushed by the structures of Romish power. It ends:

> Fair she was as any rose,
>   But more pale than lilies white,
> Her eyes full of deep repose
>   Seemed to see beyond our sight.
> Hush, she is a holy thing:
>   Hush, her soul is in her eyes
>   Seeking far in Paradise
> For her Light, her Love, her King.[38]

What Rossetti made of the finished picture she did not reveal: she would in any case scarcely have assessed it 'merely' as the production of an artist – it was the creation of someone with whom she had been romantically involved and in whose private religious dramas she had shared.

That Rossetti retained a strong sense of identification with the PRB is shown by her applying to it, with a healthy helping of irony, her default themes of failure and demise in a comic obituary-sonnet of November 1853, 'The P.R.B. is in its decadence'. Here she lists the diverging paths of the original Brothers, concluding: 'So rivers merge in the perpetual sea, / So luscious fruit must fall when over ripe, / And so the consummated P.R.B.'[39] Rossetti continued to visit, every so often, the main London exhibitions where the Pre-Raphaelites showed their work. In 1852 she saw the exhibition of the National Institution of Fine Arts at the Portland Gallery on Regent Street, where Collinson's *Saint Elizabeth* had been shown the previous year, and was inspired by a picture she found there to write the poem 'Books in the Running Brook' (originally 'After a Picture in the Portland Gallery').[40] The poem describes someone revelling in the beauties of a spring day in the country ('It is enough') before a darkening of the landscape impresses her with an uneasiness that she realises can only be stilled by entering God's presence. The National Institution offered a space in the capital for artists who were less well connected; in 1852, a remarkably high proportion of these seem to have been Welsh. With few exceptions, the pictures shown there cannot now be traced. One of any number of landscapes exhibited that year might have provided the starting point for Rossetti's poem, and it seems fitting that, on this rare occasion when she apparently took a picture for inspiration, she used one impossible to identify and, in changing her poem's title, hid all trace of the nature of the source. Were there other such cases? David Bentley has suggested that the long narrative poem 'The Prince's Progress' had its germ in a painting by the Liverpool Pre-Raphaelite William Lindsay Windus, *Too Late* (1858).[41] Both share the theme of a suitor arriving to find his beloved respectively dead or dying, but beyond that the association can only be speculative. It is hard to imagine the resolutely independent Rossetti allowing it to be seen that she had borrowed an idea for a major poem from a painting familiar to her friends.

Rossetti was consistently struck by the ambition of Holman Hunt, who had used her face as one ingredient in a disparate range of models for the head of Christ in his *Light of the World* (fig. 2.13: see Chapter Two). But she would surely have had misgivings over his tour to the Holy Land in order to apply Truth to Nature to the scenes of the life of Christ, given her doubts regarding the wisdom of travel for artists, and her preference for a symbolic treatment of Jesus. In 1861, when Hunt's *Finding of the Saviour in the Temple* (fig. 1.10) was causing a sensation, Rossetti visited his studio, reporting afterwards that 'Mr. Hunt's paintings are so high above my puny praise that I may well keep silence concerning them.'[42] As on many other occasions, the writer's ostensible diffidence leaves us feeling that much more, possibly of a less deferential nature, has been left unsaid.

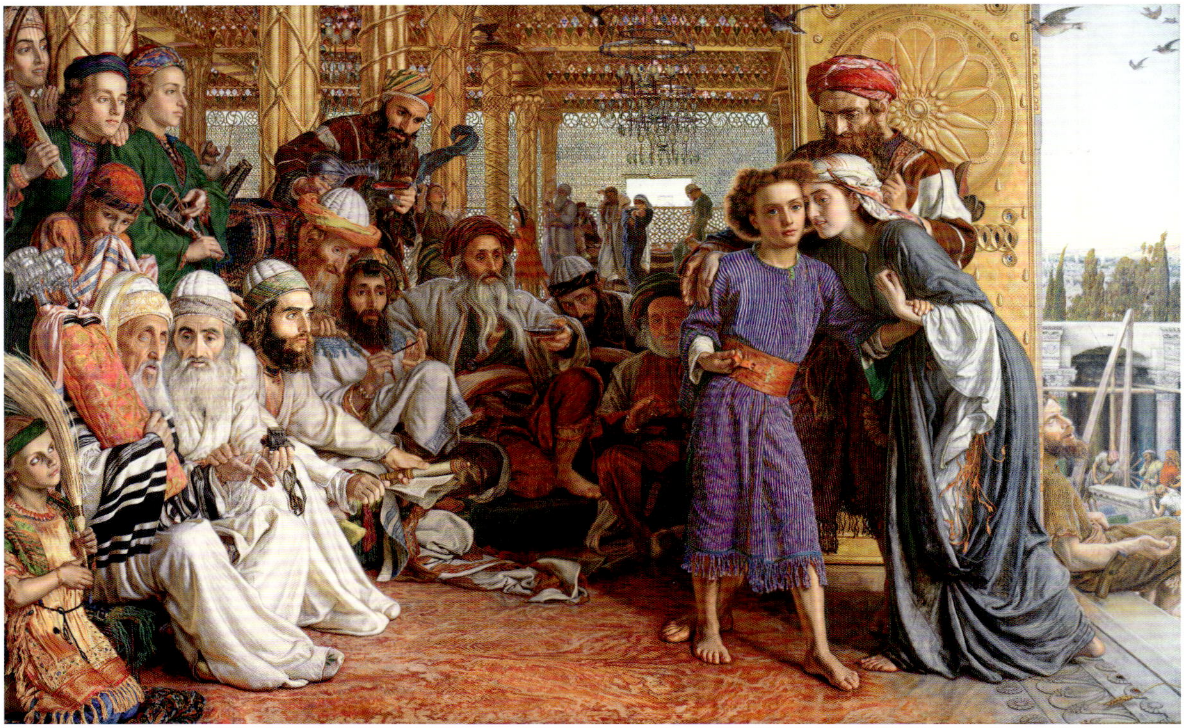

1.10 William Holman Hunt, *The Finding of the Saviour in the Temple*, 1854–60, oil on canvas, 85.7 × 141 cm. Birmingham Museum & Art Gallery.

About Millais, Rossetti was both guarded and, on occasion, critical. His worldly narratives were not to her taste. *The Order of Release* (1853) seems to have offended with its suggestion of a Jacobite rebel's freedom having been bought at the price of his wife's honour; while the objection that a churchgoing woman might take to the theme of a respectable child shown snoozing through *My Second Sermon* (1864) was evident enough.[43] In 1859, Millais became one of Rossetti's early illustrators, with a design to accompany 'Maude Clare', a romantic narrative ballad, in *Once a Week* (see Chapter Four).[44] Looking back on this from our knowledge of the great wealth of later visual interpretations of Rossetti's verse, this image, the literal style of which looks like the kind of thing we would associate with the illustration of, say, Thackeray, seems distant from the poetry.

In outline: Rossetti's pictorial aesthetic

Rossetti came to maturity as a poet as a partner in the Pre-Raphaelite enterprise. Rarely, if ever, has a major poet grown up so deeply embedded in an avant-garde visual culture. Yet she seems actively to have resisted the lure of the world of images, preferring to live and write, as Bell liked to think she did spontaneously, out of her own mind. The works of art – or reproductions of artworks – that she allowed to remain physically with her were, in most cases, present as points of connection to those she loved. She was a poet who had a reputation, not undeserved, for needing to have things arranged in exactly the ways that suited her. She barred the door literally but also metaphorically, not wanting to allow into her imagination the visual images of others. Perhaps she was not so very different in this regard from other poets of her era who were famous enough to face the problem of rival interpretations of their inventions being offered to the public. Tennyson, for example, reacted badly to his illustrators – who had included the leading Pre-Raphaelites – in the 1850s.[45] But it does not seem far-fetched to say that Rossetti especially needed to keep a clear distance between herself and pictures precisely because of the proximity at which she had lived with the Pre-Raphaelites. As suggested above, she actively edited the visual culture around her as one strategy for the preservation of her own imaginative space. Rossetti certainly developed an aversion to much, or even most, of the visual arts – an aversion that we can fairly represent as being partly due to her deeply held religious beliefs. At the same time, certain images were made an exception of and allowed into her imagination; her scruples, and her occasional enthusiasm for a picture, combine to construct something approaching a 'taste'.

First, we should accept that there was much in Rossetti's way of looking that was, after all, Pre-Raphaelite. Many of her contemporaries found echoes between her way of expressing herself and that of the predominantly male painters of her brothers' circle. The critic Edmund Gosse saw in her verses a 'brilliant simplicity' that he compared to an early Italian painting 'in which each saint or angel is robed in a dress of one unbroken colour', while the graphologist John Ingram believed he could trace such a character in her very manuscripts, in which every letter was fully finished 'and all evince quite a pre-Raphaelitishness of execution'.[46] At their beginning, the Pre-Raphaelites had been inspired by the crisp lines of the early Renaissance artists working in fresco and tempera, by the startling clarity of the early Netherlandish and German masters and, importantly, by line engravings after such models. There was also, for Dante Gabriel Rossetti at least, Blake. On these terms, there is an identifiable Pre-Raphaelite preference in Christina. Visiting Longleat, seat of the Marquess of Bath in Wiltshire in 1850, she writes of having particularly admired there 'a certain German favourite of mine' among the pictures (which included her brother's portrait of her in *The Girlhood of Mary Virgin*: fig. 2.7). It seems plausible that this phrase would fit one of the several portraits at Longleat by, or attributed to, Holbein of Henry VIII and some of the leading aristocrats of his reign.[47] With its austere linearity, Holbein's work was a respected art-historical model for the Pre-Raphaelites. Brown in particular adopted him as an exemplar, subtitling one of his own portraits *A Holbein of the Nineteenth Century*.[48] A later portrait by Brown, again with something of the flavour of Holbein, fixed itself in Rossetti's memory. This was the depiction of John Osborne Riches, commercial manager of the Ocean Steam Colliery Company in Cardiff (fig. 1.11). Rossetti saw it at Brown's studio, presumably around 1874 when it was completed, and recalled it years later in a letter to Brown's daughter Lucy, mentioning in particular the diamond ring on the sitter's finger.[49] This detail, with its suggestions of

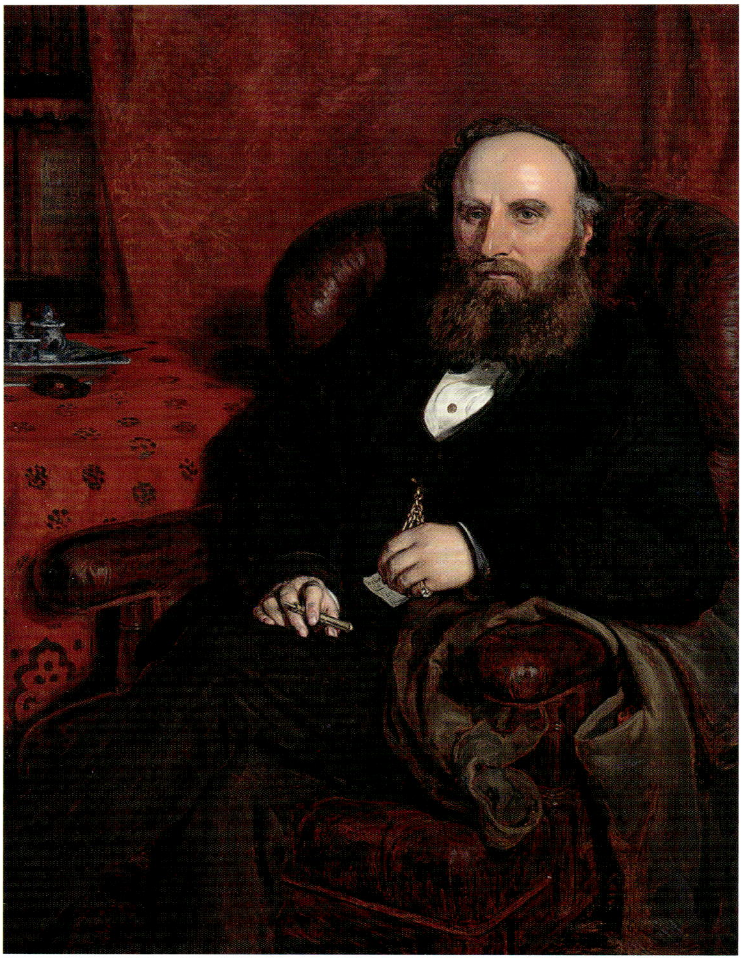

1.11 Ford Madox Brown, *John Osborne Riches*, 1874, oil on canvas, 114 × 89 cm. Private collection.

glamorous ostentation amid a hard-working industrial environment, and of the relationship between diamonds and coal, must have lent this wonderfully bourgeois image a symbolic character in Rossetti's eyes (her poem 'A Diamond or a Coal?' had appeared in *Sing-Song* in 1872).

An even stronger connection to a picture was alleged by William Michael Rossetti to have existed in the case of a once well-known German painting, *Christmas Eve*, showing the Christ Child being brought to earth through the darkness by a trio of angels (fig. 1.12). The first angel, holding Jesus who is playfully brandishing his martyr's palm, is shown cheerfully completing her task; but her two following colleagues, holding a cross and a crown of thorns, contemplate the terrible suffering that will be part of his incarnation. Heinrich Maria von Hess, based in Munich, was associated with the Nazarene group of Catholic German painters. On a print after the painting in the British Museum, William wrote: 'My Sister takes this Picture for part of the subject of her Poem called Christmas Eve', which first appeared as the entry for 24 December in *Time Flies: A Reading Diary* in 1885:

1.12 Gottlieb Bodmer after Heinrich Maria von Hess, *Die Christnacht*, *c.*1829, lithograph, 16.9 × 21 cm. British Museum, London.

William Michael Rossetti's annotation reads 'My Sister takes this Picture for part of the subject of her Poem called Christmas Eve.'

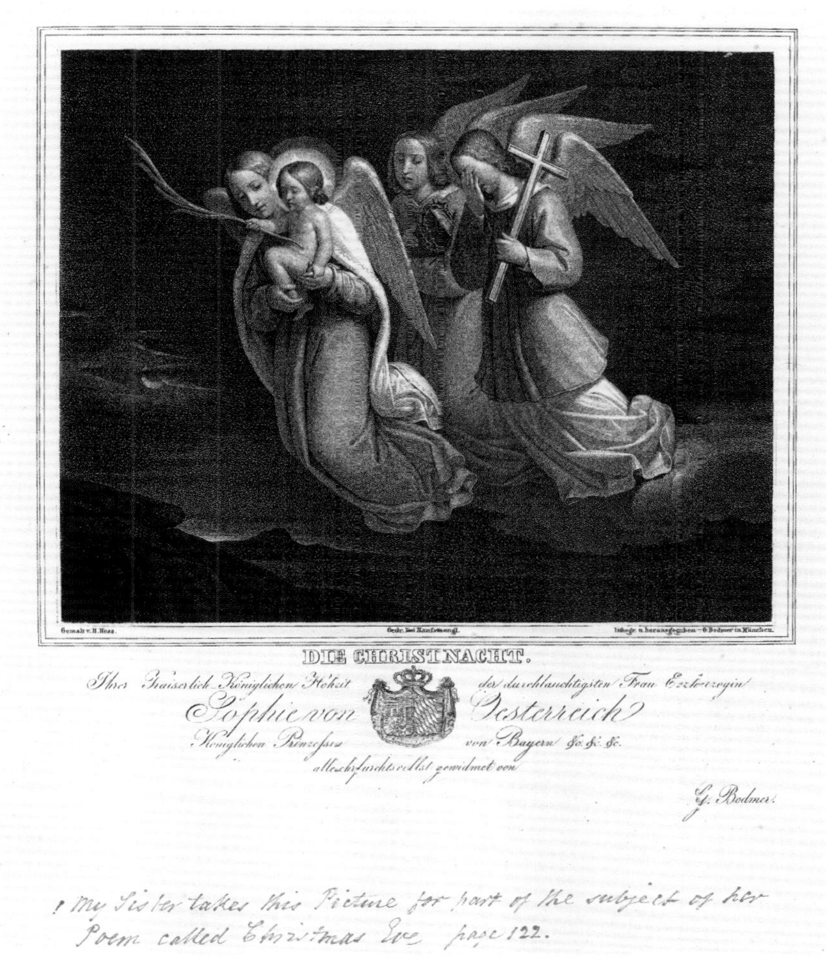

Christmas hath a darkness
   Brighter than the blazing noon
Christmas hath a chillness
   Warmer than the heat of June,
Christmas hath a beauty
   Lovelier than the world can show:
For Christmas bringeth Jesus,
   Brought for us so low.

Earth, strike up your music,
   Birds that sing and bells that ring;
Heaven hath answering music
   For all Angels soon to sing:
Earth, put on your whitest
   Bridal robe of spotless snow:
For Christmas bringeth Jesus,
   Brought for us so low.

The awkward grammar of William's inscription confesses the ambiguity of the relationship: did Christina really 'take' the poem from the image? If so she has hardly been a plagiarist, for none of the details are copied. Or did she rather find in this allegorical image the emotional ambiguity of hurt and joy that her lines evoke?[50] This emblematic Christian picture, expressed in the print almost sculpturally in black and white, has close affinities with another engraving that prompted Rossetti's single most enthusiastic recorded response to any kind of picture (fig. 1.14). In *Time Flies* she wrote: 'There is a design by William Blake symbolic of the Resurrection. In it I behold the descending soul and the arising body rushing together in an indissoluble embrace: and this design, among all I recollect to have seen, stands alone in expressing the rapture of that reunion.'[51] Rossetti's apparent attraction to the printed image extended to humorous caricature, which she seems to have enjoyed. She was even able to laugh at her own family when Dante Gabriel Rossetti's circle's penchant for blue-and-white pottery was the subject of satire in *Punch* magazine (fig. 1.13).[52]

These few examples help us see that for Rossetti, pictures were most powerful when describing figures in a strong linear style. As we have seen, she appears to have been sceptical of the picturesque model of art whereby an attractive slice of nature was accurately transcribed. Rossetti's theology emphasised the visible world as a language of signs of the divine. If we follow Christ's language and thought, then 'the two worlds, visible and invisible, will become familiar to us ... as double against each other'.[53] Representational art can only get in the way of this imaginative operation, muddying rather than clarifying. As we have already noted, Rossetti suggested that turning away from the arts in this life brings nearer the eventual satisfaction of beatific vision. How much worse when art aspired more literally to the reproduction of nature in the form of sculpture. Sculpture, like architecture, is something Rossetti virtually never comments upon, although she does recall a visit to a waxworks display (Madame Tussaud's?) at which she was disturbed by the quasi-human forms, and later reproved herself for her weakness in being distracted by such phantasms: 'Will we not rise above an awe of waxwork?'[54] Although a great admirer of Plato, whose idealist philosophy did not contradict her Christian precepts, for Rossetti the classical world – characterised artistically through its lifelike sculpture – was horribly devoid of hope. Her antiquity is one of dead cities and pagan despair, its legacy still alarmingly to be found in some un-Christian elements of modern culture.

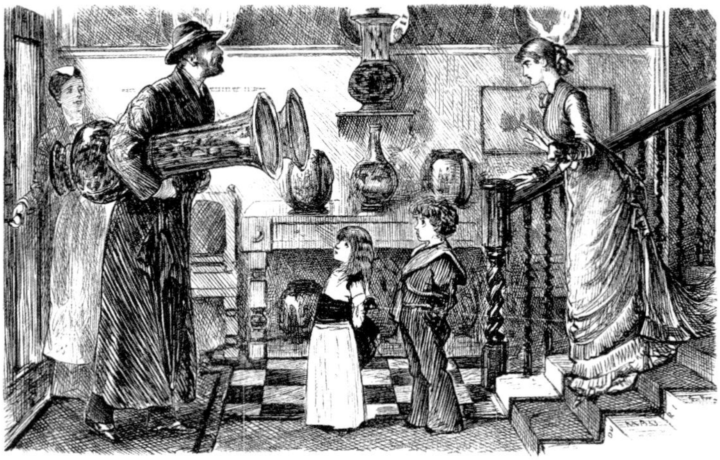

1.13 After George du Maurier, *Aptly Quoted from the Advertisement Column, Punch*, 15 December 1877, wood engraving.
Punch Magazine Cartoon Archive.

The cartoon makes fun of the enthusiasm for Oriental art, in particular blue-and-white china, made fashionable by artists associated with the Aesthetic Movement.

1.14 Luigi Schiavonetti after William Blake, *The Reunion of the Soul and the Body*, illustration to Robert Blair, *The Grave*, 1813, engraving, 28.6 × 22.2 cm.
Metropolitan Museum of Art, New York.

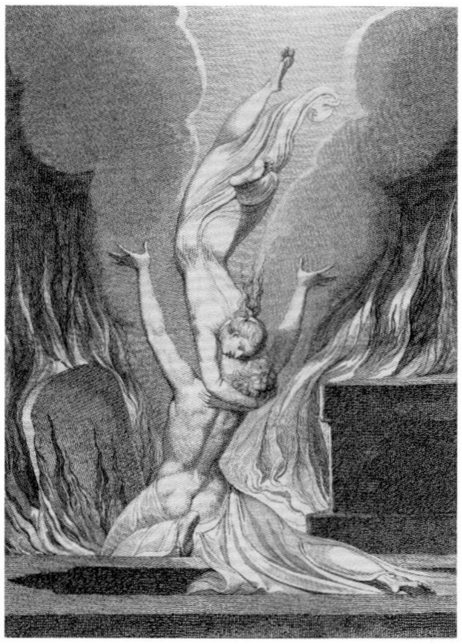

1.15 Emily Gertrude Thomson, *They Stole Little Bridget for Seven Years Long*, illustration to William Allingham's poem 'The Fairies' in *The Fairies: A Child's Song* (London: Thomas De La Rue, 1883), colour lithograph. Private collection.

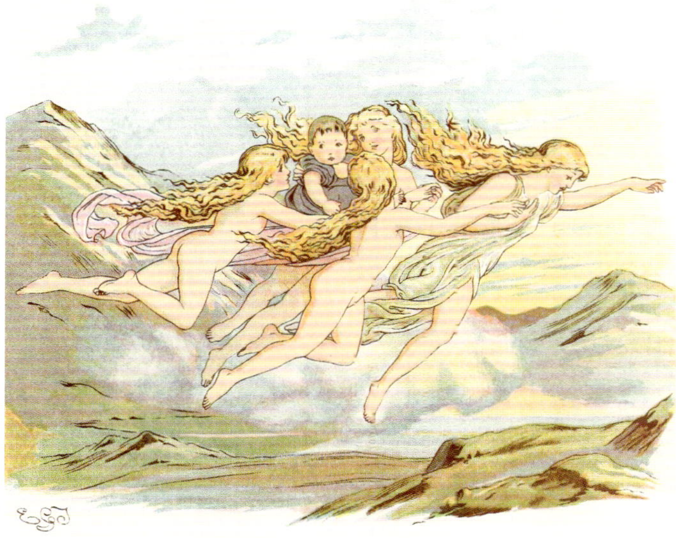

In 1883, Rossetti was invited to admire the new illustrations to William Allingham's poem 'The Fairies' by Emily Gertrude Thomson, a *protégée* of her friend Shields, but she was not amused (fig. 1.15). Angels, as in the Von Hess picture, were one thing; but the Victorian taste for images of sexy little fairy-nymphs – a disturbingly paedophilic neoclassicism – was not to her liking. Rossetti's antipathy was surely exacerbated by her involvement at this time in the campaign to have the age of consent for girls raised from its current level of just thirteen.[55] Rossetti also disapproved, following the Second Commandment against making graven images, of pictures purporting to show God (we should recall that Rossetti was the author of a volume of *Notes on the Commandments*, the subtitle of *Letter and Spirit*, 1883). Hence she commended, despite her own admiration for Blake, her sister Maria's refusal to look at his magnificent illustrations to the Book of Job.[56]

A divine perspective

The study of Rossetti has been enormously enhanced in recent years by a focus upon her religious life. Indeed, the theological turn in Rossetti studies is much to be credited with encouraging a revival of serious thinking about Christianity in Victorian culture generally. The poet was strongly affiliated to the High Church wing of the Anglican, Protestant Church of England.[57] The churches Rossetti attended, the theological texts she studied and the clergy she was close to all demonstrate a sympathy with the Tractarian Movement, which began in Oxford in 1833 as a revolt against the expanding British state's perceived coercion of the established church. Enthusiastic revivalists within the Church, the Tractarians were named after the controversial *Tracts for the Times*, and were also known as the Oxford Movement, Puseyites, Anglo-Catholics or High Church party. They represented in many ways the other side of the coin to the earlier 'low church' evangelical revival, which insisted on the Gospel being the first and only criterion of action and worth, and on the immediate political duties of the Christian. The Tractarians' emphasis was upon the Church itself, however – its buildings, rituals, traditions, music and language – as well as its capacity to improve the lives of the poor and outcast. They encouraged an ecclesiastical and liturgical culture that demanded precedence over political or economic life. There was an element of rarefied exclusivity evoked by the intimidating scholarship of the leading Oxford figures such as John Keble, Edward Pusey and John Newman, and by the doctrine of reserve, according to which the holy mysteries were to be revealed gradually, not hawked about for all to see.[58] Added to this heady mixture was a flavour of rebellion, or even principled treason, for Newman and others gradually came to the conclusion that the Anglican Church was truthfully Protestant only in name, and that to put conscience first meant, ultimately, becoming a Catholic.

The likely appeal of the Oxford Movement to any aspiring teenage poet is obvious. To one such as Rossetti, who was of Catholic heritage and who, as a young woman, could have little or no professional aspiration within the polity against which the Movement had raised its standard, it must have been all the more irresistible. In 1845 Rossetti was presented for confirmation at Christ Church in Albany Street near her London home, a leading centre of Tractarian thought and practice. This was the year of Newman's conversion and of Rossetti's unexplained illness, a malady that one doctor described as 'religious mania'.[59] There was plenty to get excited about at Christ Church. The incumbent during the 1840s was the Reverend William Dodsworth, who combined High Church zeal with a passion for biblical prophecy. He oversaw a surpliced choir (a novelty) and allied to his church, from 1845, was the first formal sisterhood of Anglican nuns to be seen in England for many generations.[60]

In her apparently autobiographical story *Maude: A Story for Girls*, written about 1849–50 (but not published during her lifetime), Rossetti describes the tormented conscience of a teenage poet longing for, but feeling unworthy of, communion at her church. Her sense of spiritual failure seems to derive from nothing more than the shame of having shared her poetry and hearing it praised. Maude's inner struggle with vanity – perhaps with having contravened the principle of reserve – is the story's drama. The spectre of self-love haunts even her churchgoing. Visiting the very 'high' new church of St Andrew's in Wells Street to enjoy its famous music, Maude finds that while 'I listen to the holy antheming', her heart sees that 'Vanity enters with thee, and thy love / Soars not to Heaven, but grovelleth below'.[61] For Maude there is no escape into Tractarian aesthetics from such 'wire-drawn' self-criticism, any more than there perhaps was for Rossetti herself.[62] Rossetti seems to have taken little interest in church decoration, and perhaps part of the appeal of Christ Church was that it was in fact a notoriously plain building despite its ritualistic reputation.[63] It did however boast a

1.16 Simeon Solomon, *A Deacon*, 1863, oil on canvas, 35 × 25.4 cm. Birmingham Museum & Art Gallery.

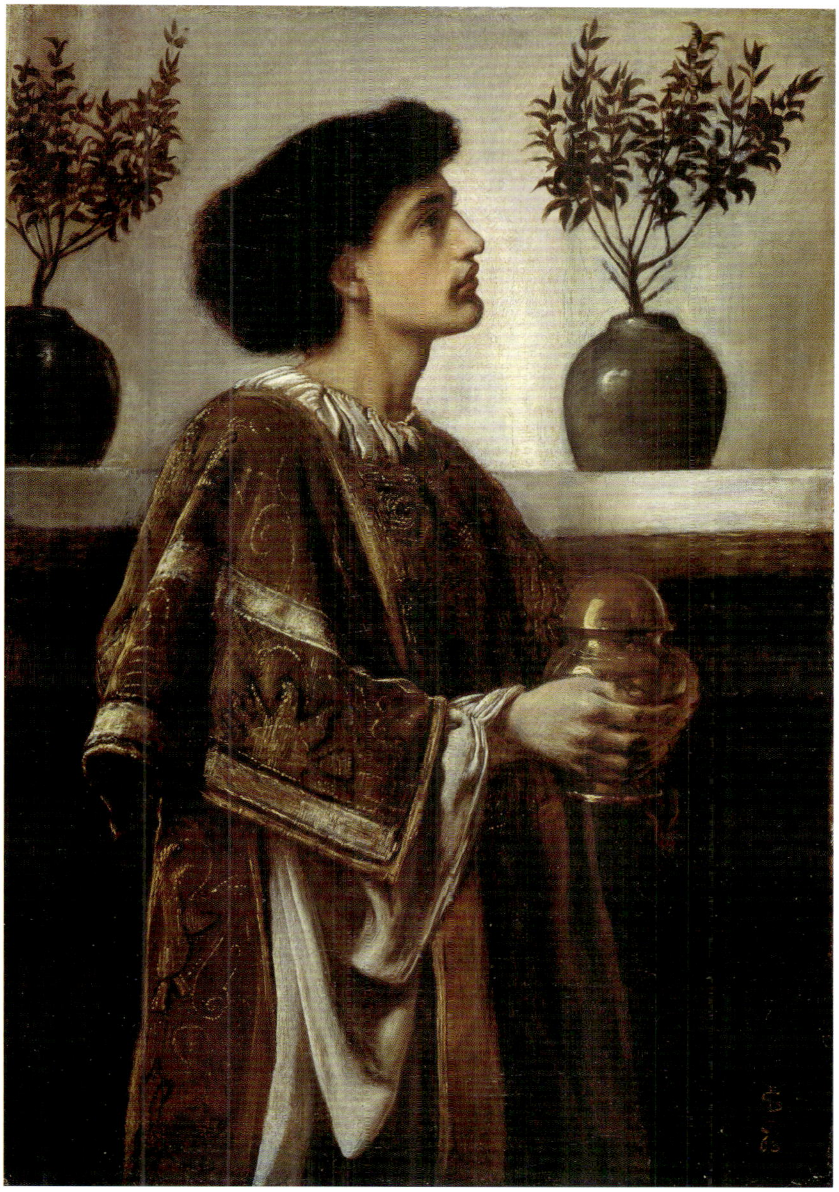

proper altar picture, a copy of Raphael's *Transfiguration* by the Welsh painter Thomas Brigstocke, made not long before the opening of the church in 1837.

Providing such pictures for new London churches had become relatively common in the post-Waterloo years and was not an especially Tractarian feature. The Oxford Movement intellectuals had little to say about pictorial art *per se*: their rhetorical efforts were reserved for the defence of the church and its services *in toto* as forming a kind of romantic *Gesamtkunstwerk*.[64] If asked what a 'Tractarian picture' looked like, many in the 1850s would have pointed to the Pre-Raphaelites, indeed to pictures such as Gabriel's *The Girlhood of Mary Virgin* and *Ecce Ancilla Domini!* (figs 2.7 and 2.10), both featuring Christina. She herself admired the pictures of Simeon Solomon in which ritual, both Christian and Jewish, is celebrated for its aesthetic appeal. At the Royal Academy in 1864, Rossetti especially picked out Solomon's *A Deacon* (fig. 1.16) in which a soft young man performs an ambiguous liturgical ceremony. Unmanliness became a standard charge against the ritualists, but Solomon had no qualms about celebrating the male dressing-up that was one aspect of the Tractarian disturbance of gendered roles. Rossetti, who, it has been argued, found her own gender-based constraints liberated to some extent through her church life, was perhaps drawn to such images partly for this reason.[65] Certainly the doctrine of reserve seems to help us understand something of her attitude towards pictures. As already suggested, presumably Holman Hunt's *The Finding of the Saviour* (fig. 1.10), purporting to really reveal the scriptural scene, and toured around the country in a one-picture travelling exhibition, cannot have been to her taste. It seems fitting that Rossetti's sole extended text about a picture, her short story 'The Lost Titian' (1856), should be concerned with a seductive Renaissance masterpiece that is overpainted and mislaid – its message muted, but not destroyed, awaiting the adept who is worthy to identify its truth.[66]

Image and emblem

The Rossetti scholar Emma Mason has shown how, for the poet, the colour white was symbolic of the doctrine of reserve. Rossetti uses white in her poetry to symbolise the highest degrees of sacredness, and explains this in *The Face of the Deep*, her devotional commentary on the Apocalypse, or Book of Revelation (1892): 'At the first moment *whiteness* does not suggest *colour*: yet all colour being latent in it, we finally discern in its train every lovely hue and gradation of hues ... whiteness is not an absence but rather a compendium of colour.... Thus colourless light paints the rainbow.'[67] Mason connects this theological take on Newton's prism – through which white light is refracted into the hues of the rainbow – with the astonishingly monochrome *Ecce Ancilla Domini!*, which thereby becomes a kind of manifesto of humility, both theological and chromatic. I think we can extend the attraction of the immaculate palette to the idea of the picture book, of the image contained within text: this was the context in which Rossetti encountered, for example, Blake's *The Reunion of the Soul and Body*, an illustration to Robert Blair's *The Grave* (fig. 1.14). The white page retains all possible colours, its glorious potential undisturbed by the linear (as opposed to painterly) pictorial intervention of a book illustration.

The archetypal integration of text and image, in a devotional context, is the emblem book tradition that flourished in Britain in the seventeenth century, uniting verse with engraving.[68] The influence of the emblem is clearly visible in the simply executed but powerful pencil illustrations that Rossetti added to a number of books, including some of her own (see Chapter Three). Few of these are accessible today, but the illustrations made by Rossetti in her copy of Keble's *The Christian Year* – first published in 1827, and probably the single most popular book of nineteenth-century Christian poetry – create what was perhaps for her an ideal balance of text and picture.[69] With an emblematic design added to the head of every poem or hymn in the book – one for each Sunday of the year plus many others for feasts of the Church – Rossetti created a unique kind of illustrated text in which the pictures are original, playful, enigmatic and yet subservient both to an existing text and, in the case of the Keble volume, to the liturgical calendar.

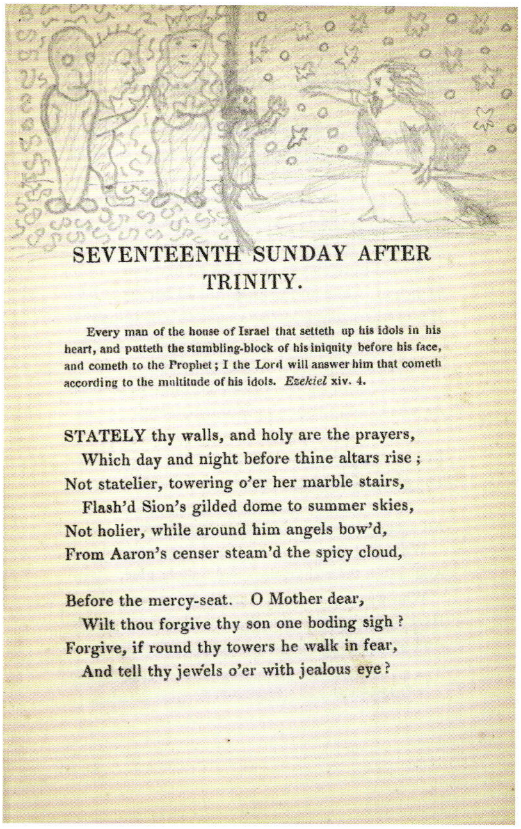

SEVENTEENTH SUNDAY AFTER TRINITY.

Every man of the house of Israel that setteth up his idols in his heart, and putteth the stumbling-block of his iniquity before his face, and cometh to the Prophet; I the Lord will answer him that cometh according to the multitude of his idols. *Ezekiel* xiv. 4.

STATELY thy walls, and holy are the prayers,
Which day and night before thine altars rise;
Not statelier, towering o'er her marble stairs,
Flash'd Sion's gilded dome to summer skies,
Not holier, while around him angels bow'd,
From Aaron's censer steam'd the spicy cloud,

Before the mercy-seat. O Mother dear,
Wilt thou forgive thy son one boding sigh?
Forgive, if round thy towers he walk in fear,
And tell thy jewels o'er with jealous eye?

1.17 Christina Rossetti, pencil illustration added to 'Seventeenth Sunday after Trinity' in her copy of John Keble, *The Christian Year* (Oxford: Parker, 1837). Private collection, on loan to British Library, London.

Rossetti was, furthermore, one of her own first illustrators. William writes in his 1904 edition of her *Poetical Works*: 'At some date – it may have been towards 1850 – Christina took it into her head to make some little coloured illustrations' in a copy of her privately printed *Verses* of 1847.[70] These images William terms 'devices', appropriately evoking something personal and bespoke. His valuable descriptions of the illustrations suggest the same mixing of whimsy and cosmic symbolism that characterised the emblem book tradition. 'On the Death of a Cat' has, as its illustration or device, 'a cat, in a rather sentimental attitude of languor, extending its right arm over a kitten. The cat is sandy and white, the kitten tabby', while 'The Martyr' has 'the soul ... received into heaven by an angel. Between the angel's wings are a series of red and white curves, symbolizing (I suppose) the nine heavens, as in Dante'.[71] Christina also made a long sequence of illustrations in a copy of *Goblin Market and Other Poems*, her first major collection, published in 1862.

This volume, plain as can be typographically, was introduced by two full-page illustrations after designs by Dante Gabriel Rossetti (see Chapter Four). In the frontispiece, the goblins that tempt the two sisters with fruit are imagined, prompted by the text, as 'brisk fruit-merchant men', yet with the heads of the different animals they each resemble. In the title-page image, the sisters sleep, indistinguishable, as the poison of the goblins' fruit begins to take hold. The goblins themselves appear now in procession within the circular detail of the upper left. Here their brutish faces, miniaturised, appear deformed and disturbing rather than quaintly anthropomorphised as in a fairy-tale illustration. They resemble, in fact, one of the grotesque figures imagined by Rossetti in her Keble volume illustration to the passage in Ezekiel where the raising of false idols is condemned (fig. 1.17). Her own illustrations to 'Goblin Market', untraced but described by William Rossetti, sound similar to both the little figures in Gabriel's roundel and the Ezekiel image: 'She draws several of the goblins – all very slim, agile figures in a close-fitting garb of blue; their faces, hands, and feet are sometimes human, sometimes brute-like, but of a scarcely definable type.'[72] Rossetti's own goblins, as visualised by herself, are thus well removed from fairyland, and perhaps suggested to their author the idea of idols – apparently fearsome objects of a fragile authority, easily overcome by love. From what we can presently reconstruct of Rossetti's own emblematic creations, it was, as we would have imagined, the idea that mattered, not any naturalistic description.

Included in the first edition of the *Goblin Market* volume was the 1856 sonnet 'A Triad' – three women lose their inner, or actual, lives to worldly love through different routes. Gabriel made a drawing of the subject, which was it seems never developed into anything finished (fig. 5.1). The poem also drew the attention of one of his hangers-on, the obscure George Chapman, who had wished to make a portrait of his friend's sister. Dante Gabriel Rossetti helped Chapman sell his painting inspired by 'A Triad' to one of his wealthy industrialist patrons, James Leathart, but it is now untraced. William Rossetti believed it was probably this painting that caused Christina to worry that her poem was open to moral exception, perhaps for representing comfortable marriage as no more life-affirming than other forms of love. In any case, she removed 'A Triad' from future collections of her poetry.[73] This was not a promising start to the tradition of artists creating paintings inspired by Rossetti's verse (the subject of Chapter Five). Anyone seeking to put flesh on her words, so to speak, risked contradicting the images in her own mind's eye – as recorded, to some extent, by the little drawings she added to a selection of her poems. Among her black-and-white illustrators, Laurence Housman's Art Nouveau treatment of 'Goblin Market' of 1893 (figs 4.21 and 4.23) was not well received by the poet, but Arthur Hughes, a Pre-Raphaelite associate, did become an accepted illustrator. His few images accompanying *Speaking Likenesses* (1874) are, for once, the match of the text, which represents an intriguing but opaque response to the *Alice* stories of Rossetti's friend Lewis Carroll, who was also responsible for making the most appealing of the photographs of the poet to have survived (figs 1.18, 2.23 and 2.24). Hughes's frontispiece to *Speaking Likenesses*, showing the sensible little Maggie tempted to join in the frolics of 'a party of children [who] were sporting together in the very freest and easiest manner possible', is an overlooked early British response to Goya, a jarring but memorable conflation of the Spanish master's tonal etching style with the chunky linearity of Victorian children's illustration (figs 1.19 and 1.20).[74] Unfortunately, evidently wishing to liven up this offer to the Christmas market, the publisher, Macmillan, titled this image 'Maggie meets the fairies in the wood', earning a stiff rebuke from Rossetti, who was not pleased to see naughty children confused with fairies – two types of being, for her, of entirely distinct moral natures.[75]

The most comfortable union of text and image in one of Rossetti's books is probably achieved in her 1881 volume of hagiography, *Called to be Saints: The Minor Festivals Devotionally Studied* (fig. 1.21).[76] With each saint given his or her own emblematic plant or flower, this is the nearest thing Rossetti published to an emblem book. The botanical illustrations are careful and literal, but in this specific context

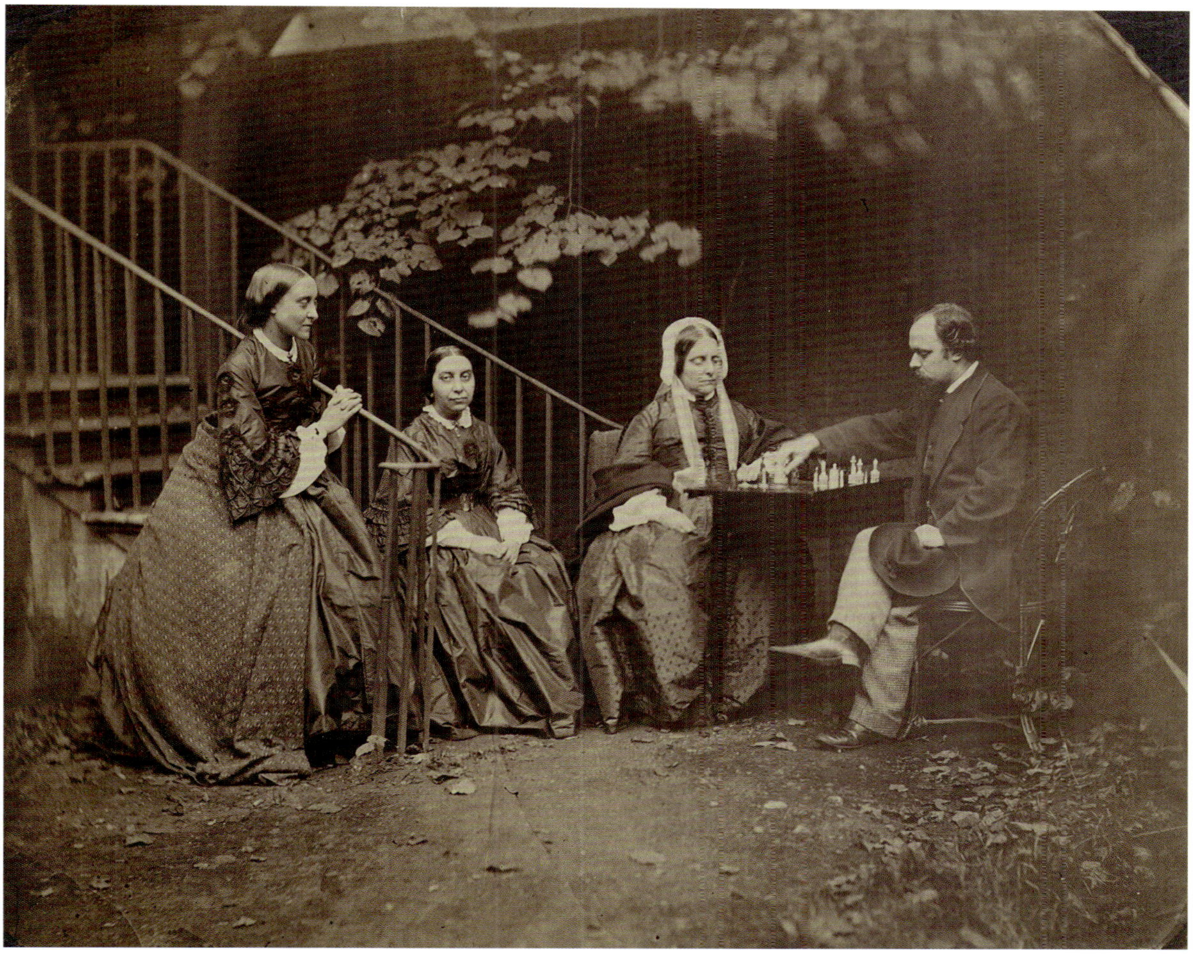

1.18 Lewis Carroll (Charles Lutwidge Dodgson), *The Rossetti Family*, 1863, albumen print, 18.8 × 23.8 cm. Harry Ransom Center, The University of Texas at Austin.

understood to be, at the same time, entirely symbolic – charming ciphers of another level of experience. The picturesque finally finds its purpose within Rossetti's visual world once it submits to an allegorical role. In the decades ahead, many of the most compelling visual responses to Rossetti's verse likewise seek after analogy rather than to translate words directly into pictures. In 1888, *Atalanta*, a monthly magazine for girls, opened its October number with a reproduction of Edward Poynter's 1882 drawing of the singing head of an androgynous youth alongside Rossetti's poem 'Exultate Deo' – one of her meditations in white. Many other artists, as varied as Arthur Hughes and the great Belgian Symbolist Fernand Khnopff (figs 5.6 and 5.7), created poetic, melancholic pictures that do not illustrate Rossetti but reach into her emotional world, with fragments of her verse taken for titles, or appended to an exhibition catalogue entry like the motto accompanying the image in an emblem book. Musical settings of Rossetti's poems became common from as early as the mid-1860s, just at the time that painters first began looking to her work.[77]

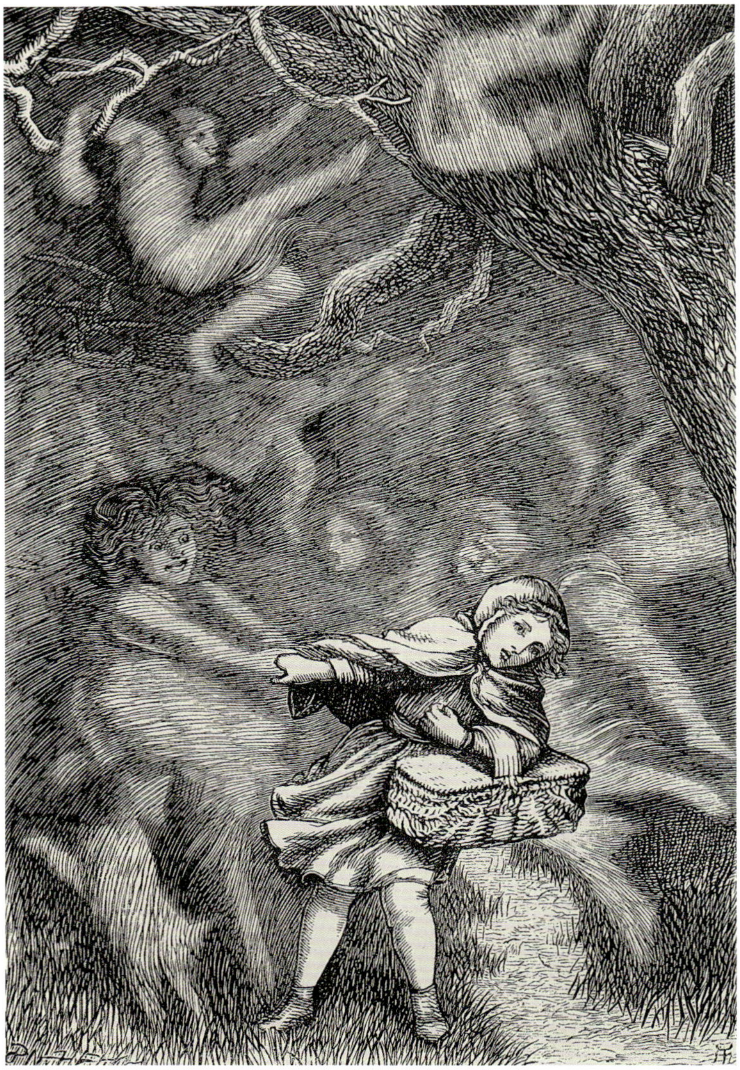

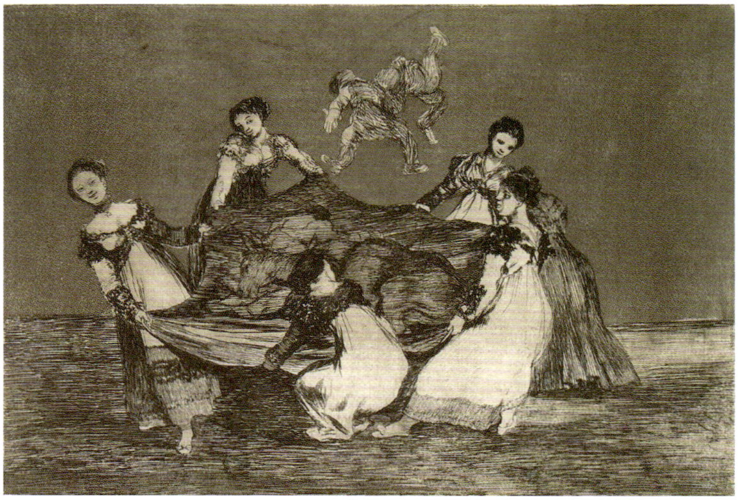

1.19 Left:
Dalziel Brothers after Arthur Hughes, *Maggie in the Woods*, frontispiece to Christina Rossetti, *Speaking Likenesses* (London: Macmillan & Co., 1874), wood engraving. Collection of Stephen Calloway.

1.20 Below left:
Francisco de Goya, *Pesa mas que un burro muerto (Disparate femenino)* [*Heavier Than a Dead Donkey (Female Folly)*], c.1816–23 (published 1864), etching with aquatint, 33.4 × 48.2 cm. Metropolitan Museum of Art, New York.

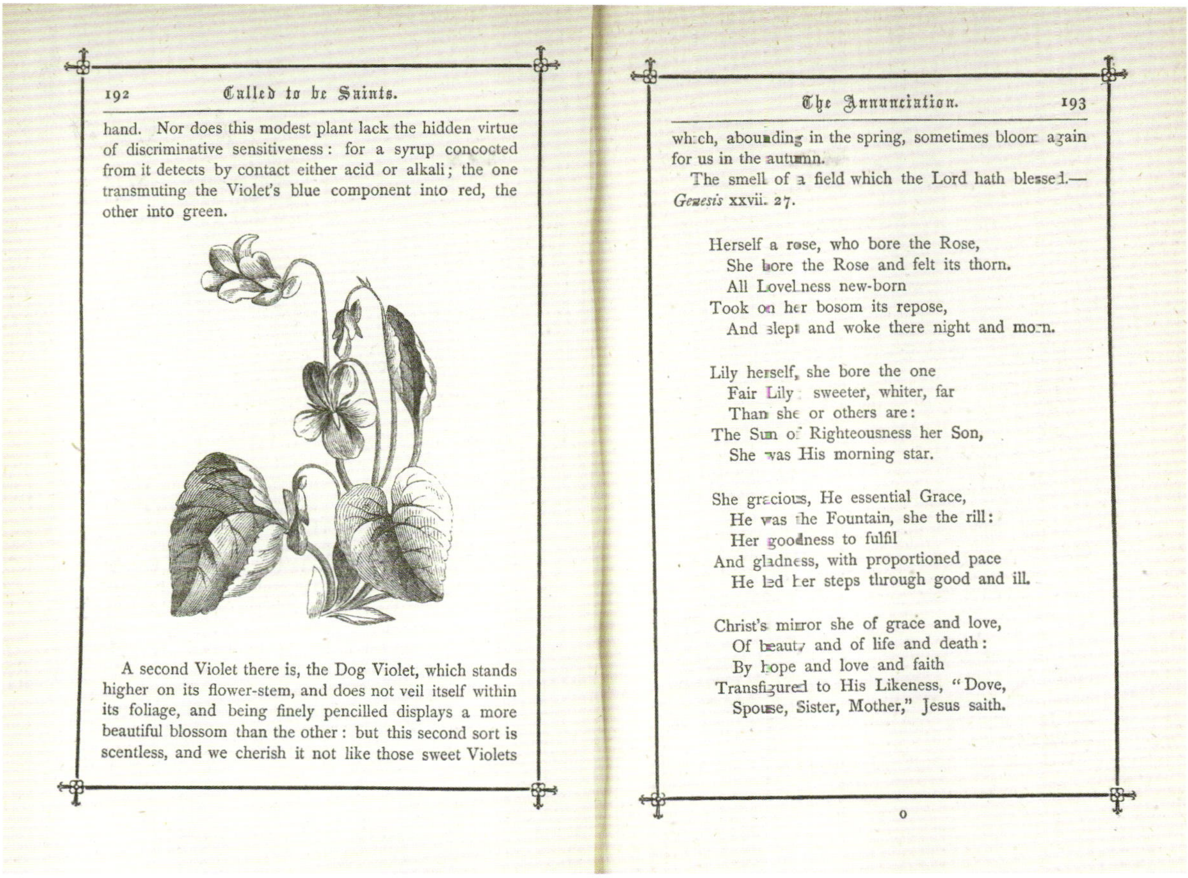

192 Called to be Saints.

hand. Nor does this modest plant lack the hidden virtue of discriminative sensitiveness: for a syrup concocted from it detects by contact either acid or alkali; the one transmuting the Violet's blue component into red, the other into green.

A second Violet there is, the Dog Violet, which stands higher on its flower-stem, and does not veil itself within its foliage, and being finely pencilled displays a more beautiful blossom than the other: but this second sort is scentless, and we cherish it not like those sweet Violets

The Annunciation. 193

which, abounding in the spring, sometimes bloom again for us in the autumn.

The smell of a field which the Lord hath blessed.—*Genesis* xxvii. 27.

Herself a rose, who bore the Rose,
She bore the Rose and felt its thorn.
All Loveliness new-born
Took on her bosom its repose,
And slept and woke there night and morn.

Lily herself, she bore the one
Fair Lily; sweeter, whiter, far
Than she or others are:
The Sun of Righteousness her Son,
She was His morning star.

She gracious, He essential Grace,
He was the Fountain, she the rill:
Her goodness to fulfil
And gladness, with proportioned pace
He led her steps through good and ill.

Christ's mirror she of grace and love,
Of beauty and of life and death:
By hope and love and faith
Transfigured to His Likeness, "Dove,
Spouse, Sister, Mother," Jesus saith.

o

1.21 Christina Rossetti, 'The Annunciation' in *Called to be Saints: The Minor Festivals Devotionally Studied* (London: SPCK, 1881). British Library, London.

Rossetti's apparent rejection of the world became legendary. The almost self-destructive tendencies complained of by her brothers suggested a latter-day Sappho, the suicidal archetypal poetess of antiquity, and her consequent failure to provide a heroic model for later women writers has suggested the epithet 'Anti-Muse' to one critic.[78] Hers was certainly no practical, professionalised model of artistic creation: in her book, each writer and artist individually carried a terrible responsibility to an authority far beyond the world of critics, periodicals and art galleries. The inner world of Christina Rossetti may not have been a comfortable place, somewhere from which pictures generally found themselves barred out. But for the artist with their own vision, a few borrowed lines of her poetry could be enough to help generate something newly alive.

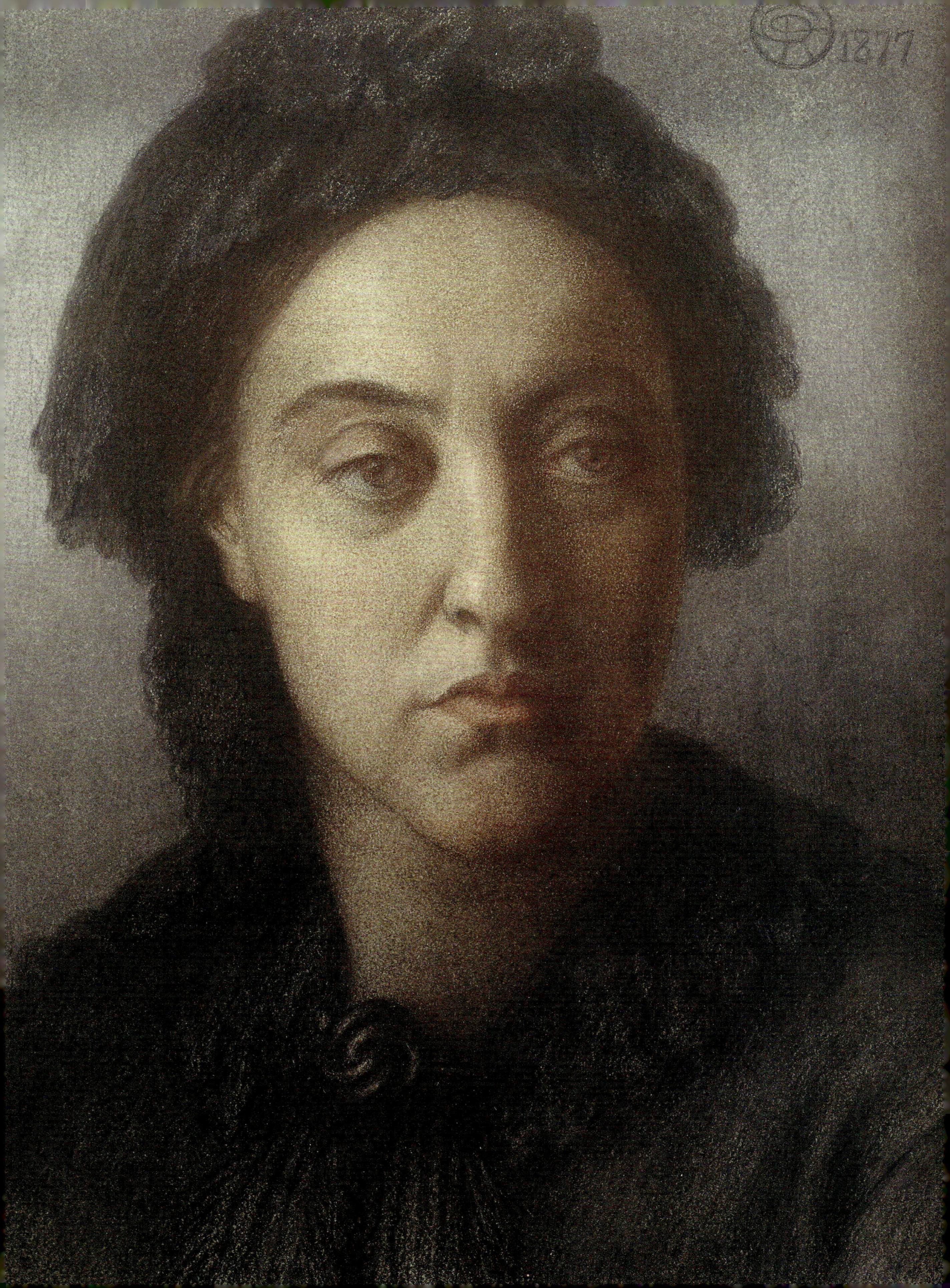
1877

One face looks out from all his canvasses

2 The Appearance of Christina Rossetti

SUSAN OWENS

WHAT did Christina Rossetti look like? Her face appears in an unusually large number of portraits: there she is as a young woman, drawn by her brother in severe linear profile; there as the mature poet, depicted as though in a moment of inspiration; there again, in a late photograph, her features altered by ill health. But if we came across these portraits out of context, would we realise it was the same person? No satisfyingly definitive image has ever come forward with a claim to being the representative likeness. It is as though she slips smilingly out of the room whenever we try to get a good look at her.

A further irony is that Rossetti should have left so rich a visual legacy at all, because despite her fame she avoided publicity and was, if not reclusive, then certainly retiring, a tendency that increased with age – 'My tastes are somewhat *stay-at-home*', she would write to a friend at the age of just twenty-one.[1] Had it not been for her familial background and artistic milieu, we would surely have been left with little record of her appearance. As it was, her most frequent portraitist by far was her brother Dante Gabriel Rossetti; others included her sometime fiancé James Collinson and another suitor, John Brett. All represent her in very different ways, as though striving to understand her enigmatic personality. And her presence in visual art is not limited to portraits: in her late teens and throughout her twenties she acted as a model, mostly for Gabriel but occasionally for other members of the Pre-Raphaelite Brotherhood too. As a result, her features – or versions of them – are woven into some of the most significant of their early works.

Early likenesses

When Christina Georgina and her elder siblings Maria Francesca, Dante Gabriel and William Michael were children, the Rossetti home in Charlotte Street – a red-bricked terraced house in what was then a 'dingy' corner of London just south of Regent's Park – was a hub for Italian expatriates 'of all classes, men of high cultivation and others of

Detail of fig. 2.27

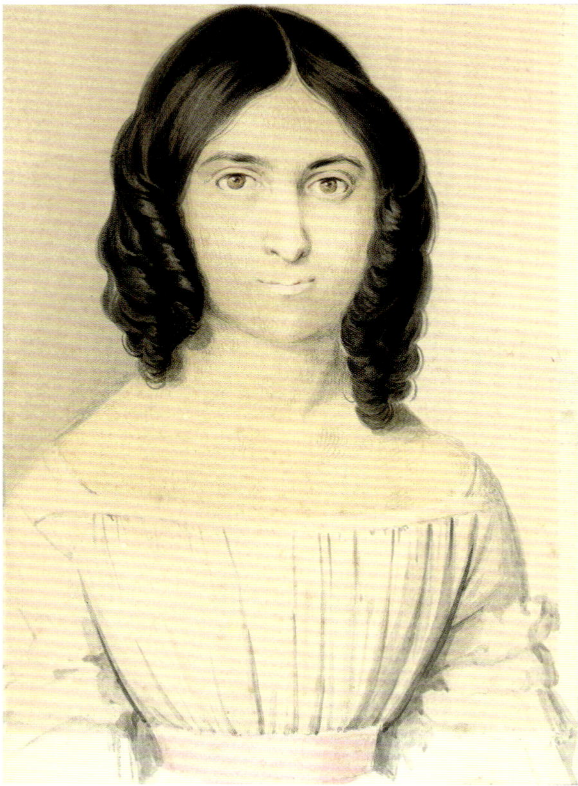
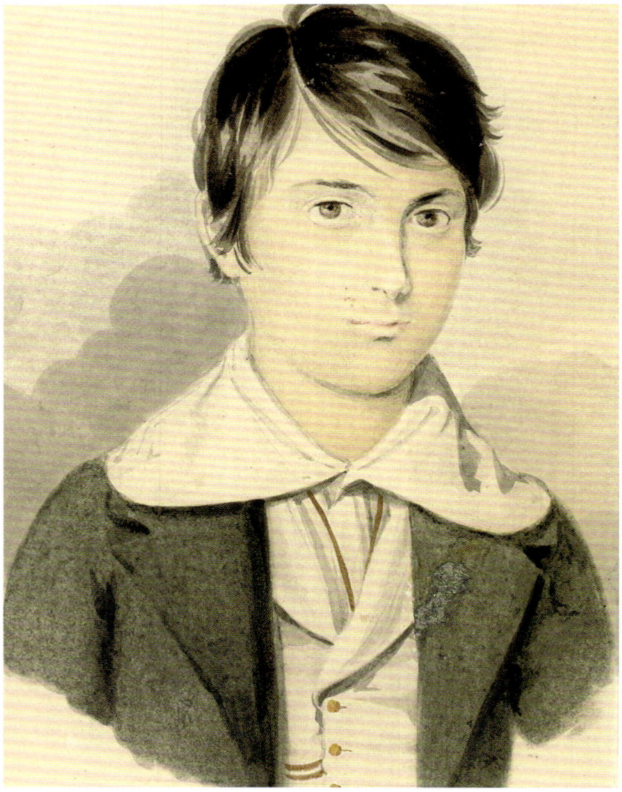
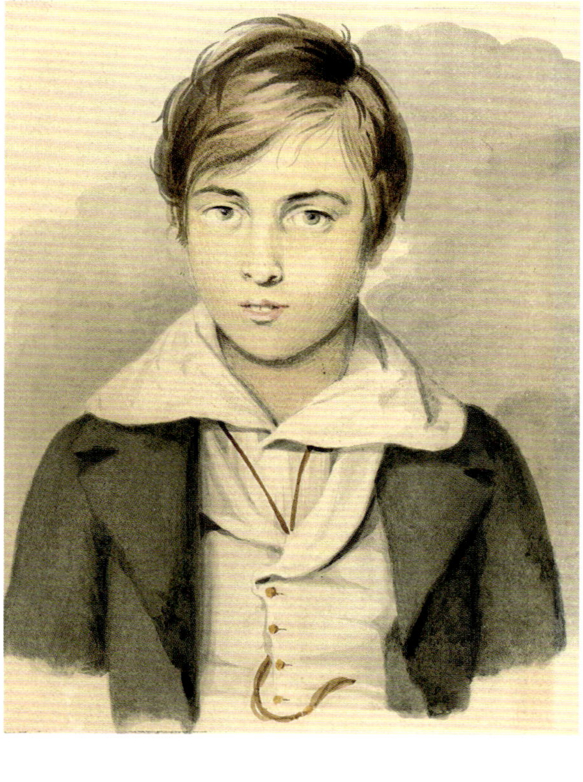
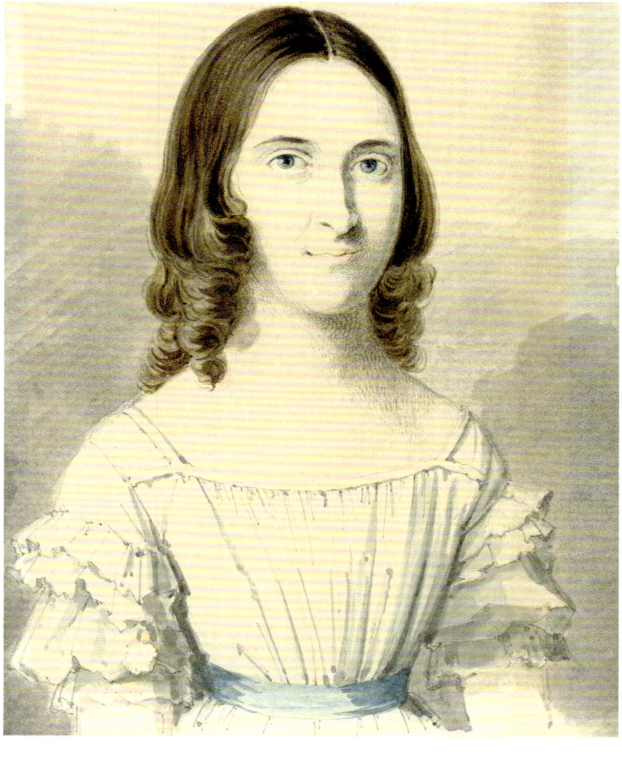

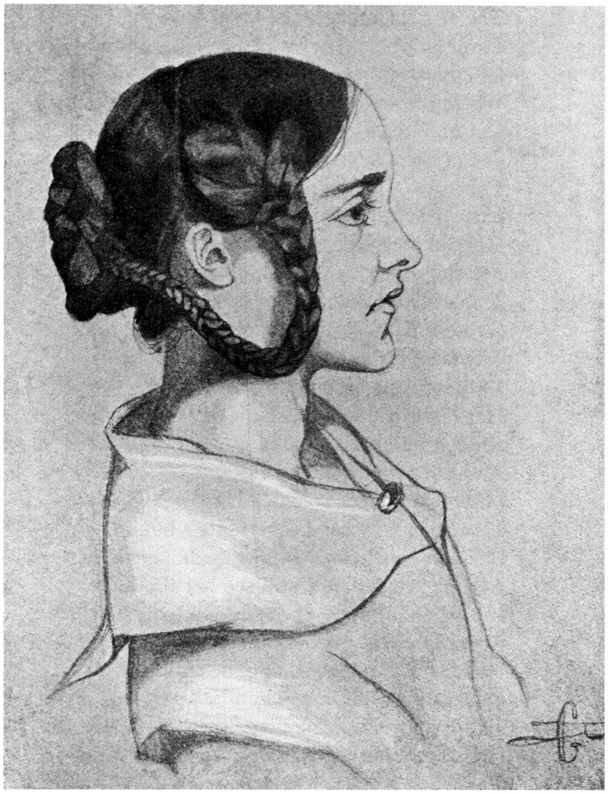

very little' with political views 'of the ultra-liberal and sometimes of the revolutionary kind'.[2] These men came to visit their father Gabriele Rossetti, a Neapolitan patriot in exile from Vasto, who had come to England in 1824 and later married Frances Polidori, daughter of Gaetano Polidori, another political exile. We first catch a glimpse of Christina as a rather solemn seven-year-old, and later at twelve or thirteen in watercolour portraits by one of these Italian friends: Filippo Pistrucci (fig. 2.1).[3] Pistrucci was a painter and engraver who had been active in Rome in the early years of the nineteenth century but who, like Gabriele, had been forced to leave Italy and who had come to London in 1822, where he taught grammar and history at a school in Holborn.[4] The later watercolour, one of a set representing each of the Rossetti children, presents a rather stiff, doll-like image, more like an illustration in a book than a living, breathing girl. It was not an auspicious start. When he listed the portraits of Christina in his memoir of 1904, her brother William called it 'a woful [*sic*] failure', and noted that the artist had misdrawn her mouth, giving her 'a conceited smirking expression'.[5]

2.1 Left:
Filippo Pistrucci,
Portraits of the Rossetti Children: William Michael, Christina Georgina, Dante Gabriel and Maria Francesca [clockwise from top right], *c.*1843, pencil and watercolour on paper, each 16.2 × 12.4 cm.
Private collection.

2.2 Above:
Dante Gabriel Rossetti,
Portrait of Christina Rossetti, *c.*1846, pencil on paper, 22.9 × 17.8 cm.
Private collection, reproduced in *Gabriele Rossetti: A Versified Autobiography*, ed. and trans. William Michael Rossetti (London: Sands & Co., 1901).

Gabriel drew the first of many portraits of his sister around 1846, when she was fifteen (fig. 2.2). This drawing shows her in profile, poised and self-conscious, her hair arranged in fashionably looped plaits. The heavy lids of her eyes and short upper lip prefigure the ideal of female beauty that was to dominate his later paintings and drawings, particularly those representing his principal muse of the 1860s and 70s, Jane Morris. The drawing also reflects the style Gabriel had adopted at the time; despite being in his first year as a student at the Royal Academy Schools, where painstaking shading and modelling were a requirement, he demonstrated his independence from the Academy's strictures by employing a supple, incisive line.

William was fond of this portrait, and deemed it to be 'a good likeness', although, in his view, not quite doing justice to her 'attractiveness'.[6] But how does it compare with written descriptions of Christina's appearance at around this time? In 1847, the painter and poet William Bell Scott, who was to become a close friend of the family, encountered her when for the first time he visited the Rossetti home. He also drew attention to the contours of her features, describing 'a slight girl with a serious regular profile, dark against the pallid wintry light' standing by the window and writing at a tall desk.[7] Scott presents her like a work of art, a cameo profile sculpted from dark stone and set against a pale background.

Perhaps it is inevitable that an older artist should, especially in writing about it later, describe a sixteen-year-old girl in aesthetic terms.

But how did Christina regard her own appearance? One might point to her story *Maude: A Story for Girls*, written when she was in her late teens. Early in the narrative Maude's appearance is described:

> Her features were regular and pleasing; as a child she had been very pretty; and might have continued so but for a fixed paleness, and an expression, not exactly of pain, but languid and pre-occupied to a painful degree. Yet even now, if at any time she became thoroughly aroused and interested, her sleepy eyes would light up with wonderful brilliancy, her cheeks glow with warm colour, her manner became animated, and drawing herself up to her full height she would look more beautiful than ever she did as a child.[8]

Maude is about a teenaged girl, a gifted poet who suffers a carriage accident and, with a few pious and thoughtful words to her attentive cousin Agnes, decorously dies. The melancholy drama has an autobiographical dimension – Maude is, like Rossetti herself at that age, serious, rather stiff in company, impatient with girlish frivolity, proud of her poetic ability and deeply devout. She introduces her cousins and their friends to the game of *bouts-rimés*, in which one person supplies the last word of each line of a sonnet, and the other has to invent the rest; it was a game she frequently played with her brothers, particularly with William. Quite how much of herself Rossetti revealed through Maude is a moot point. But without taking her description of her fictional creation to be an uncomplicated self-portrait, distinct parallels may be drawn between their appearance as well as their characters.

Maude was not published in Rossetti's lifetime. But when William edited it for publication in 1897, three years after her death, he chose for the frontispiece a nearly full-face study of Christina (fig. 2.3) that Gabriel had made around the time she might have begun her story – in an inscription on the back he noted that it must be 'quite early say 1847', although on the frontispiece an inscription dates it 'towards 1848'. In his list of portraits of his sister William remarks upon 'some archness of expression' here, adding that it was a quality in which she 'was by no means deficient.'[9] This portrait is unfinished, as fragmentary as the earlier profile was definite: the right side of Rossetti's face is more definitely drawn than the left, which is lightly sketched with the position of the eye not quite resolved. She rests her chin on an almost imperceptible hand and gazes out at the viewer with her one completed eye with a slight air of resignation. She looks as though she is slowly coming into being – which, in a sense, she was.

Did Christina herself prefer to be depicted in profile? When Gabriel drew her twice in this manner in 1847, both portraits were intended to be seen in public – and indeed one was made in public. This was a gift for a friend; at the bottom of the sheet Christina has inscribed it 'affectionately' to her 'dear Mrs Heimann' (fig. 2.4). Mrs Heimann's husband taught German at University College School,

2.3 Dante Gabriel Rossetti, *Portrait of Christina Rossetti*, c.1847–8, pencil on paper, 17.1 × 11.4 cm. Ashmolean Museum, University of Oxford.

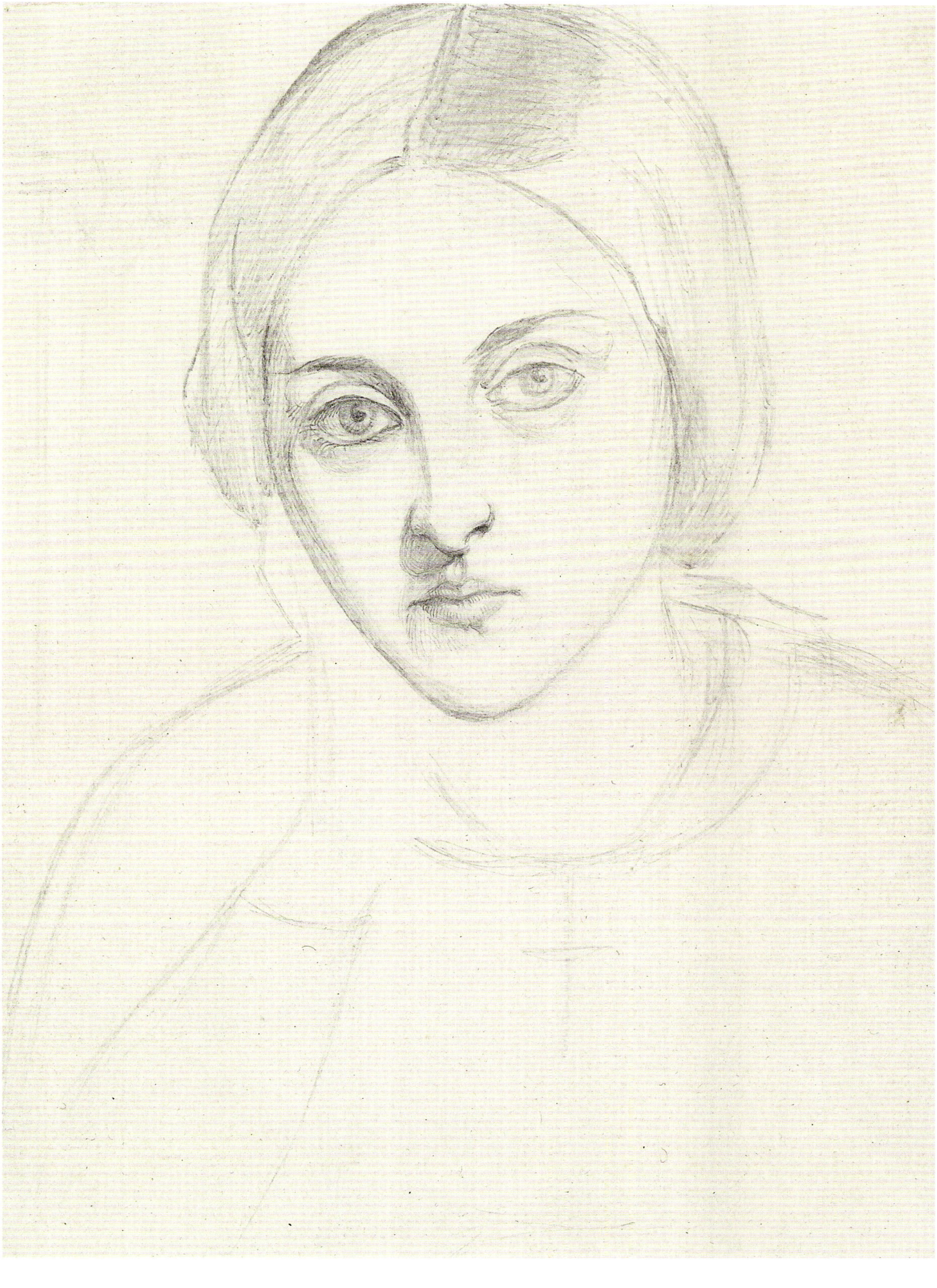

and was teaching the language to the Rossetti children in exchange for Italian lessons from Gabriele. Christina had been close to Amelia Heimann since 1843, when Dr Heimann first took his young bride to meet the family, and they remained friends throughout their lives. A note in the V&A's acquisitions register records that Gabriel drew the portrait at Mrs Heimann's house at 57 Gordon Square.[10] The other portrait drawing was bound in as a frontispiece to her first collection of poetry, *Verses*, which had been privately printed by her maternal grandfather, Gaetano Polidori, in 1847. In addition, Gabriel made three full-page pencil drawings illustrating different poems that were also added to this copy of the book, now housed in the Harry Ransom Center at the University of Texas. Of the two surviving letters Christina wrote that year, one (probably dating from July) is addressed to Mrs Heimann, and was written to accompany a presentation copy of *Verses*, or, as she calls it with ironic self-deprecation, 'my famous little book'.[11]

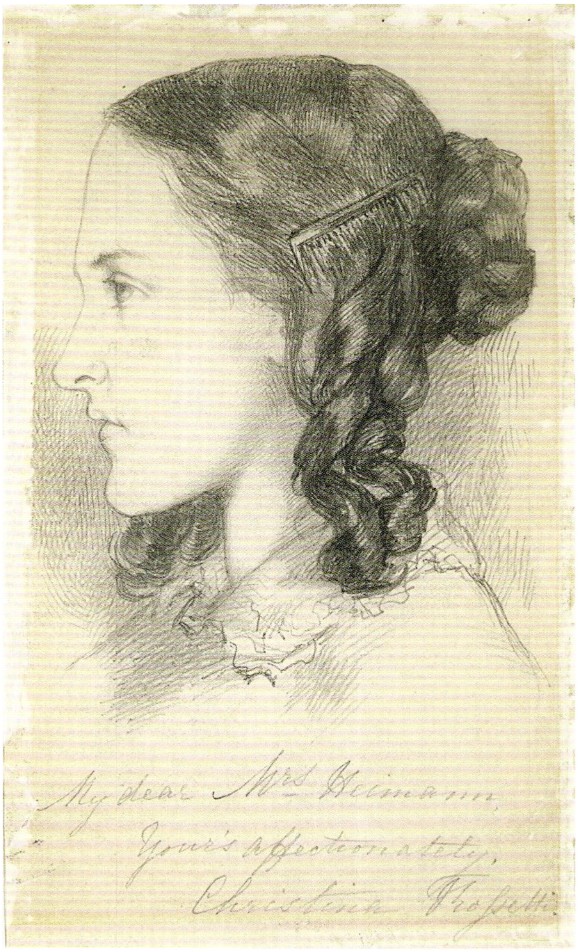

2.4 Dante Gabriel Rossetti, *Portrait of Christina Rossetti*, 1847, pencil on paper, 11 × 8.4 cm. Victoria and Albert Museum, London.

The similarity of Gabriel's two drawings would seem to indicate that one portrait was based on the other, although slight differences in the arrangement of Christina's hair suggests that the secondary version was also drawn from life. Did Christina show Mrs Heimann her special copy of *Verses* with Gabriel's drawings bound in, and did her friend request her own portrait to celebrate its publication? Whatever the order of production, in terms of self-representation, this was evidently the image Rossetti herself wanted to present to the world – whether it was in the context of a gift to an affectionate friend, or a way of establishing her identity as a serious and accomplished poet.

Why did Rossetti choose a profile for her 'official' portrait? As a portrait type, the profile is ambiguous: it presents the face as an object for admiration – we feel as viewers permitted to stare without engaging with the sitter as intimately as we do when confronted with a full-face portrait. Pared down as it is to essential contours, it also reminds us of the nobility and seriousness inherent in portraits on coins and medals. But paradoxically it is also a type that allows the sitter a degree of self-effacement because it necessitates a modest aversion of the gaze. As such, it was perhaps the ideal type of portraiture for a girl who was both proud of her achievements (though one who felt guilty about this) and, like many adolescents, awkward in company, her shyness often expressing itself in excessive formality.[12]

Gabriel made more portraits of Christina in the following year, 1848. One was a black chalk drawing of her face in three-quarter profile, carefully shaded this time and more in keeping with the style approved

2.5 Right:
Dante Gabriel Rossetti,
Portrait of Christina Rossetti, 1848,
black chalk touched with white
on paper, 28.8 × 21.5 cm.
British Museum, London.

2.6 Below:
Dante Gabriel Rossetti,
Portrait of Christina Rossetti, 1848,
oil on canvas, 16.5 × 14.6 cm.
Private collection.

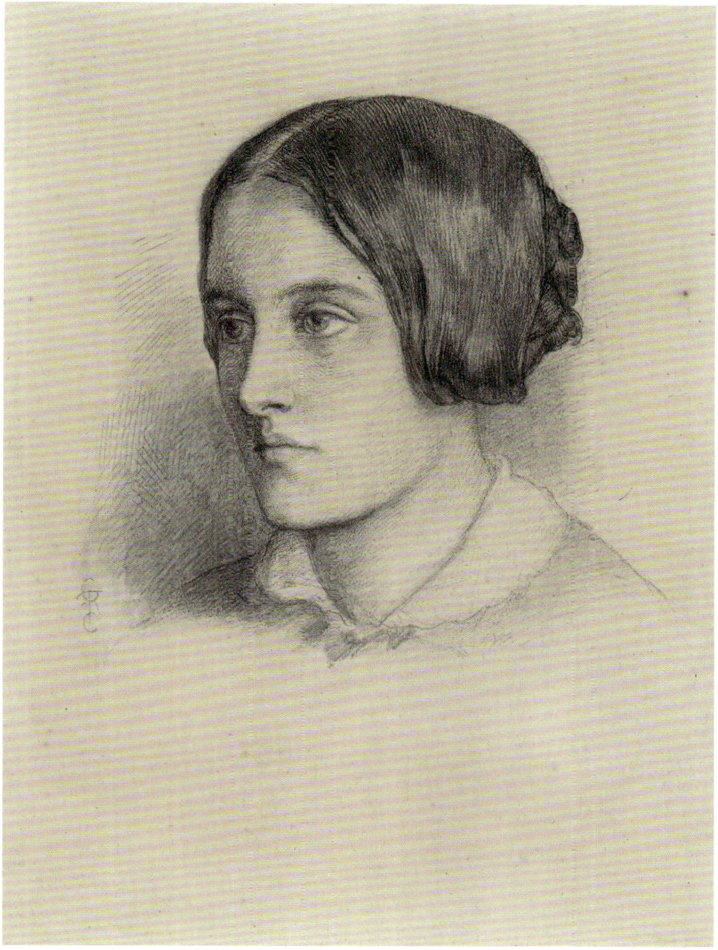

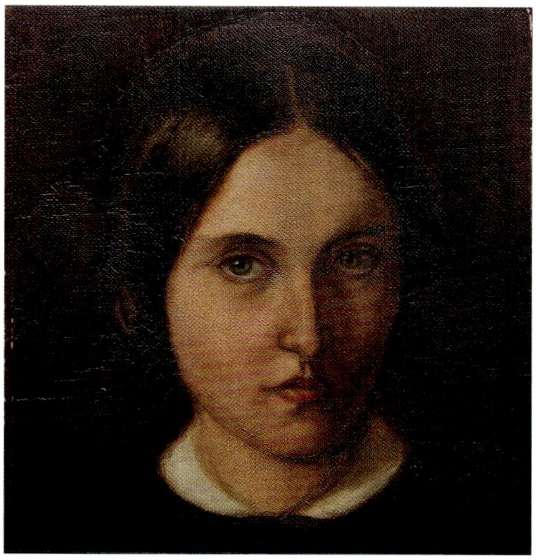

by the Royal Academy Schools, in which she gazes intensely off to the side; it was 'a most truthful likeness, and a highly pleasing one', according to William (fig. 2.5).[13] The other was a little oil painting that William thought 'the first coloured work that [Gabriel] completed', and also 'a true likeness' (fig. 2.6).[14] In this picture she looks out rather warily at the viewer. As with the unfinished full-face pencil drawing of Christina, executed either in 1847 or 1848, only one side of her face is clearly shown; in this case the other is in deep shadow, giving her appearance an enigmatic, almost mystical air.

A 'double sisterhood'

In the summer of 1848, the Rossetti brothers and friends, including the painter William Holman Hunt, the sculptor Thomas Woolner and other artist-writers Walter Deverell and James Collinson, formed a literary group. Gabriel naturally imagined Christina being involved along with 'all the nice chaps we know who do anything in the literary line', as he breezily described them to Hunt in a letter of July 1848.[15] As the author of a book of verses she was, after all, a more accomplished and prolific poet than any of the 'chaps' in question. In the event, however, she declined to join, for reasons Gabriel went on to explain:

> When I proposed that my sister should join, I never meant that she should attend the meetings, to which I know it would be impossible to persuade her, as it would bring her to a pitch of nervousness infinitely beyond Collinson's. I merely intended that she should entrust her productions to my reading; but must give up the idea, as I find she objects to this also, under the impression that it would seem like display, I believe – a sort of thing she abhors.[16]

The literary club itself was short-lived, and towards the end of 1848 some of the members, with the addition of John Everett Millais, re-formed as the Pre-Raphaelite Brotherhood (PRB). Although Christina was never an official member of the PRB, she did, however, refer jokingly to additional rights conferred by what she called her 'double sisterhood' when writing to William in April 1849.[17]

How serious was Christina about this 'double sisterhood'? If we skip four to five years into the future, to the year in which she lived in Frome in Somerset, we have the advantage of a greater volume of correspondence, and her numerous letters from that time are alive with excited enquiries and observations about the PRB's paintings and exhibitions. 'How sorry I am you missed seeing the Exhibition', she exclaims to Mrs Heimann in August 1853, 'I cannot now call upon you to admire Mr Hunt's *Sheep*, or *Claudio and Isabella*, or Mr Millais' *Cavalier*: for his Scotch picture my admiration is less cordial'.[18] Her letters to William in particular are full of requests for news that reveal the closeness with which she was following the production and exhibition of particular works of art: 'nearer still looms the satisfaction of the opening Exhibition; pray let us know some of its glories'; 'Has Mr Munro really managed to make his medallion of Scotus [William Bell Scott] too quaint? ... I shall like to see the portrait of Ruskin'; 'I suppose Mr Hunt's devout picture will not then be in town?'[19]

Returning to the earliest years of the PRB, during this time Christina justified her claim to a 'double sisterhood' by making contributions that were both literary and visual. On the literary side she was an active contributor to the PRB's journal *The Germ*, with her poems 'Dream Land' and 'An End' published anonymously in the first number of January 1850, 'Song', 'A Pause of Thought' and 'A Testimony' (under the pseudonym Ellen Alleyn) in the second and 'Repining' and 'Sweet Death' in the third. What is less well known is her contribution to the PRB's iconography. As the art historian Ronald Parkinson has observed, her thin face and slight figure seem to have been strong influences on the look of early Pre-Raphaelite pictures: 'it was as much the appearance of Christina Rossetti that determined the emaciated and angular style of the Brothers as any return via Lasinio's engravings to the Pre-Raphael frescoes in the Campo Santo at Pisa'.[20]

2.7 Dante Gabriel Rossetti, *The Girlhood of Mary Virgin*, 1848–9, oil on canvas, 83.2 × 65.4 cm. Tate, London.

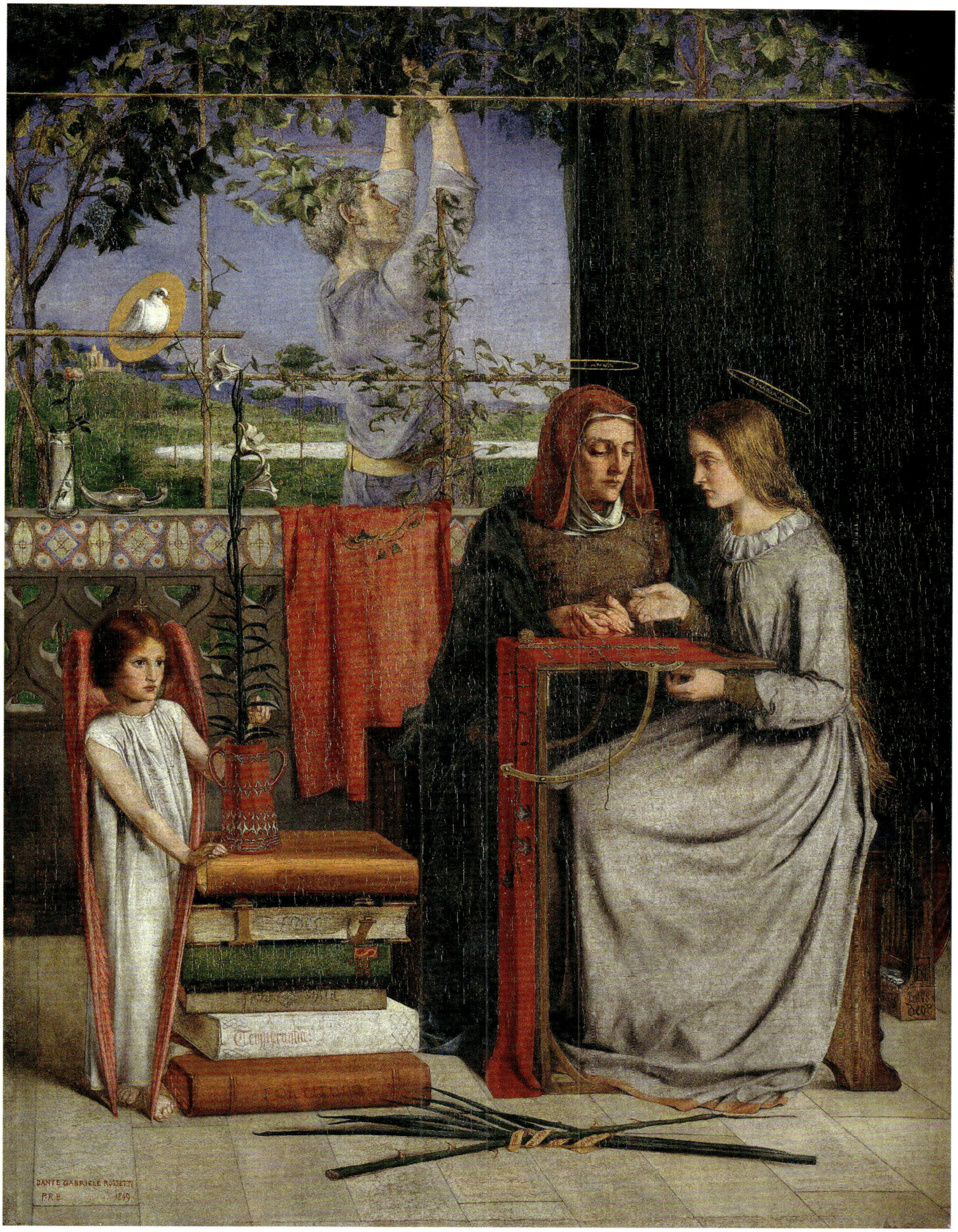
DANTE GABRIELE ROSSETTI
P.R.B. 1849

From the outset, the earnest aims of the PRB and the religious subject matter of their pictures chimed with Christina's devout Christian faith, and must have conduced to her willingness to act as a model, which she did not only for Gabriel but also for Collinson and Hunt – something we might imagine she would otherwise have refused on the grounds that it 'seem[ed] like display'. Helping her brother to create a moving composition of the Virgin Mary as a girl bending diligently over her embroidery was evidently acceptable, however, and she sat for Gabriel's first major composition, *The Girlhood of Mary Virgin* (fig. 2.7). Their mother, moreover, added her imprimatur, sitting for the Virgin's mother, St Anne. In a letter of 14 November 1848, Gabriel explained to his godfather Charles Lyell that he had made several studies and drawn the design on the canvas 'and a portion of the figure of the Blessed Virgin, for which Christina sits to me; her appearance being excellently adapted to my purpose'.[21] Apart from her hair, that is, which Gabriel transformed into a bright, coppery gold. She is represented in profile,

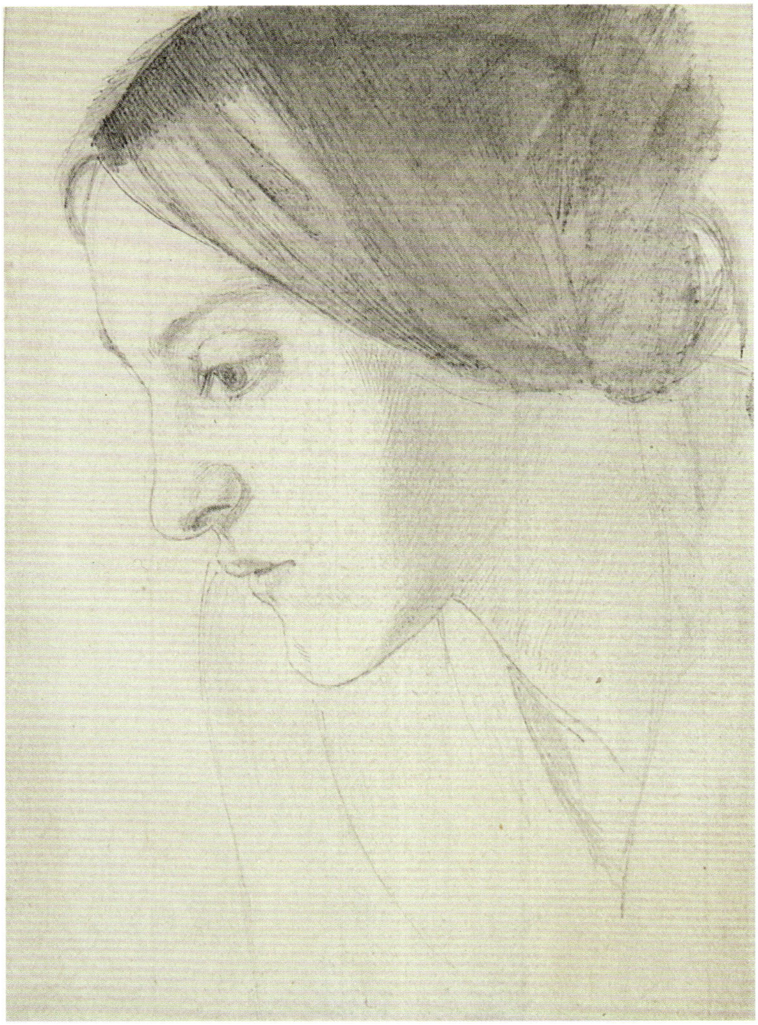

2.8 Dante Gabriel Rossetti, *Portrait of Christina Rossetti*, c.1848–50, pencil on paper, 14.9 × 11.4 cm. Private collection.

looking up from her embroidery as though caught in a moment's apprehensive contemplation of her future role. A sensitive pencil drawing Gabriel made of his sister (fig. 2.8), perhaps at around this time, may have been a preparatory study for the picture. The drawing's emotional tenor is quite different from the other portrait drawings to this date. These two siblings – the 'two storms', as their father called them, contrasting them with the 'two calms' of Maria and William – had a sparring relationship, and William recalled that Gabriel (along with Maria) was 'inclined at times to treat her *de haut en bas*' because of their difference in age.[22] Freed from the obligation of negotiating his sister's character, however, Gabriel produced a drawing of remarkable grace and tenderness. As with Christina's description of Maude, the oblique view can sometimes be the most revealing.

The Girlhood was, in part, inspired by 'The Child Jesus', a poem written by James Collinson, another member of the PRB, and published in the second issue of *The Germ*. As Jan Marsh has pointed out in her biography of Christina, 'poem and painting seem to be interlinked', with Gabriel incorporating details such as the vine-pruning from Collinson's poem for his composition.[23] Collinson, a member of the congregation at Christ Church, Albany Street, where Frances and her daughters worshipped, was drawn into the Rossetti circle in another way in the autumn of 1848: he and Christina became engaged. Collinson painted her portrait at this time, producing an image of a thin-faced, dour young woman with stooping shoulders (fig. 2.9). William deemed it 'a true likeness of Christina', but went on to describe the portrait as 'an ordinary one, done by an artist whose eye for beauty was not keen, and whose style was stinted.'[24] Elsewhere he wrote that 'so far from being "flattering", it does not do justice to her face, though fair enough as a likeness'.[25] Nevertheless, in November of that year he took it with him, with a copy of Christina's *Verses*, as a proxy for her presence when he made a visit to Collinson's mother and sister at their home in Pleasley Hill, near Mansfield in Nottinghamshire. 'I wish', wrote Christina to William during his stay, 'that they could be convinced that the celebrated portrait is flattering, and that "the thoughtful and pleasing expression" of my face is indeed "as developed in the portrait".'[26] She is presumably quoting remarks and enquiries made by Mrs or Miss Collinson, as reported to her by William. We know his low opinion of James Collinson's portrait; with the alarming prospect of a visit of her own to the Collinson family looming, was Christina hoping that her brother would not put her in an embarrassing position by suggesting that she was more attractive in the flesh?

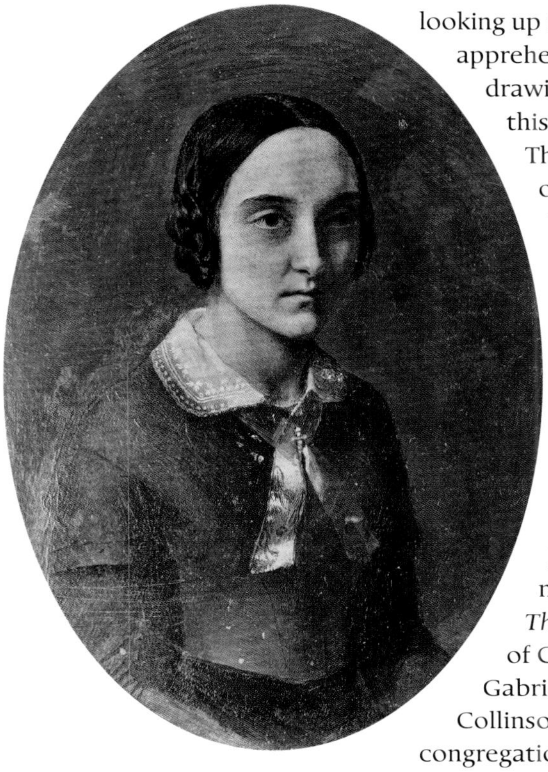

2.9 James Collinson, *Portrait of Christina Rossetti*, 1848, oil on canvas, 18.5 × 15.5 cm. Untraced; photograph National Portrait Gallery, London.

The following year, in the November of 1849 – some three months after her own stay with the Collinson family at Pleasley Hill – Christina was transformed for the second time into the Virgin Mary. Gabriel turned to his sister again for his second major painting, the Annunciation

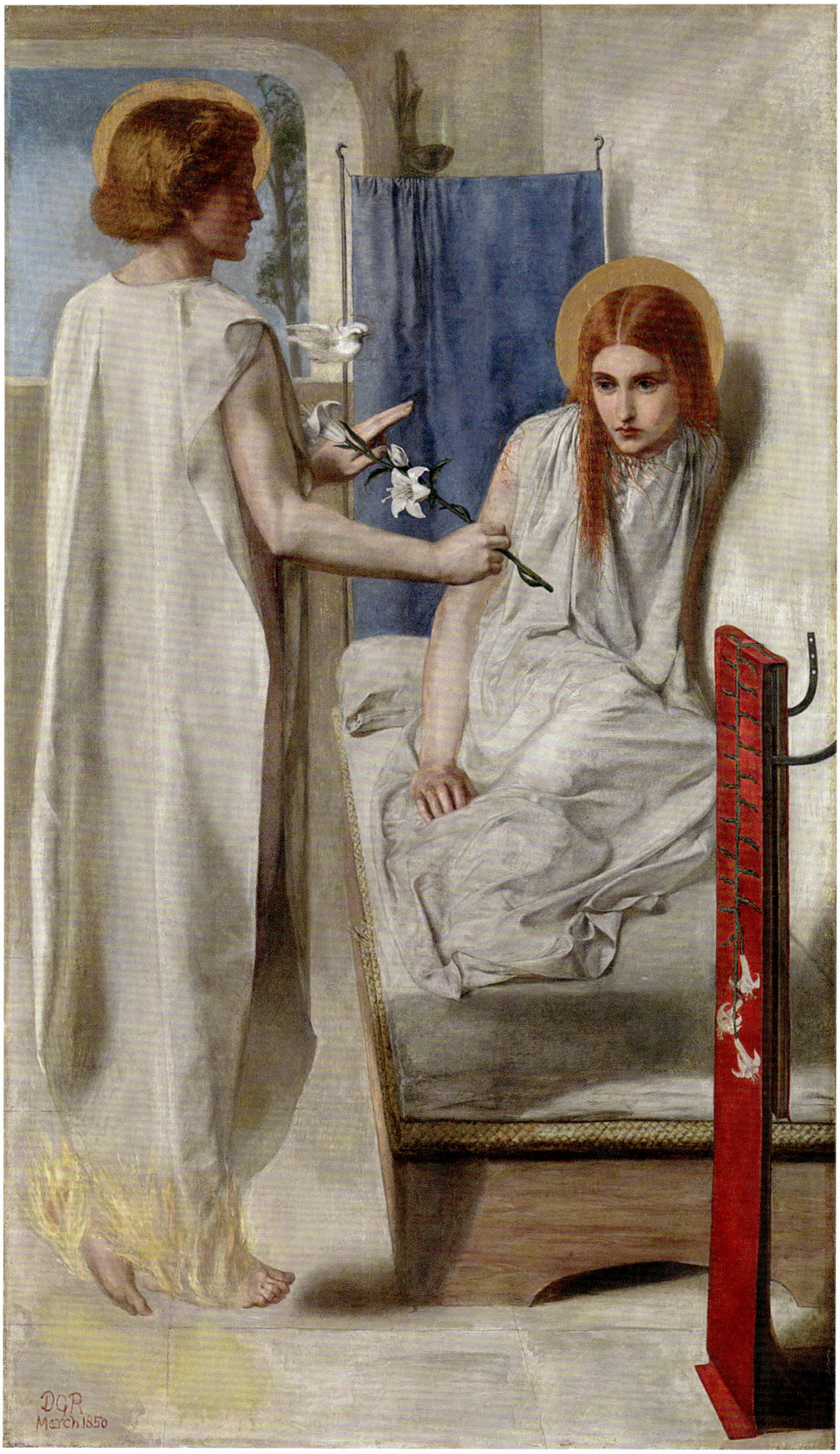

2.10 Dante Gabriel Rossetti, *Ecce Ancilla Domini! (The Annunciation)*, 1849–50, oil on canvas, 72.4 × 41.9 cm. Tate, London.

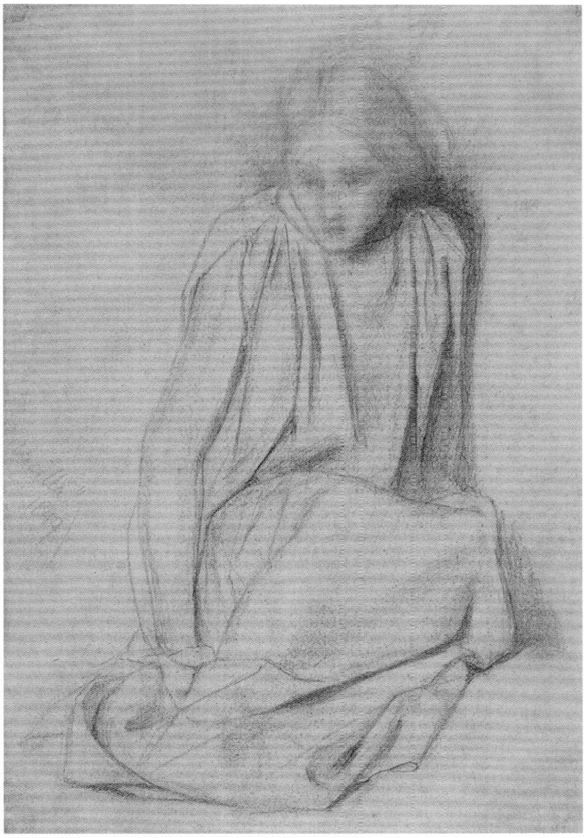

2.11 Dante Gabriel Rossetti, study for *Ecce Ancilla Domini! (The Annunciation)*, c.1849, pencil on paper, 19.4 × 13.7 cm. Tate, London.

scene *Ecce Ancilla Domini!* ('behold the handmaid of the Lord'), which he began to design on 25 November 1849 (fig. 2.10).[27] As with *The Girlhood*, with its subtle capturing of a moment's premonition, the Virgin's face in *Ecce Ancilla Domini!* is a study of psychological tension – fear, apprehension and wonder. This time, however, the Virgin's face caused him protracted problems. At some point, either in late 1849 or early 1850, Christina posed for him, hunching her shoulders and looking apprehensive (fig. 2.11).[28] Gabriel used soft pencil and, perhaps tellingly, he smudged his drawing of her face to make his sister's features less distinct. The 'PRB Journal' that William kept during this period catalogues Gabriel's work on *Ecce Ancilla Domini!*. On 23 March 1850 he was 'at work repainting the Virgin's head in his picture', and nearly a week later, on 29 March, he had a model, Miss Love, 'to sit for the Virgin's hair, and is also repainting the head entirely'; he returned to the picture on 5 December when he 'painted on the head of the Virgin in his last picture'.[29] According to this tally, he painted the head no fewer than four times. William later remarked that 'it presents some substantial resemblance to Christina, and that the expression of *her* face more than any other is realised in it', but concludes: 'a portrait it is not, and does not affect to be'.[30]

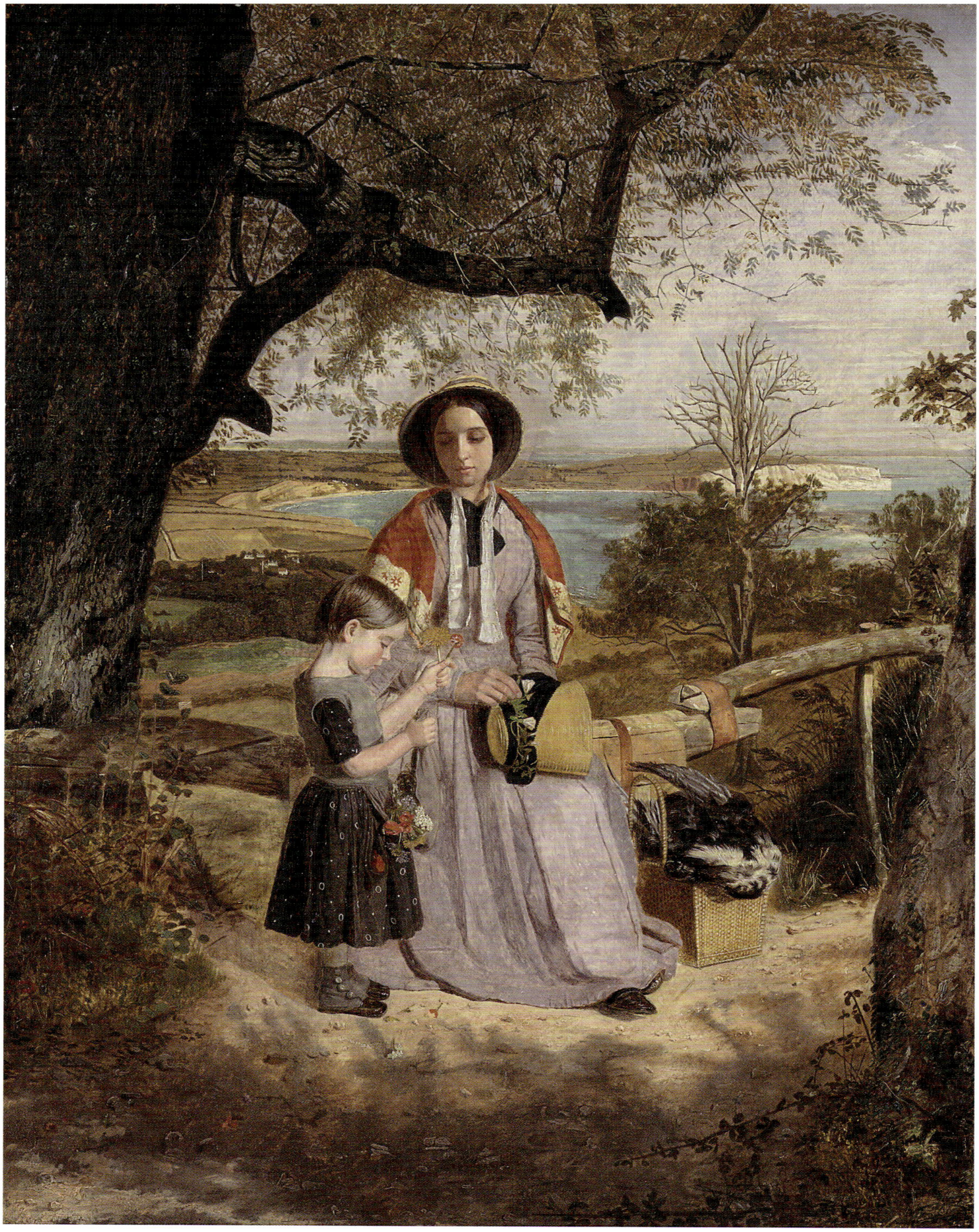

2.12 James Collinson,
Mother and Child by a Stile, with Culver Cliff, Isle of Wight, in the Distance,
c.1849–50, oil on panel, 52.7 × 42.2 cm.
Yale Center for British Art, New Haven.

A brother's close attention was one thing; Collinson's was quite another. Sittings created opportunities for the young couple – however closely chaperoned – to spend time together, and would have allowed the rather timid James to gaze at Christina in a way that would not in any other situation have been possible. She seems also to have modelled for his painting of 1849–50, *Mother and Child by a Stile, with Culver Cliff, Isle of Wight, in the Distance* (fig. 2.12); with her attention absorbed by her child's activity and oblivious to the glorious landscape around her, the female figure looks the very picture of devoted maternal care.[31] It seems as though in his choice of subject Collinson was projecting a desired role onto her – in which case, the picture can be seen as an emotional vision of the future. But if Christina ever shared his dream, she abruptly awoke. Collinson's reconversion to Catholicism gave her, a committed Anglican, little choice but to make the painful decision to break off their engagement, which she did in the spring or early summer of 1850. With a certain grim appropriateness, Collinson was at this time working on *An Incident in the Life of Saint Elizabeth of Hungary* (fig. 1.9; see Chapter One), about a thirteenth-century saint who gave up her worldly life and entered a convent. Had Christina expected to sit for the figure of the saint herself?[32] She later learned that Collinson was intending to use the same model for St Elizabeth as he was using for one of the saint's maids of honour; 'is this the case?' she asked William, adding 'I hope not...'.[33]

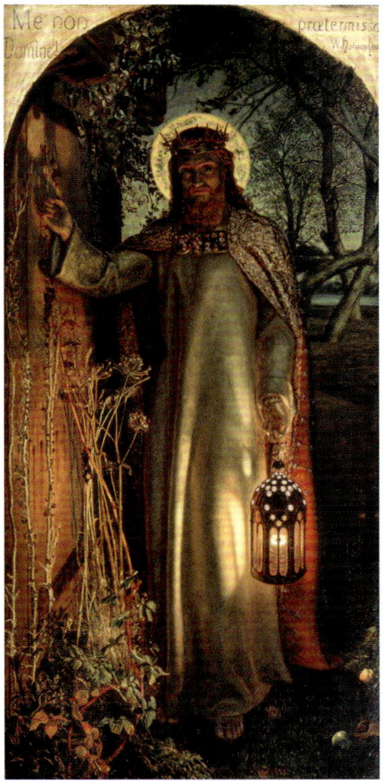

2.13 William Holman Hunt, *The Light of the World*, 1851–3, oil on canvas, 125.5 × 59.8 cm. Keble College, Oxford.

Christina's empathy for the artist's model and her understanding of the relationship between observer and observed are expressed in a sonnet she composed on Christmas Eve, 1856. She wrote 'In an Artist's Studio' after a visit to Gabriel's working room, during which she was struck by the repeated image in his pictures of the face and figure of Elizabeth Siddall, his muse and later wife. The first lines of the poem consider the same system of transformation Christina herself had undergone for the sake of her brother's art:

> One face looks out from all his canvasses,
>   One selfsame figure sits or walks or leans;
>   We found her hidden just behind those screens,
> That mirror gave back all her loveliness.
> A queen in opal or in ruby dress,
>   A nameless girl in freshest summer greens,
>   A saint, an angel; – every canvass means
> The same one meaning, neither more nor less.

There was, however, one major difference. It is notable that the majority of the characters for whom Christina posed are sacred.[34] Even so, one of her most surprising roles was as a model for the face of Christ in William Holman Hunt's *The Light of the World* (fig. 2.13). She was not alone in this, but one of a number of different people from whom Hunt took some element: by using a wide variety of models and even existing portraits, he aimed to distil the essence of friends and family as well as 'many departed heroes'.[35] 'I felt very determined to make the figure mystic in aspect and not suggesting any single person', he said.[36] Having 'secured the male character in the head' he turned to two women: Elizabeth Siddall, for 'the effect of the light and shade on her beautiful copper-coloured locks'; and Christina for her 'solemn expression' – she 'promised to help me with some shade of earnestness I aimed at getting', he explained. Accompanied by her mother, she went for a single sitting at Hunt's Chelsea studio.[37]

Another painting on a religious theme with which Christina has been connected is *Jesus Washing Peter's Feet* by Ford Madox Brown, a close associate of the PRB and a friend of the Rossettis; William would marry his daughter Lucy in 1874.[38] It was a painting begun in the autumn of 1851 during the time Christina was attending the North London School of Drawing and Modelling in Camden Town, where Brown was headmaster (although being in the women's school, she was rarely taught by him).[39] Brown used various different models for the disciples who sit around a table looking on, including William, Hunt and Gabriel.[40] Many years later, in 1894, Christina denied having modelled for the figure of St John, depicted in near-profile on the extreme right. 'William very likely sat for the head of St John', she wrote to Frederic Stephens, one of the founding members of the PRB; 'but I am not certain: not I, certainly. Indeed, I never did sit to Mr Madox Brown for any head'.[41] Brown's grandson and biographer Ford Madox Hueffer and Stephens himself, who sat for Christ, however, both thought she had.[42] Whatever the case, the fact that both believed she might have played a part, and that neither considered it out of the ordinary, is telling in itself.

Christina played quite a different role in a composition of 1853, *Hesterna Rosa* (*Yesterday's Rose*) (fig. 2.14). Gabriel based this elaborate

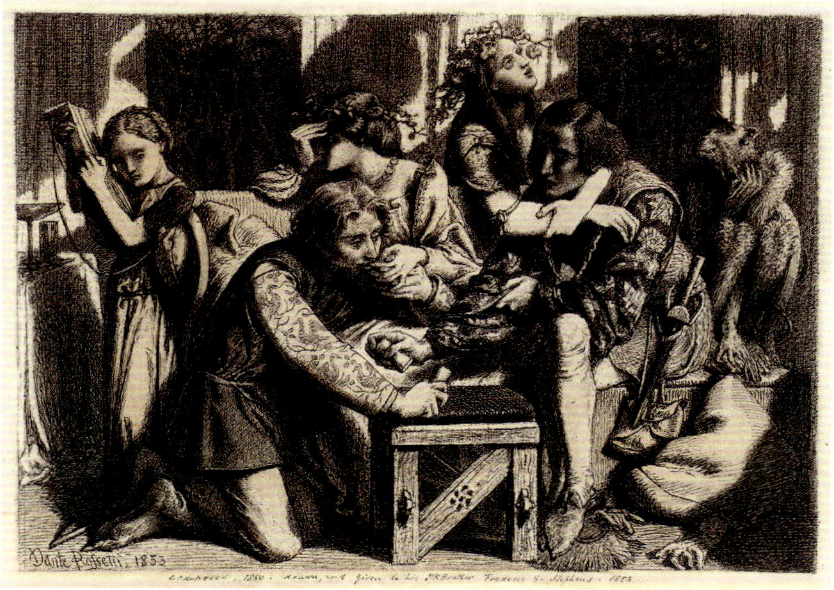

2.14 Dante Gabriel Rossetti, *Hesterna Rosa* (*Yesterday's Rose*), 1853, pen and ink on paper, 19 × 23.5 cm. Tate, London.

2.15 Dante Gabriel Rossetti, *Portrait of Christina Rossetti*, 1852, pencil on paper, 22.8 × 16.5 cm. National Trust, Wightwick Manor, Wolverhampton.

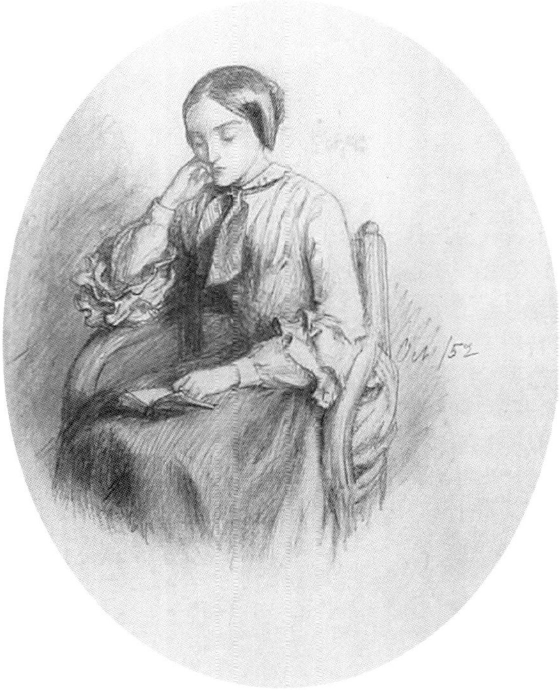

pen-and-ink drawing on a song in a play of 1834 by Sir Henry Taylor, *Philip van Artevelde*:

> Quoth tongue of neither maid nor wife,
> To heart of neither wife nor maid:
> 'Lead we not here a jolly life
> Betwixt the shine and shade?'
>
> Quoth heart of neither maid nor wife
> To tongue of neither wife nor maid:
> 'Thou wag'st, but I am worn with strife,
> And feel like flowers that fade.'[43]

The composition contrasts innocence with depravity: a young girl who plays a lute on the left symbolises innocence, a monkey on the right lechery. One woman drapes her arms around her lover's neck, while in the centre a second woman, apparently modelled by Christina, turns away in shame, hiding her face with one hand while her lover kisses the fingers of the other.[44] She is yesterday's rose, overcome by the realisation of her situation much in the manner of the woman in Hunt's precisely contemporaneous painting *The Awakening Conscience*. Christina, it seems, was happy to pose for the figure of a 'fallen woman' as long as the picture in question pointed a clear moral.

As time went on, Gabriel's drawings of Christina began to lose the self-consciousness that was such a marked feature of the earlier portraits. One drawn in October 1852 (fig. 2.15), which shows her reading, has a quiet restraint that speaks of growing maturity on the part of both artist and sitter. It can be seen as a precursor to the extraordinary sequence of portraits representing Elizabeth Siddall, also often executed in pencil and on a similarly small scale, that Rossetti drew almost obsessively in the mid-1850s. William later wrote of this portrait that it 'affords an extremely good idea of the composed, orderly look of Christina in day-by-day life; modestly self-withdrawn, as incapable of parade in mental gifts as in toilet – but not incapable of making those gifts apparent when the occasion arose'.[45]

Two months earlier, however, Gabriel had sketched a scene showing a less solitary side to his sister's character. During July and August of 1852, Christina had been invited to stay at Darlaston Hall in Staffordshire, home of the poet and former MP Swynfen Jervis, in order to tutor one of his daughters in conversational Italian. Jervis was, as William later noted, a literary figure, 'something of a Shakespearean commentator, and something also of a verse-writer'.[46] Gabriel wrote to Christina in August, including a cartoon of her sitting earnestly at Mr Jervis's feet, pen poised over a pad of paper, as – leaning against a bust of Shakespeare and adopting the pose of the eighteenth-century monument to the playwright in Poet's Corner, Westminster Abbey – he holds forth (fig. 2.16). As Gabriel facetiously explains in his letter:

> On the opposite page is an attempt to record, though faintly, that privileged period of your life during which you have sat at the feet of one for whom the ages have probably been waiting.... On *his* countenance is a calm serenity, unchangeable, unmistakable. In yours I think I read awe, mingled however with something of that noble pride which even the companionship of greatness has been known to bestow. Are you here transcribing from his very lips the title-deeds of his immortality, or rather perpetuating by a sister art the aspect of that brow where poetry has set up her throne? I know not.[47]

The first known photographic portrait of Christina, a studio photograph in which she poses with her mother and sister, dating from 1855 or 1856, shows the same sweeping jaw and pointed chin that Gabriel caricatures here (fig. 2.17).

Over the next decade Christina continued to model for Gabriel sporadically. Her features appear twice in his design *King Arthur and the Weeping Queens* (fig. 2.18), which he had been commissioned to produce for a lavishly illustrated edition of Tennyson's poems, published by Edward Moxon in 1857. According to William, 'The first face here (from the spectator's left) is taken from Christina, but is less

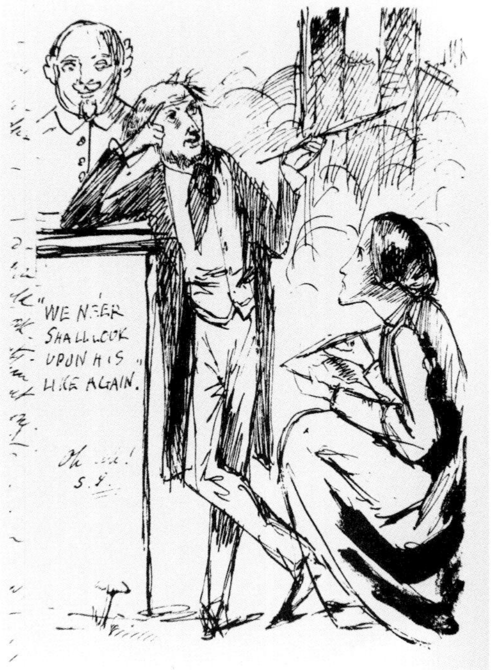

2.16 Above:
Dante Gabriel Rossetti, *Christina Taking down the Verses of Swynfen Jervis*, 1852, pen and ink on paper, 17.8 × 11.4 cm. Private collection, reproduced in *The Family Letters of Christina Georgina Rossetti*, ed. William Michael Rossetti (London: Brown, Langham & Co., 1908).

2.17 Right:
Anonymous photographer, *Portrait of Christina, Maria and Frances Rossetti*, *c.*1855–6, reproduced in Gabriele Rossetti, *A Versified Autobiography* (London: Sands & Co., 1901).

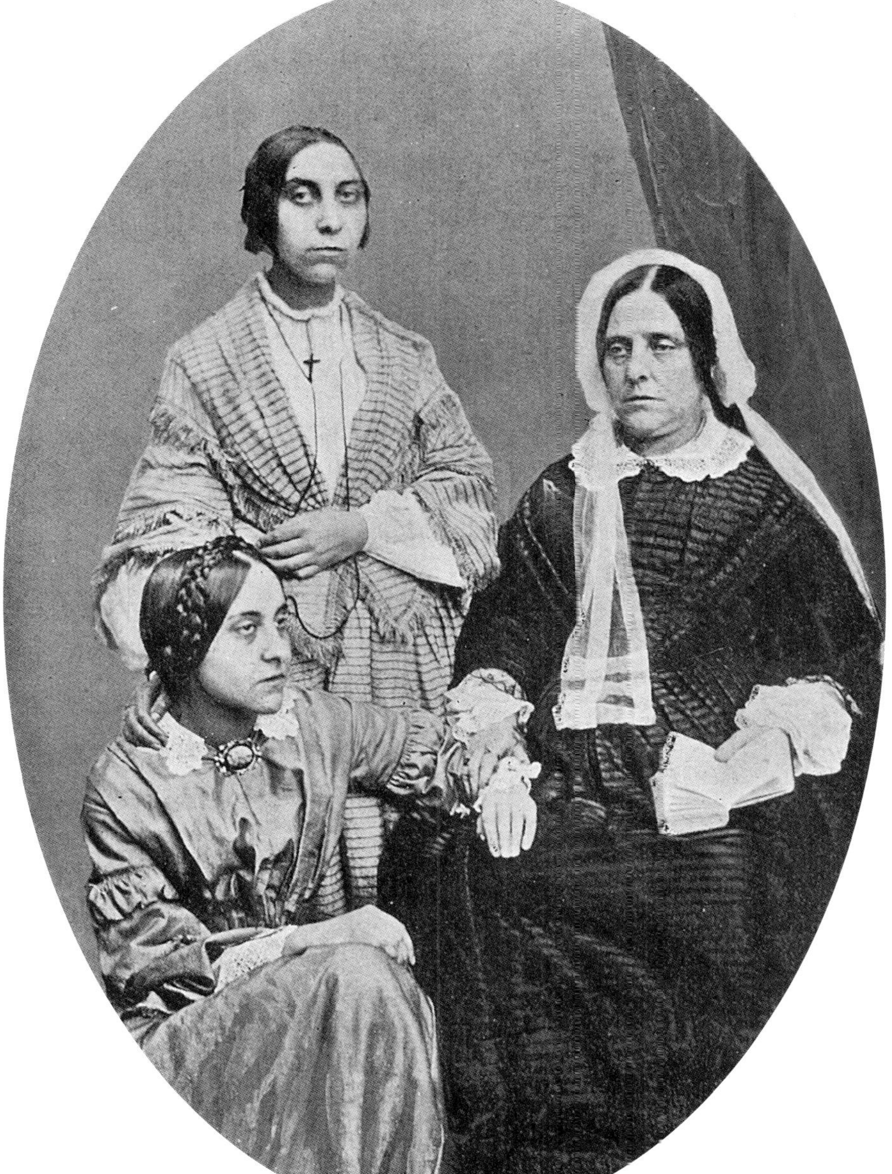

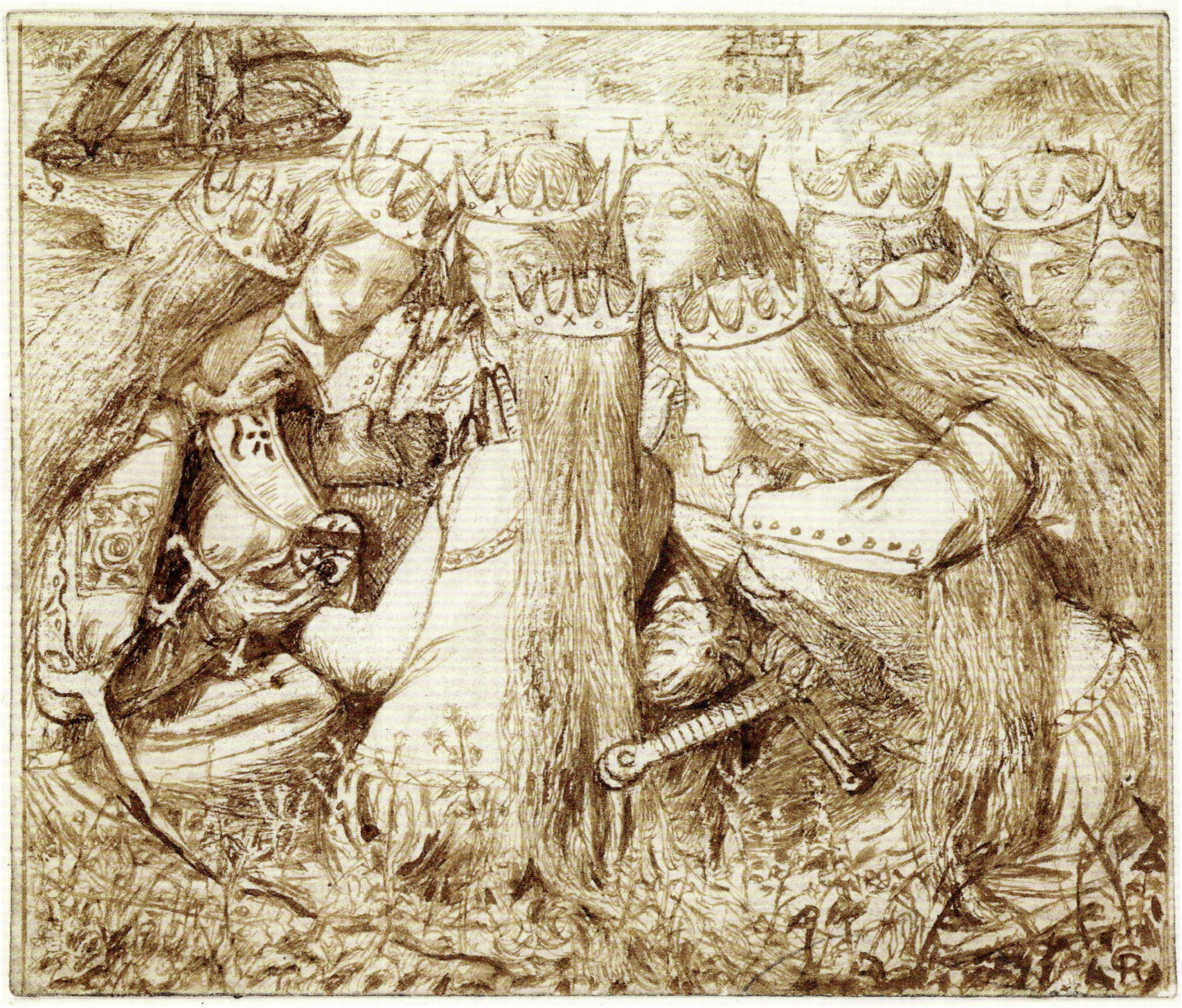

like her on the engraved page than in the original drawing; she must also have sat for the profile to the extreme right, which is a very faithful likeness'.[48] In 1861, Gabriel gave the Virgin Mary his sister's features for a third time when he was planning a stained-glass design for All Saints Church, Selsley, Gloucestershire, representing the Sermon on the Mount (fig. 2.19). Christina – at least on paper – joined a gathering of various members of her brother's circle: she appears at bottom left, with Fanny Cornforth beside her as Mary Magdalene; behind them are A. C. Swinburne as St John and Simeon Solomon as St James; and on the right is William Morris as St Peter, with the art dealer Ernest Gambart, who Gabriel disliked, behind him as Judas. And did Gabriel include a surreptitious image of the author in 1865, when designing the frontispiece illustration *You Should Have Wept Her Yesterday* for Christina's book *The Prince's Progress and Other Poems* (fig. 4.7)?

2.18 Dante Gabriel Rossetti, *King Arthur and the Weeping Queens* (design for the Moxon Tennyson), *c.*1856–7, pen and ink on paper, 8.2 × 9.2 cm. Birmingham Museum & Art Gallery.

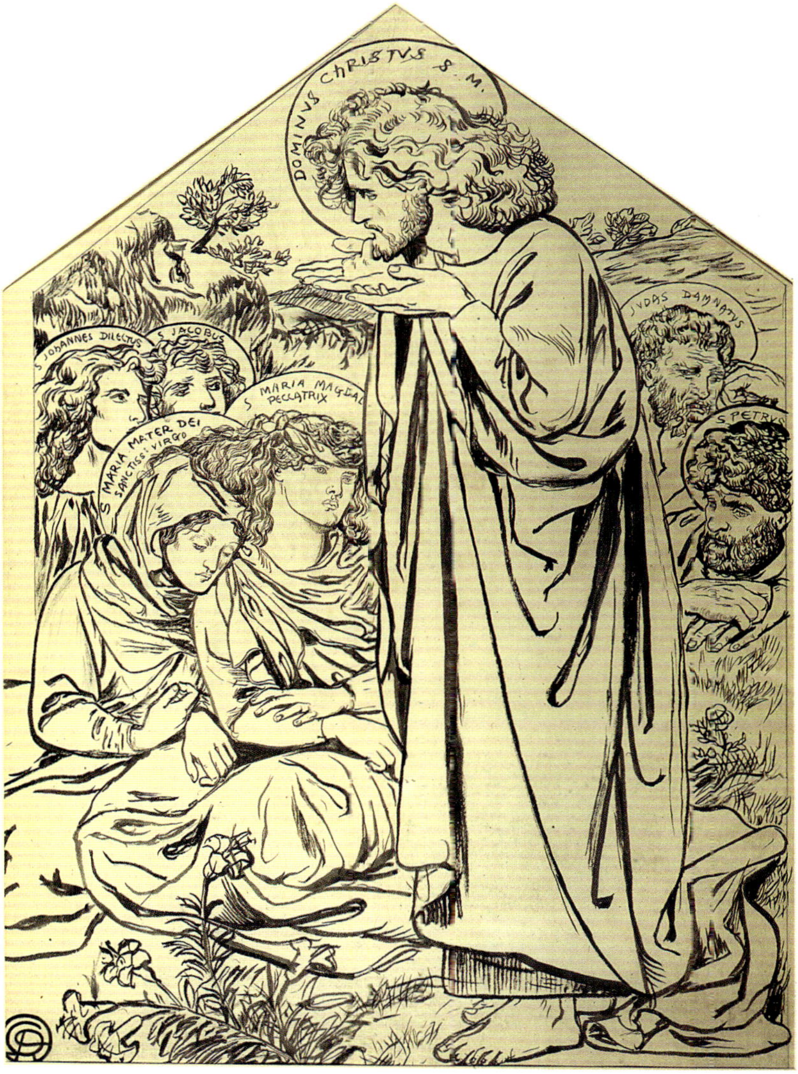

2.19 Dante Gabriel Rossetti, *The Sermon on the Mount* (design for a stained-glass window), *c.*1861, pen and ink on paper, 73.5 × 54.2 cm. William Morris Gallery, London.

In March 1865 he sent her proofs of the wood engravings for her comments. 'Surely the severe female who arrests the Prince somewhat resembles my phiz', she responded.[49] In May of that year Gabriel made a sensitive portrait of her in profile (fig. 1.6), although it is not known whether it was in connection with this forthcoming book.

It was around this time that Christina's face began to appear in murals painted by her old friend William Bell Scott (or 'Scotus', as the Rossettis called him) at Penkill Castle in Ayrshire, which belonged to his close friend Alice Boyd, and where for part of each year he lived with his wife Letitia. From 1865 to 1868 he decorated the walls of the spiral staircase with scenes from *The Kingis Quair*, written by King James I of Scotland while he was held prisoner at Windsor Castle in the 1420s. Scott introduced portraits of his friends in his scheme: Christina as Lady Jane Beaufort, and Swinburne and William as courtiers of Venus.[50]

But while, when she consented to pose as a model, Christina's own features were subsumed into the larger work, here the situation was different: she was included as a gesture of friendship. Through her image she maintained a presence in the castle – where she often went to stay with Alice and the Scotts – even in her absence.

2.20 John Brett, *Portrait of Christina Rossetti*, 1857, oil on panel, 13.3 × 10.1 cm. Private collection.

'I never said I loved you, John'

Nine years after Collinson painted his portrait of Rossetti, another artist was captivated by her appearance. But if Collinson made a drab London pigeon of her, in John Brett's imagination she was transformed into an altogether more extraordinary fowl (fig. 2.20). Brett was a painter on the fringes of the PRB who embraced Pre-Raphaelite principles of vivid colours and meticulous attention to the detail of natural form. As he recorded in his diary in May 1853: 'I am going on fast towards Preraphaelitism – Millais and Hunt are truly fine fellows. I greatly admire and honour them – Have resolved in future to go through severe course of training and close childlike study of nature. In short to follow their steps.'[51] His specialist subject matter was the landscape and the coast, but he also made portraits, principally of his family and friends, for his own pleasure – mostly to keep, rather than to sell.[52]

Brett used a small panel for his portrait of Rossetti, and painted it like a miniature, dabbing paint onto a white ground in order to increase the intensity of the colour and to achieve a luminous clarity. Behind her head to the left is the tail feather of a bronze turkey, while at the top is an unfinished sketch of a peacock feather.[53] This extraordinary, icon-like painting was, however, abandoned before it was completed, remaining in Brett's possession and subsequently being passed down within the family. He did not sign or inscribe it himself, but in later years someone, probably his granddaughter Winifred Watson, attached a slip of paper to the back bearing a note that reads: 'Painted by John Brett A.R.A. / Christina Rossetti ? Mickleham 1857', basing these pieces of information on detailed notes she had made from conversations with her mother (Brett's daughter), Daisy.[54]

Further than that, the circumstances surrounding Brett's portrait of Rossetti are a puzzle to which some of the pieces are tantalisingly missing. Was the relationship between artist and sitter a romantic one? What might the feathers – which, in the context of 1850s portraiture, are such a strange feature – symbolise? And why was the portrait never finished?

From being part of a wider circle of like-minded artists, Brett seems to have become friendly with the Rossetti family in 1856, when he was probably invited to Frances's regular Thursday evening parties, and indeed there were numerous other social, exhibition-related events at which he and Christina might have encountered each other.[55] In the summer of 1857 Brett was staying at Mickleham in Surrey while he was working on one of his best-known works, *The Stonebreaker*; they could have met in July, during a brief visit

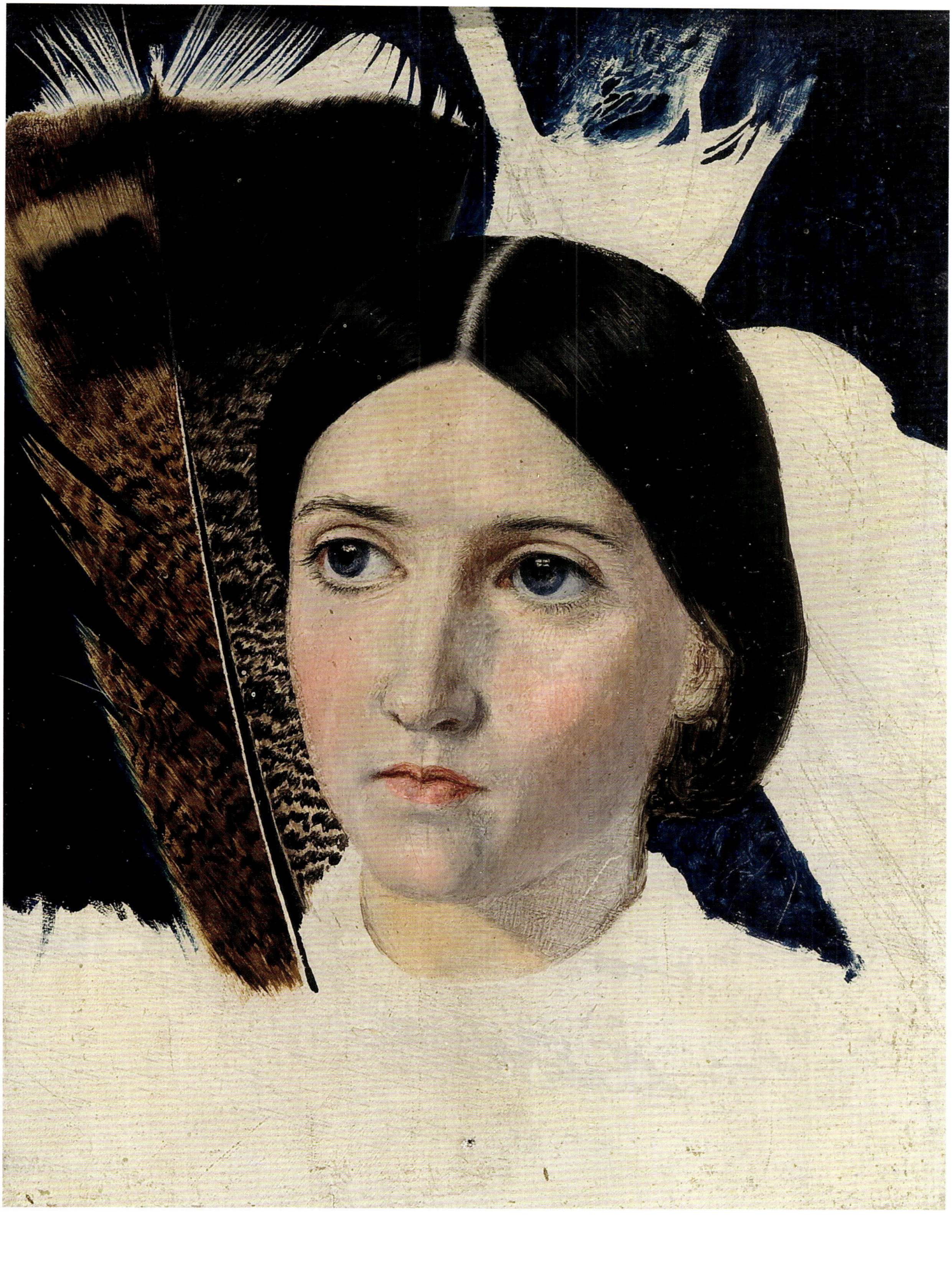

Christina and her sister paid to the Epps family at nearby Warlingham.[56] Unfortunately no letters survive that might have provided a contemporary commentary, although William later recalled that Brett 'had appeared to be somewhat smitten by Christina'.[57] Did Christina return his feelings? Was it this that inspired her to write 'A Birthday', her joyful poem about love, which she composed in November of that year?

> My heart is like a singing bird
>   Whose nest is in a watered shoot;
> My heart is like an apple tree
>   Whose boughs are bent with thickset fruit;
> My heart is like a rainbow shell
>   That paddles in a halcyon sea;
> My heart is gladder than all these
>   Because my love is come to me.

William recalled having been asked more than once if he could 'account for the outburst of exuberant joy' in the poem. 'I am unable to do so', he wrote, yet continued: 'It is, of course, possible to infer that the *Birthday* is a mere piece of poetical composition, not testifying to any corresponding emotion of its author at the time; but I am hardly prepared to think that.'[58]

If there were – at least for a time – romantic feelings on both sides, could the picture have been intended as a betrothal portrait? In which case the turkey feather could perhaps be interpreted as Brett's attribute, the peacock feather Christina's (it is worth noting that she refers to 'peacocks with a hundred eyes' in the second stanza of 'A Birthday').[59] Perhaps the portrait remained unfinished because their relationship came to an end. Elizabeth Siddall's biographer Violet Hunt claimed Brett had told her that Christina had refused an offer of marriage he made to her, while a poem Christina wrote in March of 1860, '"No, thank you, John"', is written in the voice of a woman exasperatedly rejecting a stubbornly insistent suitor.[60] Without drawing overly simple biographical conclusions, this poem does at least reveal that she had such a situation in mind at around this period: 'I never said I loved you, John: / Why will you teaze me day by day'; 'I'd rather answer "No" to fifty Johns / Than answer "Yes" to you.'

In 1875, Christina's publisher Macmillan & Co. brought out a collected edition of her verses, *Goblin Market, The Prince's Progress and Other Poems*. In December that year, she observed in a letter to Gabriel: 'The whole subject of youthful poems grows anxious in middle-age, or may at some moment appear so: one is so different, & yet so vividly the same.' Referring to her decision to include '"No, thank you, John"' in this collection, with which Gabriel disagreed, she writes: 'As to "John", as no such person existed or exists I hope my indiscretion may be accounted the less'.[61] And yet she contradicted herself in a pencilled note that she made in the margin of her own copy of her collected poems, a

2.21 Clarkington & Co., *Portrait of Christina Rossetti*, c.1863, albumen print, 9 × 5.5 cm. Victoria and Albert Museum, London.

volume eventually inherited by William. It reads: 'The original John was obnoxious, because he never gave scope for "No thank you!"'[62]

'I am not much addicted to sitting for my portrait'

With the publication of *Goblin Market and Other Poems* by Macmillan & Co. in April of 1862 – and its warm reception in the press – came public attention, and with public attention came a desire to know what this hitherto unknown author of such extraordinary poetry looked like. Initially Rossetti dealt with her publisher's request for a portrait photograph with distinct brusqueness, replying in a letter of 7 April 1862: 'I wish I had by me a photograph worthy of a place in your Magazine, but I have not at all a good one. If ever one is taken I will not forget your claim; but I am not much addicted to sitting for my portrait.'[63] A refusal to take any active steps in the matter was rather a chilly brush-off; yet a few months later, Rossetti seems to have had a change of heart. In August she wrote again to Alexander Macmillan:

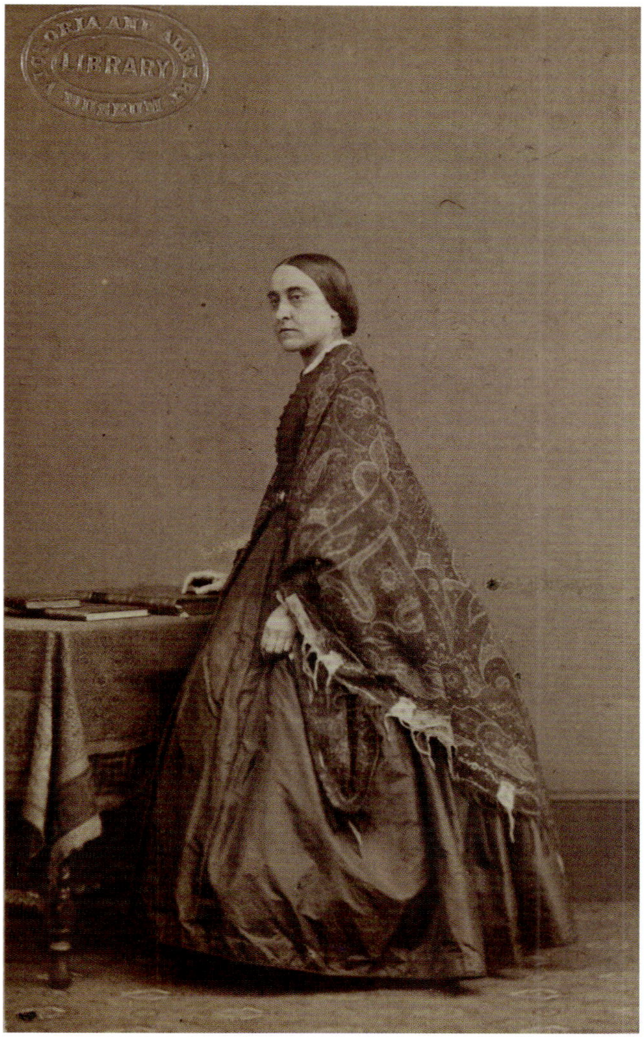

> I know not whether the photograph I enclose will appear worth inserting in your copy of the Magazine: but remembering that you once asked me for one of myself, I cannot forbear offering it. It was taken by an amateur friend in 1855, when I was much more addicted to verse writing than I am now; and is perhaps the most satisfactory ever done of me. The copy I send has only just now come into my hands.[64]

The photograph was among a group taken by Christina's friend Henrietta Rintoul, the daughter of the editor of *The Spectator*, who became engaged to William around 1856 (although in 1860 she ended the relationship). In two, Christina posed on a little balcony at the top of the house, alone in one and with William in the other. Sadly none survives; and indeed even in 1904 her brother remarked on the extent to which they had faded.[65] Macmillan, however, apparently thought the amateur photograph unsuitable: 'I have kept in mind that you did not approve of my photograph sent you a while ago', wrote Christina in December of 1863.[66] This time, however, an increasing number of requests for her photograph prompted her to have formal *carte-de-visite* studio portraits taken, two standing and one seated, for which she wore a dark silk dress over a crinoline (fig. 2.21).[67] She sent two to Macmillan for him to choose from.

'Is it troubling you too much', she asked, 'to send me back whichever of the two you reject? one is so often asked for one's photograph that every copy has its value.'[68]

One session at a photographic studio could hardly be counted an addiction, although Christina evidently liked the results well enough to send portraits to her new friend Dora Greenwell and to her old, Mrs Heimann: 'My effigy greets you and yours', she wrote to the latter in January 1864, 'with all New Year's greetings of true love, and begs a nook in your album: harbour the stranger, or rather your affectionate old friend.'[69]

While Christina was dealing with the dissemination of her photograph with fastidious caution, Gabriel had created a rather less dignified image of his sister. A review of *Goblin Market* published in *The Times* included the observation: 'Miss Rossetti can point to work which could not easily be mended'; this inspired him to make a sketch of his sister in the throes of a tantrum, stamping her feet in fury and waving a hammer in the air as she wrecks the furniture (fig. 2.22). It became a private joke between them. In a letter of March 1865, replying to one of Gabriel's in which he had offered detailed (and by no means entirely welcome) comments on the poems she had selected for her collection *The Prince's Progress and Other Poems,* she refers back to this vision of her behaviour: 'After 6 well defined and several paroxysms of stamping, foaming, hair-uprooting, it seems time to assume a treacherous calm: and in this (comparatively) lucid interval I regain speech.'[70]

In searching for Christina's image we seem to be presented with two extremes at this stage of her life: either the stiff formality of the studio portrait or the physically demonstrative caricatures of Gabriel's imagination.[71] A more natural image, however, was to be added. In the autumn of 1863 the Rossetti family gathered in the garden of Tudor House on Cheyne Walk in Chelsea, to which Gabriel had moved the previous year in the wake of his wife's death. They were there to be photographed by one of the most talented amateur photographers of the age, Charles Lutwidge Dodgson (better known by his pen name Lewis Carroll). Dodgson, a lecturer in mathematics at Christ Church in Oxford since 1855, seems to have been introduced to Gabriel by the Pre-Raphaelite sculptor Alexander Munro on 30 September 1863, the date Gabriel wrote to his mother: 'The photographer (Revd Mr Dodgson) is coming here on Wednesday to do the lot of us, – this day week.'[72] Dodgson recorded in his diary that Gabriel was 'most hospitable in his offers of the use of house and garden for picture-taking, and I arranged to take my camera there on Monday [5 October], have Tuesday for friends, and on Wednesday take him and his mother and

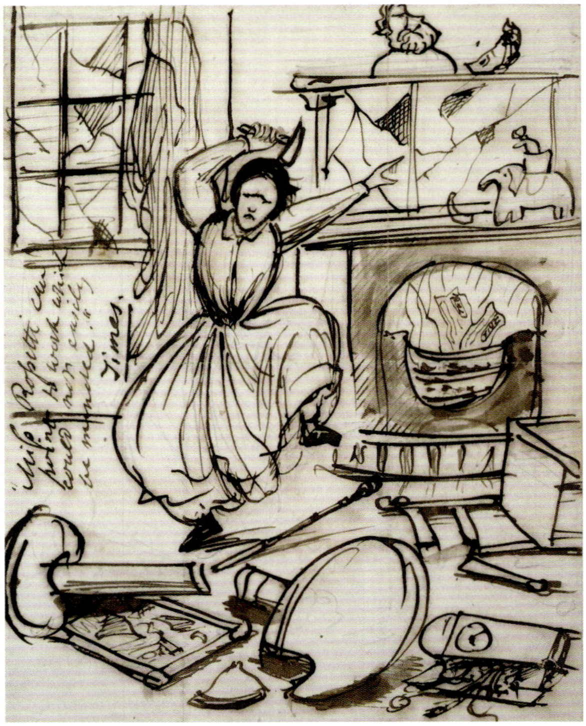

2.22 Above:
Dante Gabriel Rossetti,
'"Miss Rossetti can point to work which could not easily be mended" (Times)', 1862, pen and ink wash on paper, 22 × 18 cm.
National Trust, Wightwick Manor, Wolverhampton.

2.23 Right:
Lewis Carroll
(Charles Lutwidge Dodgson),
Portrait of Gabriel, Christina, Frances and William Rossetti, 1863, albumen print, 17.5 × 22.2 cm.
National Portrait Gallery, London.

sister.'[73] He noted that Christina, who 'seemed shy at first', sat for two portraits on 6 October, although these have not survived.[74] The next day he concentrated on photographs of the assembled Rossetti family.

At this time poses had to be held for around forty-five seconds, but despite this handicap Dodgson's portraits have a remarkably relaxed air: in a group photograph of Mrs Rossetti with three of her children taken on 7 October (fig. 2.23), Gabriel leans against the railings; Christina sits on the steps and rests her chin on her hands, looking up with a slight smile; Frances, seated on a chair, turns towards her daughter as though about to speak; and William, at the far right, stands with his hands in his pockets and one leg crossed casually over the other. Their expressions are natural – they seem cheerfully engaged with each other, as much as they are with the process taking place. A photograph of Christina looking at a book with her mother (fig. 2.24), taken the same day, seems to bring her to an even greater degree of vivid life. We see less of her face because of the oblique angle of her head – there is her profile again – but the easy intimacy of the two women and the angles of Christina's knee, elbow and wrist are expressive of character.

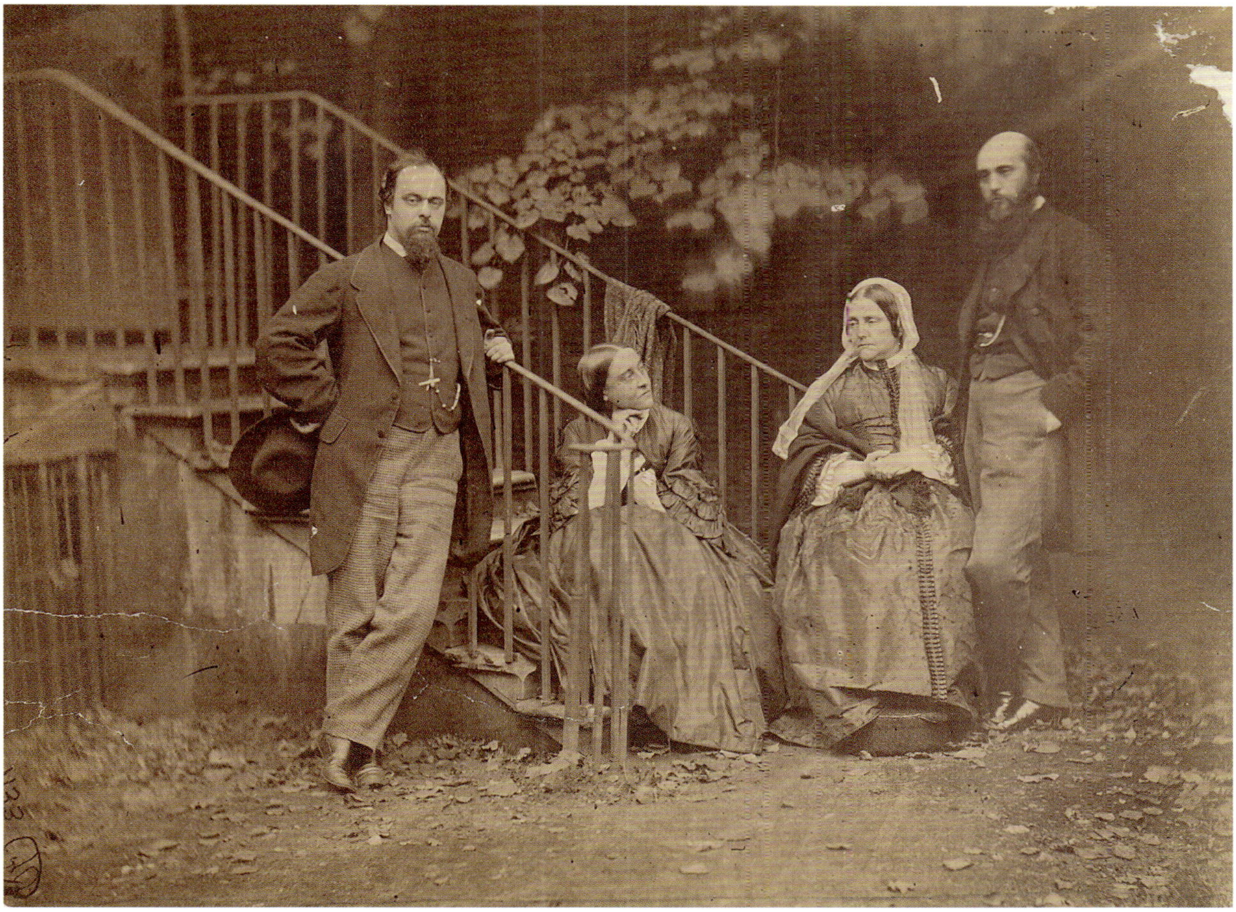

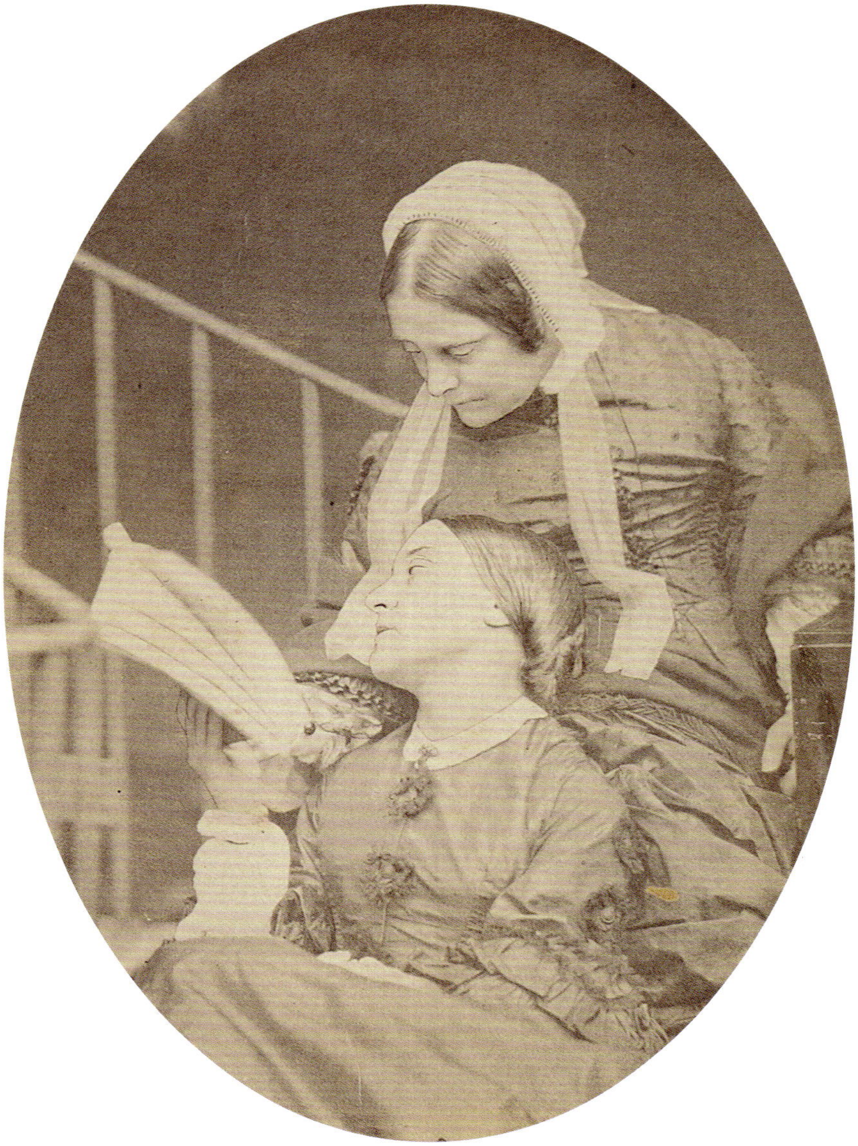

2.24 Left:
Lewis Carroll
(Charles Lutwidge Dodgson),
Portrait of Christina and Frances Rossetti, 1863,
albumen print, 14 × 10.5 cm.
Mark Samuels Lasner Collection,
University of Delaware Library.

2.25 Right:
Dante Gabriel Rossetti,
Portrait of Christina Rossetti, 1866,
coloured chalks on paper, 79 × 63.5 cm.
Private collection.

Christina's second collection, *The Prince's Progress and Other Poems,* was published in June 1866. Perhaps in recognition of her achievement, in which he had been involved not only as illustrator but also as advisor, in September Gabriel drew what is perhaps the most powerful portrait he ever made of his sister. Showing her leaning on a table and looking up from an open book as though struck by poetic inspiration, this coloured chalk drawing presents an image of a mature poet (fig. 2.25). William remarked that as well as being 'beautiful', 'chaste in outline' and 'distinguished in expression', it would also 'be hard for any likeness to be more exact'.[75] Gabriel himself remarked that 'every one seems to think [it] a good likeness'.[76]

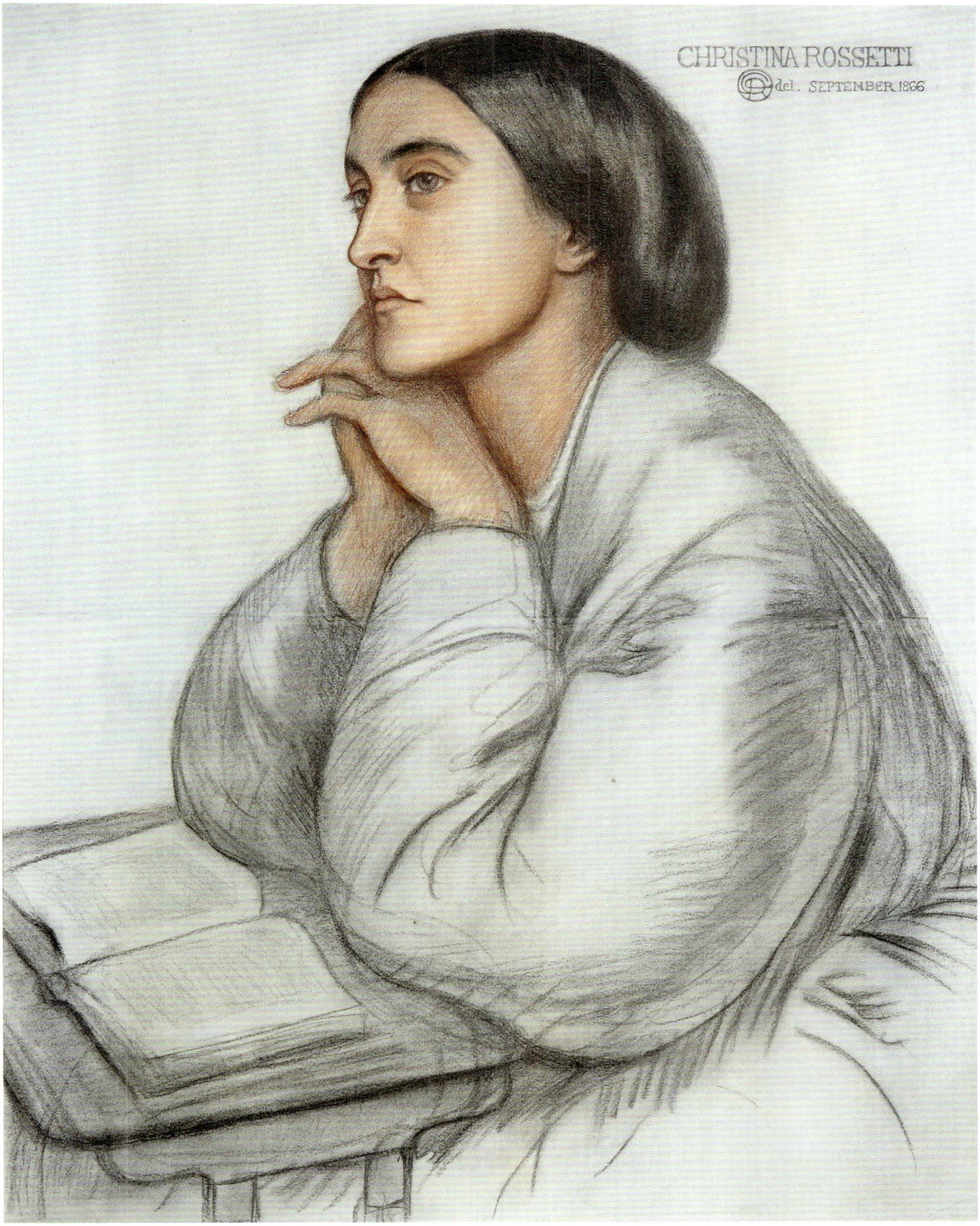
CHRISTINA ROSSETTI
del. SEPTEMBER 1866

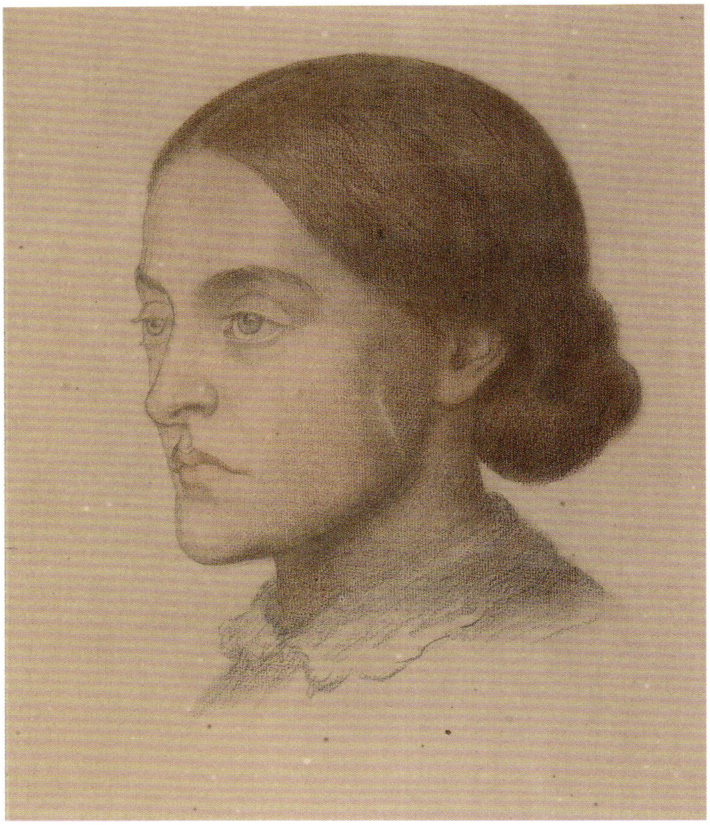

2.26 Dante Gabriel Rossetti,
Portrait of Christina Rossetti, c.1866,
coloured chalks on paper,
48.9 × 43.2 cm.
Fitzwilliam Museum, Cambridge.

Yet it is more than a portrait; as a half-length representation of a female figure dreamily absorbed in her own thoughts, it can also be compared with some of the sensual compositions Gabriel was painting in the 1860s, such as *Aurelia (Fazio's Mistress)* (1863) or *Sibylla Palmifera* (1865–70); or even *Beata Beatrix* (c.1864–70), a hybrid work, part posthumous portrait of Elizabeth Siddall and part response to Dante's *La Vita Nuova*. At around the same time Gabriel drew another portrait of Christina in coloured chalks, in the same near-profile but with a slightly different tilt of the head (fig. 2.26), which was possibly made in connection with the larger drawing or to celebrate the publication of *The Prince's Progress*.

In August 1866, shortly before Gabriel drew the half-length portrait, Christina had received another proposal of marriage, this time from a friend to whom she had been close since 1862. He was Charles Bagot Cayley, described by William as 'a close and abstracted scholar, a man of singular unworldliness', who had first become known to the family when he began to study Italian with Gabriele in 1847.[77] Despite warm feelings towards Cayley, Christina declined his proposal, apparently on the grounds of his atheism, but the two remained close until the former's death ('if he *likes* to see me,' she wrote to William shortly after her refusal, 'God knows I like to see him').[78] Cayley wrote a sonnet about a portrait of Christina, in all likelihood the half-length of September 1866, which was eventually published in his 1880 collection *Poems and Translations*:

> Ah noble aspect, sweet, and firm, and true,
> The folded bud of love's and honour's pink –
> Whose aspect? Well, 'twas Eivir's you might think,
> Ere with wild Harold to the woods she flew;
> Or hers, whom fatally the Tarquin knew,
> Or Sappho's ere she learnt Love's fire to drink;
> Or someone's, who should join, with fittest link,
> Such virtues, that so widely parted grew.
> Fine blood of England, Hellas, Italy,
> And pure, and quick and soft as each hath been,
> Show'd in the lips alone its majesty,
> Veil'd in the features with a light-brown sheen.
> Ah golden hours, that saw a brother trace,
> With art so reaching, such a sister's face![79]

Cayley supplies the rich narrative dimension at which Gabriel only hints – one could argue that together they create what the latter termed a 'double work of art', a drawing and a poem working together. Christina is compared to Eivir, the brave Danish maiden from Walter Scott's long verse narrative *Harold the Dauntless* (1817), who disguised herself as the hero's servant Gunnar and was eventually to marry Harold; to the virtuous Roman noblewoman Lucretia, who committed suicide after being raped by Sextus Tarquinius; and to the ancient Greek lyric poet Sappho, who, according to legend, threw herself into the sea when rejected by her lover Phaon. But she is like these figures, 'ere' the moments occur that precipitate their passionate dramas; they are images of overwhelming emotional potential, as yet unrealised. For Cayley, Christina remained 'a folded bud', a tantalisingly untapped resource.

The drawing became, for a time, something approaching an official portrait, and Gabriel had photographs taken of it that allowed Christina to send copies to her friends.[80] 'Please accept the unworthy little phiz as the phiz of a friend', she wrote, for example, to Alice Boyd in 1870, 'or at least as Gabriel's version of such phiz.'[81] The portrait itself hung in her drawing room at 30 Torrington Square, the room in which she died.[82]

Apart from Gabriel, if any artist of the time was equipped to create the definitive image of Christina Rossetti, it was Julia Margaret Cameron, who brought an unprecedented visionary intensity to portrait photography. They became friends in 1866, the year of Cameron's composition *The Minstrel Group* (fig. 5.3; see Chapter Five), which was inspired by lines from Rossetti's poem 'Advent'. In a letter to William from Penkill, where she was staying with Alice Boyd and the Scotts, Christina describes having recently seen her:

> Mrs Cameron called one day (of course in London) with a portfolio of her magnificent photographs, of which she kindly presented 5 to Mamma, Maria, and self. Maria and I returned her visit at Little Holland House, where we saw the gigantic Val [Prinsep], Mr [G. F.] Watts, Mrs Dalrymple, and got a glimpse of Browning, besides of course seeing Mrs Cameron.[83]

2.27 Dante Gabriel Rossetti, *Portrait of Christina Rossetti*, 1877, coloured chalks on paper, 38.7 × 29.8 cm. Private collection.

Cameron photographed Christina around 1867, inscribing the lid of one of her negative boxes: 'no. 24 Christina Rossetti profile'. Frustratingly, the location of this box is currently unknown and no print has been identified.[84]

'Seized by a burning desire to have her portrait drawn'

It was more than ten years before Gabriel drew Christina's portrait again, and when he did brother and sister were both changed by illness. In the early 1870s Christina had been dangerously ill with a thyroid condition, Graves' disease, that discoloured her skin, made her neck swell and eyes protrude and left a permanent mark on her features; in 1872, Gabriel suffered a nervous breakdown from which he never completely recovered.

The final portraits Gabriel created of Christina resulted directly from his illness. In the summer of 1877, Gabriel's heavy dependency on the drug chloral had brought about a new crisis in his health, and in August he was persuaded to leave Chelsea in order to recuperate at Herne Bay in Kent, where a secluded farmhouse had been found. Frances and Christina joined him there, followed by Gabriel's friend Theodore Watts (later Watts-Dunton). One of the delusions that beset Gabriel at this time was the idea he was no longer able to draw. One day, however, conversation turned to the sudden hair loss experienced by their old friend William Bell Scott. 'Sketch Scotus's bald pate for us', suggested Watts, at which Gabriel took up a piece of chalk and made a bravura drawing. 'Of course', wrote Watts,

> we made no comment upon the fact of his powers of work being suddenly restored, but the next day Christina was seized by a burning desire to have her portrait drawn in chalk. Simultaneously Mrs. Rossetti was seized by a burning desire to possess a portrait of Christina in chalk. When Rossetti declared that he could not even hold a piece of chalk, Scotus's bald pate was pointed to. The result of the little plot was a very successful chalk portrait group, of Christina and her mother ... followed by another portrait of Christina, then by a portrait of Mrs. Rossetti and then another of Christina.[85]

The portraits (figs 2.27, 2.28 and 2.29), made between the end of September and the end of October, are an extraordinarily powerful group, with a psychological depth that perhaps resulted not only from Gabriel's own suffering but also from his realisation of the extent of

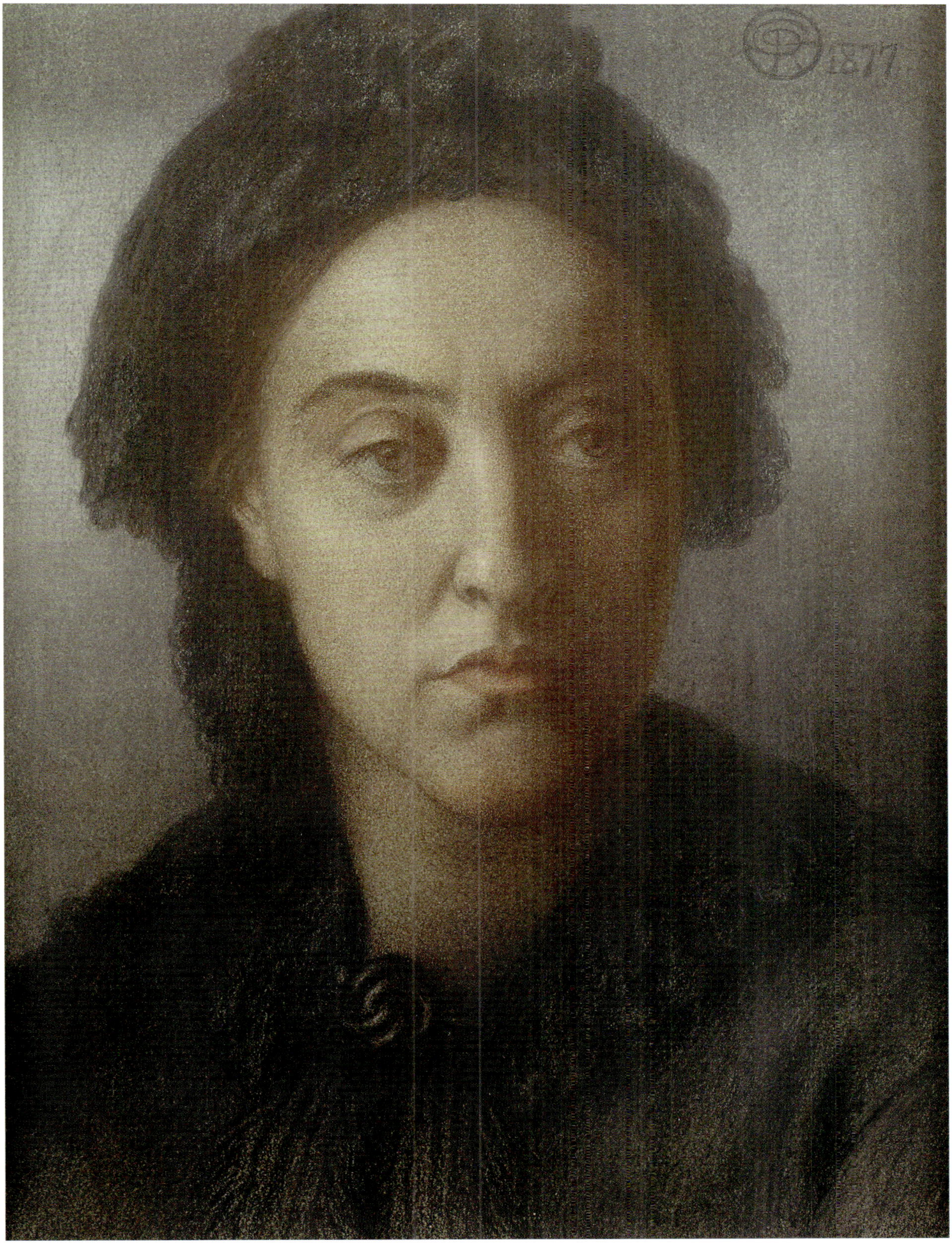

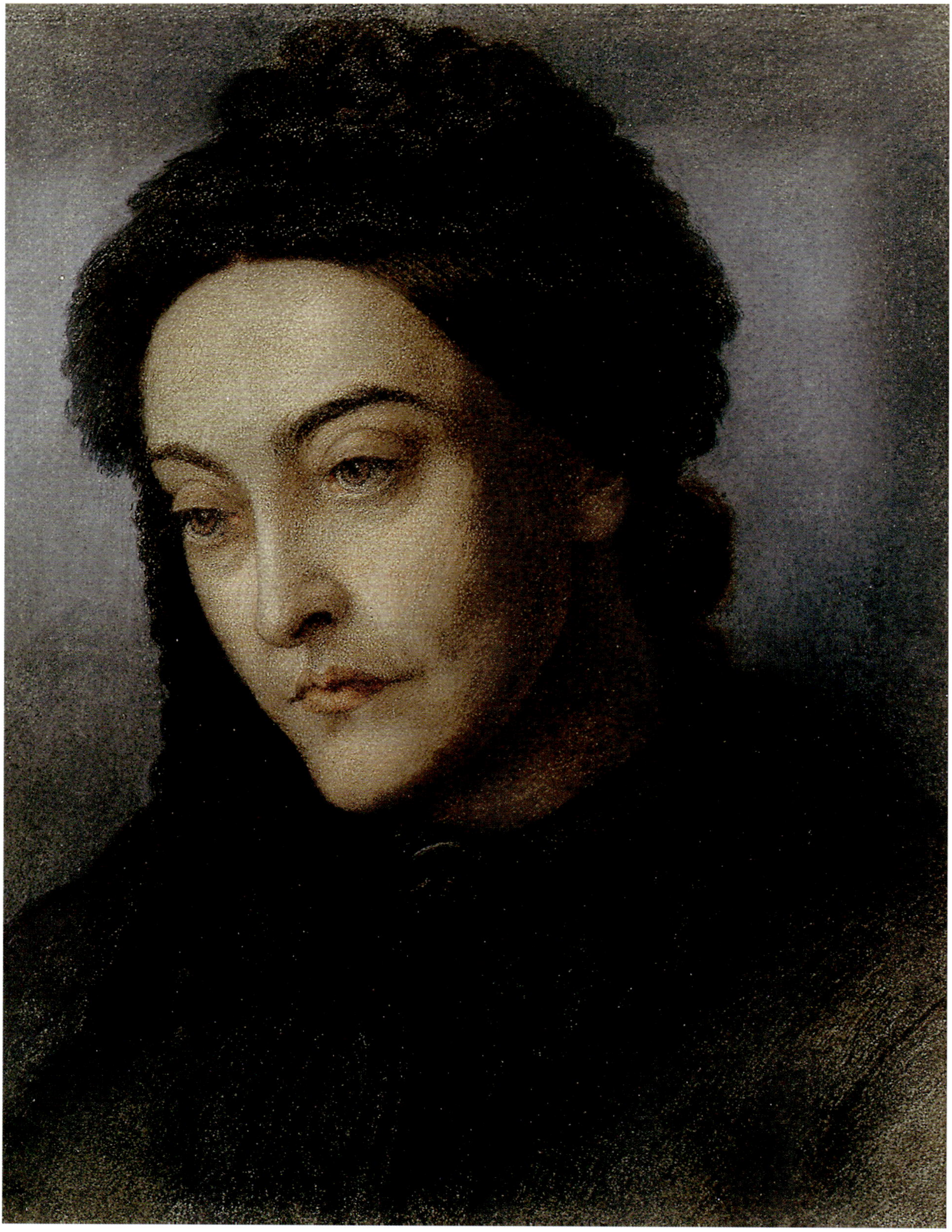

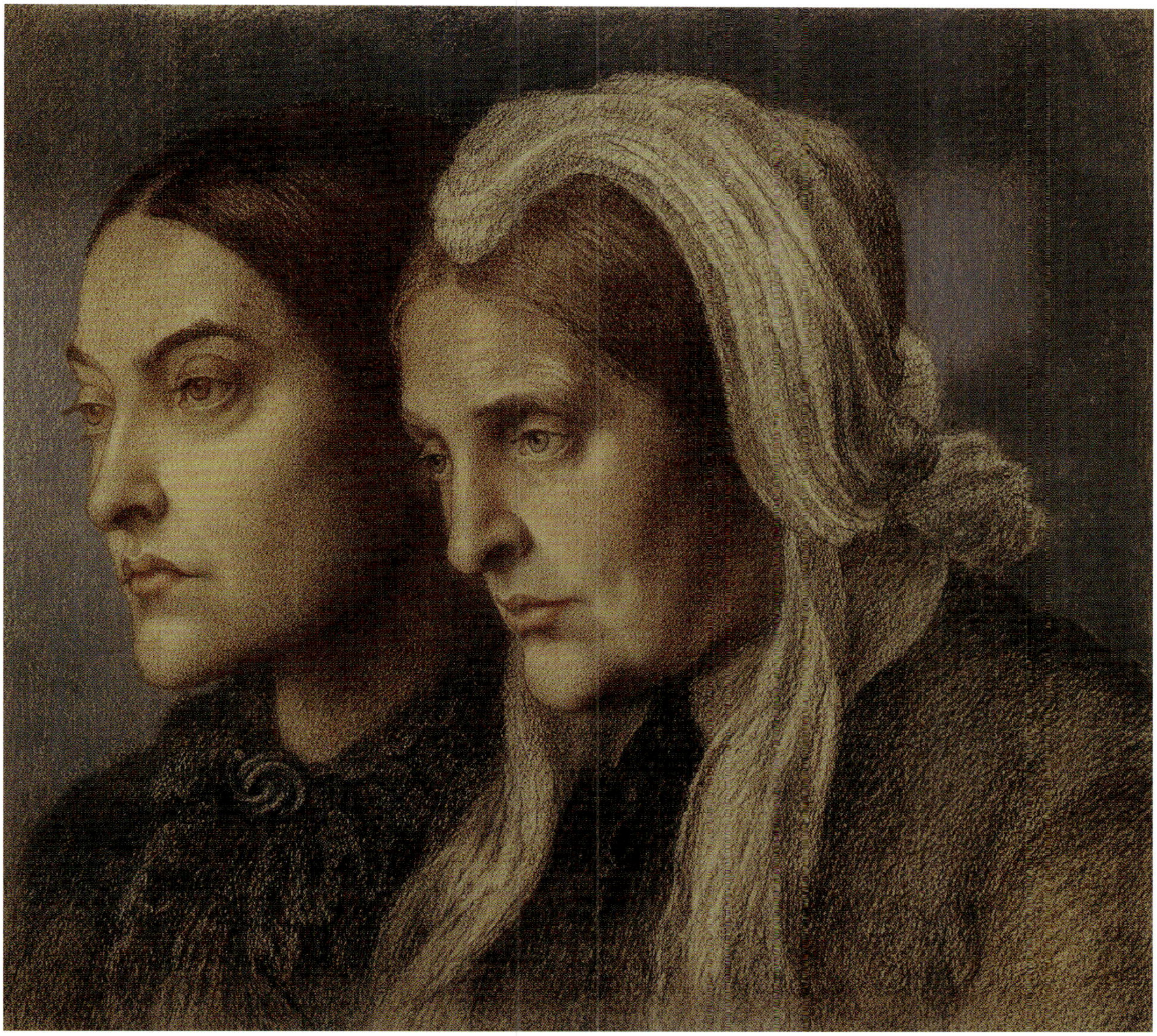

2.28 Dante Gabriel Rossetti,
Portrait of Christina Rossetti, 1877,
coloured chalks on paper, 42.5 × 34.9 cm
Private collection.

2.29 Dante Gabriel Rossetti,
Portraits of Christina and Frances Rossetti, 1877,
coloured chalks on paper, 42.5 × 48.3 cm.
National Portrait Gallery, London.

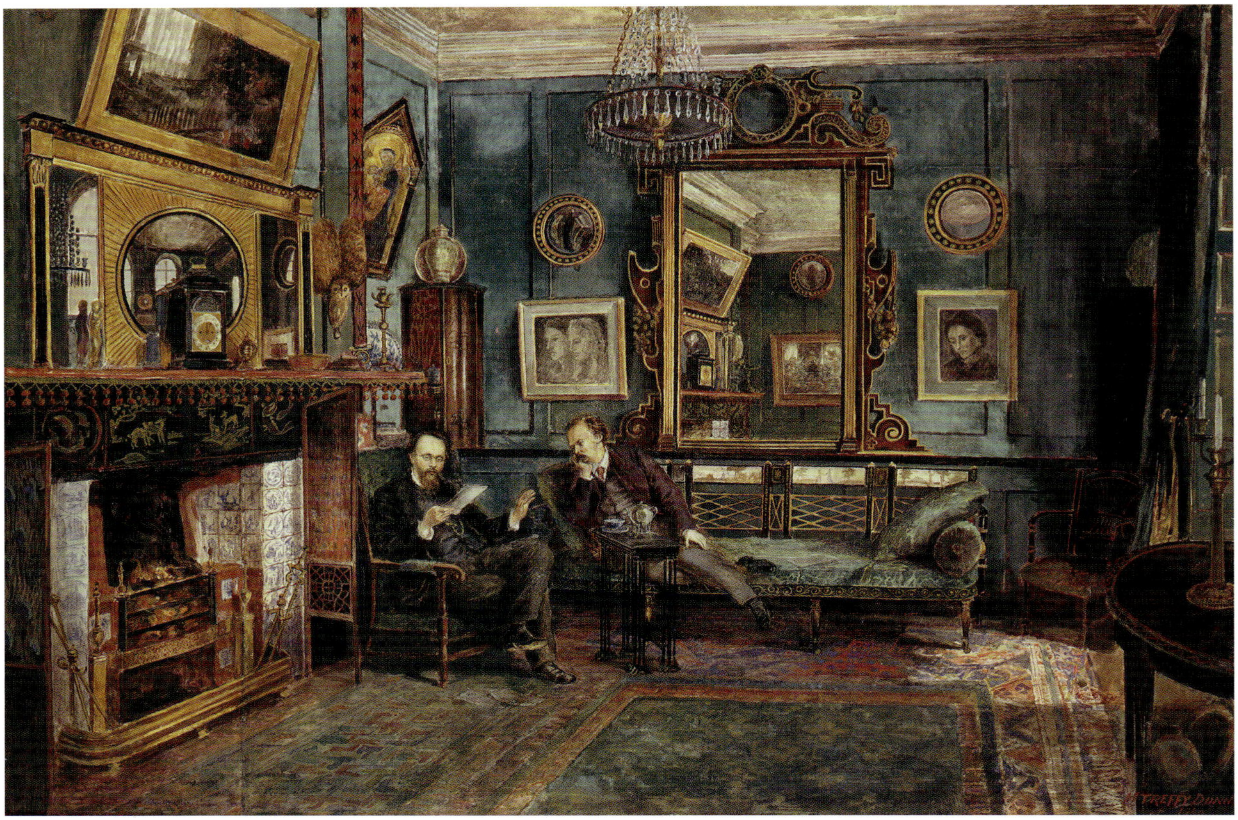

Christina's ill health – on 1 October he remarked in a letter that she was 'very far from well just now'.[86] In so far as the ruse was intended to restore Gabriel's confidence, it was a great success: 'I am now doing a drawing of my mother', he wrote to Watts on 1 October, 'which is all right & shows me there is no fear as to my present power of work'.[87] On starting to draw Christina he thought the portrait would be 'a very good likeness', and by the time he wrote to Ford Madox Brown in mid-October he was convinced it would be 'one of the best things I ever did'.[88] On 29 October he recorded that he was 'beginning yet another of Christina, whose effigy my illness will thus tend much to multiply'.[89] Gabriel kept one of the portraits of Christina and the double portrait with their mother with him for the rest of his life: they can both be seen hanging on the wall of his sitting room at Tudor House, in a watercolour painted in 1882 by his studio assistant Henry Treffry Dunn (fig. 2.30).

2.30 Henry Treffry Dunn, *Dante Gabriel Rossetti and Theodore Watts-Dunton at Tudor House*, 1882, gouache and watercolour on paper, 54.3 × 81.9 cm. National Portrait Gallery, London.

Ever since she had been in her late teens, the portraits that had been drawn or painted of Christina had been made in the context of love and affection, whether by Gabriel or by Collinson or Brett. In the second half of her life, as her reputation steadily gained ground, the public's desire to see her image was fulfilled by studio photographs or by photographic reproductions of Gabriel's portraits – his 1866 portrait and one of the drawings made during their time at Herne Bay were both

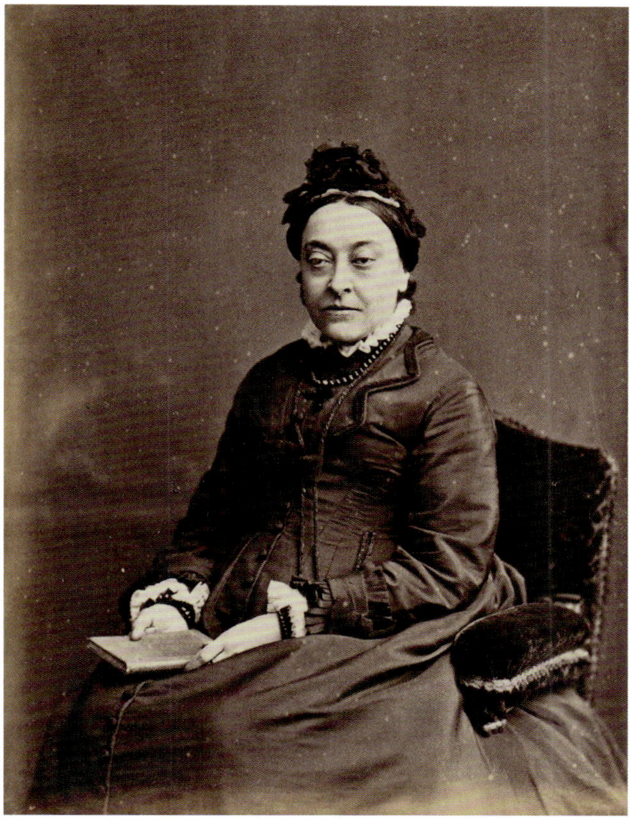

2.31 Elliott & Fry,
Portrait of Christina Rossetti, c.1877,
albumen print, 12.7 × 9.7 cm.
National Portrait Gallery, London.

reproduced and offered for sale. In 1877 Christina arranged a sitting with Elliott & Fry, a leading firm of photographers, that resulted in two three-quarter-length photographs (fig. 2.31).[90] This reversed an earlier decision: in 1867 she had been 'solicited by Elliot [*sic*] and Fry to sit for her photograph' but had declined; William speculated that her reason was 'modesty, based on religious considerations', but at that date perhaps she simply thought it unnecessary because she already had a recent likeness to circulate in the shape of Gabriel's half-length portrait.[91] Many years later, when writing to a friend who wished for a photograph, she humorously gave her a choice: if she 'aimed at beauty rather than at aught else' she could buy photographs of 'beautiful drawings by my brother D. G. R.: but', she continued, 'what between his being my brother and his overmastering love of beauty I dare not recommend these as equally faithful with Elliott and Fry's stern transcript'.[92]

But in 1892, just two years before her death, a far grander opportunity for a portrait presented itself. George Frederic Watts, who Rossetti had met in 1865 through Julia Margaret Cameron, proposed to include an oil portrait of her among the 'Hall of Fame' that he intended to present to the National Portrait Gallery, and that otherwise included luminaries such as Cardinal Manning, Thomas Carlyle, Robert Browning, Frederic Leighton and Tennyson.[93] Remarkably, Rossetti would have been the only woman included in the projected gift. In this series of portraits Watts sought a deep and intense characterisation, concentrating on the head and face rather than on dress and accessories. Having had an operation for cancer on 25 May, however, it was impossible for Rossetti to sit for Watts. William wrote in his diary on 12 June:

> I had to write today to G. F. Watts, explaining that his offer to paint Christina's portrait, to be given to the nation among the others of his gift, cannot be further taken into account for the present: a disappointment to me, and no doubt, to some extent, to Christina herself.[94]

And, indeed, to us: tantalising speculations about the insights this unrealised portrait might have offered haunt the end of the story.

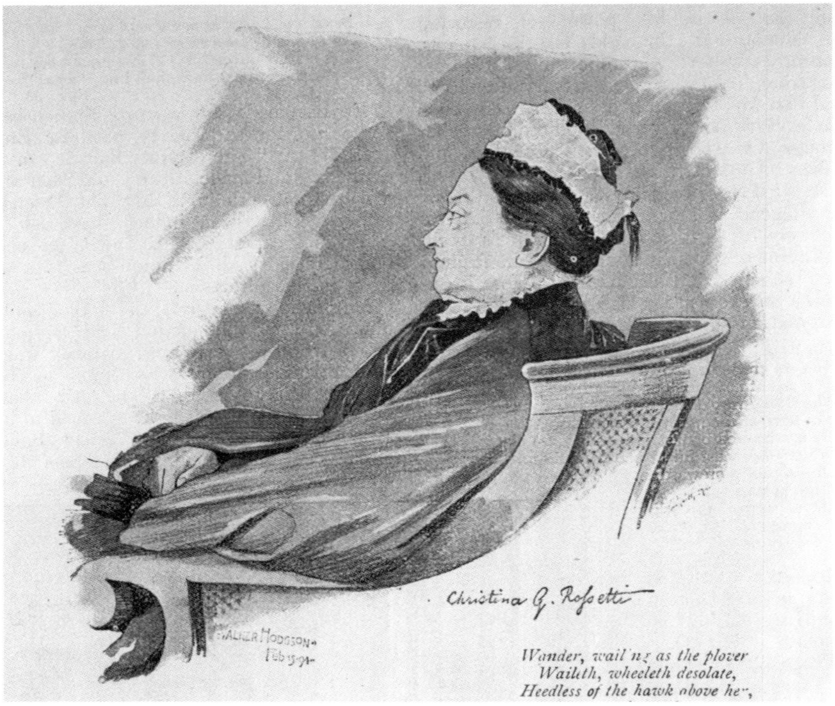

2.32 (William) Walker Hodgson, *Portrait of Christina Rossetti*, in *Cassell's Family Magazine*, May 1895, half-tone process print. British Library, London.

What happened to Christina Rossetti's image after her death on 29 December 1894? An illustrator's drawing in *Cassell's Family Magazine*, executed in February 1894 and published in May 1895 (fig. 2.32), sets a conservative tone, showing a profile view of a respectable elderly lady neatly dressed in a white cap and comfortably settled in an armchair. She gazes into the middle-distance, but looks as though her mental state is one of mature reflection rather than of poetic inspiration. It was not long, though, before authors and publishers began to turn to much earlier representations, preferring Pre-Raphaelite idealisation to later 'stern transcript[s]'. The Society for Promoting Christian Knowledge combined these with a religious theme in two of its publications: Ellen Proctor's brief biography of 1895 uses a detail from Gabriel's *The Girlhood of Mary Virgin* as a frontispiece, while the popular volume *Reflected Lights from 'The Face of the Deep'* (1900) reproduces *Ecce Ancilla Domini!*. And while Mackenzie Bell's 1898 biography of Christina reproduces the half-length 1866 portrait as the frontispiece, William, for his collected poems and biographical notes of 1904, chose the delicate profile sketch Gabriel probably made in the late 1840s when preparing to paint *The Girlhood* (see fig. 2.8). Of these four, it is remarkable that only one frontispiece can be described without qualification as a portrait. The others depict Christina either in the process of being transformed into a work of art, or after she has been transfigured, becoming someone else entirely.

I want to conclude this chapter with two versions of Christina Rossetti that emerged in the early years of the twentieth century.

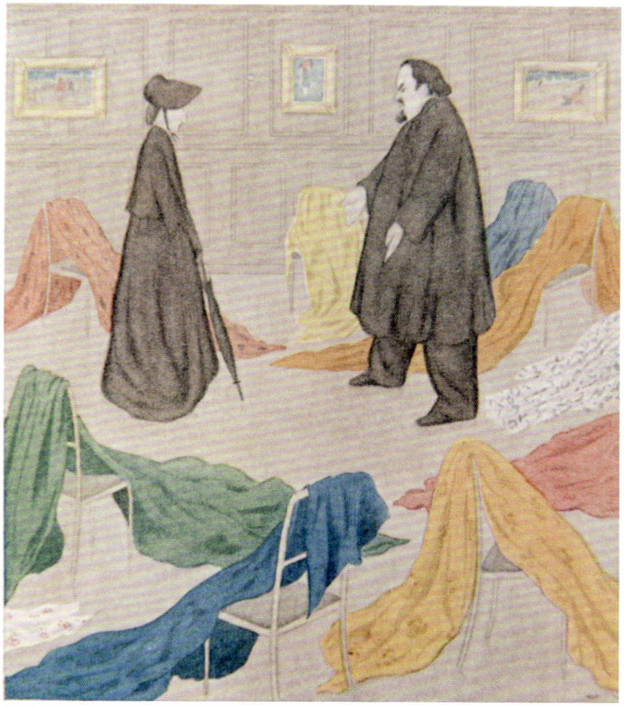

2.33 Max Beerbohm, *Gabriel and Christina,* in *Rossetti and his Circle* (London: William Heinemann, 1922), colour process print. Collection of Stephen Calloway.

The first is a caricature by Max Beerbohm, drawn in 1917, that was published in his book *Rossetti and his Circle* (1922) with the caption 'Rossetti, having just had a fresh consignment of "stunning" fabrics from that new shop in Regent Street [Liberty], tries hard to prevail on his younger sister to accept at any rate one of these and have a dress made of it from designs to be furnished by himself' (fig. 2.33). Here Beerbohm tackles the disparity between dowdy appearance and brilliant, passionate poetry head-on. Standing amidst chairs draped with gorgeously coloured fabrics are Christina and Gabriel, both dressed in black. Gabriel is saying: 'What *is* the use, Christina, of having a heart like a singing-bird and a water-shoot and all the rest of it, if you insist on getting yourself up like a pew-opener?' to which Christina mildly replies: 'Well, Gabriel, I don't know – I'm sure you yourself always dress very quietly'.

The second is Virginia Woolf's description in an essay entitled '"I am Christina Rossetti"', first published in 1930, the centenary of the poet's birth. Woolf begins by comparing the act of reading biographies to peering into an aquarium: 'Here is the past and all its inhabitants miraculously sealed as in a magic tank'.[95] But one story about Christina brings her so vividly to life for Woolf that it is as though the fish one has been watching 'suddenly dashed at the glass and broke it':

> A tea-party is the occasion. For some reason Christina went to a party given by Mrs Virtue Tebbs. What happened there is unknown – perhaps something was said in a casual, frivolous, tea-party way about poetry. At any rate, 'suddenly there uprose from a chair and paced forward into the centre of the room a little woman dressed in black, who announced solemnly, "I am Christina Rossetti!" and having so said, returned to her chair.' With those words, the glass is broken.[96]

Both Beerbohm and Woolf contrast the poet's power to surprise, even to shock, with her appearance in later life. Now we no longer think of her as that black-clad Victorian spinster; as I have suggested, however – and as the covers of recent books about her confirm – there is no more consensus about which portrait best characterises her now than there was in the years immediately following her death. But Rossetti's voice retains its dazzling colours and its disconcerting directness. As for her appearance, the wealth of portraits that can now be assembled, alongside versions of her 'phiz' in Pre-Raphaelite art, offer us images that reflect many facets of her character.

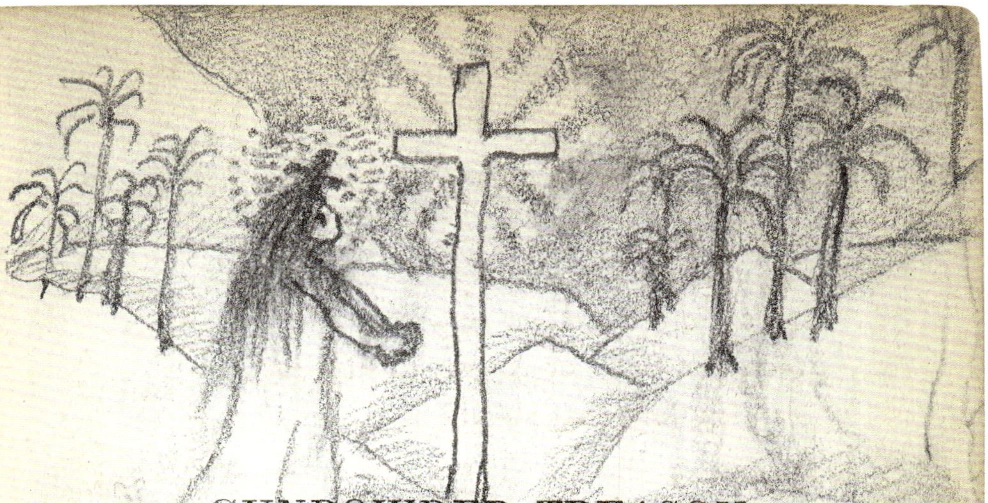

GUNPOWDER TREASON.

As thou hast testified of me at Jerusalem, so must thou bear witness also at Rome. *Acts* xxiii. 11.

BENEATH the burning eastern sky
    The Cross was rais'd at morn:
The widow'd Church to weep stood by,
    The world, to hate and scorn.

Now, journeying westward, evermore
    We know the lonely Spouse
By the dear mark her Saviour bore
    Trac'd on her patient brows.

At Rome she wears it, as of old
    Upon th' accursed hill:
By monarchs clad in gems and gold,
    She goes a mourner still.

Lord, grant us eyes to see
Within the seed a tree,
Within the glowing egg a bird,
Within the shroud a butterfly

3 'Come and See': Christina Rossetti's Illustrations for *The Christian Year*

DINAH ROE

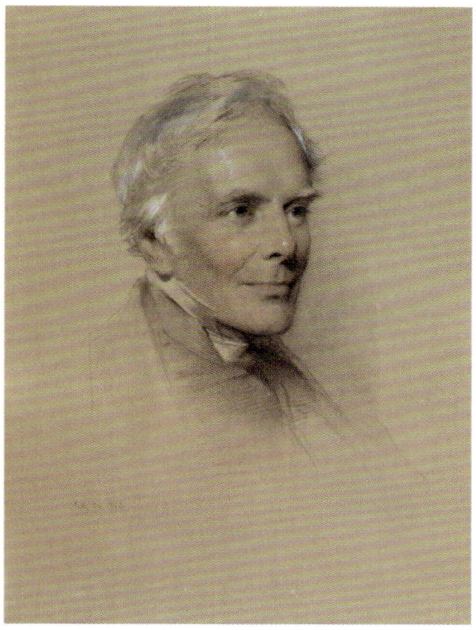

3.1 Above:
George Richmond,
Portrait of John Keble, 1863,
chalk on paper, 71.8 × 52.1 cm.
National Portrait Gallery, London.

3.2 Left:
Christina Rossetti, pencil illustration added to 'Gunpowder Treason' in her copy of John Keble, *The Christian Year* (Oxford: Parker, 1837).
Private collection, on loan to British Library, London.

JOHN KEBLE (fig. 3.1) was a Church of England clergyman, Oxford Movement leader and poet whose faithful aversion to vanity was so extreme that he wrote dull sermons on purpose. He felt that stylistic and doctrinal originality were not only self-regarding, but also potentially heretical. Keble famously advised a fellow sermon-writer 'Don't be original', an editorial suggestion that quickly became a Tractarian maxim.[1]

William Michael Rossetti's remark that Christina Rossetti 'thought *nothing* of Keble as a poet'[2] needs revisiting in light of the poets' shared commitment to the Tractarian doctrine of reserve, which, among other things, advocates artistic self-effacement in the service of faith.[3] Perhaps thinking '*nothing*' of Keble's poetry was the greatest compliment Rossetti could pay him; she was absorbed in his message rather than concentrating on his style. Like Keble, Rossetti often struggled to reconcile artistic expression with a religious practice that demands modesty, reserve and diffidence. In her devotional prose work *The Face of the Deep*, for instance, Rossetti mounts a defence of literature based on biblical precedent. She reminds us that the Bible itself is a literary endeavour, a 'text' in which God 'condescends to employ' various persuasive strategies including: 'wooing, beseeching, alluring, encouraging'. As an author, God 'lavishes beauty on the sacred text' in which 'He tells us much', 'stirs up such feelings', 'works upon us' and 'appeals in us to what we can and to what we cannot define'. For Rossetti, God is the only writer with a claim to originality. Writers who understand their own 'words and thoughts' as 'a commentary' on his work 'may lawfully' offer these as 'firstfruits' of their literary labour. This amnesty extends to all the arts: 'painting, sculpture, music', or 'any form of beauty' that allows us to 'worship God in wordless aspiration'.[4]

Rossetti's book illustrations are rare examples of her own 'wordless' worship. Unpublished during her lifetime, these amateur drawings are reserved both in the sense that they are private and in their use of humble media: pencil, crayon and occasionally watercolour.[5] William dates Christina's earliest known efforts at illustration 'towards 1850', when she added thirty-nine drawings to her own first volume of poetry, privately printed by her maternal grandfather Gaetano Polidori in 1847.[6] These drawings were done during the period of her closest association with the Pre-Raphaelite Brotherhood.[7] The results, William notes, 'are slight and amateurish – one might indeed say childish'. Even so, he detected 'a certain degree of fancy in them', pointing out that 'Dante Gabriel always considered that our sister, had she chosen to study and take pains, might have done something as an artist'.[8] In the summer of 1852, Dante Gabriel was sufficiently convinced by Christina's developing talent to warn her, tongue-in-cheek, 'not to rival' his then-fiancée Elizabeth Siddall in her artistic efforts, but to 'keep within respectful limits'.[9] Though no rival for the more accomplished Siddall, Rossetti nevertheless shared her penchant for depicting angular, intense female figures with haunted eyes and long, unbound hair. Like the women in Siddall's pen-and-ink drawings *The Nativity* (1854) and *The Lady of Shalott* (1853) and her watercolour *Clerk Saunders* (1857), Rossetti's female figures often appear in shapeless full-length shifts and adopt stilted, awkward poses (see 'Gunpowder Treason' [fig. 3.2], 'Ash Wednesday' [fig. 3.3], 'Easter Eve' and 'First Sunday After Christmas').

Like Gabriel, Ford Madox Brown identified artistic potential in Christina during the early 1850s, declaring: 'She bid fair [to] draw as well as her brother, had she continued.'[10] Brown was in a position to know; she had briefly been a student in his drawing classes sometime during 1851–2, while he was head teacher at the North London School of Drawing and Modelling. Rossetti would later remark that the school was 'better conducted now than it was in my time', because Brown had become 'the sole master both of the Male and Female Classes'.[11]

Both brother and teacher overestimated the element of choice in their generous assessments of Christina's artistic potential. Given the social, cultural and financial restrictions of the time, it is no surprise

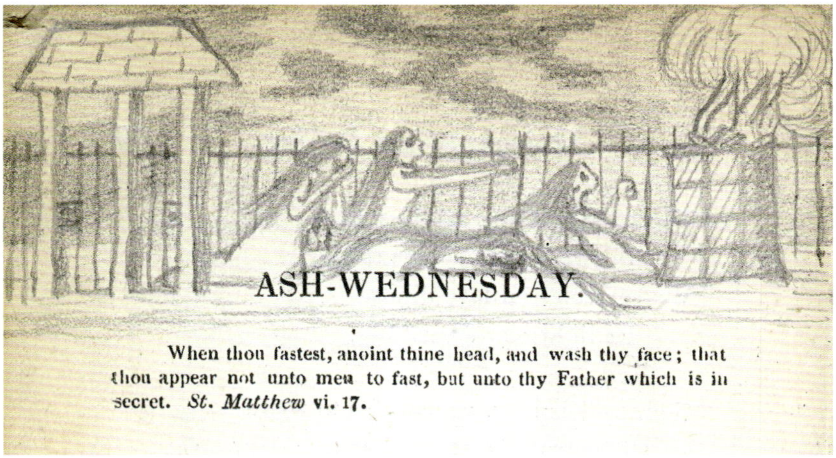

3.3 Below left:
Christina Rossetti, pencil illustration added to 'Ash Wednesday' in her copy of John Keble, *The Christian Year*, 1837. Private collection, on loan to British Library, London.

3.4 Right:
Christina Rossetti, *Portrait of Frances Rossetti in Profile*, 1853, pencil on paper, 29 × 20 cm. Private collection.

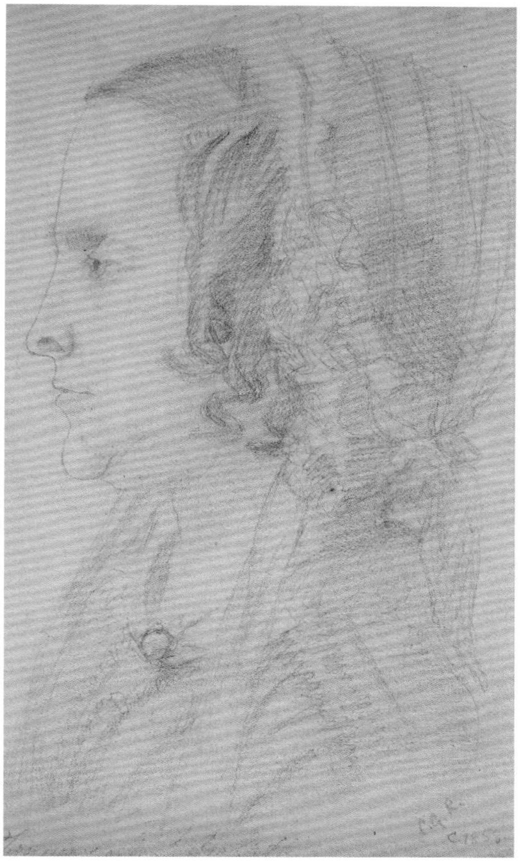

that she did not 'take pains' to become an artist. During this period, the Rossetti family was in financial crisis, brought on by their patriarch Gabriele's academic disgrace and consequent breakdown following his badly received critical writings on Dante Alighieri. Scarce funds were hardly going to be diverted to train the family's youngest female member for a career in which a woman had little hope of success. In straitened financial circumstances, the Rossetti family could only afford one artist, Gabriel, who as Christina's brother William tartly remarked 'cost something, and earned nothing'.[12] Even if there had been sufficient money for tuition, art training for young women was severely limited. Female students were not admitted to the Royal Academy, and the drawing schools to which they were admitted generally did not offer life classes. Social propriety excluded them from important male critical and artistic networks.[13] It was expensive, not to mention morally suspect, for a single woman to rent a private studio space, and domestic space was unlikely to be reserved for a household's youngest woman to hone her craft.

A lack of role models was a further hindrance to women's progress. As Victorian painter William Powell Frith observed, 'we have a long and honoured list of old masters, but no old mistresses'.[14] Frances Rossetti reflected this attitude in her remarks to Gabriel on the likelihood of her daughter's artistic success: 'should her talent be equal to her admiration of art, she will indeed prove a great artist; but in this regard small is my faith in woman kind.' Yet she did not discourage Christina from drawing, hoping that portraiture 'might prove advantageous to her in more ways than one, carrying her a little out of herself'.[15] While Gabriel admired Christina's 'pictorial eye', he was more sceptical than his mother about art as a cure for his sister's introversion, which he suspected was something of a pose.[16] He predicted Christina would reject his offer of art lessons because 'art' might 'interfere with the legitimate exercise of anguish'.[17]

Nevertheless, Christina kept practising during this period. She produced two pencil portraits of her mother in profile in the spring of 1853, when she and Frances were running their own school in Frome (fig. 3.4). William bluntly described the results as 'not good'.[18] The surviving portrait, though not as finished or accomplished as Gabriel's 1850s portraits of their mother, reflects the intimacy between mother and daughter in its realism. Christina's pencil unflatteringly depicts the double chin and unkempt eyebrows that in Gabriel's portraits are tactfully obscured. Rather than idealising their mother, Christina's clumsier attempt embraces her imperfections. She shared her mother's scepticism about her prospects as an artist, confessing in the summer of 1853 that her 'sketching' had not given her 'much faith in my own achieving greatness and fame in the Art'.[19]

Though she was not to pursue a professional career as an artist, Rossetti continued to derive personal satisfaction from adding drawings to published volumes of poetry, many of them her own. These amateur illustrations include watercolours for *Verses* (1847) and *Goblin Market and Other Poems* (1862), and pencil drawings for *Seek and Find: A Double Series of Short Studies of the Benedicite* (1879) and a manuscript version of *Sing-Song* (1872). Nor was *The Christian Year* the only devotional book by another author that Rossetti illustrated: she added pencil drawings to her copy of *The Altar* (1847), a volume of poetry by Keble's fellow Tractarian poet, Isaac Williams, and to her father Gabriele Rossetti's *L'Arpa evangelica* (*The Evangelic Harp*, Genoa, 1852).[20] William tells us that this last volume was 'profusely illustrated with pencil-designs by Christina',[21] and that it also included her two English translations of one part of 'Nell'Atto della Comunione'.[22] He dates her translations to about 1855, which may be contemporaneous with her drawings.[23] It is also possible that Christina added her illustrations earlier, in the autumn of 1853, when she received a copy of *L'Arpa evangelica* in Frome.[24]

With the exception of *The Christian Year* and *Sing-Song*, the present locations of Rossetti's illustrated books are unknown.[25] William describes some of the illustrations from *Verses* and *Goblin Market* in the notes to his 1904 edition of her *Poetical Works*, while Rossetti scholar Linda Schofield discusses unpublished notes recording her examination of Rossetti's illustrated copies of *Verses*, *Goblin Market* and *Seek and Find*. While they only represent a small proportion of her output, the illustrations that we do have represent Rossetti's most sustained engagement with the visual arts, a practice that is inextricably bound up with poetry.

Rossetti's copy of *The Christian Year*

John Keble's *The Christian Year* was one of the most successful devotional works of the age. Keble's appointment to the Chair of Poetry at Oxford University in 1831 is largely credited to the volume's positive reception. First published in 1827, this collection of 109 verses set to the annual cycle of worship was reprinted many times throughout the century. Inspired and structured by the Book of Common Prayer, Keble's poems celebrate seasons such Advent, Epiphany, Easter, Christmas and Lent, as well as marking the various feast days, saints' days and occasional services that make up the Anglican liturgical calendar. During the author's lifetime alone it ran to ninety-five editions, ranging from lavishly illustrated gift books to cheap reproductions small enough to fit in a waistcoat pocket. Commenting on its unprecedented popularity, Kirstie Blair's book on nineteenth-century religious poetry tells us the astonishing fact that 'almost every literate Victorian household would have possessed at least one copy'.[26] The Rossettis' copy dates from a period when religious poetry outsold secular poetry, a state of affairs that persisted until 1870, and which challenges the accepted opinion that religion was in decline in the Victorian era. Favourite verses were lovingly transcribed into commonplace books and letters of condolence, and the book was a popular gift. Keble's volume addressed an aspect of Victorian lives that was in danger of neglect in the wake of rapid industrial, social and technological change: their emotions. Writing about the poems' nineteenth-century readership, Samantha Matthews observes that 'Feeling rather than intellect explains *The Christian Year*'s value to its Victorian readers.'[27] The appeal of the volume is largely lost to modern readers no longer familiar with, let alone comforted by, the rhythms of a Christian liturgical cycle.

Christina owned the sixteenth edition of the volume, originally a birthday gift to her older sister Maria from their maternal aunt Charlotte Polidori. The inside cover is inscribed: 'Maria Francesca Rossetti from Aunt Charlotte', and is dated 'February 17, 1839', the date of Maria's twelfth birthday. Employed by the Dowager Marchioness of Bath, Charlotte was an unmarried, financially independent governess who, along with her sisters Eliza and Margaret, represented a way of life that exemplified the virtues of female self-sufficiency. This formidable Polidori trio helped their sister Frances Rossetti in the early days with the everyday, unpaid work of looking after her four lively and challenging young children. Charlotte and Eliza lived on and off with the Rossetti family throughout their lives, ending their days in Christina's house on Torrington Square. Charlotte's inscription to Maria speaks to the lifelong closeness among the women of the family, one that was domestic, spiritual and literary. The gift of *The Christian Year* is meaningful in this context, as its stated purpose is to guide spiritual development through regular reading practice at home. In his 'Advertisement' to the volume, Keble makes sure to draw his readers' attention to the 'personal and domestic nature' of his verses.[28]

Intended to be read in conjunction with the Book of Common Prayer, Keble's verses employ ritual patterns of repetition and allusion as a corrective to the hectic demands of contemporary life. Keble urges Victorian readers to 'discipline' their 'thoughts and feelings' by cultivating a mindful, regular reading practice that will help to restore the 'sound rule of faith' and 'sober standard of feeling' promoted in the Liturgy. He worries that the virtues of 'practical religion' are at risk 'in times of much leisure and much unbounded curiosity, when excitement of every kind is sought after with a morbid eagerness'. His poems, by contrast, are designed to emulate the '*soothing* tendency in the Prayer Book', an aspiration his many readers felt it achieved.[29] Indeed, Keble's fellow Tractarian John Henry Newman describes *The Christian Year* as 'the most soothing, tranquillizing, subduing work of the day'.[30]

We do not know when Maria's copy of *The Christian Year* passed to Christina, nor precisely when she added her illustrations. After the book passed to him upon Christina's death, William added an undated note beneath Charlotte Polidori's inscription: 'From Christina Rossetti's books illustrated by her.'[31] In her groundbreaking article on Rossetti's illustrations, Diane D'Amico persuasively speculates that the volume may have come to Christina in 1873, when her sister entered the All Saints' Sisterhood.[32] She may alternatively have inherited it on Maria's death in 1876. Bearing in mind that the volume was designed to comfort its readers, Rossetti may have found the labour of producing 109 illustrations a welcome distraction from her sister's absence. However, the drawings could have been done before the book officially became Christina's. Until Maria joined the Sisterhood, Frances Rossetti and her daughters lived together all their lives, sharing not only a domestic space and possessions, but also a deep religious faith and a love of poetry. Maria often acted as amanuensis for Christina, copying her sister's finished poems into notebooks in her fine, neat hand. It is not unimaginable that she might have encouraged Christina to draw in her books, or that Christina might have made the drawings as a present. When Maria published her scholarly commentary on Dante's *Commedia, A Shadow of Dante* (1871), Christina added pencil illustrations to the beginning of each chapter and presented her with a copy, inscribed: 'To my dear Sister / Christina G. Rossetti / with much love. / 13 October 1871'.[33]

3.5 Top right:
Christina Rossetti,
pencil illustration added to 'Second Sunday After Trinity' in her copy of John Keble, *The Christian Year*, 1837.
Private collection, on loan to British Library, London.

3.6 Middle right:
Christina Rossetti,
pencil illustration added to 'Eighteenth Sunday After Trinity' in her copy of John Keble, *The Christian Year*, 1837.
Private collection, on loan to British Library, London.

3.7 Bottom right:
Christina Rossetti,
pencil illustration added to 'Third Sunday in Lent' in her copy of John Keble, *The Christian Year*, 1837.
Private collection, on loan to British Library, London.

Spiritualised eyes

The drawings in Rossetti's copy of *The Christian Year* give us an insight into the poet's own reading practice: a Pre-Raphaelite attention to the mystical, the beautiful and the dramatic is mediated by a Tractarian faith in the meditative power of the word. Her illustrations are at once an interpretation of Keble and an exploration of the major themes that characterise her own literary work: religious faith, women's lives and the natural world.

Rossetti does not attempt to unify the page by blurring the boundaries of text and image. No foliate borders, decorated initials or floating figures appear in the margins or between lines, nor does Rossetti incorporate the letters themselves into her design. Each pencil drawing appears at the head of the poem, restricting itself to the rectangular space created by the gutter, poem title and top and right margins. Like the images from emblem books of the seventeenth century, Rossetti's drawings are generally meditations on Keble's poems rather than literal illustrations of the events and characters they describe.

While Rossetti's traditional page design encourages the thoughtful, meditative approach advocated in the 'Advertisement' to *The Christian Year*, the apocalyptic content of her pictures resists its soothing tone. The 'excitement' and even perhaps the 'morbid eagerness' that Keble warns against characterises many of her most memorable and compelling images. Women and angels battle mythical and exotic creatures, including dragons, lions and tigers in 'Second Sunday After Trinity' (fig. 3.5), 'Eighteenth Sunday After Trinity' (fig. 3.6) and 'Third Sunday in Lent' (fig. 3.7). On his knees with arms outspread, the titular martyr is stoned by three men in 'St. Stephen's Day' (fig. 3.8). Four women prostrate themselves before a flame-belching furnace in

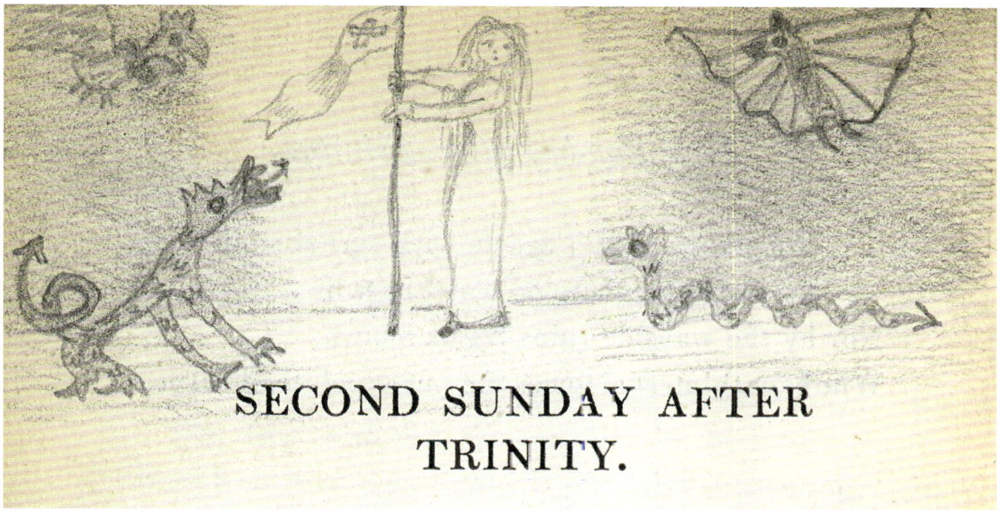
SECOND SUNDAY AFTER TRINITY.

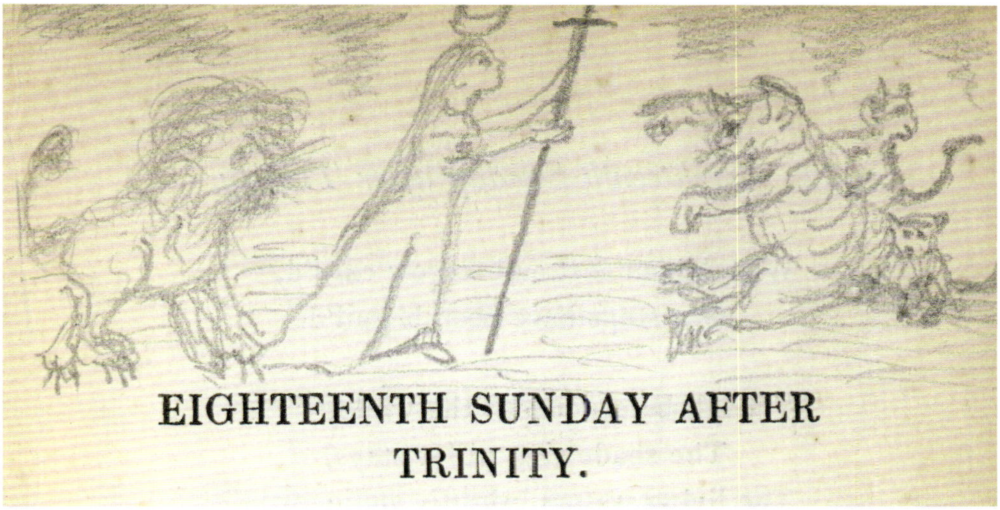
EIGHTEENTH SUNDAY AFTER TRINITY.

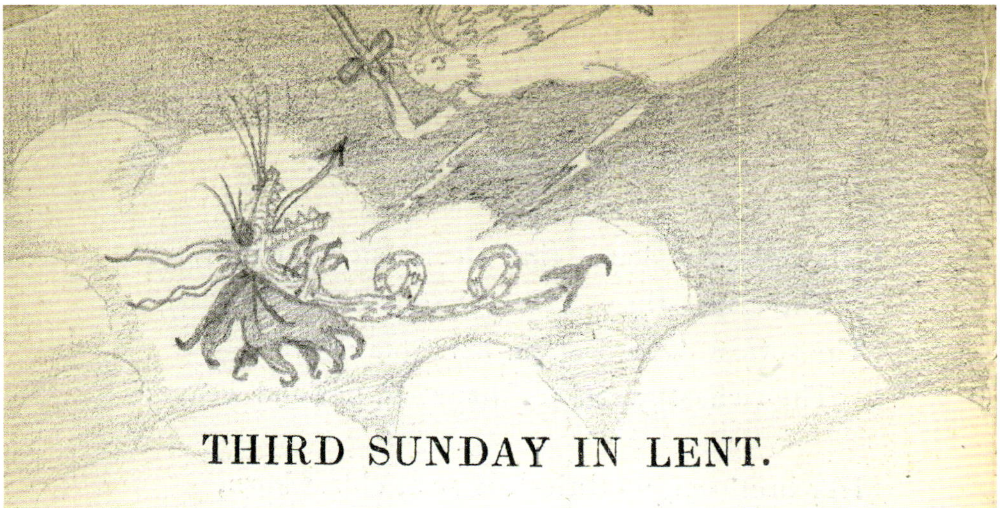
THIRD SUNDAY IN LENT.

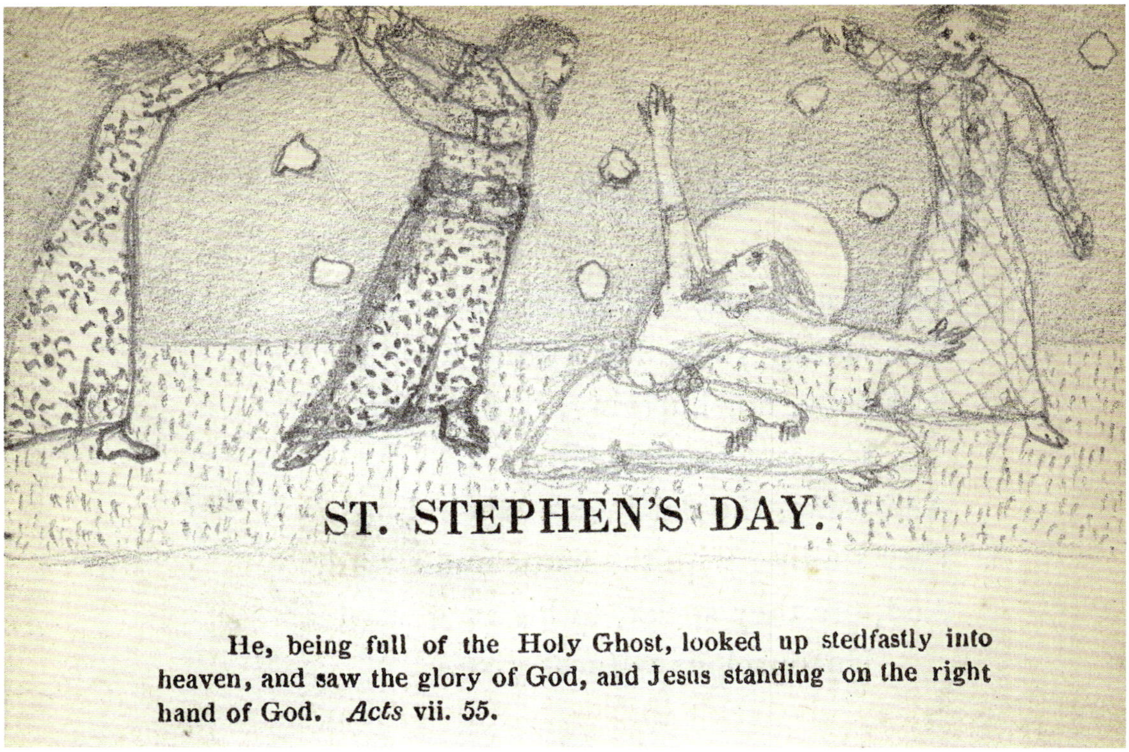

ST. STEPHEN'S DAY.

He, being full of the Holy Ghost, looked up stedfastly into heaven, and saw the glory of God, and Jesus standing on the right hand of God. *Acts* vii. 55.

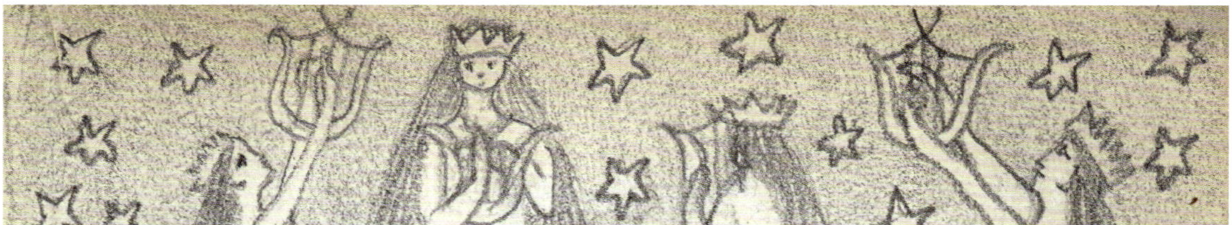

PALM SUNDAY.

And he answered and said unto them, I tell you that, if these should hold their peace, the stones would immediately cry out. *St. Luke* xix. 40.

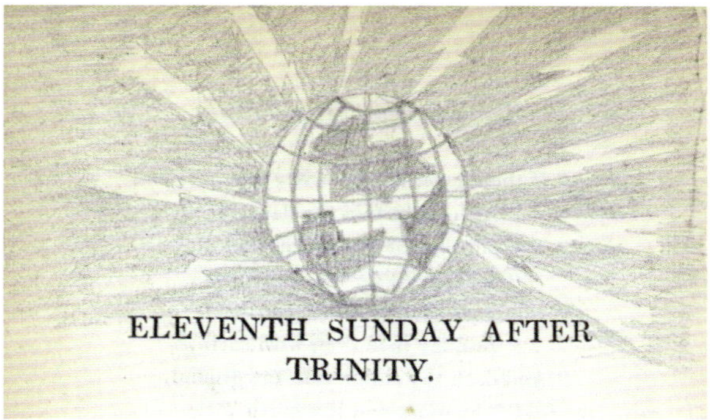

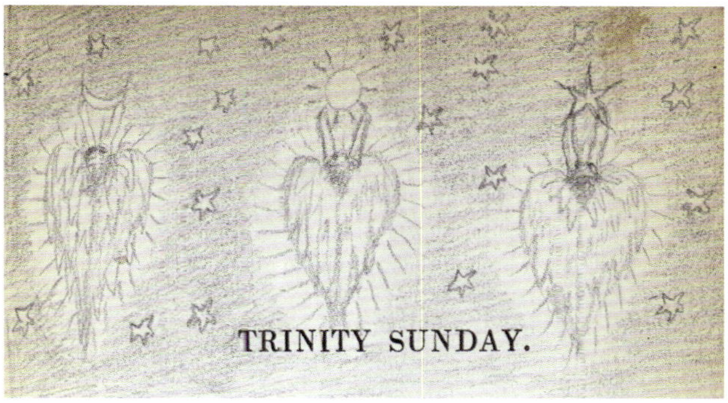

3.8 Opposite top:
Christina Rossetti, pencil illustration added to 'St. Stephen's Day' in her copy of John Keble, *The Christian Year*, 1837. Private collection, on loan to British Library, London.

3.9 Above left:
Christina Rossetti, pencil illustration added to 'Eleventh Sunday After Trinity' in her copy of John Keble, *The Christian Year*, 1837). Private collection, on loan to British Library, London.

3.10 Opposite bottom:
Christina Rossetti, pencil illustration added to 'Palm Sunday' in her copy of John Keble,*The Christian Year*, 1837. Private collection, on loan to British Library, London.

3.11 Above right:
Christina Rossetti, pencil illustration added to 'Trinity Sunday' in her copy of John Keble, *The Christian Year*, 1837. Private collection, on loan to British Library, London.

'Ash Wednesday' (fig. 3.3). Dramatic astronomical events are common. Jagged lightning bolts shoot into a globe in 'Eleventh Sunday After Trinity' (fig. 3.9). Christ's disembodied hand extends from a blazing sun in 'St. Thomas' Day'. Starry skies are the backdrop to ecstatically dancing and embracing haloed figures in pictures like 'St. Andrew's Day', 'St. Mark's Day' and 'St. Philip and St. James'. Even Rossetti's portrayal of music is far from soothing: trumpeters lead sword-wielding men in 'First Sunday After Trinity'; women musicians playing pipes are superimposed on a globe in 'Advent Sunday' and crowned female figures playing lyres hover in a sky filled with stars in 'Palm Sunday' (fig. 3.10). Rossetti's illustration to 'Trinity Sunday' (fig. 3.11) daringly substitutes female figures for the expected 'Almighty Trine' of Father, Son and Holy Spirit. Three female angels with their backs to the viewer hover in a starry sky, light emanating from their folded, heart-shaped wings. The first angel holds aloft a crescent moon, emblem of the Virgin Mary; the second a sun, symbolising Christ; and the third a star, symbol of the Christian worshipper.

Although William Blake's work does not influence Rossetti's page design, it can be detected in these striking, ecstatic figures. Rossetti's figures do not exhibit Blake's interest in the detailed musculature of the physical body, yet they incorporate Blakean dynamic poses, dramatic settings and cosmic backdrops to reflect the passion of holy union at odds with the reassuring, regular metrics of Keble's poems. As Chapter One of this book tells us, Rossetti knew Blake's work, and in particular admired his ability to convey divine rapture. Writing about Rossetti's devotional work, Emma Mason points out that the poet's 'vision in ... late writings' such as *Time Flies* and *The Face of the Deep* 'finds a visual analogy in William Blake's "The Reunion of the Soul and the Body", engraved for an 1808 edition of Robert Blair's *The Grave* (1743) in which two bodies entwine against the backdrop of a burning cemetery' (fig. 1.14).[34] Preoccupied with the dangers and delights of seeing, looking and vision, Rossetti's late writings also find a visual analogy in her own drawings for *The Christian Year*.

Rossetti's later writing makes a distinction between looking and perceiving that is based on a Tractarian understanding of the world

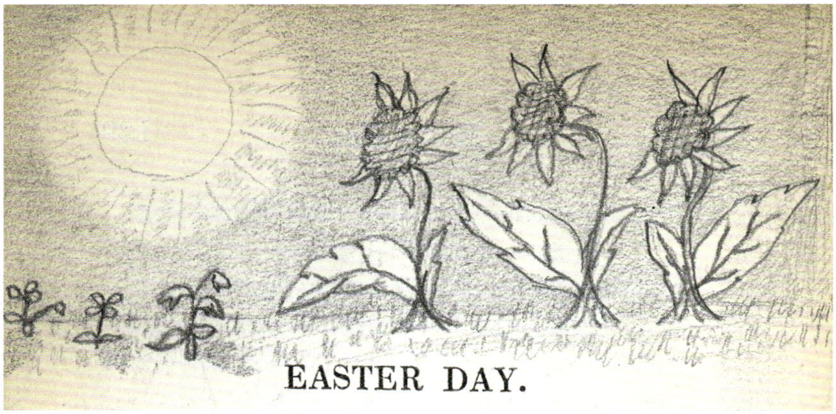

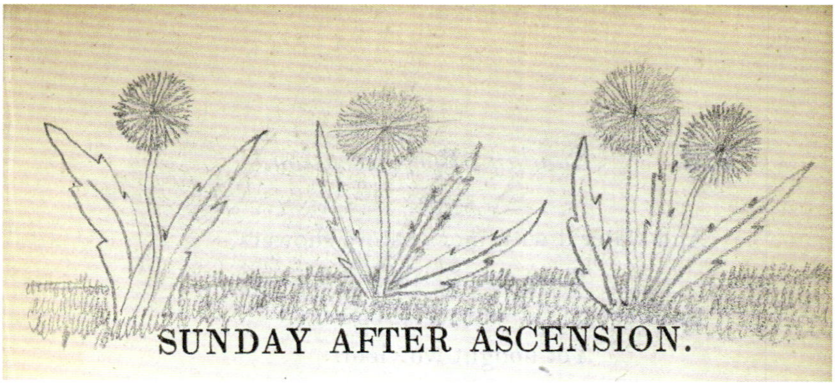

3.12 Left:
Christina Rossetti, pencil illustration added to 'Easter Day' in her copy of John Keble, *The Christian Year*, 1837. Private collection, on loan to British Library, London.

3.13 Below left:
Christina Rossetti, pencil illustration added to 'Sunday After Ascension' in her copy of John Keble, *The Christian Year*, 1837. Private collection, on loan to British Library, London.

as an analogue of the divine.[35] Keble and his followers believed that the visible world could reveal invisible holy truths to those who knew where and how to look. In *The Face of the Deep*, Rossetti writes of the discriminating 'spiritual eye', which differs from the 'natural' eye in that it 'fixes' itself 'on matters worthy of insight: it sees something, it may gradually perceive more and more'. She gives the example of 'Pharaoh's daughter', who initially 'discerned only an ark of bulrushes; next one of the Hebrews' children; at last Moses'.[36] Here, Pharaoh's daughter's keen observation of the physical world reveals its symbolic significance. Elsewhere Rossetti writes of 'eyes that have been supernaturalized' so that they can 'recognize' the significance of the natural world 'not literally only, but likewise in a figure'.[37]

Intended to appeal to the 'supernaturalized' eye, Rossetti's drawings of flora, fauna and landscapes in *The Christian Year* interest themselves in the symbolic function of nature. Rather than 'rejecting nothing, selecting nothing, and scorning nothing' as Ruskin recommends, Rossetti selects, edits and scrutinises the natural world for signs of the divine.[38] Her simple drawings are not technically sophisticated, nor do they strive to exhibit botanical accuracy or Pre-Raphaelite attention to detail. Yet their simplicity conveys an affection and sympathy not always apparent in Rossetti's drawings of human figures. William records this appeal in his notes on his sister's illustrations to 'Goblin Market' when he identifies 'the simplest, as of fruit-branches, being the prettiest'.[39]

Christian emblems, such as the pomegranate, rose, thorn, bulrush, grapevine and palm, are common in Rossetti's drawings for *The Christian Year*. Illustrations of poems celebrating renewal, such as 'Morning' and 'First Sunday After Christmas' include the pomegranate tree, emblem of the resurrection. Grapevines, symbolising Christ and his followers, appear in illustrations depicting acts of prayer, such as 'Fourth Sunday After Easter' and 'Sexagesima Sunday'. Sunflowers with faces turned towards the sun represent devotional piety in 'Easter Day' (fig. 3.12), while blown dandelions symbolise Christ's passion in 'Sunday After Ascension' (fig. 3.13), alluding also to the 'scatter'd seed' whose growth the poem anticipates. Rossetti's illustrations to *The Christian Year* include sixteen landscapes, and many more instances of natural symbolism than can be recorded here. Closer study of Rossetti's use of the Christian emblem tradition would enrich future investigations of the relationship between ecology and faith in her work.

The natural world is not the only training ground for developing 'spiritualized' eyes; books themselves can help to sharpen Christian vision. Tractarians like Keble believed in poetry as a vehicle for

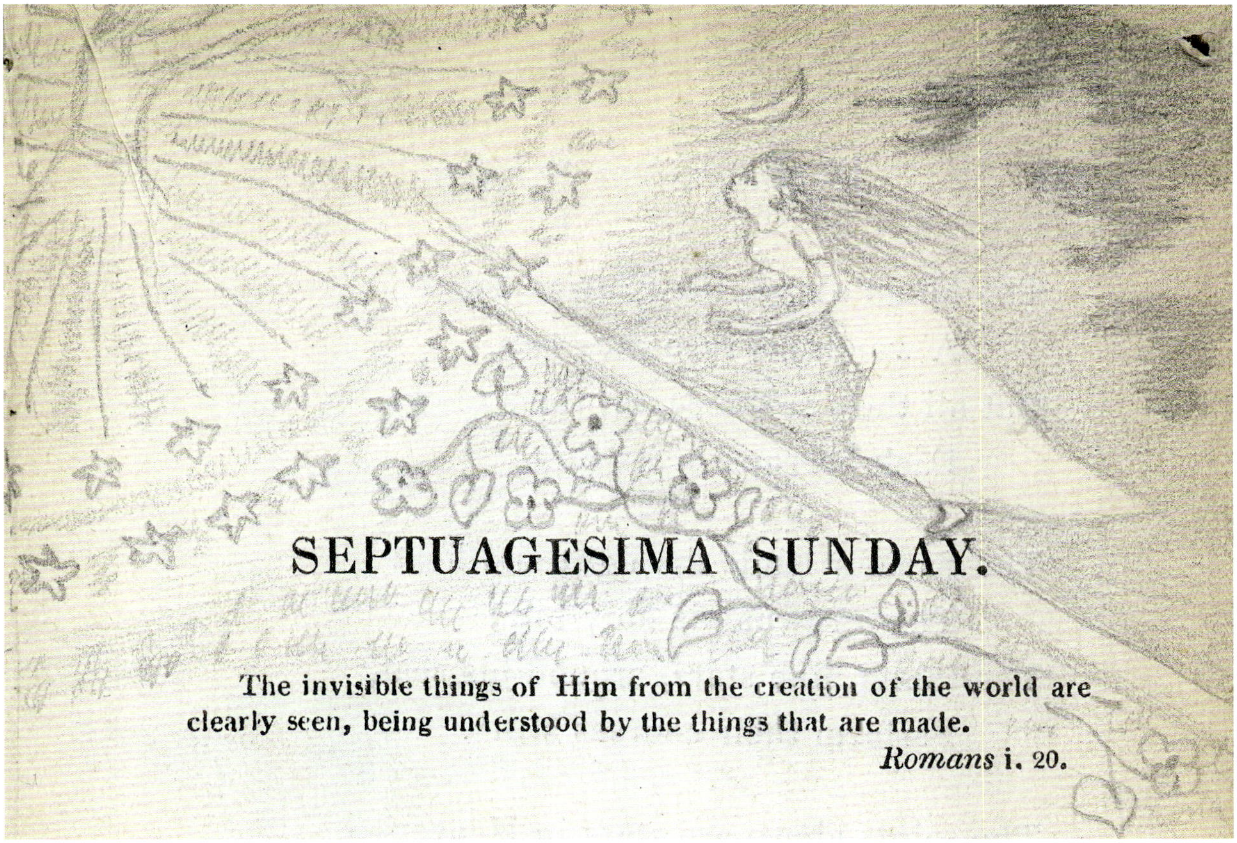

3.14 Christina Rossetti, pencil illustration added to 'Septuagesima Sunday' in her copy of John Keble, *The Christian Year*, 1837. Private collection, on loan to British Library, London.

communicating divine truth. Poetry, like divine revelation, cannot be readily understood, but reveals itself gradually to those who persist, an idea that Rossetti's illustration to 'Septuagesima Sunday' (fig. 3.14) explores. Keble's poem teaches readers not only how to read the world around them, but also how to read *A Christian Year*:

> There is a book, who runs may read,
> Which heavenly truth imparts,
> And all the lore its scholars need,
> Pure eyes and Christian hearts.

The 'book' turns out to be the natural world, its phenomena 'pages in that book, to shew / How God himself is found'.

At first glance, Rossetti's drawing for 'Septuagesima Sunday' seems to have very little to do with Keble's poem about looking for signs of God in the world. It shows a woman with outstretched arms running up a steep incline toward a Christ figure waiting to embrace her; he emanates rays and stars, illuminating the night sky. D'Amico's article on Rossetti's illustrations to *The Christian Year* marks the disparity between picture and poem, noting that where Keble's poem emphasises 'the point that we see God while still on earth by seeing him in his creation', Rossetti illustrates 'the journey away from earth towards Christ'.[40] Yet Rossetti's page itself enacts the interpretative process Keble's poem describes by shifting the emphasis back to the material book, taking literally the poem's request to God: 'Give me a heart to find out thee / And read thee everywhere.'

Rossetti's illustration does not seek God in the natural world, but rather finds him in books, or more precisely, Keble's book itself and its biblical source. In her influential book about Christina Rossetti and illustration, Lorraine Janzen Kooistra notes that this drawing 'invites the reader/viewer to interpret its visual motifs in the same way Keble asks its audience to interpret the objects of the material world: as visible

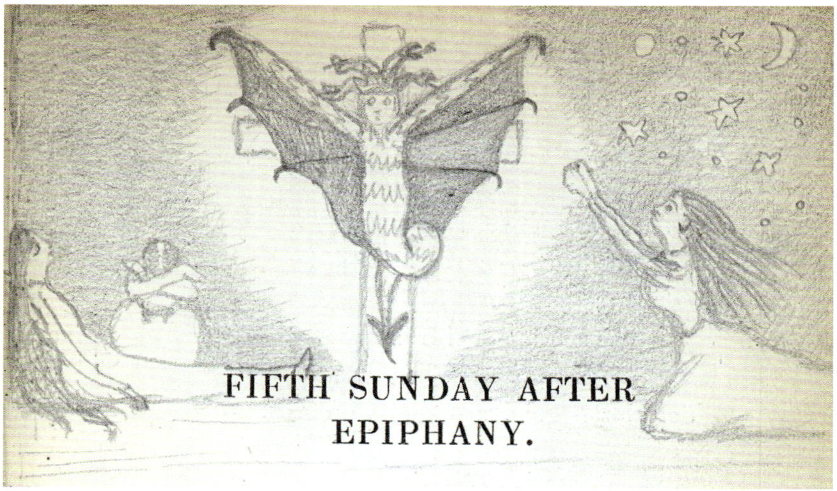

3.15 Christina Rossetti, pencil illustration added to 'Fifth Sunday After Epiphany' in her copy of John Keble, *The Christian Year*, 1837. Private collection, on loan to British Library, London.

signs betokening an invisible reality'.[41] Kooistra notices that Rossetti's illustration is inspired not as much by Keble's poem as by the biblical instruction to which its first line alludes: 'Write the vision, and make it plain upon tables, that he may run that readeth it' (Habakkuk 2:2).

The biblical verse asserts that prophetic vision must be written accessibly and legibly, in a simple 'plain' style that will not detain the reader. Keble's use of the verse in his poem connects readers' ability to 'run' their eyes over the text unhindered with interpretative freedom – to 'run' with their own interpretations, as it were. Quoting Habakkuk 2:2 in *The Face of the Deep*, Rossetti extends this privilege to women, writing, 'God helping us, we all great and small can and will run'. Here, Rossetti extends the democratic spirit of Habakkuk 2:2 to include women, defending their right to interpret the Bible:

> the symbolic forms of prophecy being set before all eyes, must be so set for some purpose: to investigate them may not make us wise as serpents; yet ought by promoting faith, fear, hope, love, to aid in making us harmless as doves.[42]

Her assertion that women's desire to investigate divine prophecy is 'harmless' authorises her own devotional writing, respects the interpretative capabilities of her female readership and subtly identifies male gate-keeping as an act of fear rather than love.

In portraying a woman 'who runs' with her own interpretation of the world and the book, Rossetti's illustration includes women among the poem's 'scholars' who 'may read' the 'heavenly truth'. Her own poem on the same holy day, 'Septuagesima', explicitly characterises the journey toward salvation as both a race and a scholarly pursuit, beginning: 'One step more, and the race is ended / One word more, and the lesson's done'.[43]

Dazzled eyes

Keble's lament that 'Sin' obscures our vision so that we are unable to 'descry / The mystic heaven and earth' in our worldly surroundings tempers the optimism of 'Septuagesima Sunday'. This idea informs Rossetti's other visual responses to *The Christian Year*. As D'Amico observes, Rossetti's illustration for 'Fifth Sunday After Epiphany' (fig. 3.15) depicts Sin interfering with the human ability to detect the divine. Here, the 'demonic figure that appears to be hanging on the Cross' is an 'embodiment of human sin ... that blocks out the saving power of the Cross'.[44]

The figures of 'Fourth Sunday in Advent' (fig. 3.16) struggle to detect evidence of the divine presence on Earth with 'unworthy', 'wishful', 'dazzled' and 'weak' eyes. Indicating its concern with flawed human vision, the poem's subtitle, 'Dimness', is taken from Isaiah 32:3: 'The eyes of them that see shall not be dim ....' Seated on a rock before a palm tree, the woman on the left is reading, or rather misreading, the large book on her lap. The figure corresponds with stanza two of Keble's poem:

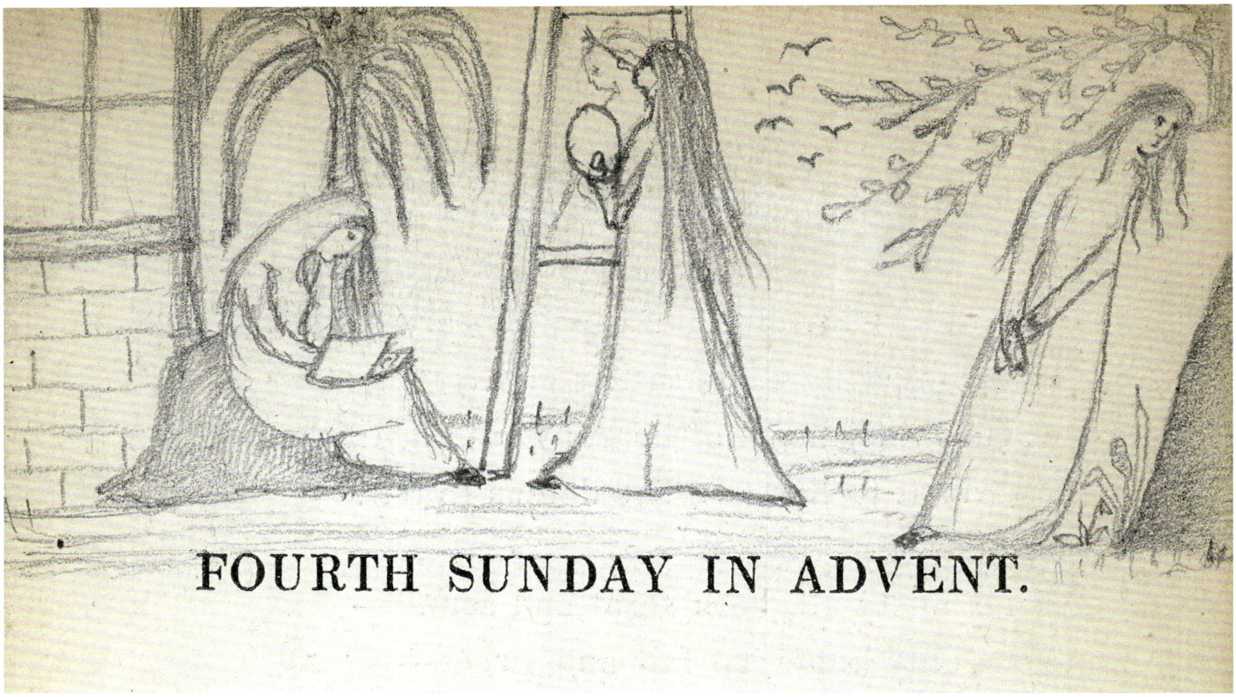

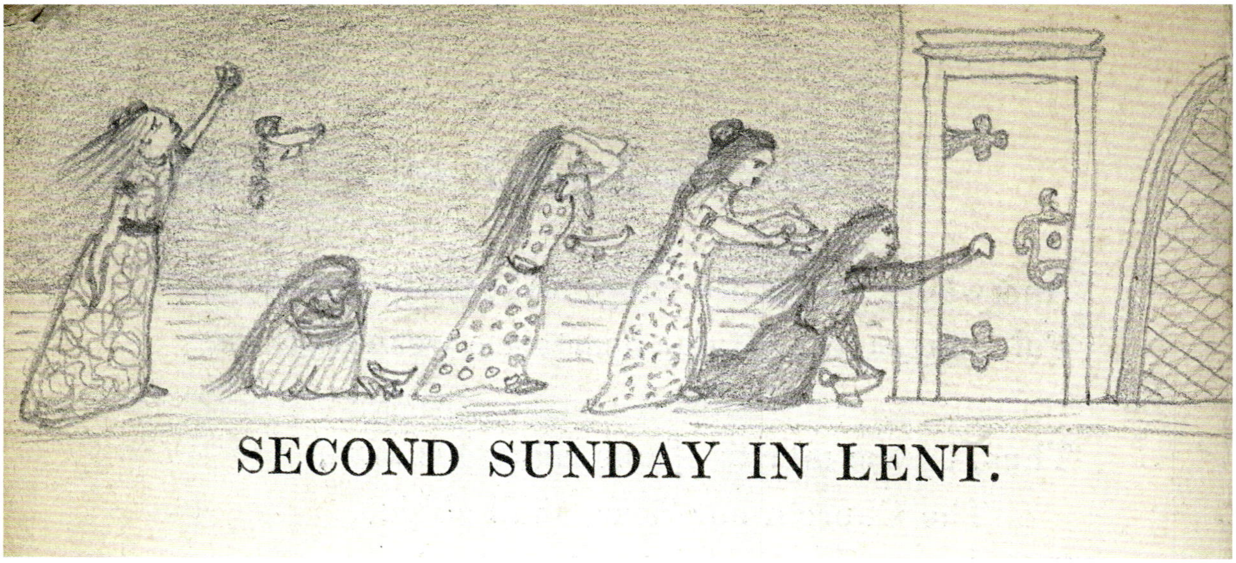

Mine eye unworthy seems to read
One page of Nature's beauteous book :
It lies before me, fair outspread –
I only cast a wishful look.

In Rossetti's drawing, 'Nature's book' appears as a material book that is a half-closed rather than an 'outspread' object of the figure's 'wishful

3.16 Opposite top:
Christina Rossetti, pencil illustration added to 'Fourth Sunday in Advent' in her copy of John Keble, *The Christian Year*, 1837. Private collection, on loan to British Library, London.

3.17 Opposite bottom:
Christina Rossetti, pencil illustration added to 'Second Sunday in Lent' in her copy of John Keble, *The Christian Year*, 1837. Private collection, on loan to British Library, London.

look'. The woman only 'seems to read'; her interpretative process is affected by her 'unworthy' eye. Painting offers no more consolation than reading. Palette in hand, the woman in the centre paints a female figure in profile on an easel. She represents Keble's speaker who:

> ... cannot paint to Memory's eye
> The scene, the glance, I dearest love –
> Unchang'd themselves, in me they die,
> Or faint, or false, their shadows prove.

Rossetti portrays the effort to recall 'The scene, the glance' as a failed artistic endeavour. Paintings cannot successfully reproduce the visions of 'Memory's eye' because they are 'faint' and 'false' 'shadows', inauthentic products of vain, fallen human perception. The woman on the right of the picture exhibits the dimmed vision to which the poem's subtitle alludes. Her darkened, unfocused eyes recall the speaker's 'eyes ... dazzled now and weak'. Hands folded before her, she leans dramatically towards a tree that disappears into the margin. Disorientated by her 'misty' inability to perceive the 'fair and sweet' world around her, she corresponds to Keble's speaker 'wandering on enchanted ground / With dizzy brow and tottering feet'.[45]

The problem for the women of 'Fourth Sunday in Advent' is that they are not looking at the right things in the right way. They look with 'natural' rather than 'spiritualized eyes', and thus fail to perceive the deeper, symbolic significance of their surroundings. They are also looking in the wrong direction. 'Advent bids us look forward and upward, for "Behold, the Bridegroom cometh"', Rossetti writes in *Time Flies*.[46] Absorbed in worldly occupations (reading, painting, listening), none of the women in this illustration looks forward or upward in anticipation of the arrival of Christ, the Bridegroom.

The women of Rossetti's illustration to 'Second Sunday in Lent' (fig. 3.17) are also looking the wrong way, though in this case it is their lack of insight into themselves, rather than a focus on external things, that prevents them from seeing their Bridegroom. In *Time Flies*, Rossetti writes that 'Lent turns our eyes backward and inward, for except we repent we shall all likewise perish.'[47] The five women in Rossetti's illustration are looking everywhere but 'inward', busy bemoaning their fate when they should be examining themselves in order to repent. Rossetti's illustration takes its cue from lines 23 and 24 of Keble's poem, which allude to the Parable of the Ten Virgins: 'Nor need th' unready virgin strike her breast, / Nor wait desponding round the bridegroom's door'.[48] In this parable, instead of being prepared for their bridegroom's arrival, five virgins go out in order to buy oil to fuel their dwindling lamps. When they return, they find the door barred against them as their master has arrived in their absence. Rossetti's selection of this episode for illustration seems out of keeping with the focus of Keble's poem, which concentrates on Esau's trade of his birthright to Jacob, only mentioning the Parable of

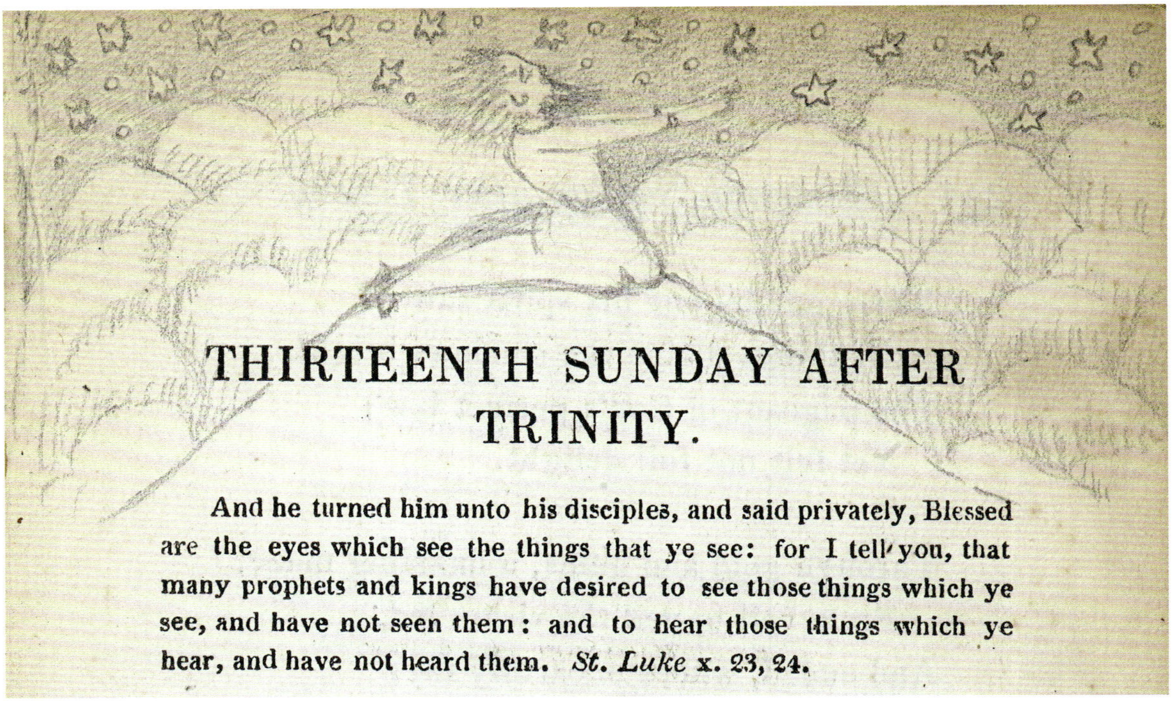

THIRTEENTH SUNDAY AFTER TRINITY.

And he turned him unto his disciples, and said privately, Blessed are the eyes which see the things that ye see: for I tell you, that many prophets and kings have desired to see those things which ye see, and have not seen them: and to hear those things which ye hear, and have not heard them. *St. Luke* x. 23, 24.

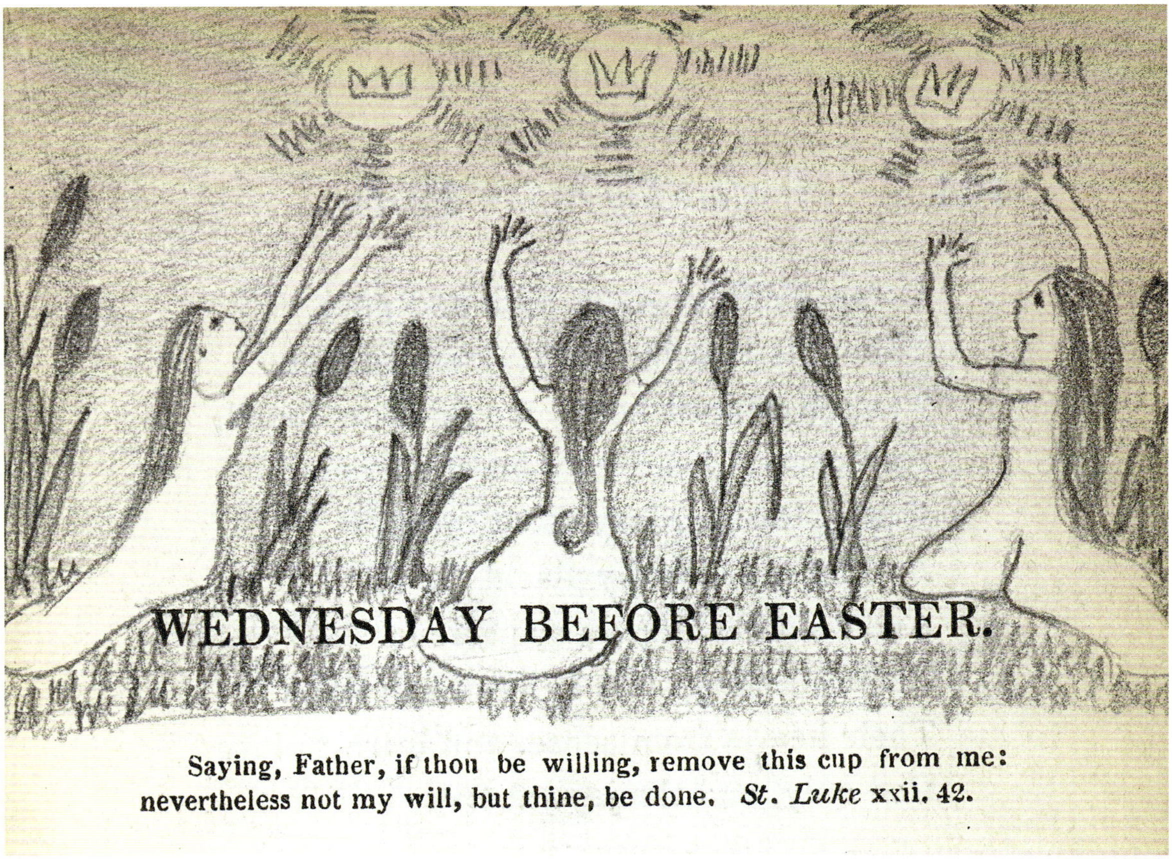

WEDNESDAY BEFORE EASTER.

Saying, Father, if thou be willing, remove this cup from me: nevertheless not my will, but thine, be done. *St. Luke* xxii. 42.

3.18 Opposite top:
Christina Rossetti, pencil illustration added to 'Thirteenth Sunday After Trinity' in her copy of John Keble, *The Christian Year*, 1837. Private collection, on loan to British Library, London.

3.19 Opposite bottom:
Christina Rossetti, pencil illustration added to 'Wednesday Before Easter' in her copy of John Keble, *The Christian Year*, 1837. Private collection, on loan to British Library, London.

the Ten Virgins in passing.[49] Like many of Rossetti's drawings for *The Christian Year*, this one shifts the poem's emphasis from a male to a female experience.

Rossetti's illustration arranges the five virgins in a straight line outside the locked door. The detailing on the women's clothing is significant here; dresses are form-fitting and display patterned fabrics (swirls, stripes, circles, dots), suggesting that vanity may play a part in the virgins' downfall. Rossetti's illustrations tend to identify elaborate costume with sin. Nebuchadnezzar's robe boasts a starry pattern in 'Nineteenth Sunday After Trinity', while the three men who are stoning the martyr in 'St. Stephen's Day' (fig. 3.8) wear robes decorated with suns, dots and a harlequin design.

Seen in profile, the women of 'Second Sunday in Lent' are in various postures of distress: the first knocks at the door; the second fiddles with her lamp; the third covers her eyes in despair; the fourth huddles on the ground with eyes downcast; the fifth throws her lamp away and shakes her fist at the heavens. Each bemoans her fate, but none looks inward to identify herself as the source of her own misfortune, which is the key to repentance.

Rossetti's drawings also celebrate human figures looking in the right direction and at the right things. In her drawing for 'St. Stephen's Day' (fig. 3.8), the martyr endures his stoning by beaming beatifically upwards. Rossetti's illustration valorises this upward gaze, which she also praises in *Time Flies*: 'while undergoing his agony his face was glorified as the face of an angel. His eyes gazed fixedly on heaven, his countenance remained unruffled'.[50] Moses adopts a similar posture in her illustration for 'Thirteenth Sunday After Trinity' (fig. 3.18). Surrounded by clouds and stars, he kneels on the top of Mount Sinai with arms outstretched, gazing up at the heavens 'in prayer and trance', waiting for 'one dear glance' from God.[51] God's 'glance' turns out to be the words of the Ten Commandments, which effectively transform Moses himself into a book. Unlike other sinners whose 'eye in smiles may wander round / Caught by earth's shadows', Moses knows enough to look up, preparing himself so that 'his breast / Might duly take and strongly keep / The print of heaven'.

Aspirational vision is not the exclusive preserve of holy men; the three kneeling women in Rossetti's illustration to 'Wednesday Before Easter' (fig. 3.19) look to the sky with the 'upward gaze' of those 'who know the life divine'. Each woman stretches her arms toward a crown hovering in the sky. Keble's poem tells us that this 'radiant coronet', which is intended to reward 'virgin souls', is 'too dazzling for a sinner's sight'. Here, sexual purity is rewarded with purity of vision. In portraying female virgins, Rossetti deviates from Keble's poem, which specifies in a note that this coronet is meant for men 'who have not defiled themselves with women'.[52] Though once again her drawing shifts the focus from men's experience to women's, Rossetti's positive portrayal of female virginity is very much in keeping with Tractarian thought, which controversially

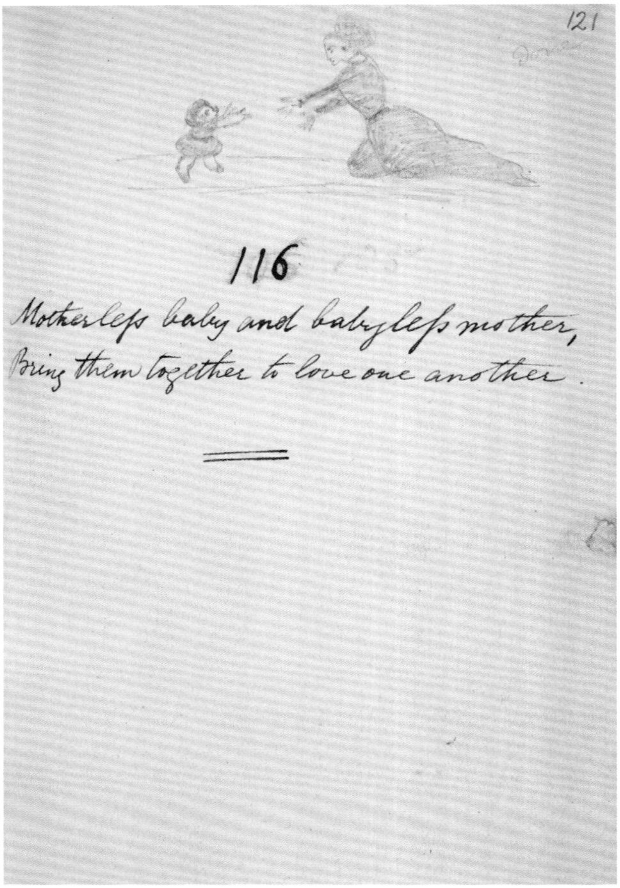

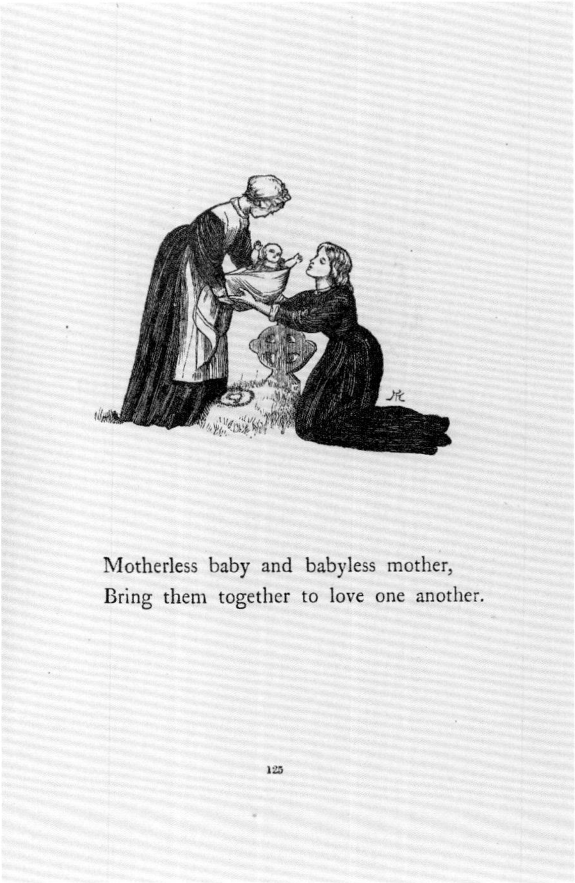

promoted chastity for both sexes. Elective virginity was a particularly radical choice for women in an age that expected them to become wives and mothers. Rossetti's unambiguously positive illustration portrays virginity as a holy choice endorsed by the natural world. Straining toward the heavens, the bulrushes growing between the female figures mimic their poses. Associated with Moses's rescue by Pharaoh's daughter, bulrushes both symbolise spiritual salvation and suggest a socially acceptable alternative identity for women in which chastity might be maintained: adoptive motherhood.

3.20 Above left:
Christina Rossetti, pencil and coloured crayon illustration added to 'Motherless baby and babyless mother' in the manuscript of *Sing-Song*, 1868–70.
British Library, London.

3.21 Above right:
Dalziel Brothers after Arthur Hughes, *Motherless Baby and Babyless Mother*, illustration to *Sing-Song* (London: Macmillan & Co., 1872), wood engraving.
Collection of Stephen Calloway.

Children's eyes

The theme of adoptive motherhood recurs in *Sing-Song*, a collection of nursery rhymes illustrated by Arthur Hughes. A long-standing member of the Pre-Raphaelite circle, Hughes was a painter and experienced illustrator known for his work on George MacDonald's *At the Back of the North Wind*, which appeared in *Good Words For The Young* (1868–70), and Thomas Hughes's *Tom Brown's School Days* (1869). Rossetti's working relationship with Hughes was collaborative; he based his illustrations on the poet's own illustrated manuscript, and she was so pleased with the results that she requested him again as illustrator for her collection of short stories *Speaking Likenesses* (1874).

Less detailed than her illustrations to *The Christian Year*, Rossetti's pencil and red crayon sketches appear above each manuscript poem. Rossetti's rhymes focus on childhood's darker, ambivalent experiences; her subjects include animal cruelty, infant death and parental grief. Her exploration of motherhood is particularly sympathetic, as in 'Motherless baby and babyless mother / Bring them together to love one another' (fig. 3.20), a poem whose picture celebrates a sense of mutual salvation.[53] Rossetti's sketch shows a mother in contemporary dress, kneeling with arms outstretched to embrace the small child toddling toward her. Arthur Hughes's published illustration (fig. 3.21) maintains the tenderness of the original, but it eliminates this sense of mutuality and choice; he depicts one woman handing another a swaddled baby over a grave. Hughes's interpretation also detracts from the radical resonance of Rossetti's term 'babyless mother', which suggests that motherhood depends on choice rather than biological destiny. She expands on this in *The Face of the Deep*: '"Give me children, or else I die" was a foolish speech: the childless who make themselves nursing mothers of Christ's little ones are true mothers in Israel.'[54]

Mutual love between mother and child is conveyed via their gaze again in Rossetti's design for *Sing-Song*'s 'Love me, I love you'. Here, a woman holds an infant in her lap while both figures look adoringly at one another. Rossetti's poem portrays maternal protectiveness as a process of holding and seeing, but in featuring the child's gaze, her design stresses a reciprocity not portrayed by the lines it illustrates: 'Mother's arms under you / Her eyes above you'. By contrast, Hughes's illustration privileges the mother figure; a standing woman cradles an infant whose face is obscured by a bonnet.

Rossetti's illustrations consistently allow children agency; they are often looking in the right place, at the right thing and in the right spirit. Rossetti's design for *Sing-Song*'s poem on infant death, 'Our little baby fell asleep' (fig. 3.22) depicts three angels embracing a baby. Wearing contemporary dress, the infant faces the viewer with eyes wide open. This bold Blakean picture recalls Rossetti's treatment of supernatural figures in *The Christian Year*. The angels' spectacularly vertical hair, flaming feet and criss-crossed long wings showcase the wide-eyed baby's 'pretty look', a gaze that signifies his awakening in Paradise.[55] Hughes depicts a more conventional, solitary angel (fig. 3.23) with long, pretty hair, feathery wings and a tender, maternal gaze.

Though they might change the emphasis of the originals at times, Hughes's illustrations are on the whole sympathetic to Rossetti's poems and sketches. Rossetti was delighted with Hughes's work and grateful for his expertise, noting that his pictures 'deserve to sell the volume'.[56] Kooistra observes that Hughes's combination of 'the maternal, the pastoral and the spiritual' recalls the work of William Blake.[57] A similarly Blakean sensibility, which resists hackneyed portrayals of childhood innocence, is evident in Rossetti's illustrations in *The Christian Year*.

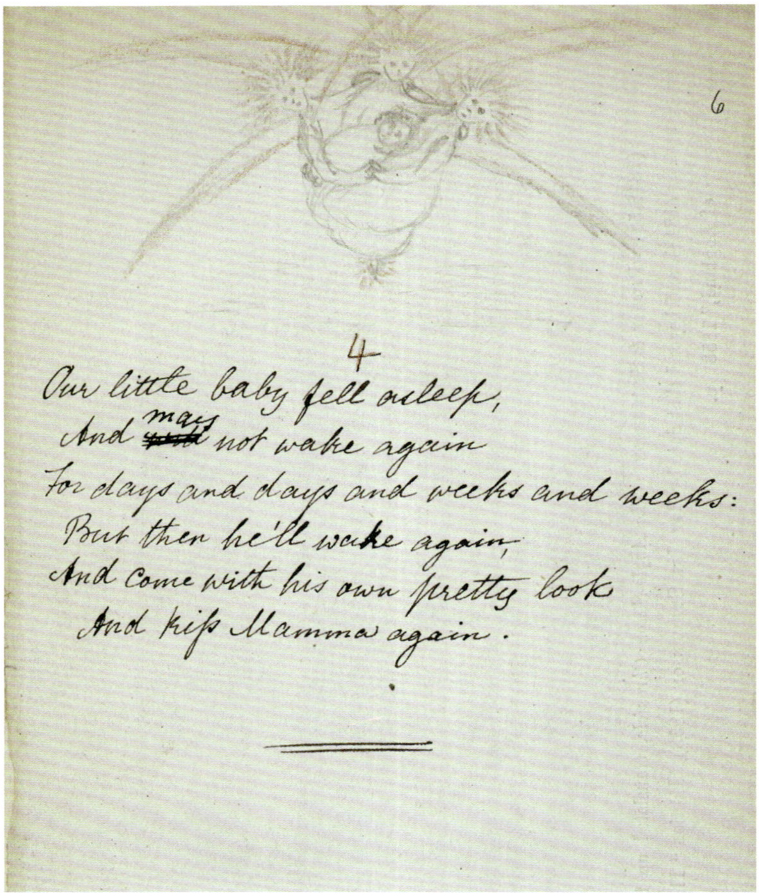

6

4

Our little baby fell asleep,
And may not wake again
For days and days and weeks and weeks:
But then he'll wake again,
And come with his own pretty look
And kiss Mamma again.

3.22 Left:
Christina Rossetti, pencil and coloured crayon illustration added to 'Our little baby fell asleep' in the manuscript of *Sing-Song*, 1868–70. British Library, London.

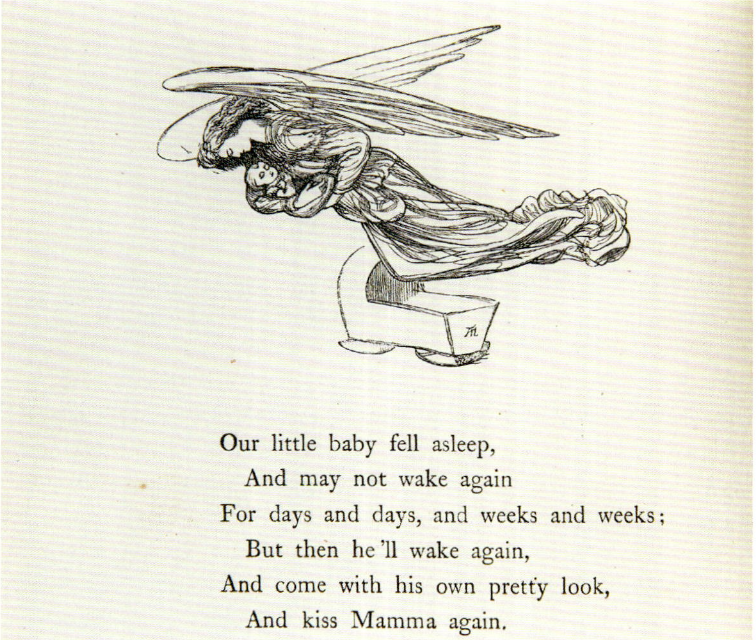

Our little baby fell asleep,
And may not wake again
For days and days, and weeks and weeks;
But then he'll wake again,
And come with his own pretty look,
And kiss Mamma again.

3.23 Below left:
Dalziel Brothers after Arthur Hughes, *Our Little Baby Fell Asleep*, illustration to *Sing-Song*, 1872, wood engraving. Collection of Stephen Calloway.

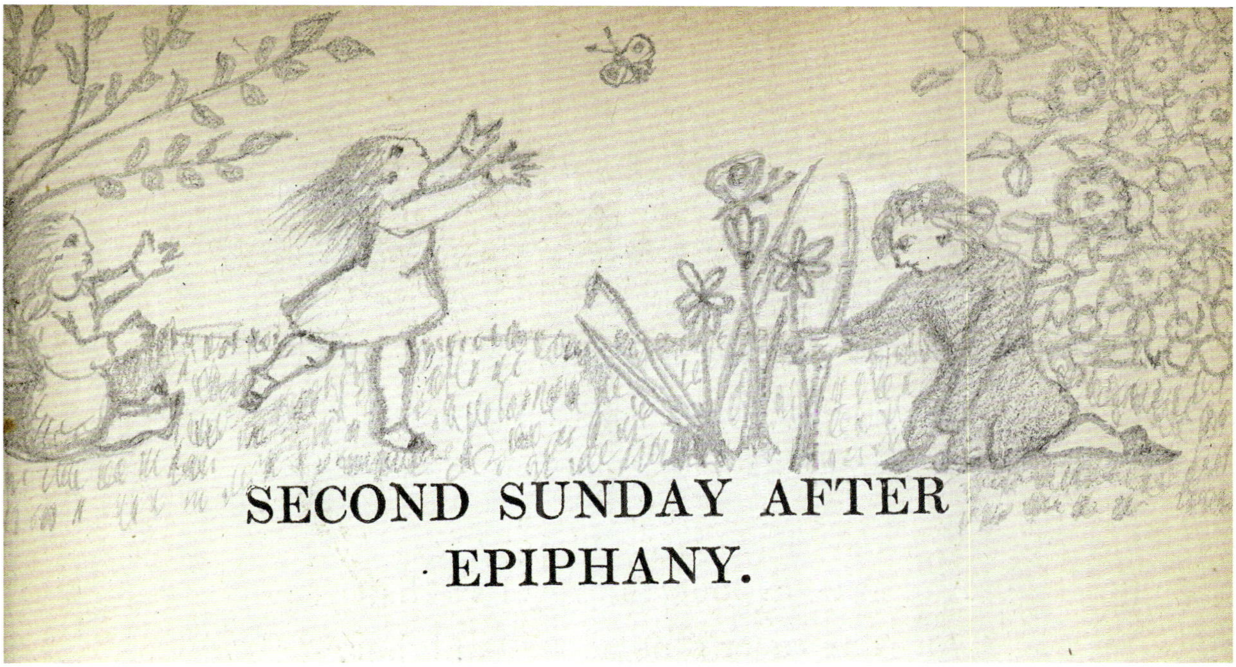

3.24 Christina Rossetti, pencil illustration added to 'Second Sunday After Epiphany' in her copy of John Keble, *The Christian Year*, 1837. Private collection, on loan to British Library, London.

In Rossetti's illustration for 'First Sunday After Easter', a mother and child unmentioned in the poem stand before a pastor. The human trio is guarded by an angel with a flaming sword. While the mother also participates in the religious ceremony, it is her child's outstretched arms and upward gaze that refocus the 'Restless Pastor' of the poem's subtitle on his ministry. While their mother's concentrated frown is directed towards the earth, the contemporary children at play in the garden of 'Second Sunday After Epiphany' (fig. 3.24) raise their arms and eyes to the sky. Reading against Keble's opening critique of the naively ignorant 'heart of childhood [that] is all mirth', Rossetti's illustration identifies childhood with qualities the poem praises. The running girl's smile indicates that she represents the loving 'hearts' who 'see all things bright / With their own magic smile', while the seated girl who looks to the heavens embodies 'Faith', who is 'Speeding her gaze o'er time and death / To realms where nought can perish'.

Animals' eyes

While Rossetti allows that sin obstructs human vision, she also shows how innocence permits beholders to see the divine in the earthly. Innocence is a quality shared by children and animals in Rossetti's poems and drawings. In *Time Flies* she includes a poem praising 'Innocent eyes not ours' belonging to 'small birds and insects'. Though they may be 'The least and last of things', they 'Have just as clear a right / to their appointed portion of delight, / As Queens or Kings'.[58] Based in biblical tradition, which sees humans as caretakers of animals and the natural world, Rossetti's sympathy for animals manifests itself not only in her

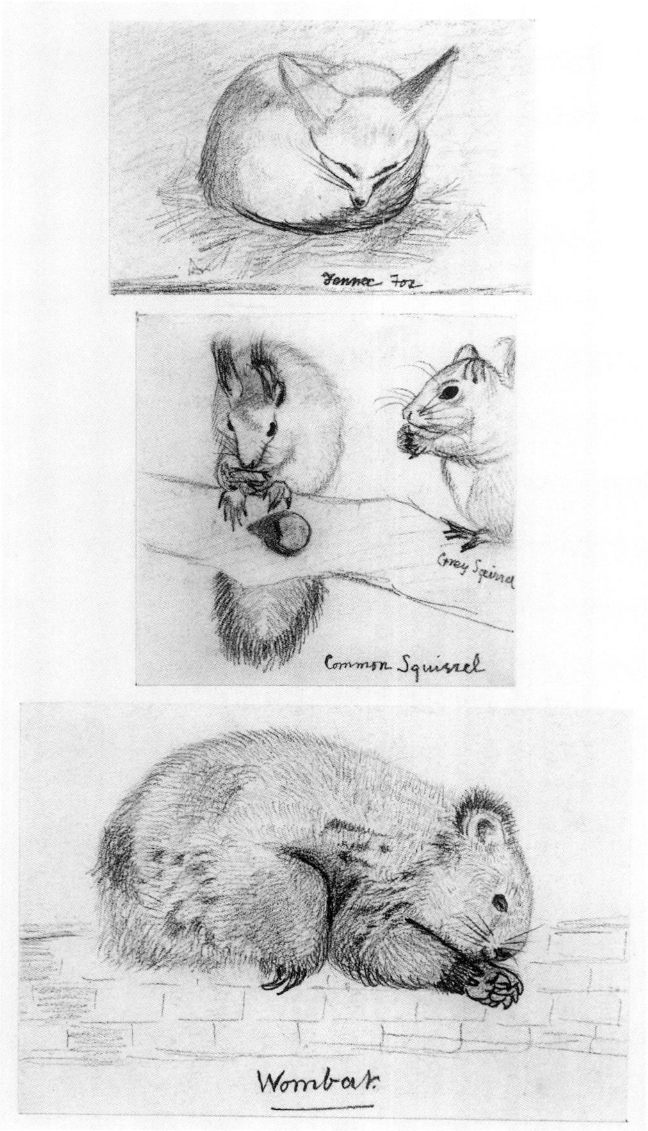

3.25 Christina Rossetti, *Three Animal Studies: A Fennec Fox, Squirrels and a Wombat*, c.1862, pencil on paper, 7 × 11 cm; 10 × 10 cm; 11 × 16 cm. Private collection.

work, but in animal activism; she was a passionate anti-vivisectionist.[59] Her affection for animals is obvious in her care for her domestic pets; Emma Mason notes that 'her last words were not adventual or apocalyptic, but simply "Don't forget about the kitten"'.[60] Her 1862 pencil drawings of a fox, squirrel and wombat in the Zoological Gardens (fig. 3.25) show an attention to character and individuality that her portraits of people struggle to convey.

Birds and insects are the animals most frequently portrayed in Rossetti's illustrations to *The Christian Year*, and, unlike the human figures, they are generally looking and moving in the right direction. 'The Purification', whose epigraph is 'Blessed are the pure in heart; for they shall see God', is illustrated by two birds perched on flower stems,

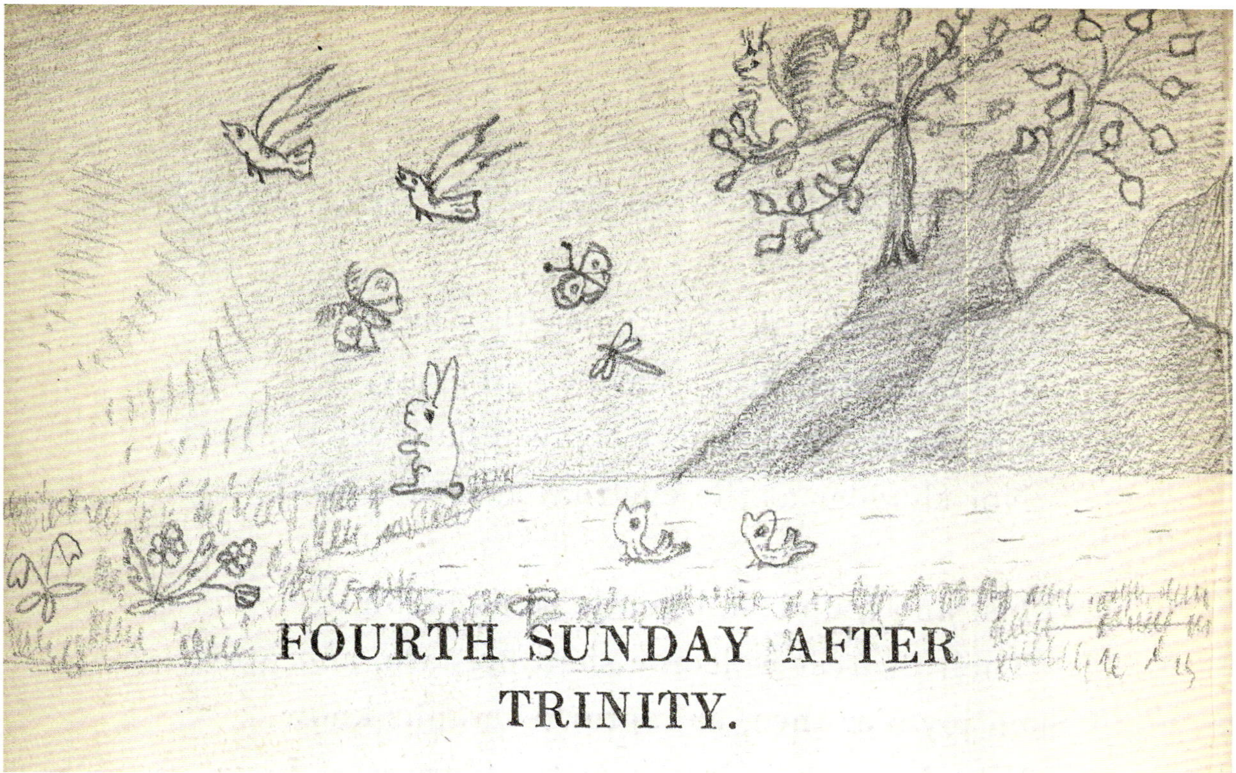

3.26 Christina Rossetti, pencil illustration added to 'Fourth Sunday After Trinity' in her copy of John Keble, *The Christian Year*, 1837. Private collection, on loan to British Library, London.

one staring out at the viewer, the other looking intently at a flower and butterfly. In 'Fourth Sunday After Trinity' (fig. 3.26), butterflies, birds, a dragonfly, a rabbit, a squirrel and even two fish in a pond look up to the sky. Birds look lovingly into one another's eyes in 'Matrimony' and 'First Sunday After Epiphany' (fig. 3.27), while the dove of 'Quinquagesima Sunday' (fig. 3.28) fixes its gaze on the viewer. In 'Third Sunday After Epiphany', a baby bird looks up from its nest towards its mother, who soars before a rainbow, eyes toward the heavens.

'Come and See': The final illustration

The 'supernaturalized' eye is the subject of Rossetti's only significant verbal intervention in her copy of *The Christian Year*. On the pastedown endpaper at the back of her copy of Keble's book, Rossetti carefully transcribes a poem, 'Come and See', by her contemporary, Elizabeth Rundle Charles. A well-known religious writer of historical fiction as well as poetry, Charles shared Rossetti's Anglo-Catholic faith and sometimes her publisher; both women's devotional prose works were released by the Society for Promoting Christian Knowledge (SPCK).

Charles's poem is an important material addition to the book, evoking the late-sixteenth-century definition of 'to illustrate': 'to use one text to shed light on another.'[61] 'Come and See' adds a female poetic voice to Keble's volume and draws our attention to the significance of vision in Rossetti's illustrations. The poem takes its title from Christ's response to his disciples' question, 'Master, where abidest Thou?' (John 1:38).[62] Each stanza closes with an invitation to '"Come and see"', the final repetition ending on a 'triumphant' exclamation point.[63]

Rossetti added 'Come and See' to her copy of *The Christian Year* not only because it intensifies the communal, intertextual reading experience Keble's volume promotes, but also because the poem deals with the vexed question of representing and interpreting the divine in word and image:

> How shall we thine image best
> Bear in light upon our brow,
> Stamp in love upon our breast?
> Still a look is all our might;
> Looking draws the heart to Thee,
> Sends us from the absorbing sight
> With the message, "Come and see."

3.27 Christina Rossetti, pencil illustration added to 'First Sunday After Epiphany' in her copy of John Keble, *The Christian Year*, 1837. Private collection, on loan to British Library, London.

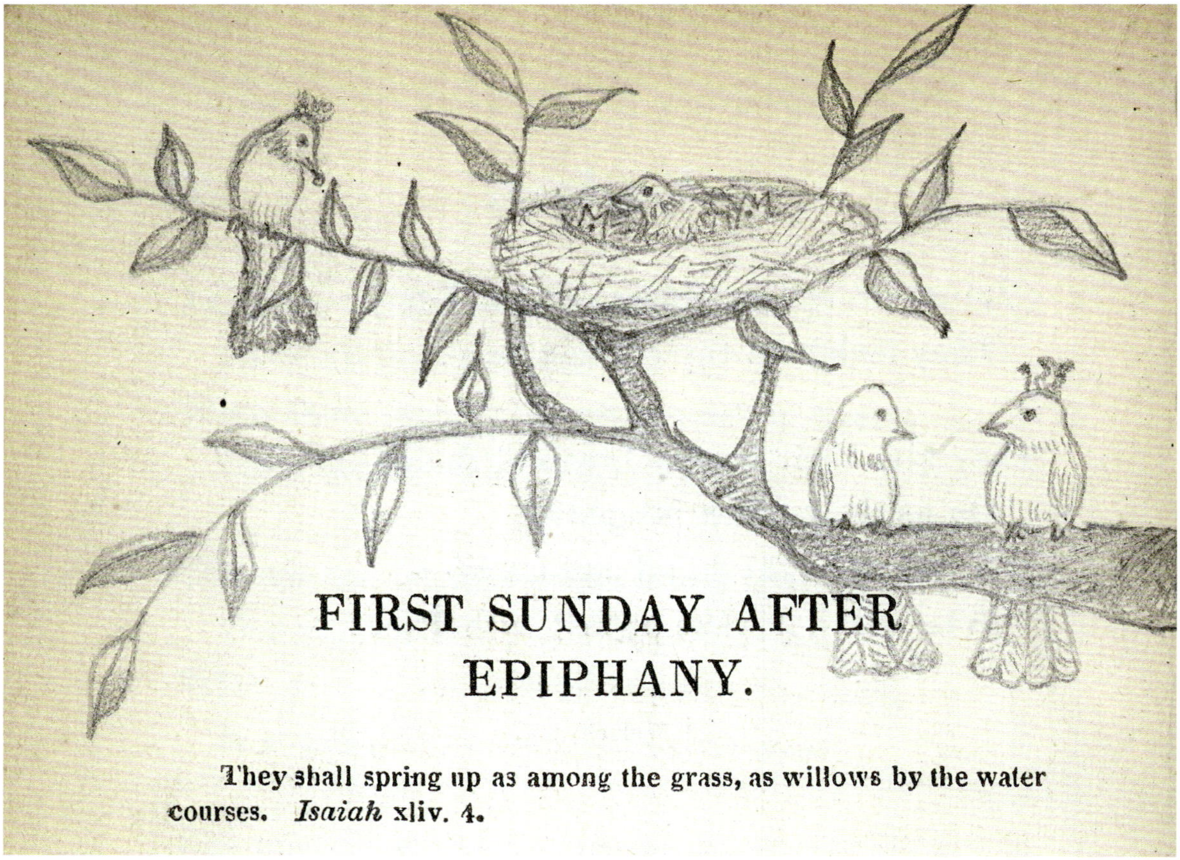

3.28 Christina Rossetti, pencil illustration added to 'Quinquagesima Sunday' in her copy of John Keble, *The Christian Year*, 1837. Private collection, on loan to British Library, London.

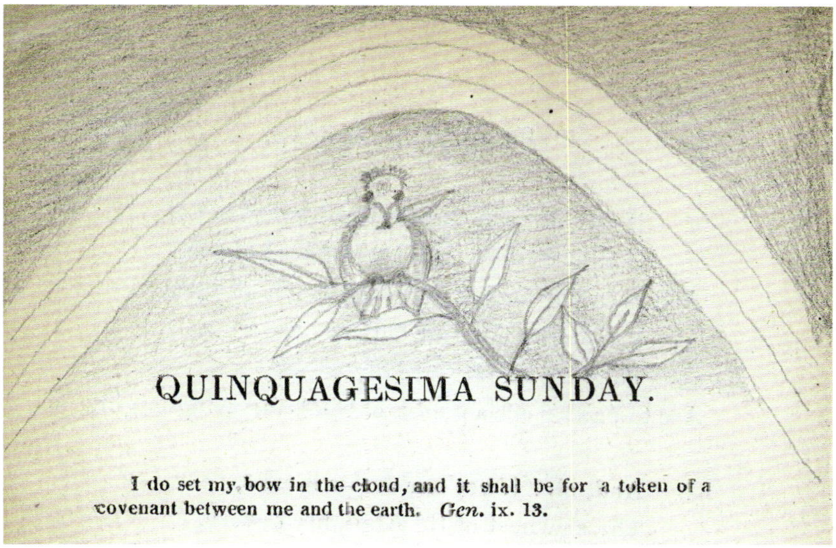

Here, an image shared is an image activated. Christian witnesses should not passively 'Bear' and 'Stamp' the divine 'image' on brow and breast; they must go 'from the absorbing sight' in order to spread the 'message', inviting others to '"Come and see"'. The human act of 'Looking' initially 'draws the heart' to God, but this individual experience acquires true power as a shared vision: 'a look is *all our* might' (emphasis mine). Made in God's image, Christians should make a concerted effort both to look like (resemble) Him and look like (as) Him.

Closing the book with the invitation to '"Come and see"' initially seems counterintuitive, or at the very least paradoxical; there is nothing more to 'see' in a book we have finished reading. Understood as a gloss on Keble's poems and Rossetti's accompanying illustrations, however, Charles's poem reminds us of the circularity of the ritual reading process itself. The reader never finishes *The Christian Year* because the ecclesiastical year always begins again. Dependent on cycles of repetition and renewal, ritual reading (and looking) supernaturalises our eyes so that, as Keble and Charles and Rossetti hope: 'Old friends, old scenes, will lovelier be, / As more of heaven in each we see'.[64]

Christina Rossetti made a habit of reading and rereading Tractarian poets throughout her life, and her illustrations to *The Christian Year* should be considered as a visual complement to that reading practice. Her methods as an illustrator are literary; she editorialises, translates and interprets, exhibiting what Keble calls 'due reserve, which always shrinks from pouring forth everything, worthy or unworthy, without selection'.[65] Rossetti's illustrations interpret Keble's poems as she would the natural world, with an eye towards discerning the invisible in the visible, the symbolic in the material. Inspired by the contemplative, intertextual reading practice *The Christian Year* promotes, Rossetti's illustrations invite us to '"Come and See"' reading as an act of looking and looking as an act of reading.

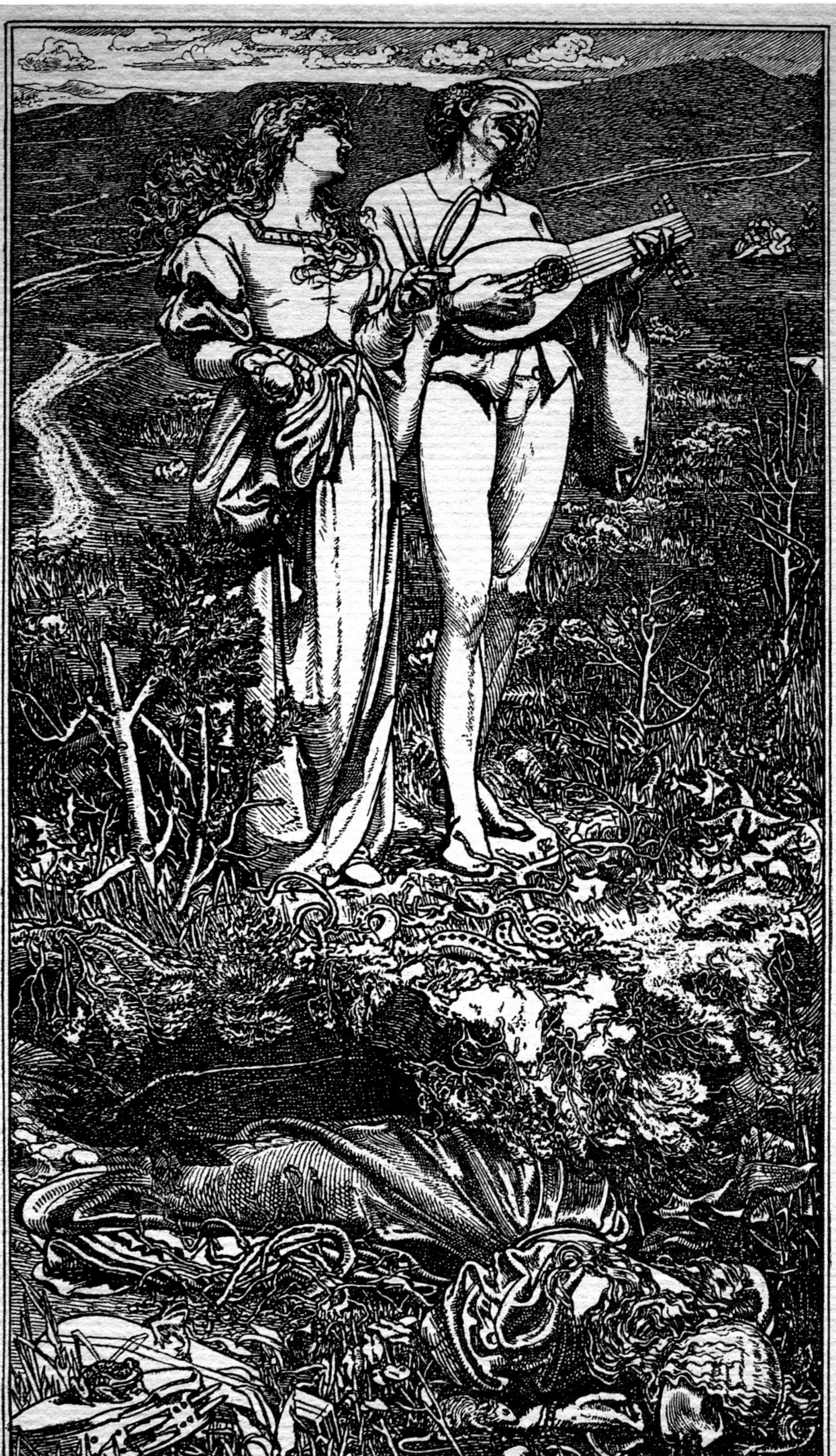

Come buy, come buy

4 Christina Rossetti's Books: The Poet, her Publishers and the Illustrators

STEPHEN CALLOWAY

COSMOPOLITAN in outlook and intellectually high-minded, revolutionary in the idealistic way of the times, boisterous and talkative, the Bloomsbury household of the Neapolitan literary scholar and political exile Gabriele Rossetti was an exciting place to grow up and a forcing ground of talent for his four clever children. Two – Christina, the youngest, and her brother Dante Gabriel – would achieve fame as major poets of the nineteenth century. Brothers and sisters alike, all four children imbibed from an early age the professor's love of letters – and in particular his devotion to Dante – but their youthful literary endeavours were also inspired and greatly encouraged by their mother Frances Polidori and her equally cultured and also part-Italian side of the family. Frances's late brother was the intriguing minor *littérateur* and physician John Polidori (fig. 1.4), friend and companion of Byron at the Villa Diodati in 1816 and the author of the sensational Gothic romance *The Vampyre*, whilst their father was Gaetano Polidori, sometime secretary to the celebrated Italian dramatist Vittorio Alfieri and, from the time of his arrival in London, a significant publisher of foreign books and the proprietor of his own private press.

Rossetti's earliest printed works

Writing and drawing illustrations to favourite books and their own poems and stories played a crucial part in the early lives of both Christina and Gabriel. Both were surprisingly sophisticated for their ages and ambitious in their creativity, and even their juvenile efforts were given serious consideration within the Rossettis' tight-knit circle of family and friends. Basking in a degree of admiration born perhaps largely of family piety, both Gabriel and Christina were indulged by their grandfather Gaetano, who generously undertook to put their first literary efforts into print. Thus Gabriel's 'legendary ballad' *Sir Hugh the Heron* appeared in booklet form – for private circulation only – in 1843.[1]

4.1 Joseph Swain after Frederick Sandys, *Amor Mundi*, the *Shilling Magazine*, vol. 2, June 1865, wood engraving. Collection of Stephen Calloway.

Precocious as this debut was, however, it had already been pre-empted by Christina's first serious effort, a short set of birthday verses written for her mother at the age of twelve. According to William Michael Rossetti, the family was, as he would write many years later, 'a little surprised' at Christina's 'coming out' as a poet and it was apparently for this reason that Gaetano 'printed the lines at once on a card'.[2] This modest offering, a single sheet the size of a postcard bearing just two stanzas, each of four lines, has the distinction of being the first item in the very extensive bibliography of the future poet's works and a remarkable literary rarity.[3]

Heartened by this small triumph but also, no doubt, inspired by some degree of sibling competition, Christina continued to work at her poetry. By 1847 she had enough pieces collected together to make a small booklet to rival her brother's. The title page of *Verses by Christina G. Rossetti, Dedicated to her Mother* prints a six-line epigraph precociously chosen from Metastasio, given in the original Italian, and bears the imprint once again of Gaetano Polidori's press in Park Village East. Containing some forty-three mostly short pieces, copies of the book were ready for circulation by July 1847; although issued in a simple, plain-paper wrapper and not technically *published*, it made Christina at least a *printed* poet at the age of sixteen-and-a-half.[4]

Although the poems in *Verses* can hardly be classed as more than juvenilia, Christina did choose to include them in her later collected volumes. And the little volume was deemed worthy to be reprinted in its entirety after the author's death and some sixty years after its first appearance, becoming one of the most attractive of all small books belonging to the great private press movement of the turn of the century (fig. 4.28).[5] For the time, however, *Verses* was an utterly conventional, which is to say unconsidered, piece of printing. Questions of typefaces, page design, layout and binding style remained as far from Christina's mind at this date as they did for her brothers and their young and earnest artistic friends.

The Germ

It has often been remarked that the Pre-Raphaelite Brotherhood, formed in the following year, 1848, the 'year of revolutions' in Europe, had aspirations that were initially as much literary as artistic. Certainly at this date Gabriel was almost as intent upon becoming a poet as a painter and he expressed his wish that Christina, though clearly precluded from joining as a full member of the Brethren, should be fully involved as one of the creative forces of their little band. Though she had an interest in drawing and never entirely gave up making small sketches and intense, if artistically amateurish, designs in the pages and margins of her books, Christina's role in the great reformation of the English art scene that was planned by the PRB would be for the most part literary, other than serving more or less willingly as a model for their pictures and drawings (see Chapter Two). Thus when, largely it seems at the instigation of Gabriel as prime mover, it was proposed to further their cause by a sort of parallel assault on the literary establishment, Christina was keen to play her part. *The Germ* was planned as a literary periodical to supplant the banal and the commonplace in the publishing world just as the early PRB pictures were intended to reform public taste for the sort of trite and sentimental paintings that clogged the walls of the Royal Academy and other major exhibition venues year after year.

The first number of *The Germ*, bearing the significantly worded subtitle 'Thoughts towards Nature in Poetry, Literature and Art', was published in January 1850.[6] Initially the names of contributors were not printed, but among the contents can be identified two of Christina's poems, 'Dream Land' and 'An End'.[7] Appropriately, the first of these unsigned pieces, 'Dream Land', appeared opposite her brother Gabriel's lines 'My Sister's Sleep'. A frontispiece in the form of an etching by William Holman Hunt set the pattern – still relatively unusual in the world of literary magazines at this time – of illustrating one of the poems within, in this case Thomas Woolner's lines on 'My Beautiful Lady'. There was however no attempt made to integrate text and image and, whatever the merits of the writing, typographically *The Germ*, with its feeble typeface, cramped layout and poor-quality paper stock, appeared as visually impoverished as most commercial offerings of the day.

In subsequent issues, again largely at Gabriel's instigation, the names of writers were identified. But with a characteristic degree of reticence, Christina chose to sign her three poems in No. 2 and a further two in the third issue with a suitably poetic or ballad-like pseudonym 'Ellen Alleyn'.[8] No contribution from Christina's pen was forthcoming to grace the next issue, and with this fourth number the publication, begun with such high-minded enthusiasm but now in debt sufficient to cause its original begetters real anxiety, ceased.

Christina Rossetti and the commercial periodicals

It would be some time before another such Pre-Raphaelite communal effort was undertaken or any further serious collaboration with her brothers entered into, but in the meantime Christina seems to have been keen to pursue her own opportunities. She continued to look for outlets for her work and began, with some success, to explore the possibilities of publishing her verses in various literary and general periodicals, both established and new. Among these, *Macmillan's Magazine* – and the interest in her work taken by its proprietor Alexander Macmillan – would prove to be of the greatest importance to Christina's subsequent publishing career.

The middle decades of the century – that is, roughly the years from the early 1840s to the mid-1860s – were an exciting period of expansion in the publishing world. The earlier 1840s had seen the establishment of many new journals (such as the *Illustrated London News* and *Punch*, to name only two of the most prominent and enduring) whose success depended to a considerable extent on their extensive employment of popular illustration. The use of engraved woodblocks, which were cut by a new breed of fast-working professional specialist and which could be economically printed on the same presses alongside type, transformed the publishing world. By the late 1850s and early 1860s publishers were enjoying a halcyon period of profit and acclaim from the creation of increasingly beautiful and sophisticated 'gift books'. Among the foremost of these productions was the celebrated edition of Tennyson's poems published by Edward Moxon. This handsome and substantial volume, which appeared first in 1857 and was several times reprinted, was the first to bring the work of the Pre-Raphaelites before a wider public. Holman Hunt and Millais both produced arresting images derived from the subjects of Tennyson's lines, but it was the group of intricately detailed designs by Dante Gabriel Rossetti that signalled a new era in illustration. Closely related to his precisely contemporary, jewel-like watercolours of medieval subjects, these illustrations were where he perfected his method of freely 'allegoris[ing] on one's own hook' in order to produce compressed images full of intense feeling.[9] His later designs for his sister's poetry would be conceived in a similar vein.

At a somewhat less exalted level of artistic intensity, even the cheaper magazines and journals of the day, such as *Once a Week* and *Good Words*, teamed poems and prose tales with high-quality illustrations, often engraved after designs by leading artists as well as a growing tribe of hack commercial draughtsmen. In this milieu, Christina's poems, mostly short, appealing in subject matter and usually metrically direct, were the sort of thing editors sought. Her first poem to be illustrated in this way was 'Maude Clare', published in *Once a Week* for 5 November 1859.[10] Gabriel would have been Christina's natural first choice of illustrator, but he had, as so often, declared that he had no time to draw out the necessary design on the block for engraving and so the job was passed – within the PRB – to John Everett Millais, who was already drawing regularly for *Once a Week*. He too must have been pressed for time, for whilst the main figure of Maude is cleverly drawn and carefully characterised, the remaining elements of the image are in the sketchy, loosely hatched manner of many of his rapidly executed contributions to the magazine. In subsequent cases, Christina would fare better with the illustration of her works.

Frederick Sandys's illustrations to Rossetti's poems

The two designs made for her poems by Frederick Sandys are generally accounted as among the very finest of the 'golden age' of wood-engraved illustration of the 1860s. The first, *Amor Mundi* – often described as Sandys's masterpiece – illustrates Christina's dark poem of the same name, which was printed in the second volume of the short-lived *Shilling Magazine* in June 1865 (fig. 4.1).[11] Sandys's design is in his most intricately linear, Düreresque drawing style, and cleverly suggests the moment of blithe indifference before a vain and worldly couple, bent on enjoyment and set upon 'the downward path', make a macabre and minatory discovery:

> "Oh what's that in the hollow, so pale I quake to follow?"
> "Oh that's a thin dead body which waits the eternal term."

In spite of Sandys's superb figure-drawing and brilliant rendition of natural details, in William Michael Rossetti's assessment, the illustration was fatally flawed because, he claimed, his sister had not intended her two protagonists to be male and female lovers, but that they should be read, as if in a sort of symbolic vanitas piece, as two aspects, both female, representing the worldly and the spiritual. Christina herself apparently made no such objection to Sandys's imagery, and whilst we do not know precisely what she thought of his illustration, it is clear from an earlier remark in a letter to Gabriel that she admired his work and was pleased that he had agreed to take on the commission.[12]

A little under a year later, in March 1866, the second of Sandys's illustrations, this time for 'If' – another poem on Christina's recurrent theme of doomed or blighted love – was printed in an early issue of the *Argosy* (fig. 4.2).[13] Here Sandys represents the figure of an abandoned woman looking out to sea in despair of her lover's return.

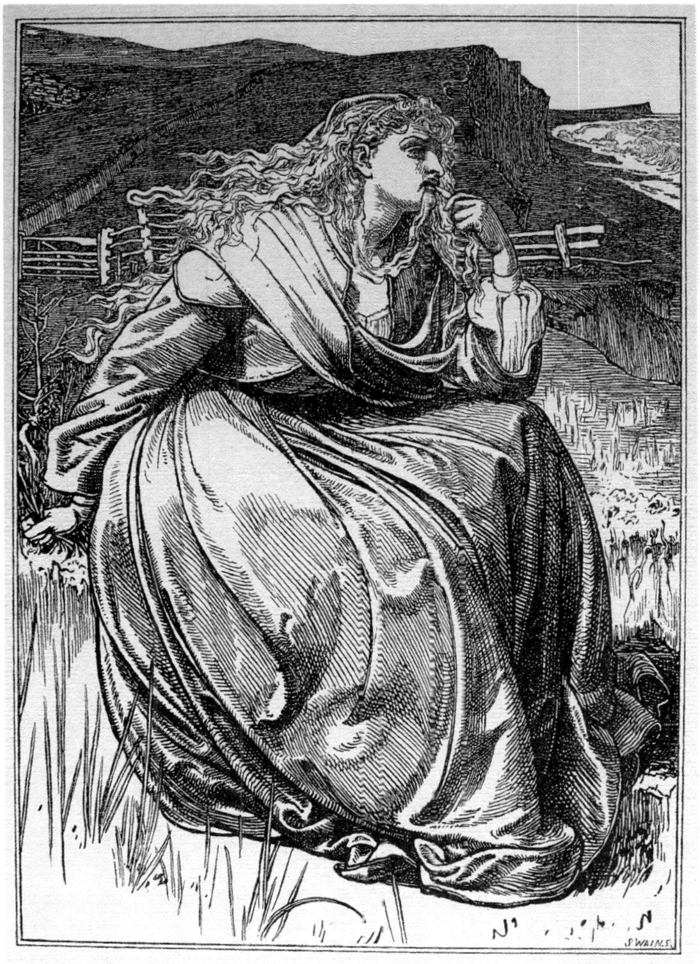

4.2 Joseph Swain after Frederick Sandys, *If*, *Argosy*, vol. 1, no. 4, March 1866, wood engraving. Collection of Stephen Calloway.

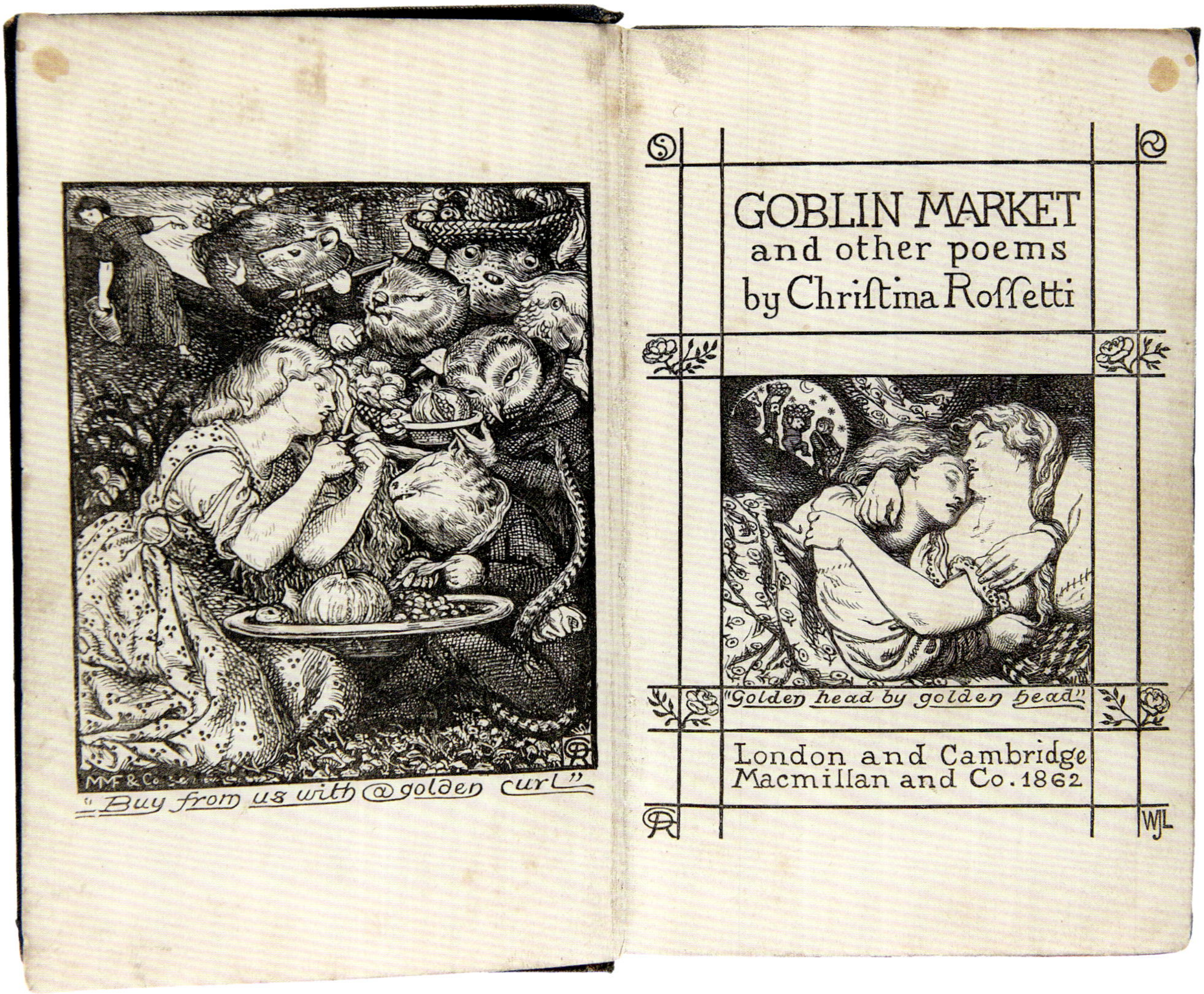

4.3 Charles J. Faulkner and W. J. Linton after Dante Gabriel Rossetti, frontispiece (Faulkner) and title page (Linton) to Christina Rossetti, *Goblin Market and Other Poems* (London: Macmillan & Co., 1862), wood engravings.
Collection of Stephen Calloway.

Sandys depicts her as voluptuously dishevelled by the wind, one hand clutching convulsively at the grass and – introducing a favourite and oft-repeated motif of his own, first seen in his painting *Proud Maisie* – biting a strand of her own hair to signify her state of heightened emotion.[14] This design, one of Sandys's most powerful, reveals a debt to Gabriel or, perhaps more accurately, the extent of reciprocal influence between the two men; they were intimate in these few years, during which Sandys became, for a while, one of the floating population of bohemian *habitués* of Gabriel's Cheyne Walk establishment. It has long been held in the Rossettian mythology that Sandys's expulsion from Tudor House and estrangement from the circle came about largely as a result of Gabriel's somewhat paranoiac imputation of plagiarism to his old friend, in whose illustrations he was said to have seen too great a resemblance to his own. In any event, Sandys made no further illustrations for Christina.

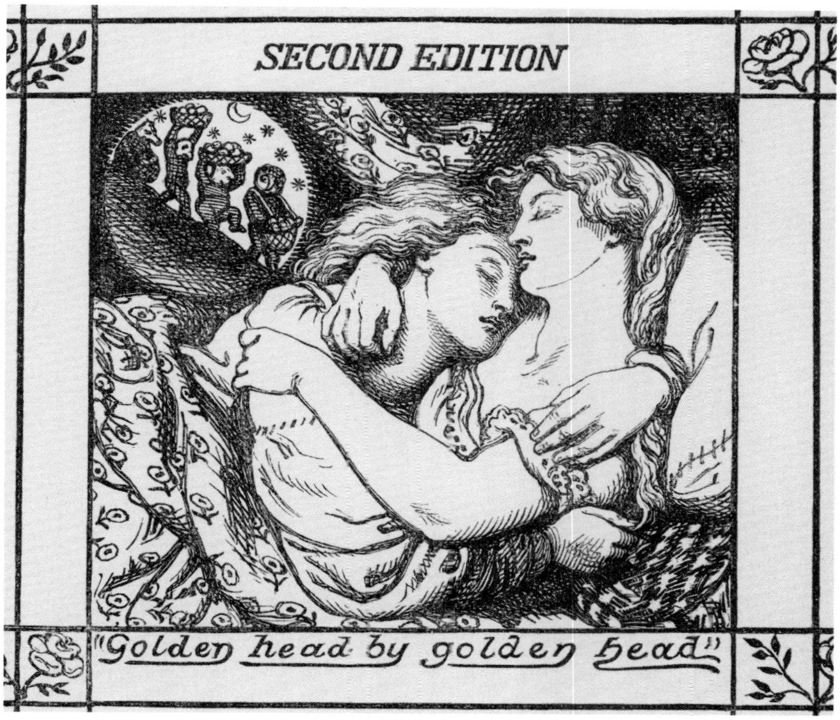

4.4 W. J. Linton and Kate Faulkner after Dante Gabriel Rossetti, *Golden Head by Golden Head*, revised title page vignette to *Goblin Market*, 2nd edn, 1865, wood engraving. Collection of Stephen Calloway.

The issue of a second edition of the book gave Dante Gabriel Rossetti the opportunity to correct the unsatisfactory reproduction of the drawing of Laura's neck by the insertion of a 'plug' into the block that was re-engraved by Kate Faulkner.

Goblin Market, 1862–1865

With the appearance in 1861 of his volume of free and inventive translations titled *The Early Italian Poets*, published by Smith, Elder & Co. with the financial backing of John Ruskin, Dante Gabriel Rossetti began to take a more serious and energetic interest in the publication of not only his own writings but also those of his friends. Always keen to promote his sister's work, he began to take an active role in helping her gather, select and prepare her verses with the idea of publishing. Thinking in terms of a volume for publication, he ordered many short pieces into two separate sequences of religious and secular subject matter, and in particular he helped her to shape a long and curious narrative piece, suggesting that she change her original title 'A Peep at the Goblins' to the more effective 'Goblin Market'. He advised that this should be the main poem for a potential volume and extended his original proposal of contributing two illustrations to include designing both the title page and binding.

On his sister's behalf, Gabriel entered into correspondence with the enterprising publisher Alexander Macmillan (who was also the proprietor of *Macmillan's Magazine*). In commercial terms, Macmillan demonstrated a cautious optimism. On 28 October 1861 he wrote to Gabriel announcing that he would 'run the risk of a small edition with the two designs which you kindly offer', adding that 'my idea is to make an exceedingly pretty little volume, and to bring it out as a small Christmas book.'[15] He offered Christina considerably generous author's terms and the book was announced in the press at the end of November.[16] But as time passed Gabriel prevaricated about the completion of his drawings, and on 11 December Christina was still writing to Macmillan to question which colour of cloth should to be used to show off his binding design to best advantage: 'The *dark* colours, especially the *puce*, *red* and *violet*, which I return, appear to me amongst the best.'[17]

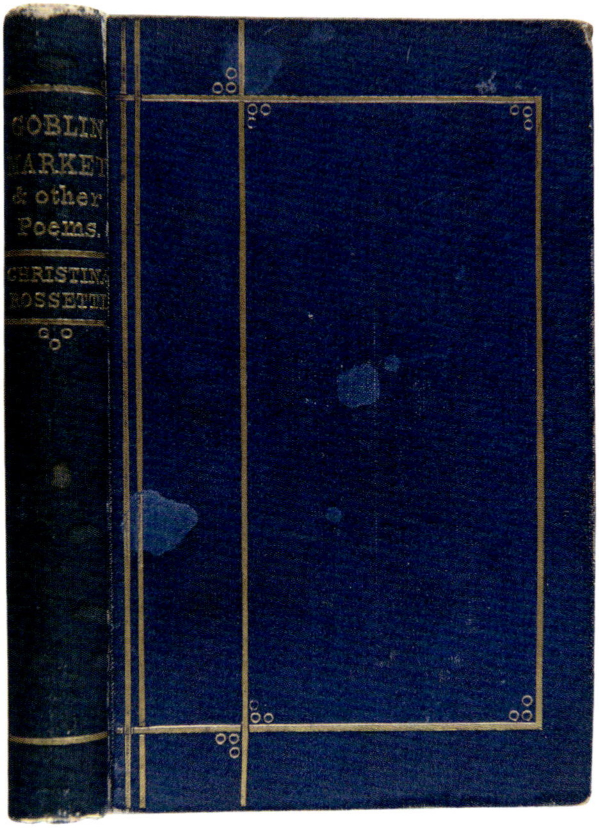

4.5 Dante Gabriel Rossetti, cover design for Christina Rossetti, *Goblin Market and Other Poems*, 2nd edn (London: Macmillan & Co., 1865), violet-blue cloth, front cover and spine blocked in gold and rear cover blind-stamped. Collection of Stephen Calloway.

Having hoped to avoid the sort of acrimonious and long-drawn-out battle that had ensued when the wood-engraving firm of Dalziel Brothers had, as he saw it, ruined his work for the Moxon Tennyson, Gabriel had enlisted instead the services of Charles James Faulkner, one of the original partners in 'The Firm' (William Morris's newly founded band of 'art workmen') to cut his frontispiece design *Buy from us with a Golden Curl* (fig. 4.3).[18] But as always, Gabriel was disappointed with the results of the cutting. The exacting task of engraving the title page with its framework of lines, hand-drawn lettering and exquisite (and as some thought, provocative) smaller image *Golden Head by Golden Head*, showing the two sisters Lizzie and Laura lying asleep in one another's arms, was entrusted to the professional engraver W. J. Linton. However even he failed to create a successful result, insufficiently capturing the nuance of Gabriel's line delineating what should have been the graceful throat of one figure and instead leaving the ugly effect of a double chin. As late as 26 February 1862, Christina wrote again to Macmillan to say that Gabriel wished him to return the block for a final attempt at improving it.

Further delays resulted from Christina's insistence upon making last-minute corrections of newly discovered textual errors when the book was already in the press, which necessitated the troublesome printing and insertion of a cancel page. As a result, the first printing of 750 copies of *Goblin Market* appeared only in March 1862, thereby missing the Christmas gift-book market from which Macmillan had hoped to profit. Even though the book was generally well received, sales were measured, and it would be three years before a new edition was called for. There can be no doubt, however, that *Goblin Market* became Christina's most popular (and most reprinted) work.

Attractive as Gabriel's illustrations are, in some ways the single most striking aspect of the volume is its binding (fig. 4.5). The *Goblin Market* cover is an improved and yet more daring version of that first conceived by Gabriel for his own *Early Italian Poets*. His concept takes as its starting point the unremarkable convention of bookbindings in which a central panel on each cover is delineated by a variety of ruled lines, often further embellished at the corners with small groups

4.6 Dante Gabriel Rossetti, *Design for a sofa*, c.1860–1, pencil, pen and ink on paper, 25.4 × 35.3 cm. Birmingham Museum & Art Gallery.

The drawing has annotations concerning measurements and manufacture added and initialled by William Morris. The sofa was made by Morris, Marshall, Faulkner & Co. and exhibited on their stand at the International Exhibition at South Kensington, 1862.

of dots, flowers or other simple ornamental elements (a convention much employed in European and especially English bindings from the seventeenth century). Gabriel's startling originality lay in the way in which he 'exploded' the framing elements of a simple panel to create a more abstract and dynamic arrangement of lines, further enlivened by the treatment of their intersections with an under-and-over weave effect and the addition of restrained groups of small circles. The bold off-centre positioning of the panel (within the context of a design tradition usually characterised by the most rigid symmetry) and the general lightness of touch in the use of line and ornament both strongly suggest the influence of Japanese design, a source of fascination and inspiration shared by Dante Gabriel Rossetti and others among his friends in the vanguard of taste, including James McNeill Whistler and the architect and furniture designer E. W. Godwin.

In this context, it is intriguing to compare Gabriel's experiments in bookbinding design with his own almost exactly contemporary design for a piece of furniture: the sofa made and exhibited among the first productions of 'the Firm' on their stand at the International Exhibition of 1862 (fig. 4.6). This extraordinary piece was perhaps Rossetti's most successful – and certainly his most startling – foray into design for the decorative arts. Taking the form of a refined and strictly rectilinear

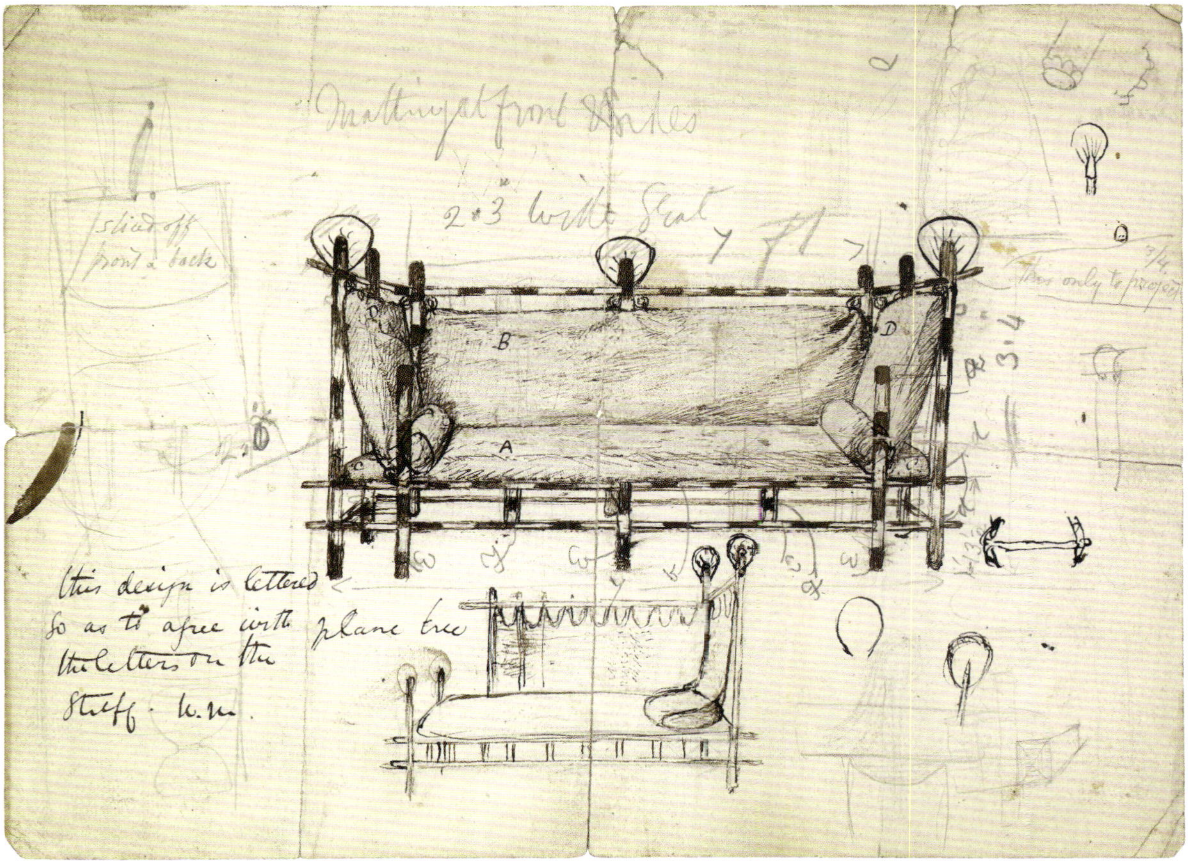

arrangement of thin, intersecting sticks painted black and highlighted in gold, the piece broke with all preconceived ideas in Victorian furnishing and was held – in as far as it was understood at all by observers – to suggest something of Japanese styling in its disregard for comfort and conventional ornamentation.[19] Considered in terms of the applied arts, or even in a more abstract light, the similarities between sofa and bookbindings seem telling in the context of any search for the origins of Aesthetic Movement design.

Tantalisingly, it is known that following the publication of the book, in one copy Christina made a sequence of watercolour illustrations (see Chapter Three). This was presumably for her own amusement or, as is perhaps equally likely, for presentation to a recipient such as her mother. The fact that the volume was described some forty years later by William Michael Rossetti in the notes to the *Poetical Works*, his definitive 1904 collected edition of his sister's verses, strongly suggests that it remained in family possession. Later the book was among the many treasures in the collection of William Michael's granddaughter (Mrs Imogene Dennis), but its present whereabouts have continued to elude the searches of Rossetti scholars and book collectors alike.

The story of the early editions of *Goblin Market* has one final twist. For, with the plan to print a second edition, Gabriel was determined to revisit the problem of the title page illustration (fig. 4.4). With time to fuss again, he had the unsatisfactory area of the woodblock cut away and a fresh piece of boxwood – known as a 'plug' – inserted to be re-engraved. Characteristically, Gabriel was furious about the way the job was done and by the 'phenomenal stupidity' of the 'plugger', writing in exasperation to Macmillan that 'there is a nautical rhyme to the word which one would like to use!'[20]

The corrective engraving was carried out at the Morris firm's Queen Square workshop by Kate Faulkner, the sister of Charles Faulkner. Requesting that Macmillan pay her, Gabriel wrote: 'I should think £2 would be right. She is a professional engraver, & I could not have thought of going to her unless with the idea that she would accept payment, as you mentioned your willingness to pay necessary expenses.'[21] At this point Gabriel also took the opportunity slightly to revise his binding design, reducing the length of some of the framing lines of the cover. This had the effect of making the design seem even more abstract and also removed the faint suggestion that the arrangement of lines resembled the projecting corners of an 'Oxford' picture frame, with the somewhat fusty connotations of that style.

The Prince's Progress

The generally favourable reception accorded in the press to *Goblin Market* and sales figures for the two editions that were sufficiently encouraging, if not exactly indicative of runaway success, made the idea of another similar volume attractive to Macmillan. Surviving correspondence from around this time between him and Gabriel and

4.7 Opposite top:
W. J. Linton after Dante Gabriel Rossetti, frontispiece and title page to Christina Rossetti, *The Prince's Progress and Other Poems* (London: Macmillan & Co., 1866), wood engravings.
Collection of Stephen Calloway.

4.8 Opposite bottom:
Dante Gabriel Rossetti, *The Long Hours Go and Come and Go*, design for title page vignette for *The Prince's Progress*, December 1865, pencil, pen and ink on paper, 9.5 × 10.5 cm.
Birmingham Museum & Art Gallery.

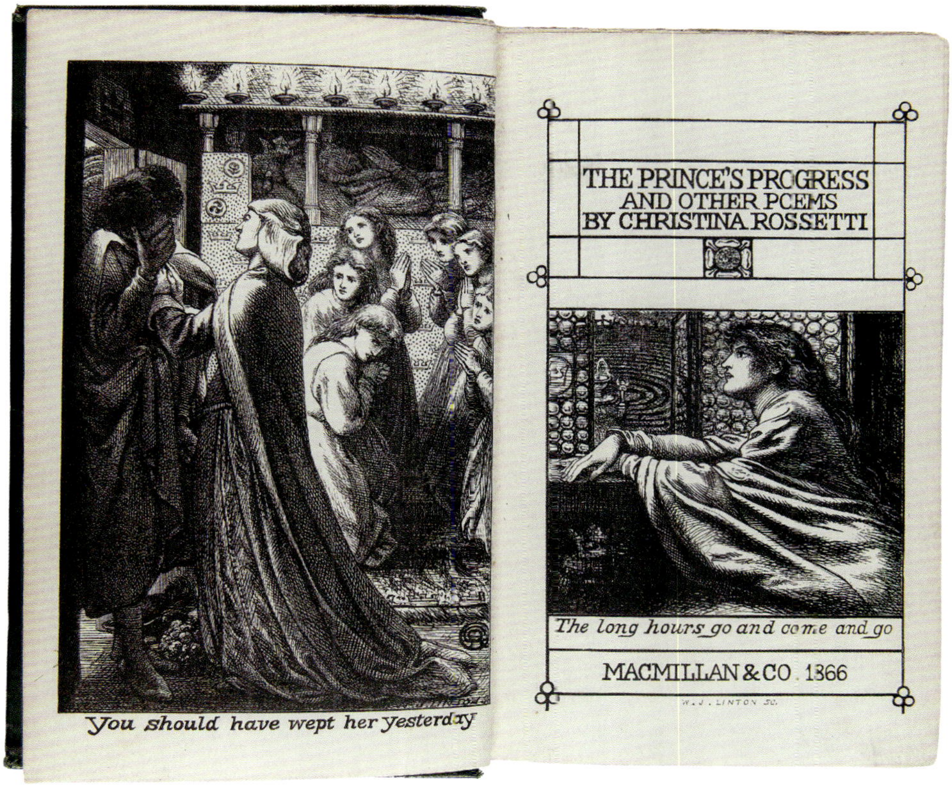
You should have wept her yesterday
THE PRINCE'S PROGRESS
AND OTHER POEMS
BY CHRISTINA ROSSETTI
The long hours go and come and go
MACMILLAN & CO. 1866
W. J. LINTON SC.

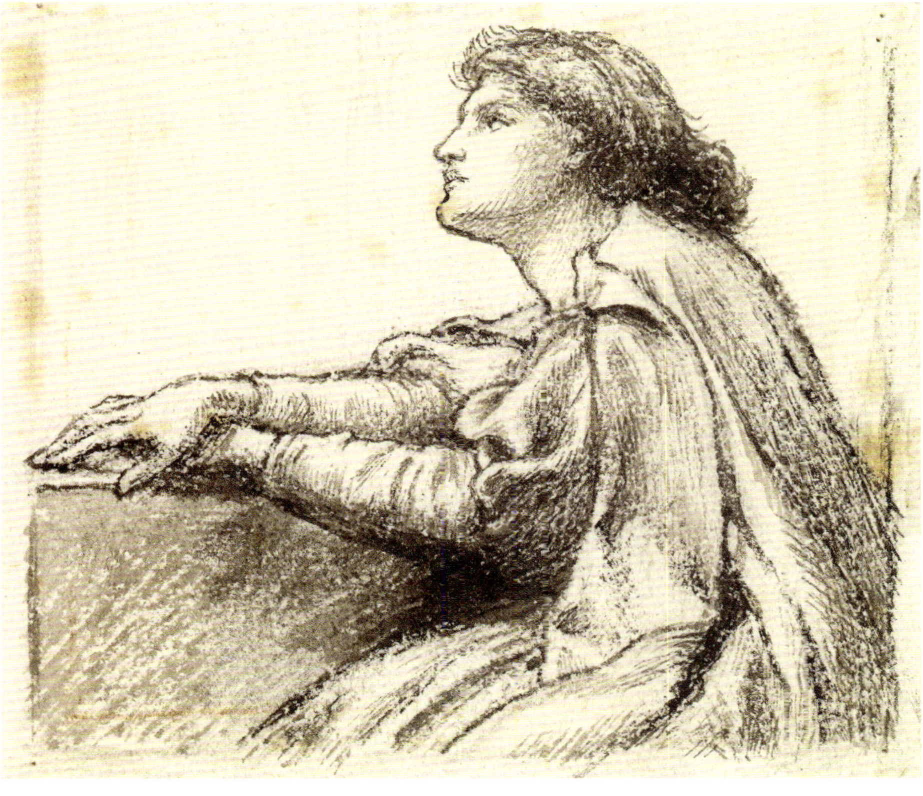

also in due course with both William and Christina reveals the extent to which he seems to have wished to become the friend as well as the publisher of the Rossetti siblings. Letters from Gabriel concern not only details about the editing and design of Christina's volumes (with, as we have seen, endless requests for small corrections and revisions), but also his attempt to persuade Macmillan to take the somewhat bolder step of publishing the poetry of Swinburne. In this we can see an attractive side to Gabriel's character, which tended, at this time especially, to a good-hearted desire to further the careers and reputations of others of his circle as much as his own. (The same altruistic enthusiasm can also be seen in his attempts to secure sales or commissions for his painter friends, such as Ford Madox Brown.)

Christina continued to write, but initially had doubts concerning both the quality and quantity of new work that she could assemble for another volume. Her brothers offered encouragement and, once again, it was Gabriel who gave her the initial stimulus and provided crucial specific guidance. He suggested that a suitable lead poem for a new book could be created by re-working and extending 'The Fairy Prince who Arrived too Late', a shorter piece that she had written in 1863 originally for the writers' circle the Portfolio Society[22] and which had been printed in *Macmillan's Magazine*.[23] Aside from his usual insistence on helping in the process of rewriting and editing – possibly not always entirely welcome to Christina – as before, Gabriel offered to contribute a pair of illustrations for frontispiece and title page and to devise a new binding design (fig. 4.7). The book was set up in type and printed by July 1865, but, once again, it would be largely Gabriel's seemingly endless delays and prevarications that held up its appearance for all but a year; only in June 1866 was the edition, again of 750 copies, actually published.[24] As with *Goblin Market*, sales were steady if not spectacular and Macmillan's records show that by 1872, with twenty-five copies still in stock, no new edition was needed.

Whilst it must be assumed that Gabriel made some or possibly many original sketches for his *Goblin Market* illustrations, only one – very close in detail to the published engraving – still exists.[25] In the case of *The Prince's Progress*, a large group of drawings (now in Birmingham City Museum and Art Gallery) survives. They reveal his creative process, in which he tried out many small variations of viewpoint, visual emphasis and detail (fig. 4.8).[26] As before, engraving of the blocks was entrusted to Gabriel's preferred professional cutter, Linton, and this time his cutting seems largely to have been met with approval. Although perhaps not as immediately visually striking as the images from the previous book, both designs have a memorable quality; that for the frontispiece being even more closely related to the best of Gabriel's watercolours, the group of highly romanticised pictures of chivalric subjects he made in the late 1850s.

A curious sidelight on the creation of such illustrations is afforded by drawings from members of the extended Pre-Raphaelite circle. The aristocratic amateur Louisa Anne Beresford, Marchioness of Waterford took desultory drawing lessons with Dante Gabriel Rossetti; her friendship with the others in the group and familiarity with their work encouraged her to make large numbers of small, often spirited ink sketches and watercolours. In about 1868 she was inspired by Christina's recently published volume to make a rapid preliminary sketch on which she inscribed lines from a stanza of 'Maiden-Song' in *The Prince's Progress*:

The king of all that country
   Coursing far, coursing near,
Curbed his amber-bitted steed,
   Coursed amain to hear;
All his princes in his train,
   Squire, and knight, and peer.

A more finished version of the design is typical of her work in the way in which it reflects not only the style of Rossetti and the young Burne-Jones but is also reminiscent – albeit on a very small scale – of the more sweeping compositions and colouristic ambitions of G. F. Watts (fig. 4.9).[27] Whilst in later years Louisa attracted something of a cult following among aficionados of 'lady amateurs', Gleeson White, the authority on late nineteenth-century illustrators, offered a more carefully modulated assessment of her abilities: 'In the designs by Louisa, Marchioness of Waterford, one encounters genius with absolutely faltering technique; and many who know how rare is the slightest touch of genius, forgive the equally important mastery of material which must accompany it to produce work of lasting value.'[28]

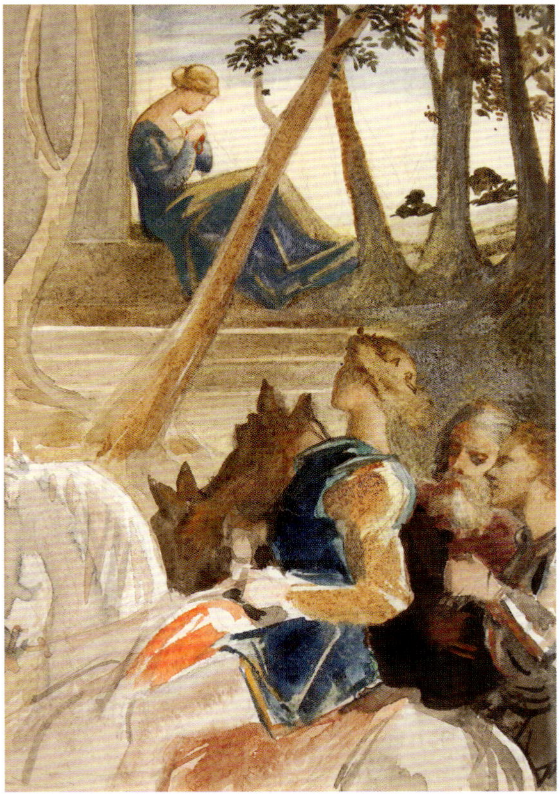

4.9 Louisa Anne Beresford, Marchioness of Waterford, *Maiden-Song*, c.1868, watercolour on paper, 18 × 13 cm. National Trust, Fenton House, London.

In spite of the attractiveness of Gabriel's illustrations for the frontispiece and title page, the more immediately arresting aspect of *The Prince's Progress*, as with *Goblin Market*, was its binding. Gabriel's new design cleverly harks back to the formal innovation and bold asymmetry of the earlier volume, but further enlivens its more static framing elements with curling lines that terminate each ruled line, suggesting not so much plant forms as spring-like coils with a positively lively tensile strength. Perhaps recalling the strength and elegance of the gothic ironwork hinges of medieval doors, the cover exudes a sense of liveliness and confidence that also derives from the way in which the design integrates the elements of both boards and the spine with so much greater assurance than before (fig. 4.10).

Always a point of dissension between designers and publishers, the question of whether to block the rear covers of books to match their fronts was one which certainly seems more often than not to have

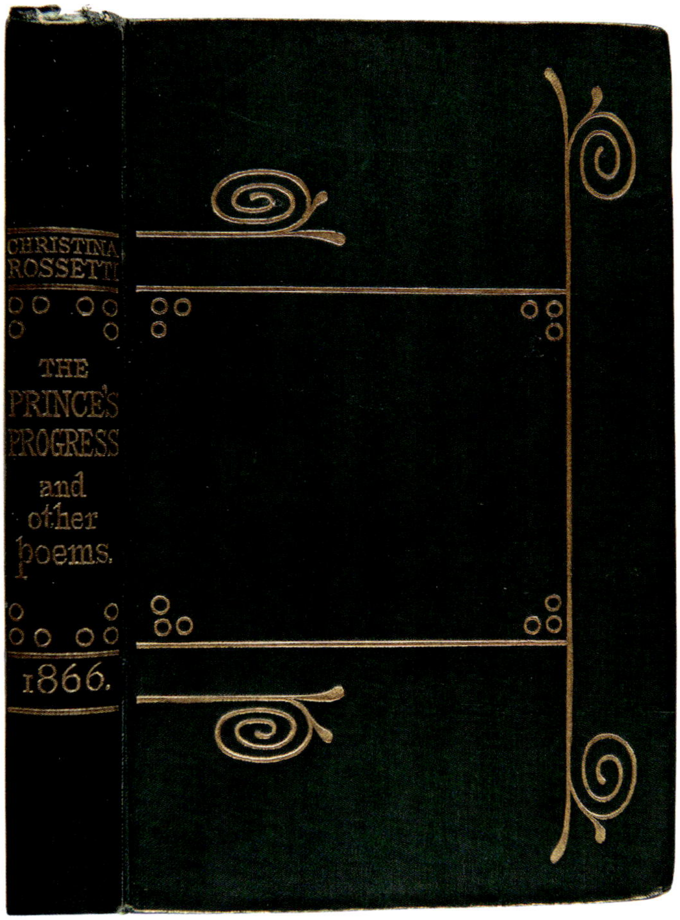

4.10 Dante Gabriel Rossetti, cover design for Christina Rossetti, *The Prince's Progress*, 1866, bright green cloth, front and rear covers and spine blocked in gold. Collection of Stephen Calloway.

been settled in favour of financial rather than aesthetic considerations. Aside from the most lavish of the 'gift books' of the 1860s, it increasingly became the norm to leave the lower cover either entirely blank, miserably blocked with the same design 'in blind' (the pattern simply impressed into the board without gold) or with nothing more than a small central device. As late as the 1890s, Oscar Wilde would still lament that 'nothing looks more vulgar and cheap than a book with an ornament on one side of the cover and the other side blank'.[29] Only in the hands of a few insistent designers, and one or two more imaginative publishers at the end of the century, was Gabriel Rossetti's concept of the binding as a whole revived. Appropriately, as we shall see, one of the most interesting instances of this attempt at the creation of the total 'book beautiful' was a new edition of Christina Rossetti's *Goblin Market* in 1893 from Macmillan.

Dante Gabriel Rossetti's 'livery' for his friends' books

In considering Gabriel as one of the most successful and innovative designers of bookbindings, it becomes apparent that, in addition to his then-unusual concern with the creation of individually beautiful volumes, he may also have had in mind a somewhat more far-reaching agenda. As I have suggested elsewhere, it seems likely that Gabriel wished to create what could be termed a sort of 'livery', not merely for his own books but also for those of all the writers of his circle.[30] This idea of a livery can be seen to a degree in the ornamentation that he designed for a good many covers, but also most significantly in the choice of colours for binding cloths that he proposed for himself or urged upon his friends. Coinciding with the point at which Gabriel adopted F. S. Ellis as his publisher (also persuading Christina to abandon Macmillan temporarily), the livery was clearly intended as a visual expression of Gabriel's notion of gathering together under Ellis's imprint 'a little knot of congenial writers'.[31]

Within the huge spectrum of possibilities available at the time, the narrow range of colours that Gabriel favoured – blacks, deep blues, sombre greens and intermediate shadings through subtle turquoise or peacock green – is most striking. Apart from his own *Early Italian Poets* (black) and his later *Poems* of 1870 (deepest peacock), the choices made by other friends that appear to have conformed to the livery over a period of years include those by both Christina and William, William Morris and William Bell Scott, Swinburne, Philip Webb, Gordon Hake and Simeon Solomon. Such signalling of an artistic and intellectual stance by the choice of colour was well understood at the time. The Aesthetic Movement adopted as something of a badge a palette of the quieter, richer, tertiary shades – olive- and blue-greens, soft Indian reds and ochres – in deliberate opposition to the strident effects that Gilbert and Sullivan castigated in *Patience* as 'Red and yellow! Primary colours! Oh, South Kensington!'

Interestingly, following the notably sombre choice made by Christina, or more likely by Gabriel, of a dark blue ribbed cloth with a dull surface for the first edition of *Goblin Market*, it seems likely that Macmillan sought to lighten the effect and thereby increase the appeal of Christina's subsequent covers by the use of brighter, smoother and, as it might have been perceived, more attractive cloths. For the second edition of *Goblin Market* published in 1865, the most noticeable difference is that the book – in other ways almost identical to the first issue – is covered in a strong violet-blue shade. Similarly striking is the almost emerald green cloth used for what would be the single edition of *The Prince's Progress*. It might be noted, in passing, that a taste for brighter and even flashy effects, made possible by the widespread adoption of harsh, newly introduced chemical dyes by textile manufacturers and the popularity of intentionally shiny weaves, is a distinct characteristic of women's dress in the 1860s. Could it be that Macmillan and possibly even Christina herself, in defiance of Gabriel's diktat and of course in contrast to her own rigid ideas of decorum in dress, sought to appeal to a market more susceptible to lighter and prettier effects; to some degree to court fashion? The appearance of Christina's next publications might give some credence to the supposition.

The books for children: *Sing-Song* and *Speaking Likenesses*

Christina's next two books, *Sing-Song: A Nursery Rhyme Book* in 1872 and *Speaking Likenesses* two years later, should be considered together. For both – unlike her other works – were aimed at a wider juvenile market, and illustrated in a recognisably children's book style by the same somewhat sentimental artist, a figure from the wider Pre-Raphaelite circle, Arthur Hughes. That the two volumes were issued under different imprints, *Sing-Song* by Routledge and *Speaking Likenesses* once again under the banner of Macmillan, is the result of an unsettling period of juggling with her publishing options in which both of Christina's brothers, no doubt with the best of intentions, muddied the waters of negotiation and offered her often-conflicting advice.

Coinciding with a period of serious illness, the complex affair caused Christina considerable upset and left her for a time without a publisher at all. Too tangled to unravel here, the initial cause of the break with Macmillan was his offer of 'obviously meagre' rewards for *Sing-Song*, Christina's collection of short verses in nursery-rhyme form; terms which Gabriel had then hoped could be bettered by a move to *his* publisher F. S. Ellis.[32] The question of who might supply the many illustrations required also led to much discussion. In a letter to Ellis, Christina dismissed a sequence of amateurish little drawings she had made herself as 'scratches', though hoped that they might 'help to explain my meaning'.[33] Several members of the wider Pre-Raphaelite circle, including Charles Fairfax Murray and also William Bell Scott's companion Alice Boyd, among others, came under consideration.[34] When Christina entered into an agreement with the Dalziel Brothers to engrave the blocks, she specifically reserved the right of approval of the choice of illustrator, but fell ill at the moment when a conclusive decision was needed. Things were happily resolved with the appointment of Hughes – a decision effectively pushed through by William Michael, but one that pleased Christina. Amid continuing uncertainty, Ellis finally declared that he was unable to bear the expense of publishing, and so it ultimately fell to the Dalziels to fix a deal with their frequent publishing associates at Routledge, the firm that had successfully taken over the proprietorship of many of the best gift books of the day, including the Moxon Tennyson (fig. 4.11).

Sing-Song was issued with an attractive cover, its design gold-blocked on a cheerful apple green (fig. 4.12). Though dated 1872, the book was issued in the previous November in order to catch the Christmas market, and the sales figures record that by March the following year the original 1,000 copies and a further 100 from a run-on printing had been sold.[35] Gabriel expressed his warm approval in a letter to Swinburne, writing: 'Christina's book is I think divinely lovely, both in itself and in Arthur Hughes's illustrations which are quite unequalled for sweetness' (fig. 4.13).[36] Always popular, the book remained in print for many years and sold quite well in various later issues, including one in a cheaper 'chaste binding'[37] and another, paper-covered, priced at just one shilling. A late, unexpected episode in the

4.11 Opposite top:
Dalziel Brothers after Arthur Hughes, frontispiece and title page vignette to Christina Rossetti, *Sing-Song* (London: Routledge., 1872), wood engravings.
Collection of Stephen Calloway.

4.12 Opposite left:
Arthur Hughes, cover design for Christina Rossetti, *Sing-Song*, 1872, bright green cloth, front cover and spine blocked in gold.
Collection of Stephen Calloway.

4.13 Opposite right:
Dalziel Brothers after Arthur Hughes, *If a Pig Wore a Wig*, illustration to *Sing-Song*, 1872, wood engraving.
Collection of Stephen Calloway.

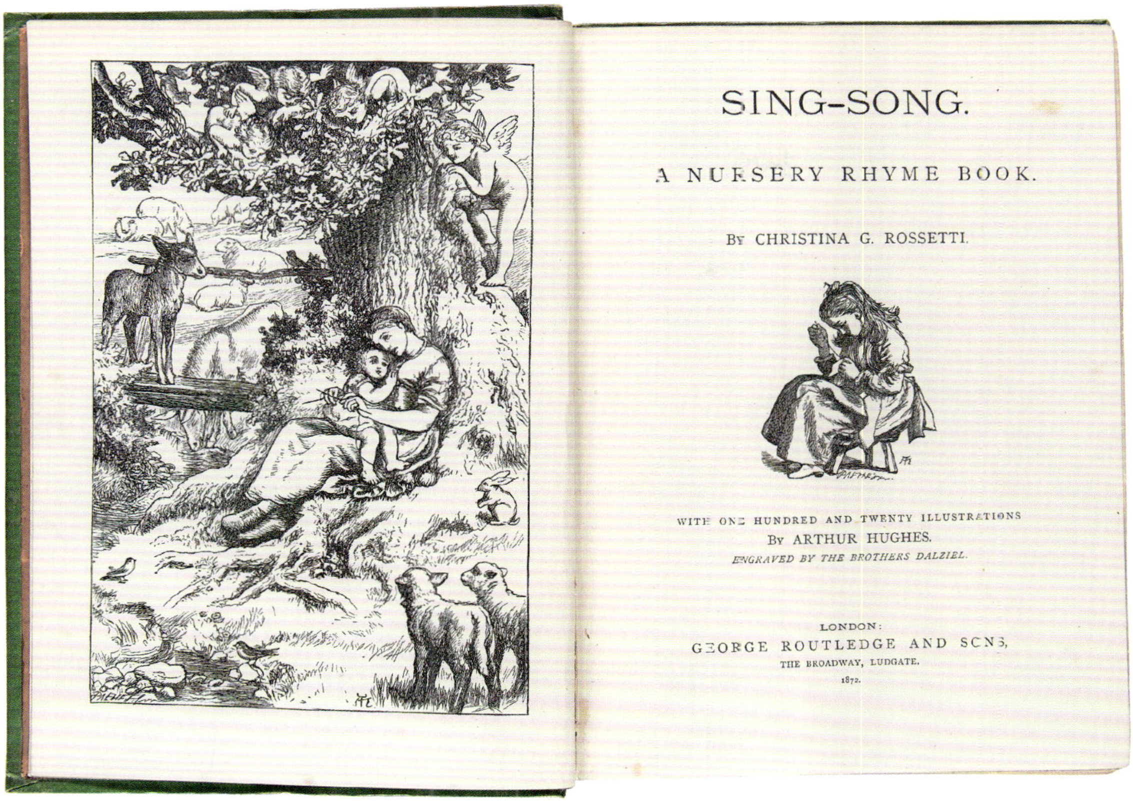
SING-SONG.

A NURSERY RHYME BOOK.

By CHRISTINA G. ROSSETTI.

WITH ONE HUNDRED AND TWENTY ILLUSTRATIONS
By ARTHUR HUGHES.
ENGRAVED BY THE BROTHERS DALZIEL.

LONDON:
GEORGE ROUTLEDGE AND SONS,
THE BROADWAY, LUDGATE.
1872.

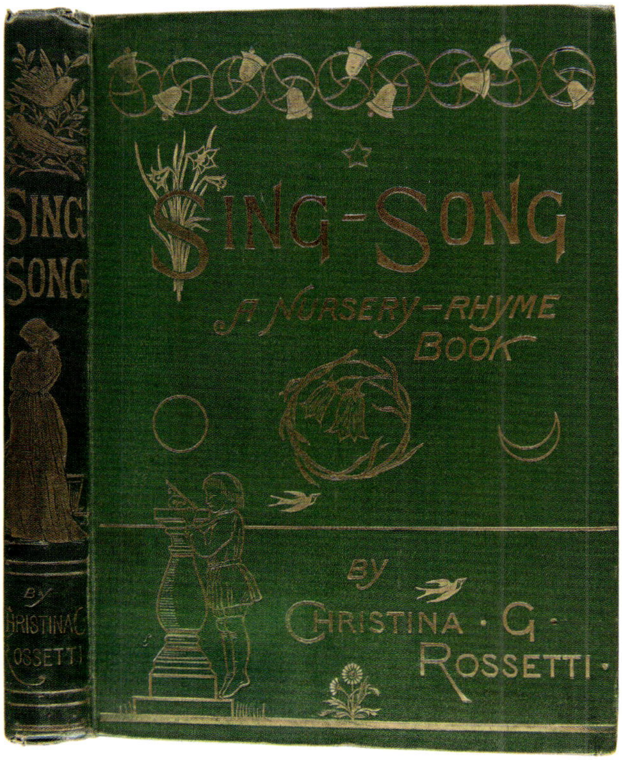

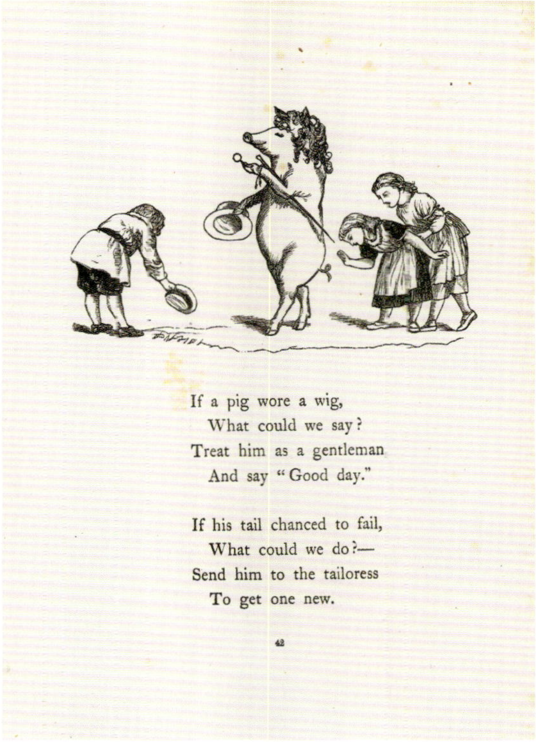
If a pig wore a wig,
What could we say?
Treat him as a gentleman,
And say "Good day."

If his tail chanced to fail,
What could we do?—
Send him to the tailoress
To get one new.

42

publication history of *Sing-Song* came with the demise of the bankrupt Dalziel firm in 1893, only shortly before Christina's own death. Showing considerable business acumen, she was able to purchase the original engraved blocks and all rights to the book and as a result, by that time long reconciled with Macmillan, she authorised a new popular edition of this perennial favourite.

Following the unfortunate rupture of relations with Macmillan back in 1870–71, Christina, to the relief of both parties, returned to the fold for her next book *Speaking Likenesses*.[38] This 'little prose fantasy', as she called it, had been first offered to her American publishers Roberts Brothers in 1873, and it was only after a whole year of delays that she concluded terms with Macmillan. He showed considerable confidence in printing an initial run of 3,000 copies for the Christmas market of 1874 (fig. 4.14). Christina again expressed the wish that Arthur Hughes illustrate the book, though in this case it seems that she had little or no direct contact with the artist as he was preparing his drawings. The cover of bright blue, gold-blocked with a curious asymmetrical design, was again clearly aimed at the market for attractively produced small gift books, and the lettering of the title, in eccentric, spiky hand-drawn letters, admirably expresses the essential weirdness of the contents (fig. 4.15). *Speaking Likenesses* is the oddest of all Christina's writings and was clearly to a considerable degree inspired by, or possibly undertaken in a certain spirit of competition with, Lewis Carroll's *Alice's Adventures in Wonderland* (fig. 4.16). The Rossettis knew and liked Dodgson, who had photographed them in Gabriel's garden at Tudor House in 1863 (figs 1.18 and 2.23), and Christina had revealed her awareness of the extent of the publishing phenomenon his book had become in a letter to Roberts Brothers in which she spoke of

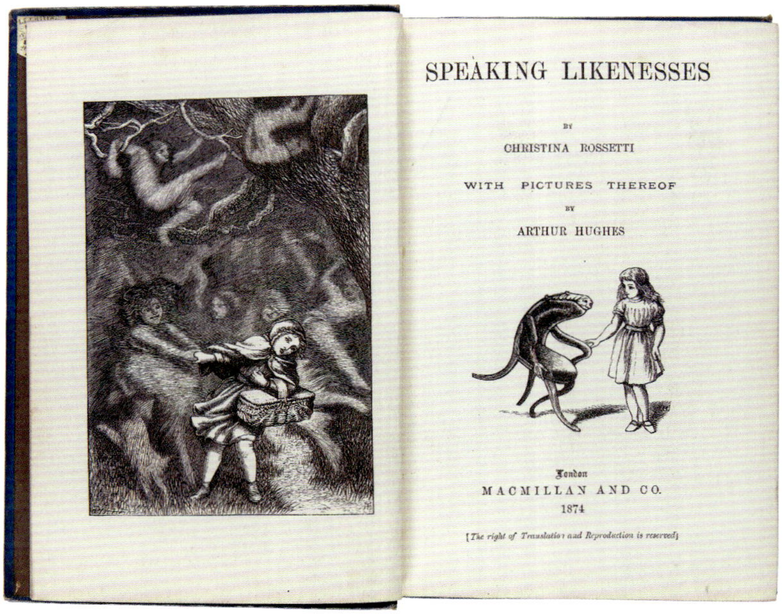

4.14 Below left:
Dalziel Brothers after Arthur Hughes, frontispiece and title page vignette to Christina Rossetti, *Speaking Likenesses* (London: Macmillan & Co., 1874), wood engravings.
Collection of Stephen Calloway.

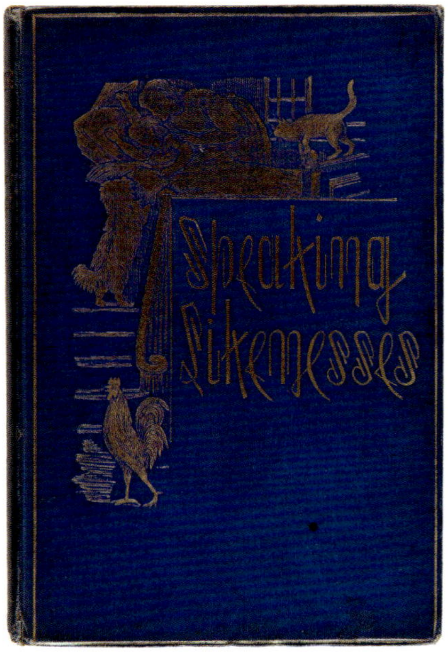

4.15 Below right:
Arthur Hughes, cover design for Christina Rossetti, *Speaking Likenesses*, 1874, deep blue cloth, front cover blocked in gold.
Collection of Stephen Calloway.

4.16 Opposite:
Dalziel Brothers after Arthur Hughes, illustration to Christina Rossetti, *Speaking Likenesses*, 1874, p. 24, wood engraving.
Collection of Stephen Calloway.

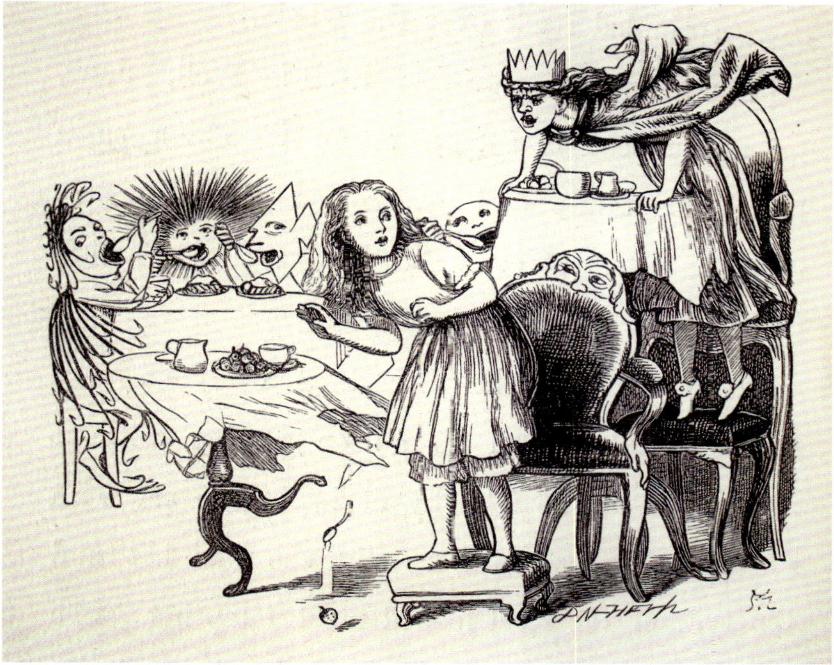

'Mr. Macmillan in whose hands "Wonderland" ... has had so appropriately a wonderful success'.[39]

Rossetti's religious poetry and devotional works

Although her forays into writing specifically for children and her explorations of a world of fantasy had absorbed her interest, as the years passed Christina Rossetti increasingly found the inspiration or perhaps, rather, the motive or emotional need for her writing in conventional piety rather than imaginative narrative. Indeed, from the later 1860s and in the 1870s, although her two books for children *Sing-Song* and *Speaking Likenesses* appeared, as we have seen, in appealing illustrated editions that were met with both popular attention and some degree of commercial success, her creative literary energies would henceforth largely be directed towards poetry and prose on specifically Christian themes. In line with this change in direction and with an ever-growing sense of religious devotion, she frequently contributed new poems to miscellaneous publications for the benefit of religious charities. Whilst previously seen and even lamented as a distinct narrowing of her scope and ambitions as a writer, recent scholarship has, on the contrary, increasingly viewed her later devotional verse, with its innovative diction and sometimes unconventional imagery, as a fruitful development of her poetic talents.

Those verses that did appear in collections under her own name – such as *Annus Domini* (1874) and *Called to be Saints* (1881) – were now issued not by her 'literary' publishers Macmillan or Routledge, but by specialist religious publishing houses (respectively James Parker and

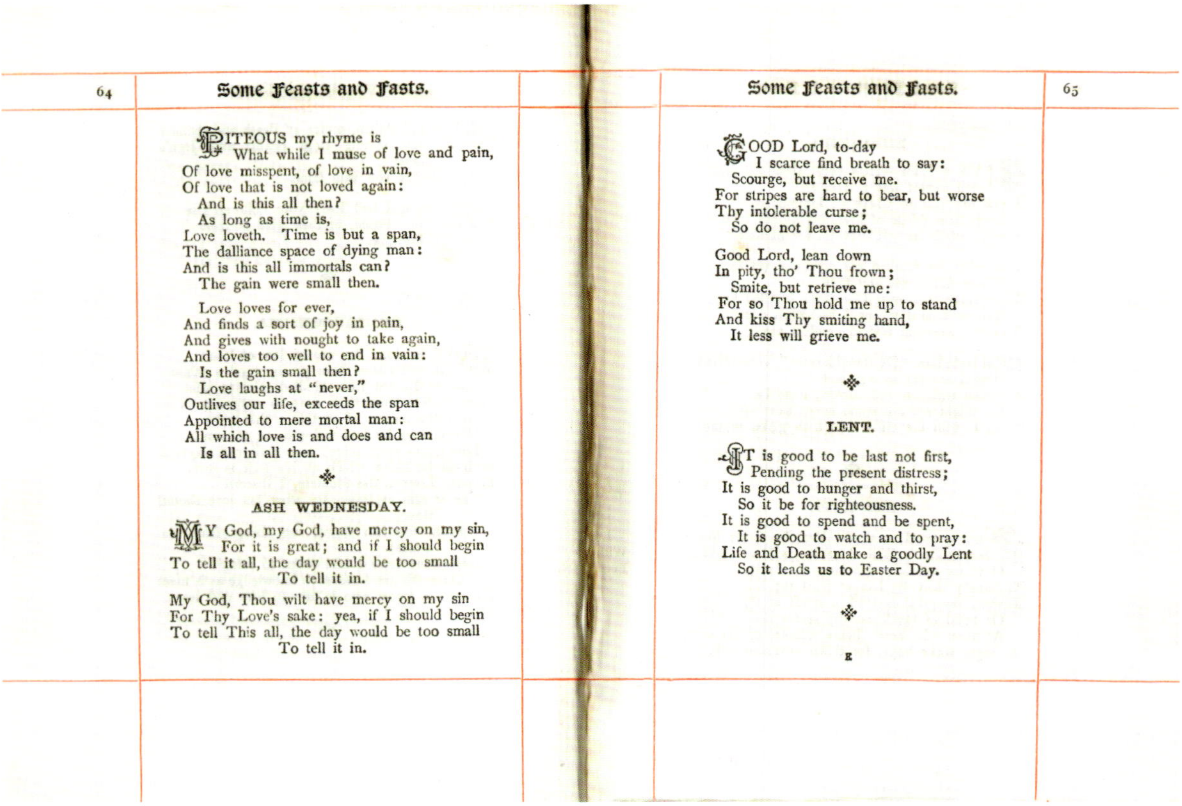

64 Some Feasts and Fasts.

PITEOUS my rhyme is
What while I muse of love and pain,
Of love misspent, of love in vain,
Of love that is not loved again:
And is this all then?
As long as time is,
Love loveth. Time is but a span,
The dalliance space of dying man:
And is this all immortals can?
The gain were small then.

Love loves for ever,
And finds a sort of joy in pain,
And gives with nought to take again,
And loves too well to end in vain:
Is the gain small then?
Love laughs at "never,"
Outlives our life, exceeds the span
Appointed to mere mortal man:
All which love is and does and can
Is all in all then.

ASH WEDNESDAY.

MY God, my God, have mercy on my sin,
For it is great; and if I should begin
To tell it all, the day would be too small
To tell it in.

My God, Thou wilt have mercy on my sin
For Thy Love's sake: yea, if I should begin
To tell This all, the day would be too small
To tell it in.

Some Feasts and Fasts. 65

GOOD Lord, to-day
I scarce find breath to say:
Scourge, but receive me.
For stripes are hard to bear, but worse
Thy intolerable curse;
So do not leave me.

Good Lord, lean down
In pity, tho' Thou frown;
Smite, but retrieve me:
For so Thou hold me up to stand
And kiss Thy smiting hand,
It less will grieve me.

LENT.

IT is good to be last not first,
Pending the present distress;
It is good to hunger and thirst,
So it be for righteousness.
It is good to spend and be spent,
It is good to watch and to pray:
Life and Death make a goodly Lent
So it leads us to Easter Day.

E

the Society for Promoting Christian Knowledge) in volumes whose conservative, intentionally dour house styles instantly identify them as belonging to the genre of pious literature (fig. 4.17). This clear break from the attractive and self-consciously 'modern' design of her earlier books can hardly have been accidental, and should, surely, be read as a subtle indicator of that shift in Christina's outlook that resulted in her growing concern with her spiritual life and consequent, if gradual, withdrawal from the world. It is a trajectory that may also be tracked in the sequence of drawings, paintings and photographs that document the small but progressive and indicative changes in her dress and personal appearance over the years.[40] All the remaining new books and reissues of her works that Christina authorised between 1875 and her death can be seen to observe what we might term a sacred/profane distinction of design. In all, she published six substantial devotional volumes, all of which appeared in unequivocally pious dress; in their ultra-conservative styling they contrast tellingly with her 'worldly' books, in which innovation and beauty are the qualities that seem always so much to the fore.

4.17 Christina Rossetti, *Verses* (London: SPCK, 1893, post-dated 1894). Collection of Stephen Calloway.

The 'Oxford' style typography was widely used for devotional works; typically, these volumes are bound in plain black cloth with bevelled edges.

The later editions of Rossetti's poetry

Christina's wish to observe a distinction between the 'sacred' and the 'profane' in her publications, though nowhere precisely enunciated, seems to have been absolute. Thus when in 1875 – no doubt partly on the strength of publicity attracted by *Speaking Likenesses* – Macmillan deemed that new editions of *Goblin Market* and *The Prince's Progress* were called for, he and Christina settled upon the idea of issuing a single volume that gathered the contents of the two books into one, agreeing that the new book should be styled following Gabriel's original design for *Goblin Market*.[41] In order to avoid the creation of a volume with the original small page size but a new and undesirably cumbersome bulk, Macmillan increased the page size a little but suggested no other significant stylistic change. As Christina requested, for the new edition Gabriel's groundbreaking cover design of simple rectilinear lines and sparingly spaced dots was gently adapted to the slightly enlarged format and blocked this time on an unusual pale violet-brown cloth. More than a decade on from its first conception, this cover design still looked unfussy and effortlessly elegant, still ahead of its time.

Christina was always especially attached to her brother's *Goblin Market* and *Prince's Progress* illustrations, doubtless in part because they recalled such an intense and happy period of creative collaboration between the siblings. One of the many surviving letters between author and publisher reveals that in the planning of her new edition, Christina's principal concern was to ensure the wood engravings by Gabriel that had adorned the earlier printings of the poems would be retained. Discussing alternative ways of positioning them on the page, she wrote to Macmillan, insisting that: 'The only plan I feel as inadmissible is to dispense with any one of the 4: but in all else I will be amenable to reason.'[42] Her judgment in this was sound, for the four illustrations – and in particular the two for *Goblin Market* – seem always to have remained extremely popular with the book-buying public.

A short, almost inconsequential entry in William Michael's diary made as far back as 12 July 1866 seems relevant here. He recorded that

> Dodgson (the Oxford man and photographer) [Lewis Carroll] writes to say that a friend of his, Rivington, would much like to illustrate either of Christina's volumes and would do it at little cost. D[odgson] sends a design by R[ivington] from *Passing Away*, which though not advanced in execution, is finely felt, and a good deal like what C[hristina] herself might do if she knew enough to draw.[43]

Christina does seem to have retained the specimen drawing that accompanied the letter (it later passed into William Michael's possession) but, unsurprisingly, nothing came of this unsolicited proposal.

In spite of what some observers have ventured to identify as a progressive state amounting to a sort of religious obsession, Christina did nevertheless continue to heed Macmillan's requests that she consider putting together a new book of 'secular' verse. She made excuses for some time, but then, in April 1881 – in spite of her misgivings as before about the quality, and sufficient quantity, of new poems that she had in hand – she finally wrote to her patient publisher 'I find I have at last enough material for another fresh volume of verse. Will you care to take it on the old terms?'[44] On the strength of his enthusiasm for her previous books Macmillan agreed to proceed sight unseen, offering as before to bear the entire financial risk of publication and promising a generous half-and-half share of all profits between author and publisher.[45]

The resulting volume comprised a miscellaneous selection of unpublished longer and shorter poems as well as a few pieces gathered from previous magazine appearances. The book takes its main title, *A Pageant,* from that of a somewhat leaden, masque-like cycle describing the months of the year, which Christina intended for recitation by children, but also includes her now more highly regarded sequence of sonnets *Monna Innominata*. Imagining the female voices of Dante's protagonists, this tight grouping of interrelated poems (here fourteen, forming a 'sonnet of sonnets') follows a poetic architecture much favoured by Christina's brother Gabriel, who employed it on an even larger scale in, for example, his monumental *House of Life* sequence. Although *A Pageant* did include some poems with religious sentiments, as a whole it falls more comfortably within the 'profane' group of Christina's works and, as such, was appropriately bound yet again with a version of the *Goblin Market* cover design. However, in this instance the choice of binding-cloth colour did not follow Gabriel's notion of uniform livery that we have come to expect, nor did it conform to Christina's preference for rich and sombre shades. Instead, copies are recorded in a variety of colours ranging from dark brown, deep red and greyish purple through to the more expected dark blue-green and a most unexpected strong orange-yellow. In fact, the explanation for this giddy burst of exuberant variety may be a simple matter of book-trade economics rather than aesthetic adventurousness: it is quite likely that Macmillan sought – as Victorian publishers often did – to cut costs by the expedient of allowing the binders to use up short runs of cloth of the kind that were often left over in the workshop from other projects. In the event, in spite of this harlequin gaiety of dress, *A Pageant* did not meet with any great sales success and was never reprinted as a single title.[46]

The 'collected works'

A continuing public interest in Christina's poetry had however resulted in steady sales of her more popular books. Following the publication in 1875 of the first 'collected' edition combining all the material from the *Goblin Market* and *Prince's Progress* volumes, a second printing appeared in 1879 and this was in turn followed by new editions in 1884 and 1888. Two years later in June 1890, encouraged by her brother William, Christina opened discussions with Macmillan about a new and more ambitious collection of her works; this was to include not only the oft-printed contents of the *Goblin Market* and *Prince's Progress* volumes but also those from *A Pageant,* together with the further addition of some extra poems, to which she referred somewhat dismissively as 'a few stray magazine pieces'.[47] The resulting fat volume was titled simply *Poems,* and described on its title page as 'new and enlarged'.[48]

Though more substantial than any of her previous volumes, this was not, as such, a true 'complete poems' for two crucial reasons. Firstly, Macmillan did not hold the copyright or have use of material from either *Sing-Song* (which had been published by Routledge for the Dalziel Brothers) or the volumes issued by the SPCK; and secondly because the commercial requirement to print much of the text from existing stereotype plates rather than newly set type precluded both revisions and, importantly, the sort of rearrangement that Christina would have considered desirable in an entirely new and restructured volume. Nevertheless, *Poems: New and Enlarged* was well received on its first appearance in October 1890. An initial print run of 1,000 copies sold quickly and was followed even before the year was out by a second impression. The Macmillan 'Edition Book' records in all a total of eleven separate printings (each of 1,000 copies) in the years immediately before and after Christina's death in December 1894.[49]

Later magazine publications

By the early 1890s Christina was ageing, failing in health, and saw and was seen by only an already small and now-diminishing circle of family and friends. However, ironically, in these final, rather tragic years her work was perhaps more read and appreciated than at any time previously. Certainly this new public interest reflected to some degree a more widespread renewal of fascination with the Pre-Raphaelites and therefore naturally enough the part that she, as Gabriel's sister and fellow poet, had played in the early days of the movement. But there can be no doubt that Christina's own fame – though not perhaps at this date pitched at the level of Tennyson or Browning – was growing apace. In some ways it could be said that she was already making that transition from being a private and individual poet in control of her own work and reputation towards that point at which writers – and in particular poets – become 'literary figures', whose work is subsumed into a wider canon of literature that is perceived as a sort of public possession. As if to signify this trajectory, it is around this time and in the following decade that a great many artists and illustrators began to take a new interest in Christina, mining her descriptive verse and rich imagery for their own, often entirely independent projects.

Two of the most interesting and, in this context, telling of such examples are to be found in the pages of the *Magazine of Art*, a newish periodical that interspersed more or less scholarly articles on the fine and applied arts with art-world gossip and pages in which popular short poems appeared embellished with drawings by both established and up-and-coming illustrators. Christina had given some assistance to the journalist and energetic editor of the magazine, Marion Harry Spielmann, in the course of his preparation of an article on Dante Gabriel Rossetti published in 1888 and, encouraged by her friendly

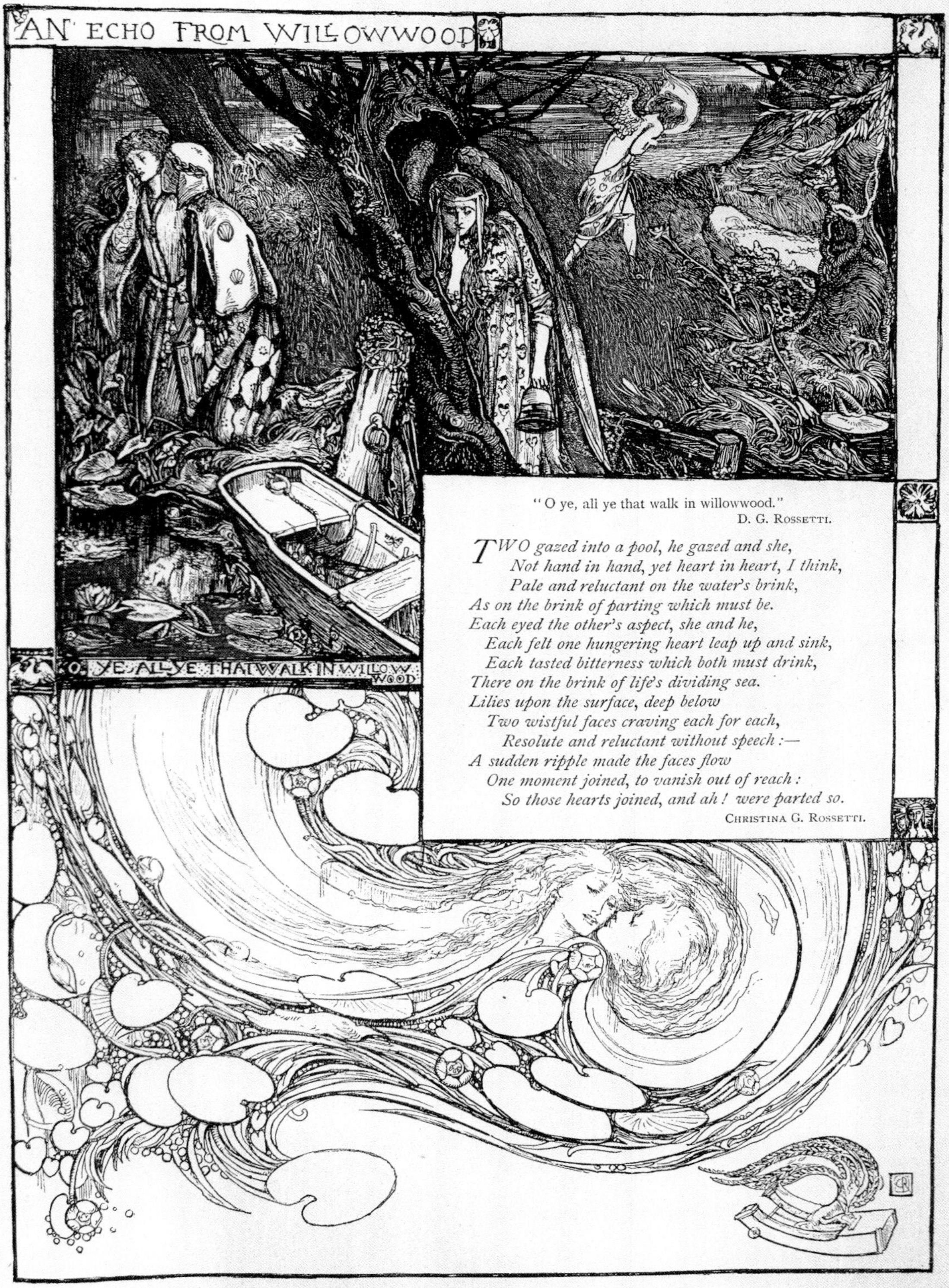

AN ECHO FROM WILLOWWOOD

"O ye, all ye that walk in willowwood."
D. G. Rossetti.

Two gazed into a pool, he gazed and she,
Not hand in hand, yet heart in heart, I think,
Pale and reluctant on the water's brink,
As on the brink of parting which must be.
Each eyed the other's aspect, she and he,
Each felt one hungering heart leap up and sink,
Each tasted bitterness which both must drink,
There on the brink of life's dividing sea.
Lilies upon the surface, deep below
Two wistful faces craving each for each,
Resolute and reluctant without speech:—
A sudden ripple made the faces flow
One moment joined, to vanish out of reach:
So those hearts joined, and ah! were parted so.
Christina G. Rossetti.

(*Poem by Christina G. Rossetti. Drawn by C. Ricketts.*)

666

4.18 Charles Ricketts, *An Echo from Willowwood*, *Magazine of Art*, 1890, p. 384, line-block. Collection of Stephen Calloway.

4.19 Below: Charles Ricketts, *An Echo from Willowwood*, 1890, pen and ink on paper, 13 × 25 cm. Private collection.

co-operation, Spielmann speculatively invited her to contribute any poems that she might care to see printed as decorated pages in the *Magazine of Art*'s house style. The first and most successful of Christina's appearances in the magazine was in the issue for September 1890. It took the form of a composite page on which two separate drawings by Charles Ricketts were juxtaposed to enclose a text panel reprinting Christina's 'An Echo from Willowwood' (fig. 4.18).[50] The poem was a reflection or emotional echo of sorts of her brother's sequence of poems of that name written many years earlier but generally held, when printed in Gabriel's 1870 volume, to be among the more approachable and evocative of his shorter verses. Christina informed Spielmann that, among her poems, she considered 'Echo' to be one 'capable of illustration'.[51]

Of Ricketts's two, not entirely comfortably balanced images, the lower depicts the mysterious pool described in the poem:

> Lilies upon the surface, deep below
> Two wistful faces craving each for each

It was drawn in a delicate style, with the precise, fine-lined penmanship that Ricketts himself referred to as 'filigree ... an almost Persian finick and finish' (fig. 4.19).[52] Already suggestive of continental Art Nouveau of the later 1890s, it thus fits very well with the more abstract, almost proto-Symbolist mood of the poem's sestet. By contrast, the upper image, which illustrates a more realistic scene of a waterside meeting of doomed lovers described in the lines of the opening octet, is conceived by Ricketts as a richer, darker image, densely worked very much in the manner of Dante Gabriel Rossetti's drawings of the late 1850s and 1860s. Ricketts would, in the few years immediately following this early

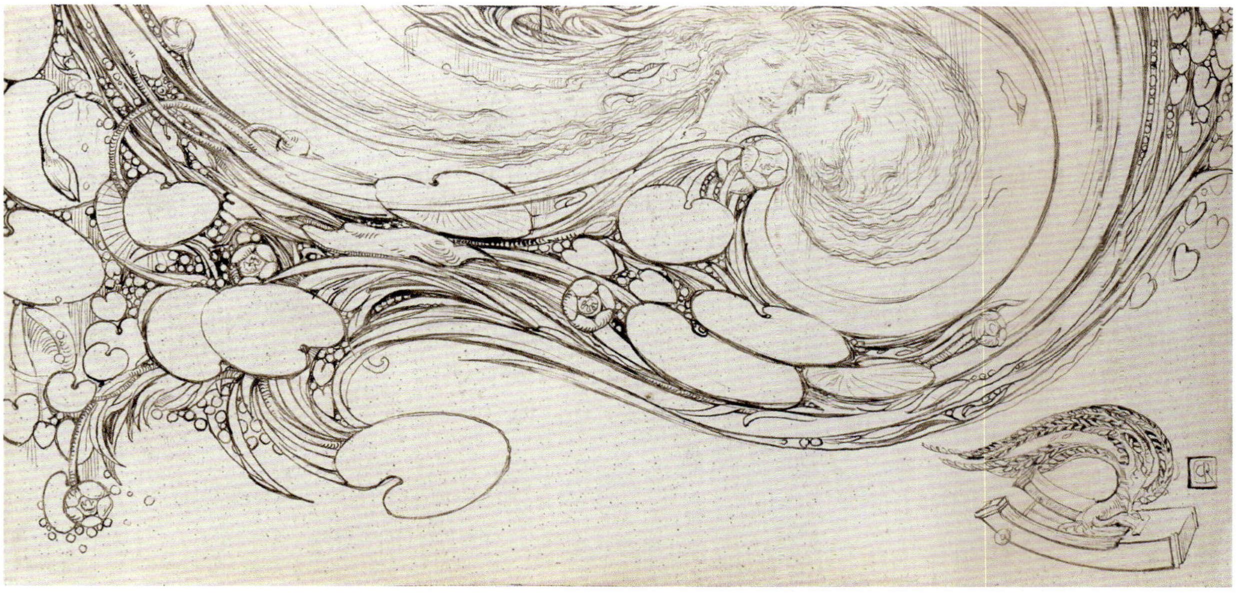

commission, go on to become one of the most admired illustrators and book designers of the 1890s, developing an idiosyncratic style that owed more to Renaissance models than to William Morris and the Pre-Raphaelites. But at this stage in his career, his admiration for Dante Gabriel Rossetti's early graphic work, greatly fostered by his acquisition of wood engravings, sketches and, later, one of the greatest large pen-and-ink drawings by his hero, was the most important single influence on his work.[53] Christina undoubtedly recognised this general connection and perhaps also other more precise visual correspondences, such as Ricketts's employment of a rectilinear framing device with small inset motifs that seems to reference Gabriel's grid-like borders for the title pages of *Goblin Market* and *The Prince's Progress*.

Christina was approving to an uncharacteristic degree about Ricketts's illustrated page and, perhaps surprisingly, responded with most enthusiasm to the lower, less 'Rossettian' half, finding it greatly in sympathy with her own intentions: 'Last night', she wrote to Spielmann, 'my sonnet came to hand interpreted by the delicate fancifulness of Mr. Ricketts. The heart-suggesting water-lily leaves are all his own, and I should like to thank him for the enrichment.'[54] Her letter is telling, not just for the indication of her pleasure at the outcome, but also for what can be read as an almost touching note of pleasant surprise, for the wording of her comment makes it clear that the editors at the magazine had not previously thought it necessary to submit Ricketts's design to the author for her approval. This pattern of such 'collaborations' between writers and illustrators was perhaps not unusual at this time. Tennyson, it must be remembered, had initially visited a few artists with Moxon the publisher, but subsequently had taken little or no interest in the progress of the wood engravings to accompany his poems for the famous 1857 edition; indeed, it was said that even when the book was published he showed scant interest beyond expressing a certain bafflement about the relationship of many of the images to his lines.

Christina's evident satisfaction with the way her poem 'An Echo from Willowwood' was illustrated by Charles Ricketts in the pages of the *Magazine of Art* encouraged her to continue sending in short pieces to this periodical – and indeed to others, such as the more recondite *Hobby Horse*, though in this latter case her lines appeared unadorned. As it would turn out, the very last of her verses to receive pictorial treatment before her death was the brief poem 'The Way of the World'.[55] This was included in the *Magazine of Art*'s number for July 1894 and the artist chosen by Spielmann to decorate the page was the now largely forgotten mural painter and illustrator William E. F. Britten. Britten, who was born in the year of the inception of the Pre-Raphaelite Brotherhood, 1848, enjoyed some degree of success for his work that rehashed themes and visual formulae associated with the PRB, intermixed later with borrowings in a would-be grand, classical style from Frederic Leighton and especially William Blake Richmond,

4.20 William E. F. Britten, *The Way of the World*, *Magazine of Art*, 1894, p. 304, half-tone process print. Watts Gallery Trust, Surrey.

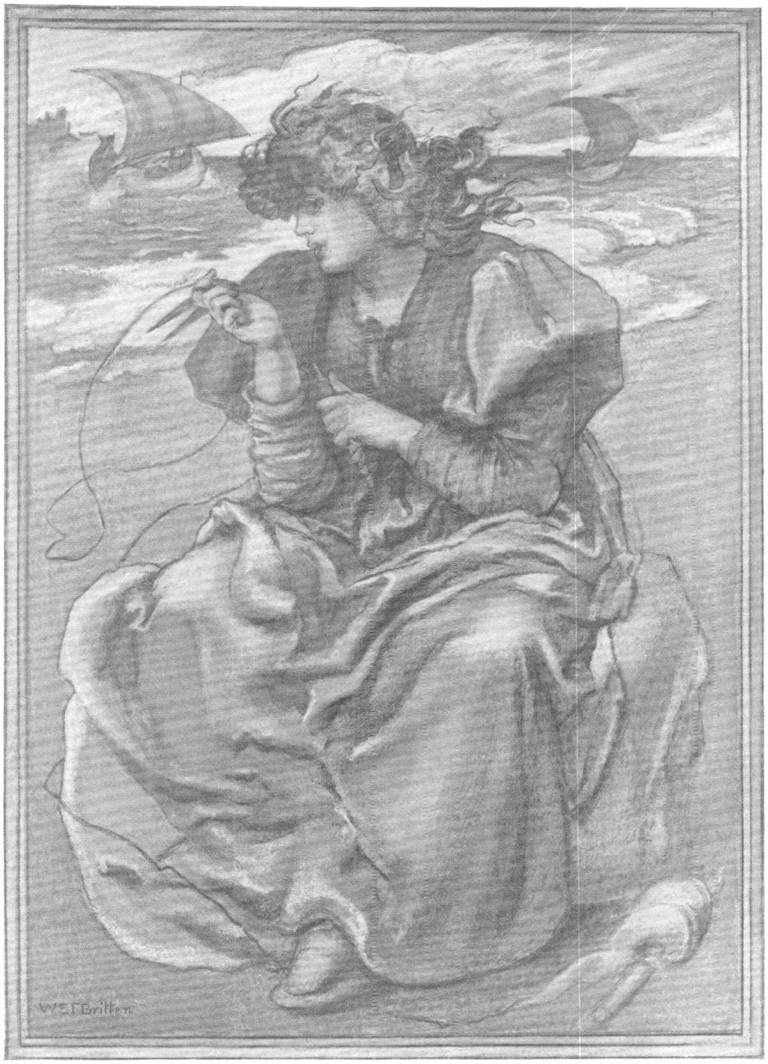

with whom Britten collaborated on decorative schemes for St Paul's Cathedral. The year before the commission to illustrate Christina's poem he had completed a set of twelve designs of *The Months* for a sequence of poems by Swinburne. Ambitious in conception, these classicising drawings reveal Britten's limitations, and it is therefore all the more interesting to see that for his illustration to Christina's 'The Way of the World', he seems to have felt it appropriate to revert to the mannerisms of his Pre-Raphaelite style (fig. 4.20). The drawing he produced almost shamelessly plagiarises Frederick Sandys's striking image drawn to illustrate Christina's poem 'If', published in the *Argosy* almost thirty years previously, but replaces the taut, controlled line of Sandys's wood engraving with the rich, somewhat slippery *sfumato* of Dante Gabriel Rossetti's late pastel drawings of sensuous female figures. The resulting image has the unfortunate feeling of parody rather than homage; Christina's opinion of this last illustration of her lines is not recorded.

Laurence Housman's *Goblin Market*

By contrast, her reactions at every stage in the protracted process of the creation of a new illustrated edition of *Goblin Market* (1893), with designs by the rising young graphic artist Laurence Housman, can be documented in considerable detail. Although by no means entirely resistant to new possibilities, as her reaction to Charles Ricketts's illustration shows, Christina played no part in the inception of Housman's project and remained reluctant and difficult throughout.

Housman had aspirations to become a popular illustrator and his designs for a hand-lettered edition of George Meredith's poem 'Jump to Glory, Jane' published by Swan Sonnenschein in 1892 had already attracted notice. Buoyed up by the reception it had gained, the young artist approached George Macmillan (son of Alexander Macmillan) with a bold proposal:

> 61 Marloes Road, Kensington, W., 20 March 1893
>
> Dear Sir,
> Enclosed I submit to you one specimen drawing and some rough sketches to show my proposed treatment of *Goblin Market*, the poem in reference to which you have previously heard from me.
>
> The sketches I have mounted, to indicate the size of page I would like to suggest, and also the arrangement, in certain cases, of illustrations facing each other and forming two halves as it were of one picture – a revival of a mediaeval usage which I think might be made effective and pleasant.
>
> As you will probably be referring these drawings to Miss Rossetti I should be glad to be allowed to say a word here in explanation of the masks which I have introduced as a pictorial allegory. I have imagined the goblins wearing animal masks in order to hide the wickedness that their own faces would reveal; this will give me the opportunity of a dramatic climax when in the poem they are finally defeated by Lizzie. I propose then to show them throwing aside their masks as they make their escape. I hope Miss Rossetti will not think this idea is in any disagreement with the spirit of her poem.
>
> It will perhaps be premature for me to make any further suggestions as to the form and amount of illustration until I hear whether what is here submitted to you meets with her approval. I trust you will be able by comparison with the finished drawing to make proper allowance for the crudeness of the other sketches.
>
> I am yours faithfully,
> Laurence Housman[56]

4.21 Below left:
Laurence Housman, illustrations to Christina Rossetti, *Goblin Market* (London: Macmillan & Co., 1893), line-block.
Collection of Stephen Calloway.

4.22 Below right:
Laurence Housman, cover design for Christina Rossetti, *Goblin Market*, 1893, light green cloth, front and rear boards and spine blocked in gold.
Collection of Stephen Calloway.

Macmillan's eventual reply offered only tepid encouragement:

> Bedford Street, Covent Garden, 18 April 1893
>
> Dear Sir,
> I had hoped to write to you before this in regard to your proposed illustrated edition of Miss Rossetti's *Goblin Market*. The matter has been under the author's consideration and as you know we could come to no conclusion until we knew her views. They are not on the whole unfavourable to the idea, but she cannot bring herself to sanction the 'masks' which you introduce in your treatment of the goblins. 'They might', Miss Rossetti writes, 'illustrate some better poem, but mine they falsify. Would not a study of my goblins as they stand supply an adequate variety and versatility of expression, a roguishness easily transformable into atrocity?' She then refers to her brother's original frontispiece. The first question then is whether you are willing to give up this part of your scheme, and to treat the goblins in some other way. If so we should be very glad to submit another specimen or two to Miss Rossetti and if she approved there would be no difficulty, I think, in arranging with you for the publication.
>
> Yours truly,
> George A. Macmillan[57]

Accommodation was achieved and Christina signalled her perhaps grudging approval in a letter of 16 May 1893 to George Craik, one of the partners at Macmillan's: 'I am fully satisfied ... I am obliged to

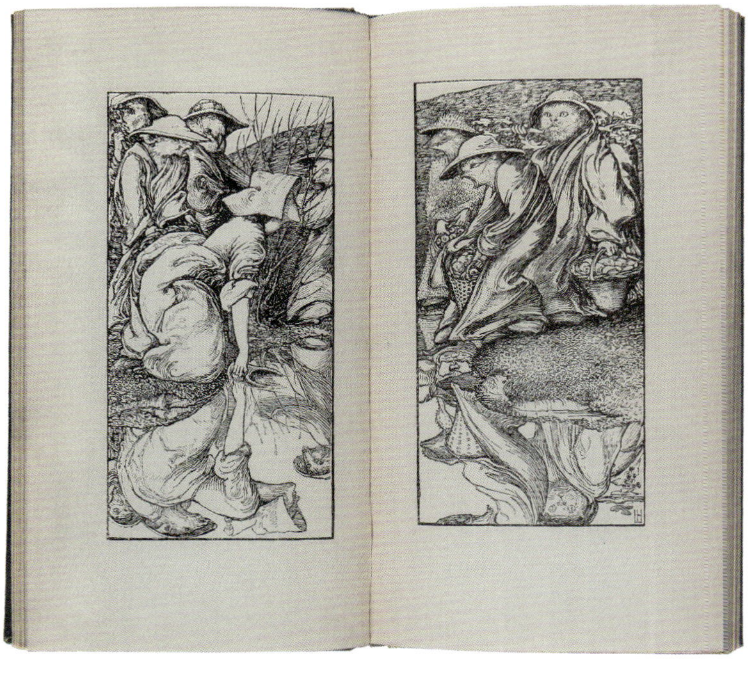

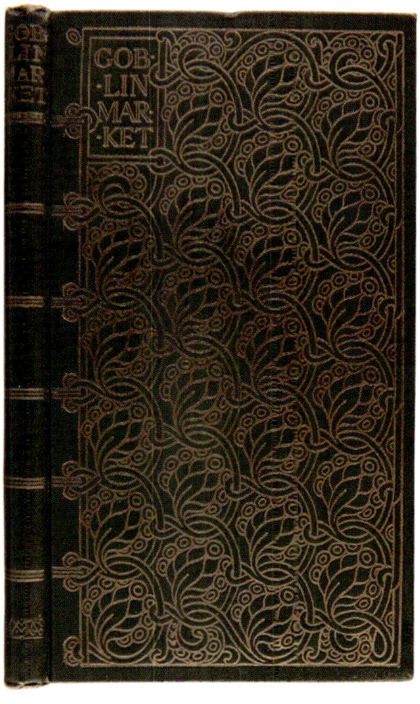

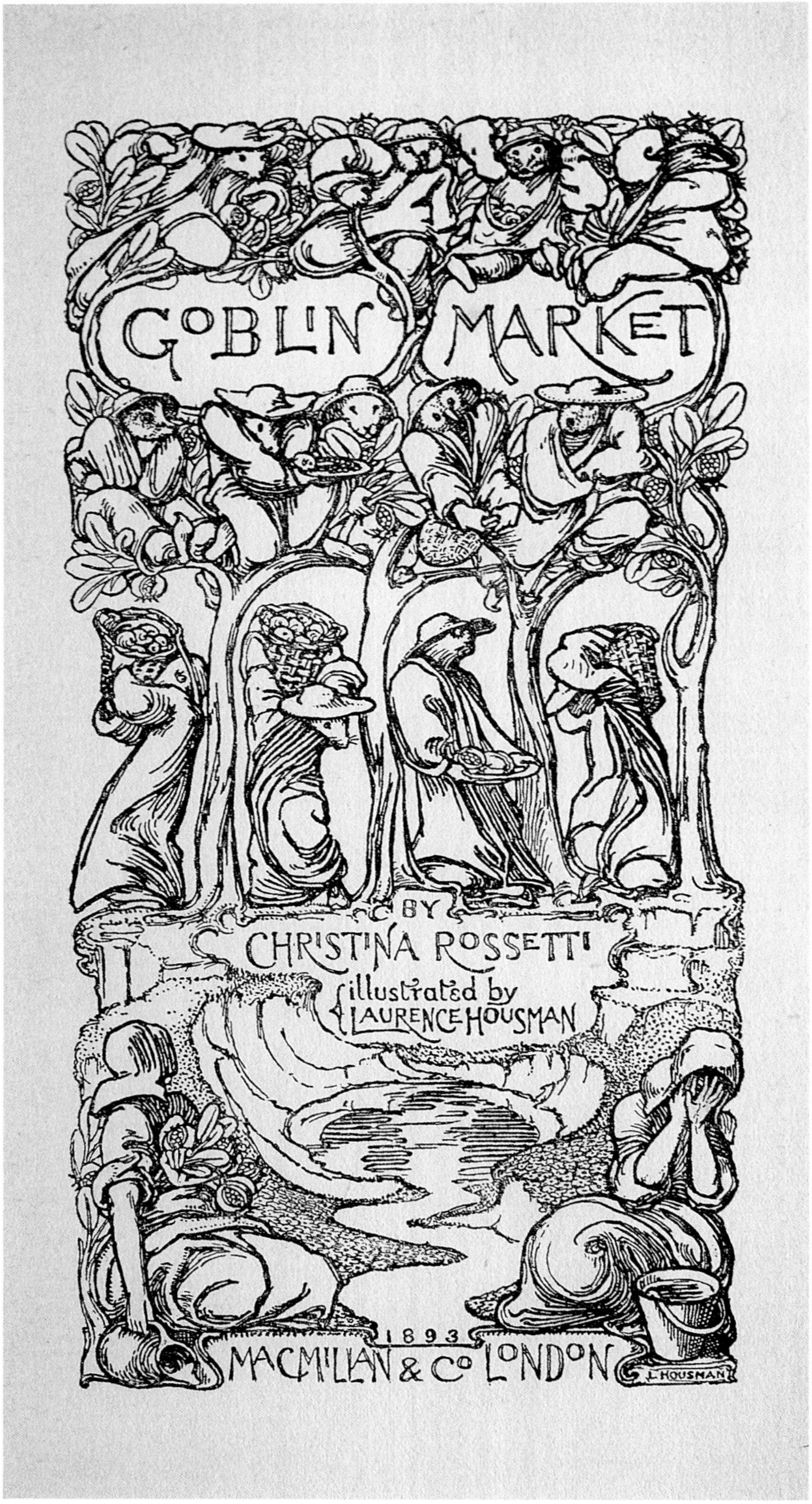

4.23 Laurence Housman,
title page to Christina Rossetti,
Goblin Market, 1893, line-block.
Collection of Stephen Calloway.

Mr. Housman for his compliance with my wish, and assure him that my goblins will keep peace with all his.'[58]

The resulting edition was printed as Housman suggested, with several of the illustrations arranged as double-page openings (fig. 4.21). The volume utilised a similar tall, narrow page proportion to Ricketts's famous design for John Gray's book of poems *Silverpoints*, also issued that year (fig. 4.23). Both volumes have intricate foliate cover designs blocked in gold (on upper and lower boards) on pale green cloth (fig. 4.22). Together these two slim volumes have been seen as quintessential books of the 1890s that heralded a new spirit of delicacy and self-conscious exquisiteness in book design. Christina, still no doubt firmly attached to her own vision of the poems that had been fixed for all time by Gabriel's original designs, clearly failed to respond to Housman's new interpretation. William Michael recorded in a poignant note: 'Mr. Housman's designs are the work of a very clever artist: but they did not correspond to Christina's notions, and I remember that, in sending me a copy of the book, she wrote on the wrapper the single word "Alas".'[59]

Gift books and illustrated editions after Rossetti's death

The second great age of the gift book, that of the colour half-tone printing era, began in the Edwardian years and was at its height around the time of the Great War, with the two leading artists Edmund Dulac and Arthur Rackham enjoying reputations far beyond those usually accorded to mere illustrators. Even after the war and well into the 1920s the market for this special genre of beautifully bound luxury editions remained buoyant. As a result, considerable numbers of illustrators, including many women artists such as Eleanor Fortescue-Brickdale and Jessie M. King, found ready employment in creating new editions of famous children's books, certain types of imaginative literature and of course poetry. One of the most successful of all such undertakings was a very large and lavishly produced volume of Christina Rossetti's poems, illustrated by Florence Harrison and published to considerable acclaim by Blackie & Son in 1910. Blackie's art director, Talwin Morris – himself a well-thought-of designer in the Art Nouveau manner – commissioned Harrison initially to supply twenty-four full-page pictures in colour, another forty-eight in black and white and enough head-pieces and odd decorations to 'prevent the pages' – nearly 400 of them – 'having an empty look' (figs 4.24 and 4.25).[60]

In the event, Harrison in fact created equal numbers of black-and-white and colour plates, thirty-six of each, as well as the handsome cover design blocked in gold on a white cloth that has seldom survived handling by children or the other more random ravages of time (fig. 4.26). Initial sales of this expensive volume were good, but the publishers went on over many years to recycle the valuable asset of Harrison's images in a number of spin-off, smaller and more economically produced editions. That these pot-boilers

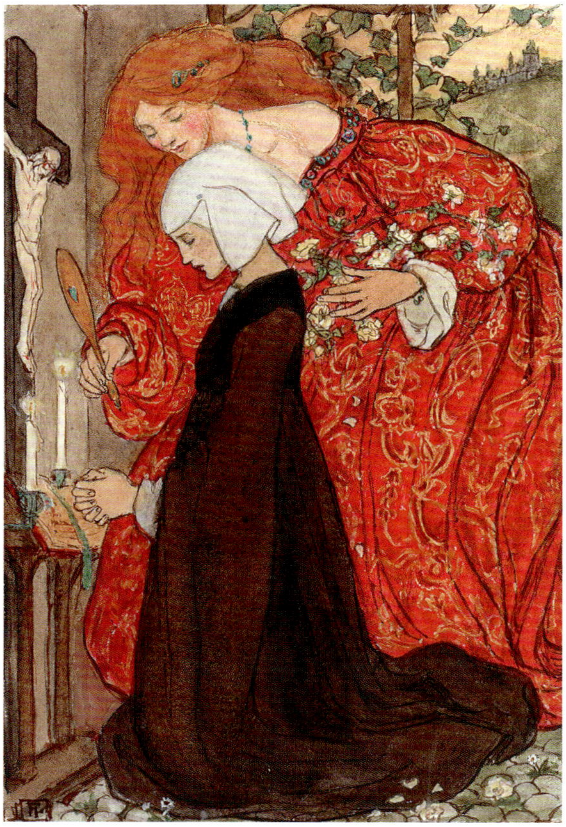

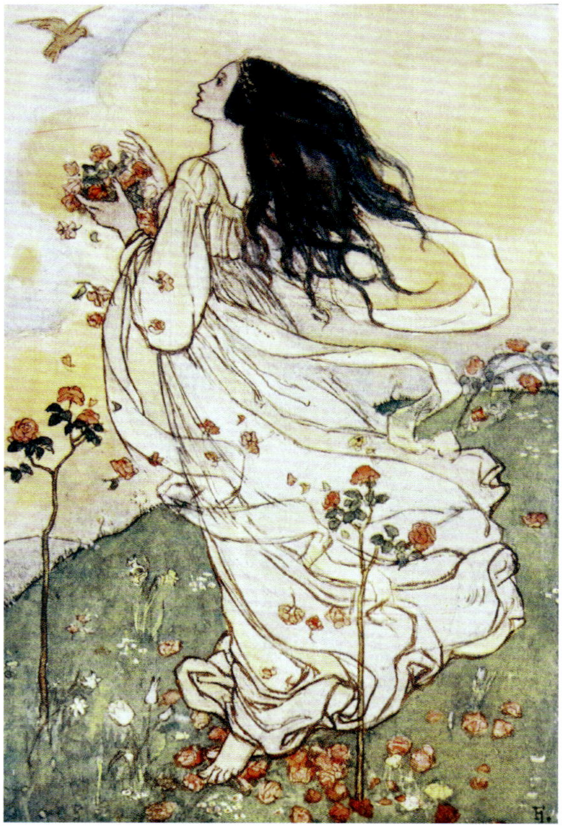

were still appearing as late as the 1920s and 30s, long after the slightly gauche Art Nouveau figure style of the black-and-white pages and the overblown sub-Pre-Raphaelite manner of Harrison's colour plates were entirely outmoded stylistically, reveals more perhaps about the enduring popularity of Rossetti's poetry than about the visual taste of the book-buying public (fig. 4.27). It is undoubtedly true to say that at no point since her death have Rossetti's writings been out of print in some format or another.

In marked contrast to the bulk of the Blackie editions, in an era in which slim volumes of poetry also enjoyed a particular vogue, one of the most attractive was the Eragny Press reprint of Christina's first book, her *Verses* of 1847. The Eragny books were in some ways typical products of the private press movement that thrived from the mid-1890s until the First World War. Self-consciously beautiful, printed on fine paper and elegantly bound in pretty patterned papers, they were issued in strictly limited editions aimed at a rarefied collectors' market. Over a period of twenty years Lucien Pissarro (the son of the Impressionist painter Camille) and his wife Esther designed and illustrated some thirty or more titles, of which Rossetti's *Verses* is one of the most sought after. Although printed with Charles Ricketts's Vale Press type, and produced very much under his influence, the Pissarros'

4.24 Above left:
Florence Harrison,
design for illustration to
Christina Rossetti, *Poems*,
(London and Glasgow:
Blackie & Son, 1910),
pencil and watercolour on paper.
Private collection.

4.25 Above right:
Florence Harrison,
illustration to Christina Rossetti,
Poems, 1910, colour process print.
Private collection.

4.26 Right:
Florence Harrison,
cover design for Christina Rossetti,
Poems, 1910, white cloth cover
and spine blocked in gold.
Private collection.

4.27 Below:
Florence Harrison,
illustration to Christina Rossetti,
Goblin Market and Other Poems
(London and Glasgow: Blackie & Son
*c.*1920), line block.
Collection of Stephen Calloway.

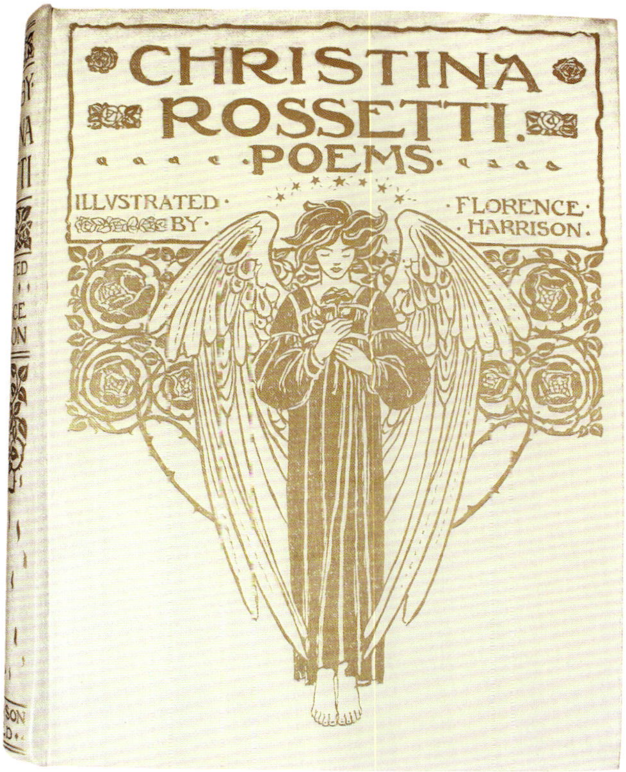

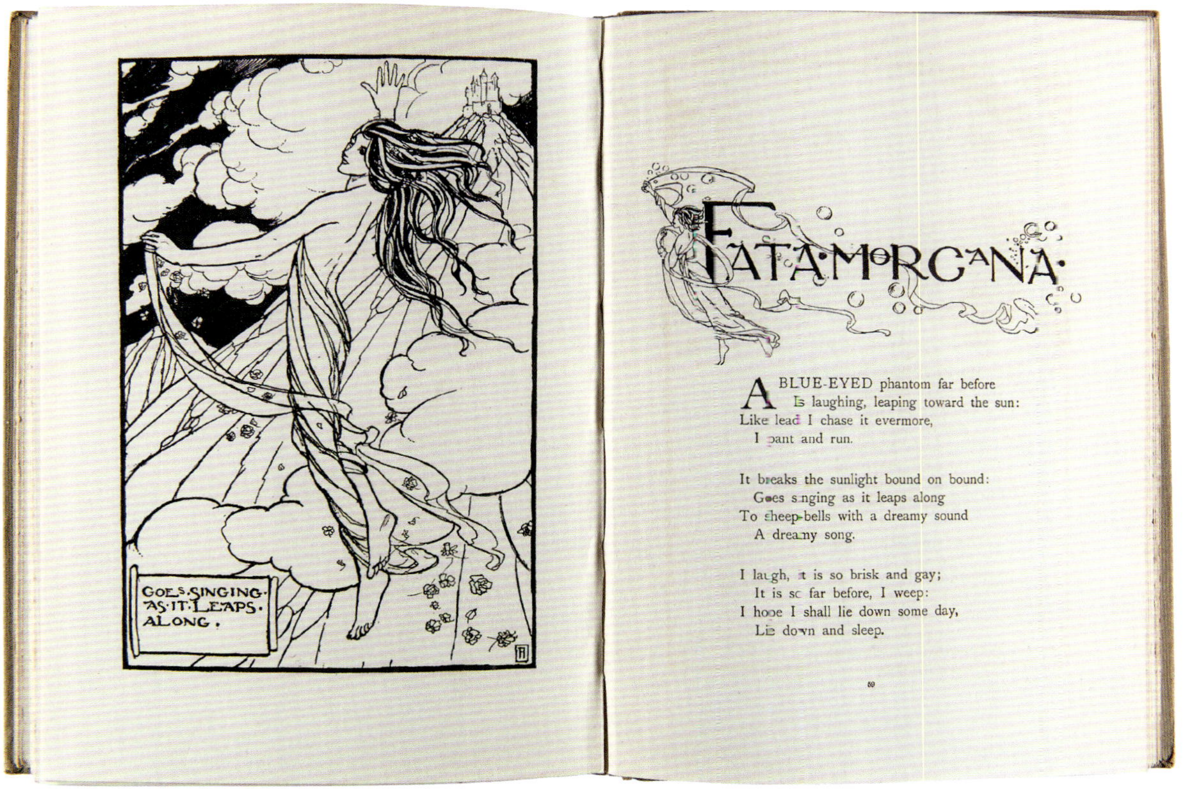

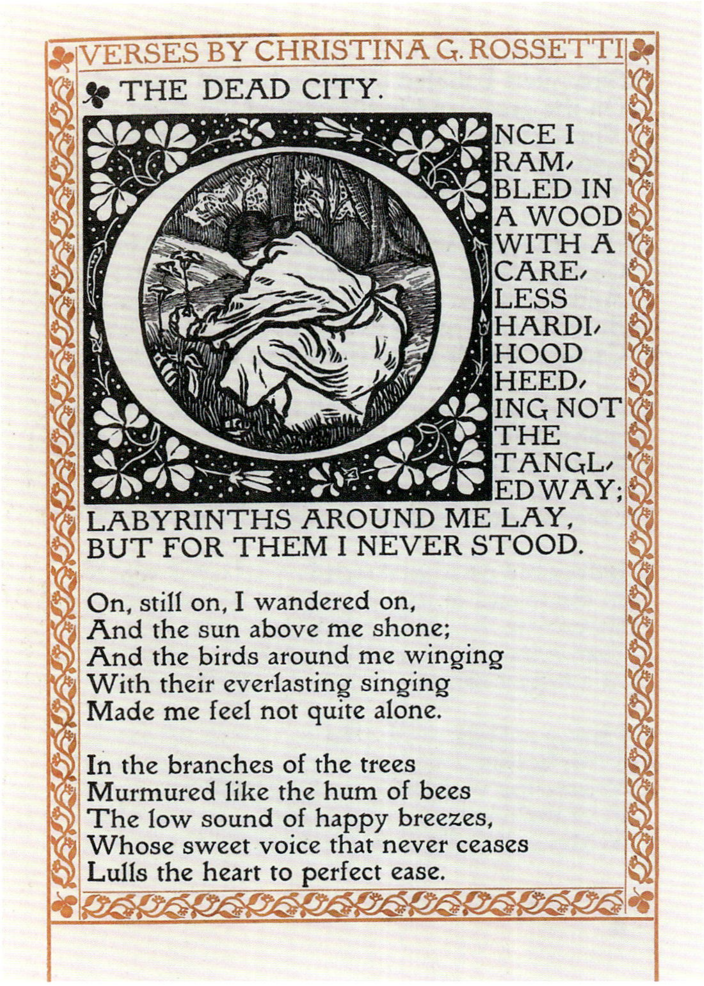

VERSES BY CHRISTINA G. ROSSETTI

THE DEAD CITY.

ONCE I RAMBLED IN A WOOD WITH A CARELESS HARDIHOOD HEEDING NOT THE TANGLED WAY;
LABYRINTHS AROUND ME LAY,
BUT FOR THEM I NEVER STOOD.

On, still on, I wandered on,
And the sun above me shone;
And the birds around me winging
With their everlasting singing
Made me feel not quite alone.

In the branches of the trees
Murmured like the hum of bees
The low sound of happy breezes,
Whose sweet voice that never ceases
Lulls the heart to perfect ease.

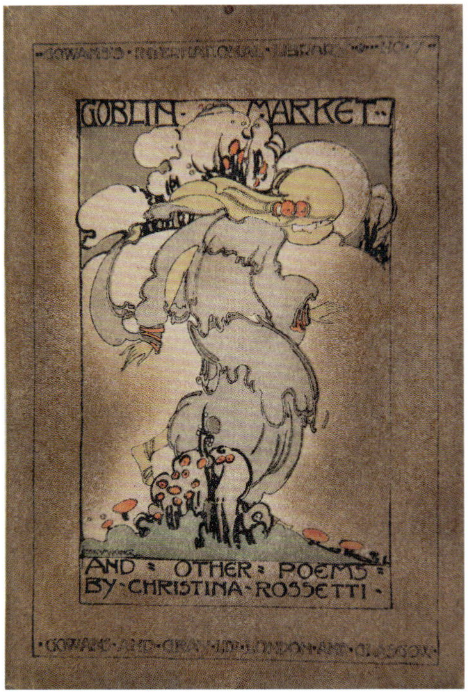

books are in one crucial respect unlike the books produced by the other fine printing enterprises of the day: their use of a range of delicate colours for illustrations and page decorations (fig. 4.28).

The popularity of poetry also tempted mainstream publishers to try harder to meet the widening demand for small, inexpensive books with popular and immediately recognisable texts. Numerous pocket editions of Christina's poems found their way into print, some illustrated or, at the least, dressed in pretty covers. One – a tiny 1907 edition of *Goblin Market* – had a vellum-paper wrapper cover (a favourite material of the day) with a single drawing by Jessie M. King (fig. 4.29); whilst another edition in booklet form with a wrapper design and a handful of small illustrations by Arthur Rackham first appeared as late as 1933 and was reprinted several times thereafter (figs 4.30 and 4.31).

Readers' interest in Christina Rossetti's works and popular curiosity about her life and character never suffered that near-total

4.28 Above left:
Lucien Pissarro,
The Dead City, illustration to *Verses by Christina G. Rossetti* (Hammersmith: Eragny Press, 1906). Ashmolean Museum, University of Oxford.

A reprint, with wood-engraved historiated initials and decorations by Lucien and Esther Pissarro, of the text of Gaetano Polidori's 1847 privately printed volume of Rossetti's early verse.

4.29 Above right:
Jessie M. King,
cover for Christina Rossetti, *Goblin Market and Other Poems* (Glasgow and London: Gowans and Gray, 1907), Japanese vellum wrappers. Collection of Stephen Calloway.

4.30 Below left:
Arthur Rackham,
cover design for Christina Rossetti, *Goblin Market* (London: George G. Harrap & Co., 1933), offset lithograph.
Collection of Stephen Calloway.

4.31 Below right:
Arthur Rackham,
frontispiece illustration to Christina Rossetti, *Goblin Market*, 1933, colour process print.
Collection of Stephen Calloway.

eclipse that befell many of the great figures of Victorian art and literature. But over time the nature of that interest changed and with it the kind of books that were published. The 1928 centenary of the birth of Dante Gabriel Rossetti has often been seen as a convenient point from which to date the revival of enthusiasm for the Victorian era.[61]

Recent illustrations and new interpretations

Most of the more recent attempts to illustrate Christina Rossetti's poems have focused on 'Goblin Market'. One of the most curious sets of illustrations, by the artist and commercial illustrator Kinuko Craft, was published as a somewhat unlikely supplement to the more usual visual fare featured in *Playboy Magazine* for September 1973 (fig. 4.32).[62] These highly wrought and colourful drawings take as their obvious starting point Arthur Rackham's 1933 interpretation, borrowing or even parodying many of the older illustrator's characteristic details and visual mannerisms (see fig. 4.31). However, they introduce a palpable sense of eroticism, which, if not entirely unthought of in previous eras, is made far more visually explicit in these few pages than in any treatment of the poem heretofore. One of the most interesting aspects of the way in which the supposed lesbian undertones of Christina's

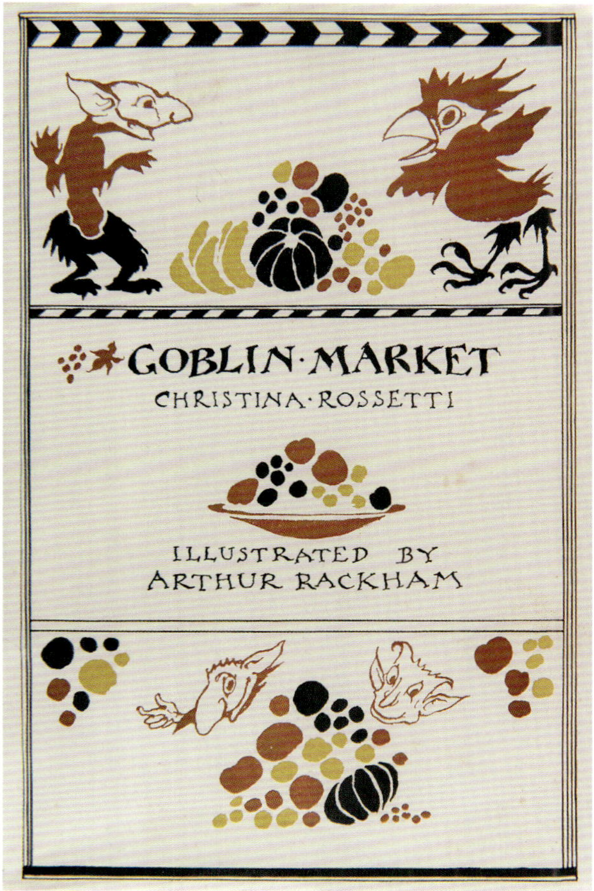

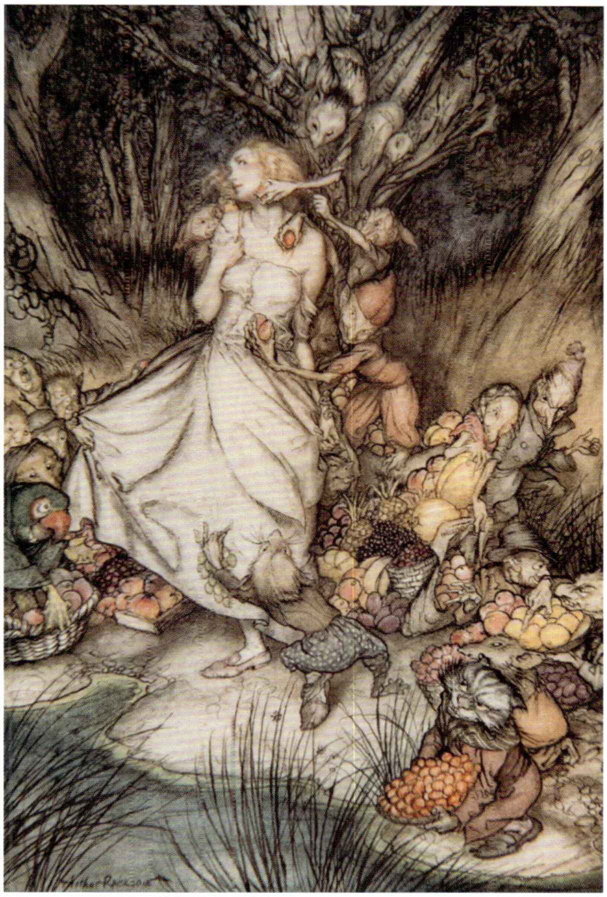

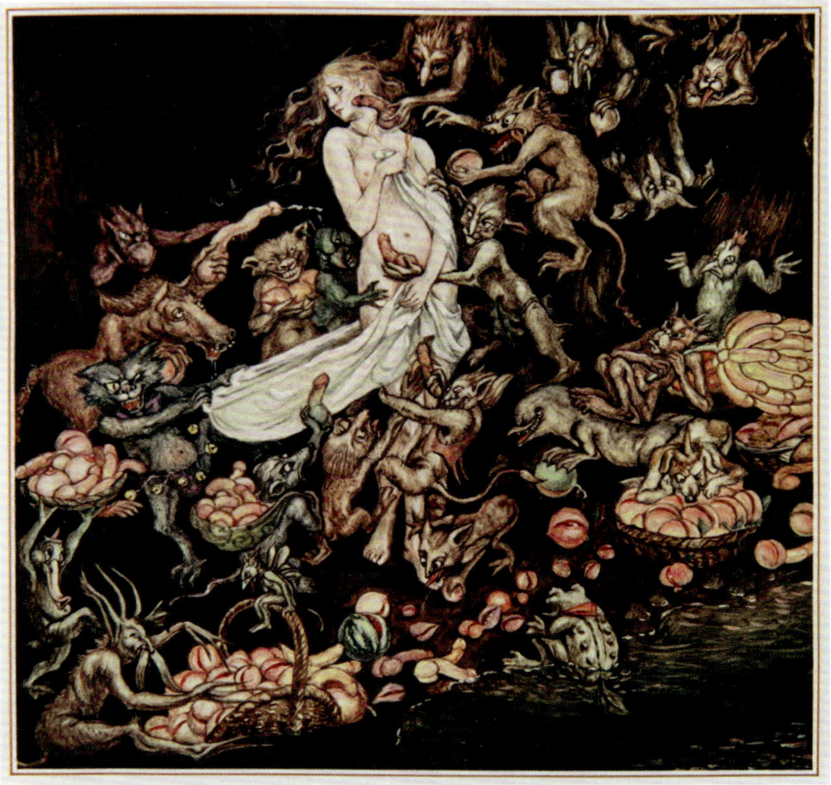

4.32 Kinuko Craft, illustration to Christina Rossetti, 'Goblin Market', *Playboy Magazine*, vol. 20, no. 9, 1973, colour process print. Archival *Playboy Magazine* material.

narrative are brought out is the fact that such an interpretation (intended deliberately here to appeal to an un-literary and, as it must be presumed, overwhelmingly male readership) appears here ahead of much of the now widespread exploration of such themes in academic studies of the poetry.[63]

Other treatments of 'Goblin Market' have ranged from the simplistic (or *faux naïf*) clearly aimed at the children's book market to the highly sophisticated. Among the latter, several artists have published their work in ordinary book form, whilst others, including Hilary Paynter and Martin Ware, working principally as printmakers, have created suites of woodcuts or etchings that are presented in the more self-consciously elite form of 'artists' books' (figs 4.33 and 4.34). In a cultural milieu different again, a more recent development in mainstream illustration, influenced by both American comic books and popular Japanese manga, has been the rise of a new genre of 'graphic novel' treatments of canonical literary texts (fig. 4.35). Not surprisingly, the poetry of Christina Rossetti, seemingly endlessly reprinted and always a rich source of inspiration for illustrative art, has been yet again reinterpreted for another generation to discover.

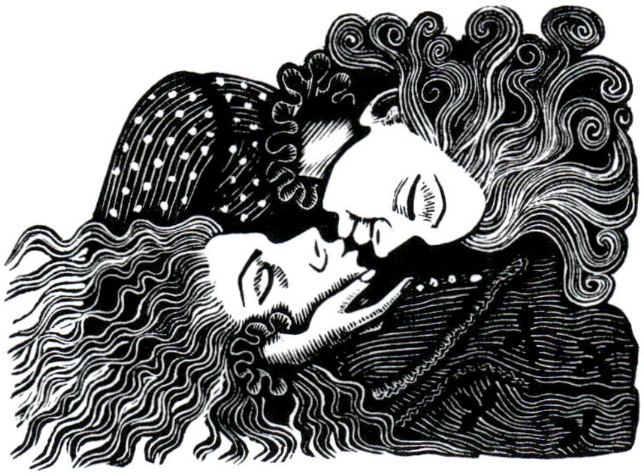

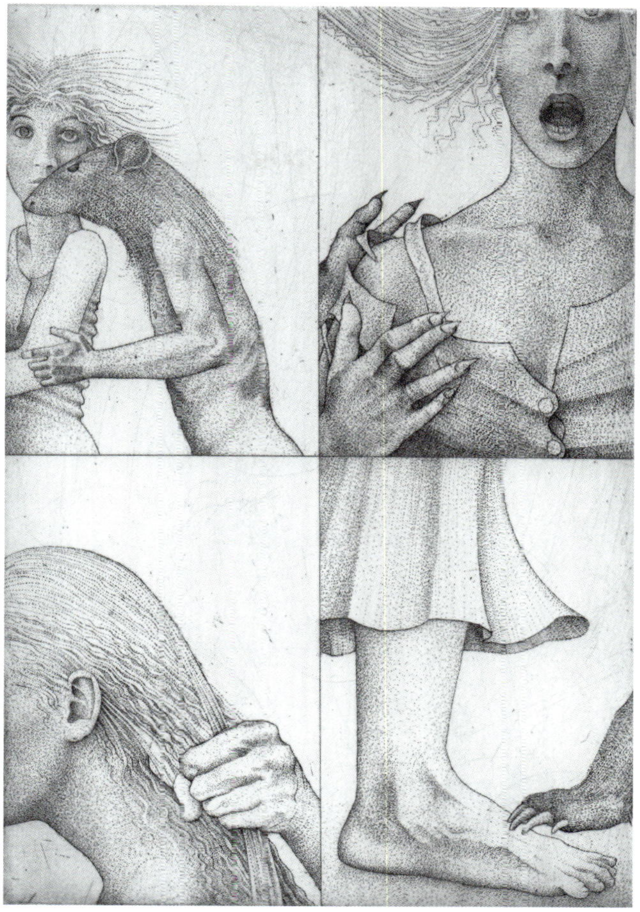

4.33 Above left:
Hilary Paynter,
illustration to Christina Rossetti, *Goblin Market* (London: Artists' Choice Editions, 2003), wood engraving.
Courtesy of the artist.

4.34 Above right:
Martin Ware,
illustration to Christina Rossetti, *Goblin Market* (London: Victor Gollancz, 1980), etching.
Courtesy of the artist.

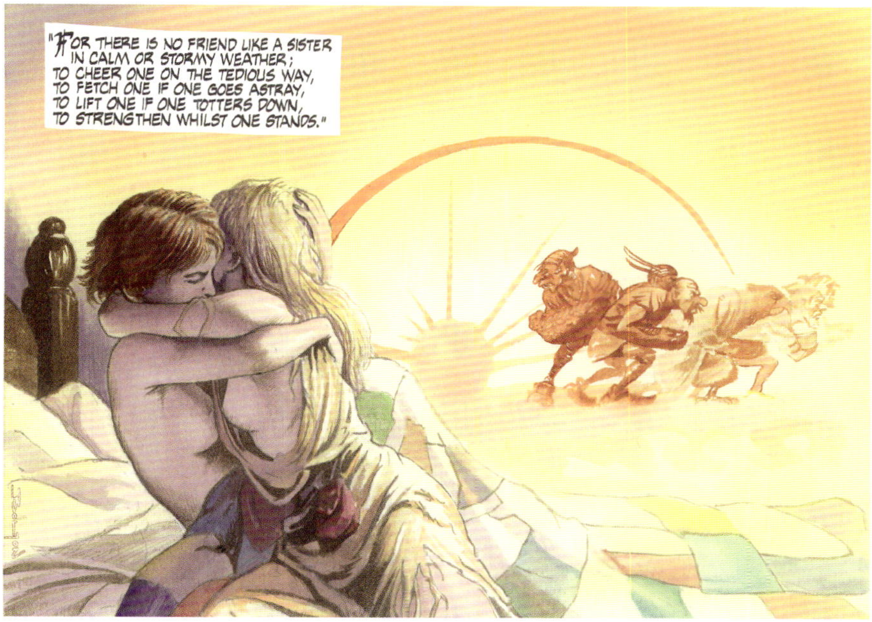

4.35 Right:
John Bolton,
illustration to a graphic novel version of 'Goblin Market' in *Pathways to Fantasy*, no. 1 (Pacific Comics, 1984), colour process print.
Courtesy of the artist.

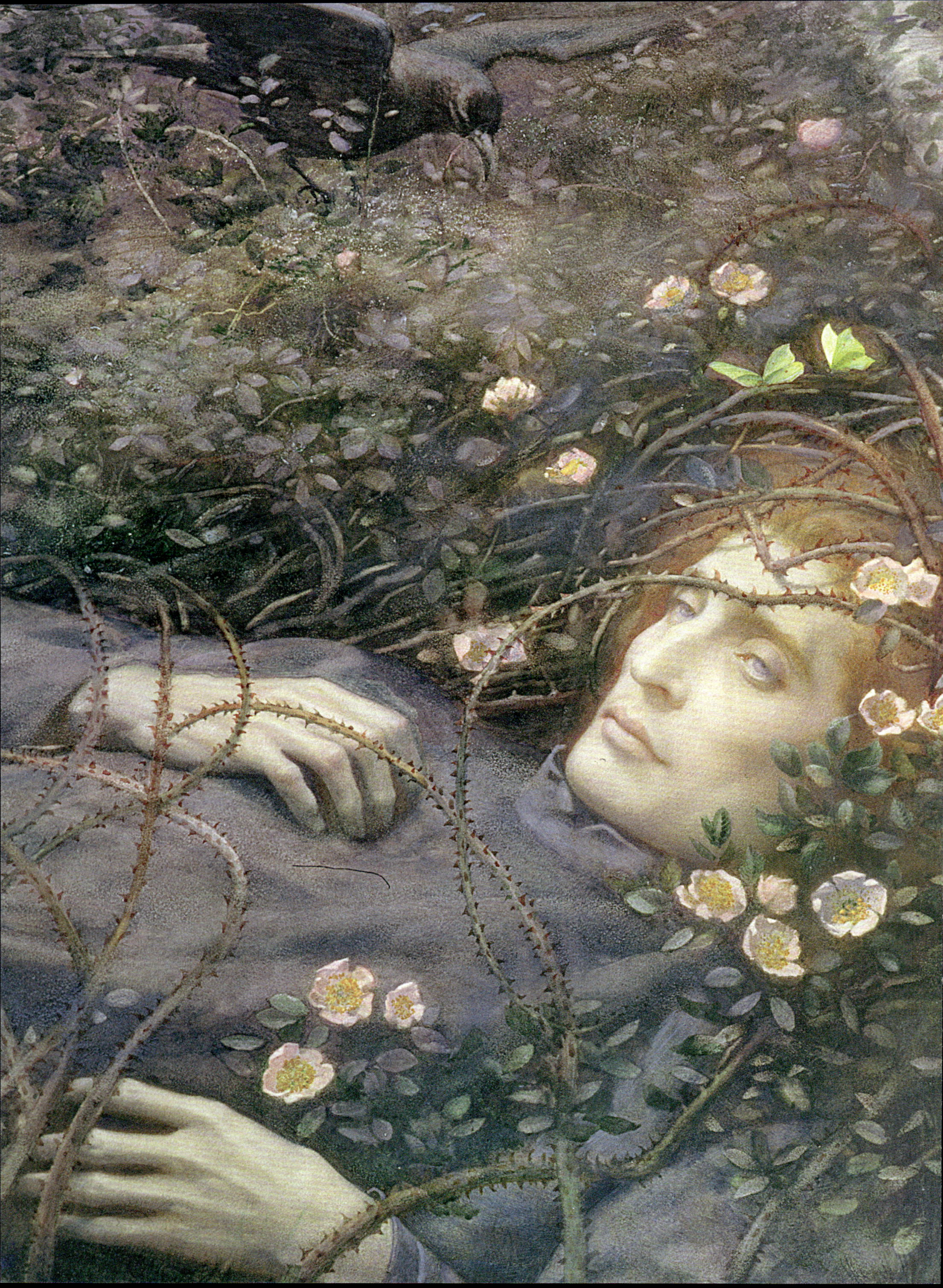

So echoes answered when her song was sung
In the first wooded vale.

5 'Pictures to the public view': Artists' Responses to Christina Rossetti's Poetry

SUSAN OWENS, NICHOLAS TROMANS AND HILARY UNDERWOOD

TRANSLATING words into visual images has often resulted in tension between artist and writer. 'The writer must die of impossible expectations', wrote George Eliot sadly on seeing Frederic Leighton's illustrations for her novel *Romola* (1862–3), while Henry James considered the very idea of illustrations in books misguided, text and image as incompatible as 'flesh and fish served on the same platter'.[1] Christina Rossetti was, in fact, unusually fortunate in her early illustrators. Her brother Dante Gabriel and their friend Arthur Hughes both proved to be amenable, translating her poetic images into visual form that, on the whole, met with her satisfaction. She was also fortunate in her publisher; when in 1893 she was unhappy with the variety of goblin imagined by Laurence Housman for a proposed new edition of *Goblin Market*, Macmillan encouraged the illustrator to return to the drawing board (see Chapter Four).

But an author's control over the interpretation of their work had its limits: there was another arena in which artists nearly always had the upper hand. In the nineteenth century an expanding urban middle class wanted pictures for their homes, and a growing army of artists was happy to oblige. A buoyant market developed for small-scale oil paintings of the kind suitable for display in ordinary domestic interiors, with subjects that were frequently anecdotal and often derived from literary sources. The heyday of this kind of genre painting was the first half of the century, but literary subjects remained popular during the following decades. Exhibitions at venues sited in the luxury shopping district of London gave artists the opportunity to show, and to sell, such paintings. The most prestigious of these was the Royal Academy of Arts, established in 1768, where, in its annual show, pictures crowded the walls from floor to ceiling. Other venues included the British Institution, the Society of British Artists, the Society of Painters in Water Colours and its offshoot, the New Society for Painters in Water Colours. Literary subjects allowed artists to dress up a composition

Detail of fig. 5.8

with cultural allusions flattering to the buyer: the authors most frequently plundered for subjects were Shakespeare, Goldsmith, Sterne, Scott, Pepys, Burns, Dickens, Cervantes and Molière. Relevant texts were often printed in exhibition catalogues, explaining the subjects and underlining the pictures' literary respectability. Living authors were not, of course, consulted; their published works were considered fair game as sources of inspiration.

Literary subjects were popular with the avant-garde as well as with those associated with the more traditional end of the spectrum, but there was a key difference. Artists connected with Pre-Raphaelitism and the later Aesthetic Movement, which transformed British painting from the 1860s onwards, were contemptuous of the triviality and sentimentality they saw in many of the popular pictures that filled annual exhibitions, and rejected the straightforwardly illustrative treatment of literary subjects so common in conventional Victorian paintings. Instead they attempted to forge a new, more equal relationship between literature and visual art, one based on shared themes.[2] Poetry was particularly well suited as inspiration: it carried less of an obligation to depict a narrative scene and offered more scope to the imagination. Subject could be allowed to recede, and mood and atmosphere to take its place. Another important factor was Dante Gabriel Rossetti's concept of the 'double work of art', in which a poem and a painting shared common inspiration but were essentially independent of one another. This idea informed his practice from the outset and was influential on that of other artists: he had composed poems to accompany his pictures from his earliest, *The Girlhood of Mary Virgin* (fig. 2.7), to his last, a version of *Proserpine*. These ideas remained influential at the end of the century, when European and British Symbolist artists sought new ways of understanding and expressing human experience and spirituality. They turned to literature, drawing in particular on the psychological insights and powerful emotional resonance of poetry, creating visual responses to literary themes rather than simply illustrating them.

So, positioned between the boisterous commercial market and the artistic avant-garde in which her brother played so prominent a part, how popular was Rossetti's verse as inspiration for independent pictures? A poet had to be well known before their words commanded sufficient recognition to be quoted in this context. Rossetti's first public recognition as a poet came in the early 1860s, following the appearance of her immediately popular 'Up-Hill' in *Macmillan's Magazine* in 1861 and her first formally published collection, *Goblin Market and Other Poems*, the following year. As a result of this timing, the imagery of her poems was picked up both by artists catering for a popular market and by painters associated with the emerging Aesthetic Movement. The rich variety of artists' responses to her verses, from all points in the artistic spectrum, is evident from the checklist that forms the last part of this chapter.[3]

5.1 Dante Gabriel Rossetti, *Three Sang of Love Together*, c.1863–5, pencil on paper, 45.1 × 32 cm. Untraced.

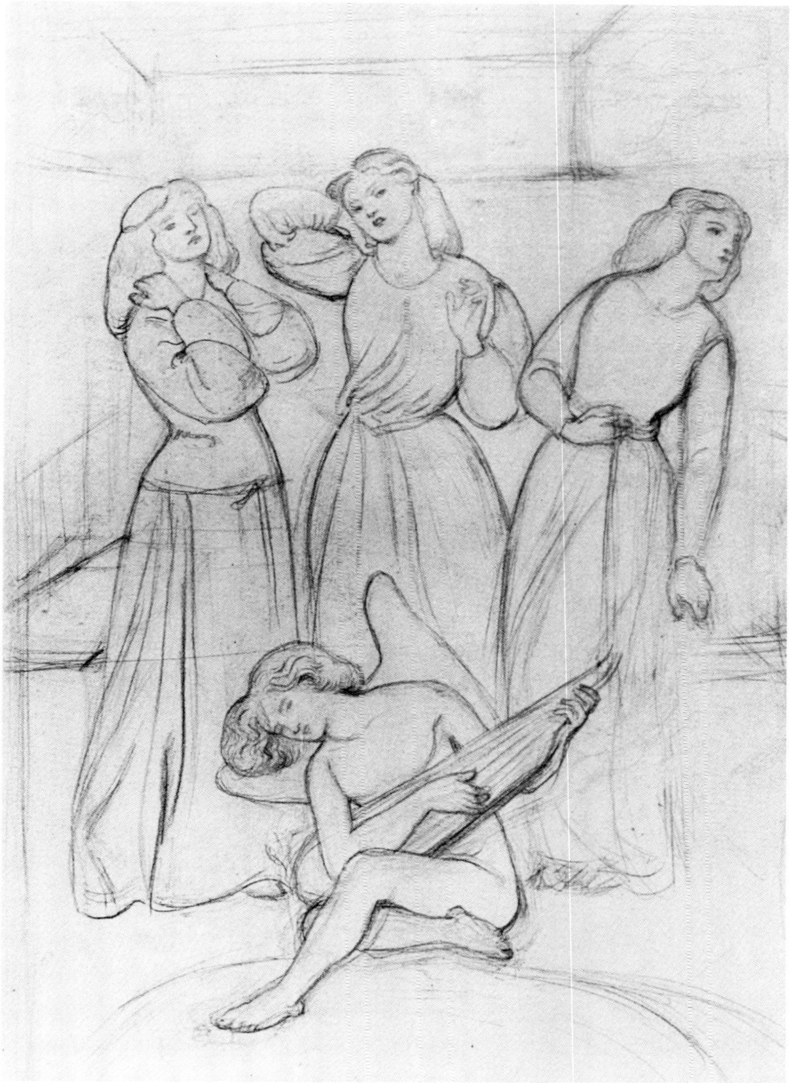

Approaching Christina Rossetti

Not long after the publication of *Goblin Market*, Rossetti received a sharp lesson in how a reader's interpretation might depart from an author's intention to a distressing degree. In 1863, a painter friendly with the Rossetti brothers, George Chapman, based his composition *Three Sisters Sang of Love Together* (untraced) on Rossetti's 'A Triad' (composed 1856; published 1862), a poem that concerns varieties of dissipated, degraded and unhappy love and voices a critical view of marriage: 'one temperately / Grew gross in soulless love, a sluggish wife'. Did the painting depict Hogarthian immorality within marriage? Or, more likely, did it use Rossetti's line 'One droned in sweetness like a fattened bee' as a pretext for a frankly sensuous depiction of a female figure, of the kind Gabriel had been painting since his watershed work

Bocca Baciata of 1859? William later described how 'something may have been said by [Chapman], or in his set, which impressed Christina with this notion of contingent misconstruction'.[4] Her reaction was surprisingly decisive: rather than accepting that, once published, a poem is out in the world and that one cannot police others' interpretations of it, she subsequently suppressed 'A Triad', cutting it from future collections of her works published in Britain.

Gabriel also sketched a composition based on 'A Triad', *Three Sang of Love Together*, but this exists only as a pencil drawing (fig. 5.1).[5] Did he plan to develop it into an oil painting, or was it an idea for an illustration? The drawing's purpose is unclear, although its composition, which represents three singing women accompanied by a seated, winged lutenist representing Love, is strongly reminiscent of an illustration Gabriel made in 1855 for William Allingham's ballad 'The Maids of Elfen-Mere'. In *Three Sang of Love Together* the women are differentiated by their facial expressions and gestures, and one might assume that they follow (from left to right) the order in which they are described in the poem: the fallen woman 'with lips / Crimson', who 'shamed herself in love'; the complacent wife 'Who bloomed like a tinted hyacinth at a show'; and the abandoned woman who 'was blue with famine after love'. In his composition Gabriel suppresses the moral overtones of Christina's poem, using it instead as an opportunity to represent three beautiful women swaying and making graceful gestures as they sing. In the light of Christina's reaction to Chapman's painting, it is not hard to imagine why it progressed no further than a pencil sketch.

An artist attuned to the rich symbolism of Rossetti's poetry, and one less likely than her brother to ignore its moral dimension, was Arthur Hughes. Ever since seeing a copy of *The Germ* in 1850, when he was still a student at the Royal Academy, Hughes had been on the fringes of the Pre-Raphaelite Brotherhood, although he never became an official member. The fresh, vivid colours, sharp detail and poignant emotional content of paintings such as *April Love* (1856) and *The Long Engagement* (1859) reveal the strength of Pre-Raphaelite influence on his work. Hughes was to become Rossetti's most prolific illustrator (see Chapter Four). But before the early 1870s, when he made designs for her books *Sing-Song* and *Speaking Likenesses*, he produced two oil paintings inspired by her poetry. The first, which he had begun by April 1864, was based on Rossetti's 'A Birthday', included two years earlier in the *Goblin Market* collection. Gabriel, who had seen this painting in Hughes's studio, wrote to Christina on 5 January 1866: 'You know he's painted a capital picture from your *Birthday*, with the poem at full length on the frame. You ought to call & see it which *wd* please him'.[6] It was exhibited under the title *The Dove* in that year's annual winter exhibition of British art held at the French Gallery on Pall Mall, a venue sympathetic to Pre-Raphaelite artists where John Everett Millais, William Holman Hunt and Ford Madox Brown had all shown their work.

In attaching Rossetti's poem to the picture's frame, presumably by inscribing it on gold paper and pasting it to the lower section,

Hughes was following a precedent set by Gabriel as early as 1849, when he pasted the two sonnets he had composed to accompany *The Girlhood of Mary Virgin* to its frame for its exhibition at the Hyde Park Corner Free Exhibition in March of that year.[7] This prominent display of the poem, and its physical incorporation into the painting's structure, made a composite work of art. It also conferred greater status on the poem than the traditional practice of printing an extract in the catalogue.

The whereabouts of Hughes's *The Dove* are currently unknown, and no visual record appears to have survived. What could a painting based on a brief lyric poem of this kind, with no narrative dimension, have looked like? The poem's list of similes – a heart like a singing bird, or like an apple tree, or like a rainbow shell – conjures up a succession of isolated images with hallucinatory vividness, none of which is easy to imagine being translated into the visual terms of a mid-Victorian figurative painting. They seem, in fact, to fit more readily into the visual tradition of sixteenth- and seventeenth-century printed emblems, which combine a title and sometimes an epigram with a symbolic image. However the painting's title, *The Dove*, hints that Hughes's composition was, perhaps, only loosely based on the poem, inspired by its powerful atmosphere rather than any specific literary image.[8] On other occasions Hughes connected a poem to a painting simply via a shared theme. For example, when *April Love* was exhibited at the Academy in 1856, a quotation from one of the songs in Tennyson's 'The Miller's Daughter' was included in the catalogue, even though the painting itself did not set out to illustrate the poem.

In 1865, the year before the public appearance of *The Dove*, Hughes exhibited another painting with a connection to a poem by Rossetti, and in this instance it is clear that he approached the text as a parallel work with a shared theme, rather than as verses to be illustrated. When *The Mower* (fig. 5.2) was exhibited at the Academy it was accompanied in the catalogue by the opening line of Rossetti's 'Old and New Year Ditties (3)' (written on the last day of 1860):

> Passing away, saith the World, passing away:
> Chances, beauty and youth sapped day by day:
> Thy life never continueth in one stay.
> Is the eye waxen dim, is the dark hair changing to grey
> That hath won neither laurel nor bay?
> I shall clothe myself in Spring and bud in May:
> Thou, root-stricken, shalt not rebuild thy decay
> On my bosom for aye.
> Then I answered: Yea.

The labourer at the centre of *The Mower* is a realistic, prosaic figure – note the corduroy trousers, braces and muscular forearm – but with his scythe that so prominently overarches the composition, slicing through the idyllic landscape, he is also a symbol of death.

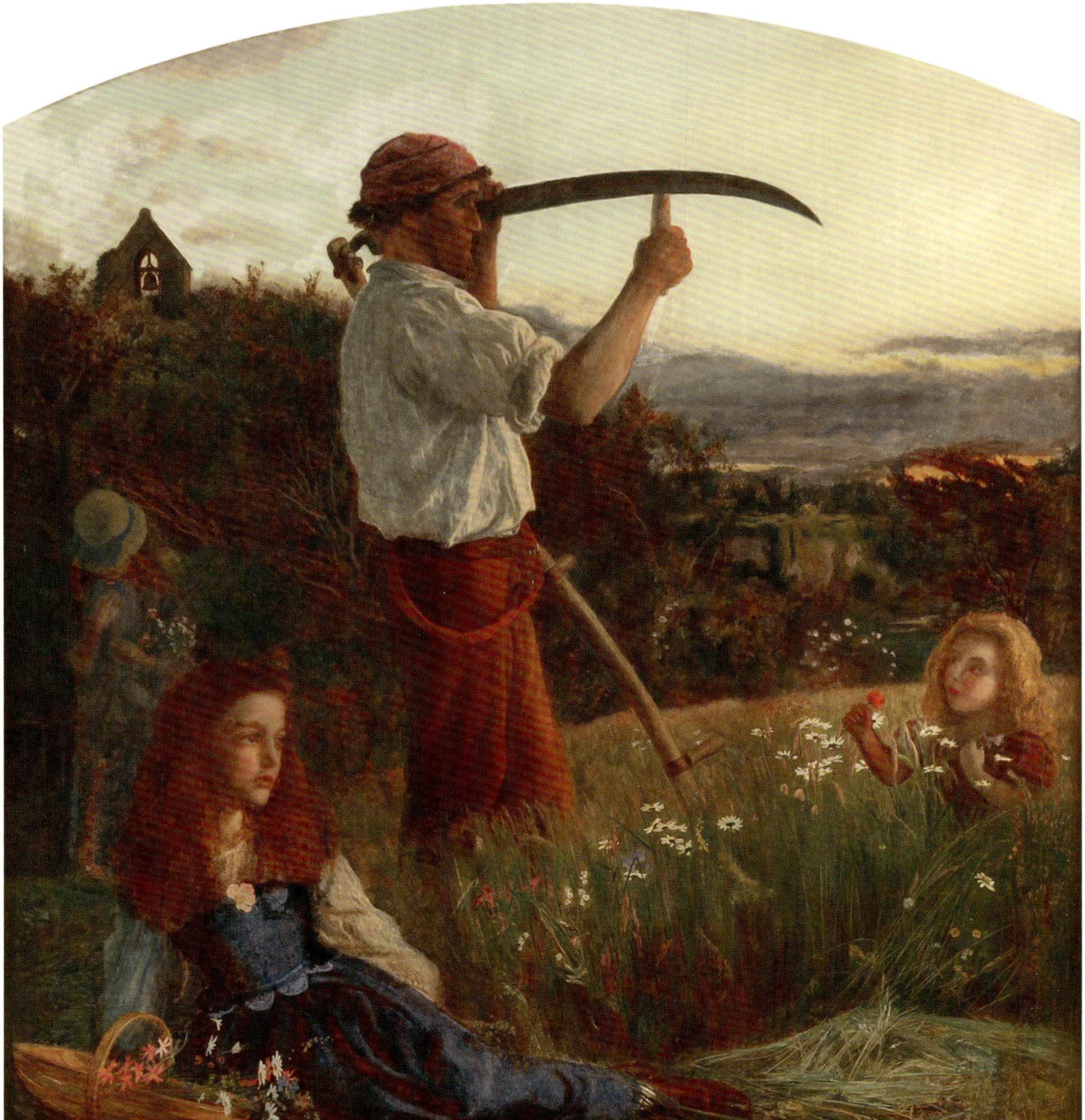

5.2 Arthur Hughes,
The Mower, 1865,
oil on canvas, 96.5 × 91.5 cm.
Private collection.

The meadow flowers, some standing, some mowed, some picked by the young girls, parallel the children's fragile beauty, while the evening light reflects the mood of transience and mortality evoked in Rossetti's poem. The musing older girl in the foreground appears aware of these connotations, and can be compared to the girls in Millais's *Autumn Leaves* (1856). In this case, the quoted line of poetry in the catalogue reflects the painting's meaning: they unite in expressing the harsh contrast between the annual renewal of nature and the single worldly growth of a human life.

Rossetti's reaction to neither *The Dove* nor *The Mower* is recorded. Several years earlier, however, in July 1858, Hughes's name arose in correspondence between her and Lady Trevelyan, a patron of Pre-Raphaelite artists, whom she had recently met through their mutual friend William Bell Scott. Rossetti explained that she only knew Hughes by sight, but remarked on her admiration for a religious painting by him that was included in that year's Royal Academy exhibition: 'It must be a privilege to know the artist of the *Nativity*', she wrote. She went on, however, to express an astute assessment of Hughes's work that is also revealing about her attitude to painting in general: 'yet I fancy that when one has gone a certain depth, one will fail to find a deeper still, intellectually of course'.[9] Within a few years, it was her own poetry that would supply intellectual underpinning and symbolic resonance to Hughes's paintings.

The photographer Julia Margaret Cameron was also inspired by Rossetti's poetry at this time. Cameron was pioneering in her approach to this still relatively new medium, and insisted on photography's status as an art form rather than a simple tool of record. In addition to the searching and unconventional portraits she made of family and friends, experimental in technique and often deliberately out of focus, she used photography to create compositions, frequently based on literary or biblical subjects, in the same way a painter might. Among these was *The Minstrel Group* (fig. 5.3), taken in 1866, the year Rossetti and Cameron met (see Chapter Two). Cameron inscribed several copies of the photograph with lines from Rossetti's poem 'Advent', composed in 1858 and published in *Goblin Market*: 'We sing a slow contented song / And knock at Paradise'.[10] Whether *The Minstrel Group* was inspired by 'Advent' or whether Cameron created it first and then found that Rossetti's poetic image chimed with her composition is not known. The lines are drawn from the sixth stanza of the poem:

> We weep because the night is long,
> We laugh for day shall rise,
> We sing a slow contented song
> And knock at Paradise.
> Weeping we hold Him fast, Who wept
> For us, we hold Him fast;
> And will not let Him go except
> He bless us first or last.

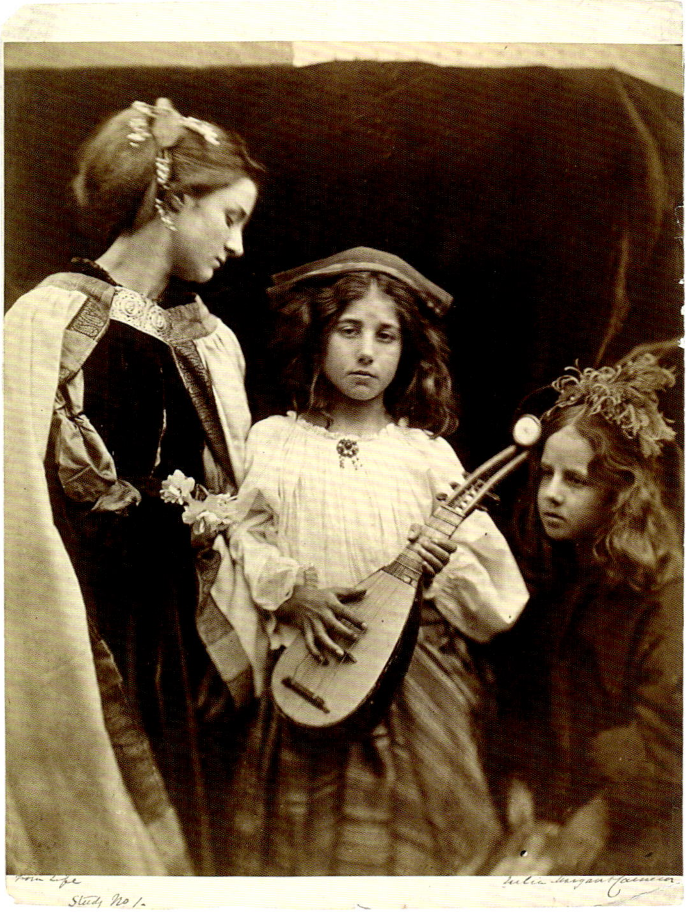

5.3 Julia Margaret Cameron, *The Minstrel Group*, 1866, albumen print from wet collodion glass negative, 34.5 × 28.5 cm. Victoria and Albert Museum, London.

Whatever the precise nature of Cameron's response to 'Advent', without the inscribed reference to Rossetti we would hardly be in a position to make the connection ourselves. Cameron's image of three young, picturesquely clad travelling musicians has no obvious religious content and Rossetti's reference to music-making is an isolated one in her poem. The link Cameron has made between picture and poem is tenuous in terms of shared subject matter, and is instead based on mood and atmosphere. Though mutually independent, when connected in this way poem and image add an extra dimension to each other, acting as a Rossettian 'double work of art'. In 1875 Charles Lutwidge Dodgson (Lewis Carroll) made a similar connection, inscribing a photograph of his teenage model Rose Laurie with lines from Rossetti's 'A Birthday'.[11]

Artists of a more traditional stamp were also attracted to Rossetti's poetry. The Royal Academy's 1865 exhibition not only included Hughes's *The Mower* but also a painting by Marcus Stone, *The Old Letters* (fig. 5.4), which was listed in the catalogue alongside a quotation from Rossetti's work. Stone was a successful painter who exhibited every year without fail at the Academy from 1858, when he was eighteen, to 1920, the year before he died. He painted episodes from British history and literature, but made his name with romantic scenes enacted between well-dressed ladies and gentlemen, usually set in the gardens and drawing rooms of large houses. It was precisely the kind of unchallenging, populist painting despised by the Pre-Raphaelites and later artists associated with the Aesthetic Movement. Marcus's father, Frank Stone, was himself a conventional genre painter and a Pre-Raphaelite *bête noire*. Holman Hunt had included a reproduction of a painting by him in the deliberately vulgar interior of his *The Awakening Conscience* (1853). Nevertheless, Marcus Stone turned to 'A Pause of Thought', published in *Goblin Market,* when he came to compose *The Old Letters,* a painting on the theme of regret over a former suitor. The poem begins:

I looked for that which is not, nor can be,
And hope deferred made my heart sick in truth:
But years must pass before a hope of youth
Is resigned utterly.

Stone's interest, nurtured by his father's great friend Charles Dickens, was primarily in storytelling, and his paintings contain clues to help us interpret them. In this case, the guitar and open volume of music suggest that the young woman has been playing a song that has reminded her of a lost love, and prompted her to open a drawer of the lacquered cabinet and re-read an old letter. Saddened, she drops the pages and kneels on the floor, absorbed in memories.

Stone's picture is a conventional one: attractive young women musing over old love letters was a common Victorian pictorial theme.

5.4 Marcus Stone, *The Old Letters*, 1865, oil on canvas, 71 × 92 cm. Private collection.

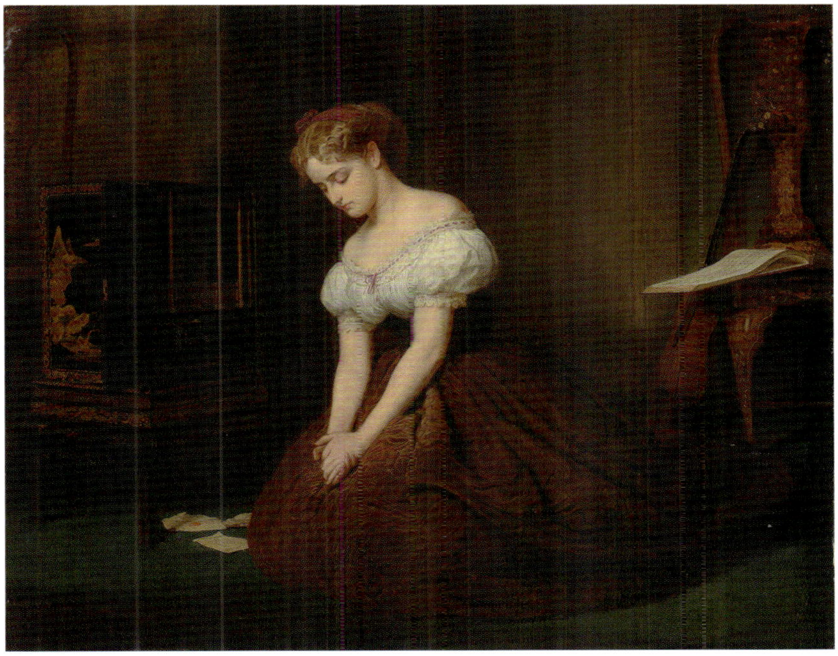

But it is an incongruous match for 'A Pause of Thought'. By introducing a back-story to explain Rossetti's pithy, heart-searching words, and adding a dominant new element – love letters do not feature in the verses – Stone sentimentalises the poem, watering down its raw emotional intensity and smoothing its jagged edges.

A transnational exchange

The development of Rossetti's reputation beyond Britain is still little understood. An intriguing fragment of evidence for that unwritten history, relevant to our subject here, comes from none other than Vincent van Gogh. In his letters to his brother from England, Van Gogh makes many references to the otherwise little-remembered painter George Henry Boughton, in particular his scenes of pilgrims and puritans. One of these, showing a pilgrim stopping to talk to a woman dressed in black, became associated in Van Gogh's mind with Rossetti's poem 'Up-Hill': both picture and poem had moved him powerfully. Indeed, in a sermon he preached at the Methodist chapel in Richmond in 1876, the young painter-preacher imagined the poem as a dialogue between the two main, or only, figures in the picture:

And the pilgrim asks her:	Does the road go uphill then all the way?
and the answer is:	"Yes to the very end"
and he asks again:	And will the journey take all day long?
and the answer is	"From morn till night my friend."[12]

The association made by Van Gogh between poem and painting is a striking example of a creative mind visualising Rossetti's verse. But the association between Boughton and Rossetti had in fact already been made, by Boughton himself. In April 1872, William Michael Rossetti visited Boughton's studio and recorded in his diary having seen there two paintings with mottos from (unspecified) lines by his sister (see p. 167).[13] We have been unable to identify these with certainty, and perhaps the mottos were dropped, but the possibility remains that Van Gogh connected Boughton and Rossetti because one or more of Boughton's pictures had been exhibited alongside lines from the poet.

The European dimension to Rossetti's reception, from an art-historical point of view, must always be centred upon two major compositions by the great Belgian artist Fernand Khnopff (fig. 5.5). Khnopff is the personification of ultra-sophisticated 1890s Symbolism – aloof, rarefied, introverted yet able comfortably to network internationally, especially in London where he was well known, making regular visits there from 1891. Like many other uncompromising European aesthetes of the period, Khnopff looked to England as the ultimate refuge of aristocratic style. His dainty but disturbing coloured-pencil drawing *Who Shall Deliver Me? (Christina Georgina Rossetti)* (fig. 5.6) borrows the title of Rossetti's poem of 1864, first published in the journal the *Argosy* in 1866 and included in her collected poems of 1875.[14] Rossetti borrowed her title from St Paul's Epistle to the Romans, the

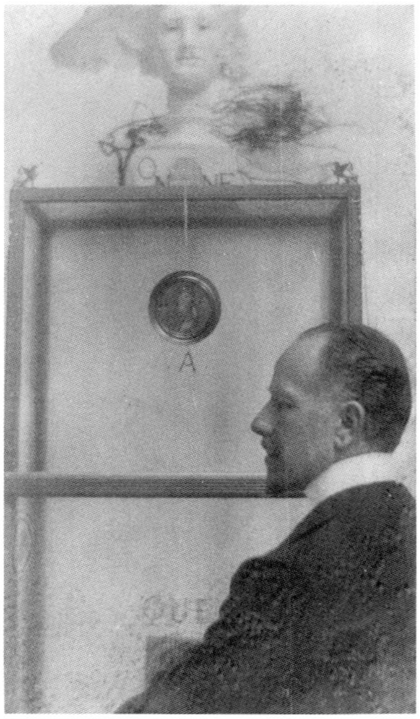

5.5 Anonymous photographer, *Fernand Khnopff Before the Altar to Hypnos in his Studio*, undated print, 24.5 × 18 cm. Royal Museums of Fine Arts of Belgium/Archives of Contemporary Art in Belgium.

5.6 Fernand Khnopff,
Who Shall Deliver Me?
(Christina Georgina Rossetti), 1890,
coloured pencil on paper,
22.4 × 13.4 cm.
Barry Friedman, New York.

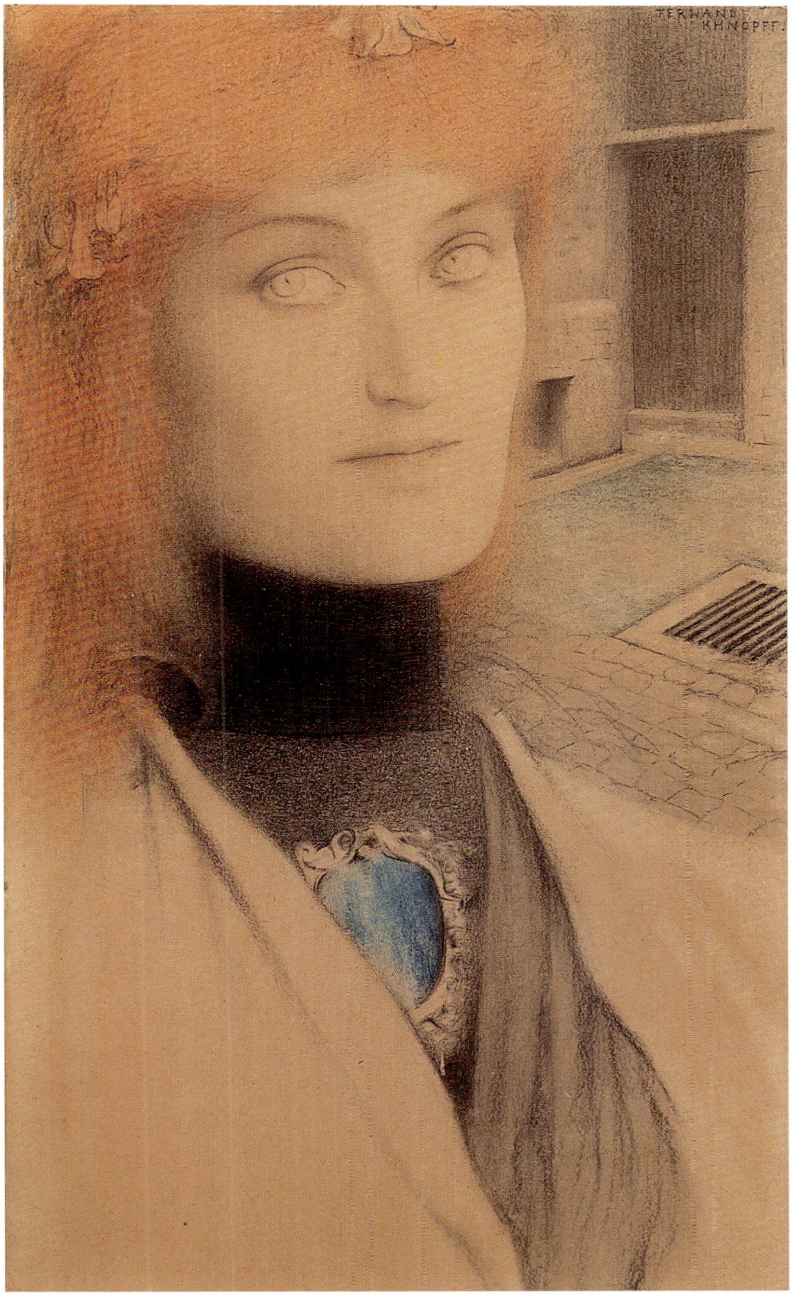

sixth book of the New Testament: 'O wretched man that I am! who shall deliver me from the body of this death?' In Khnopff's drawing a ghostly streetwalker stares out at us, a transparent apparition wearing a huge brooch that offers a glass window into emptiness. The ghost seems to be seeking the redemption begged for in the poem (quoted above, p. 20), and indeed in the biblical text, while the drain cover behind – its corner turned by perspective into a razor edge pointing dangerously at the

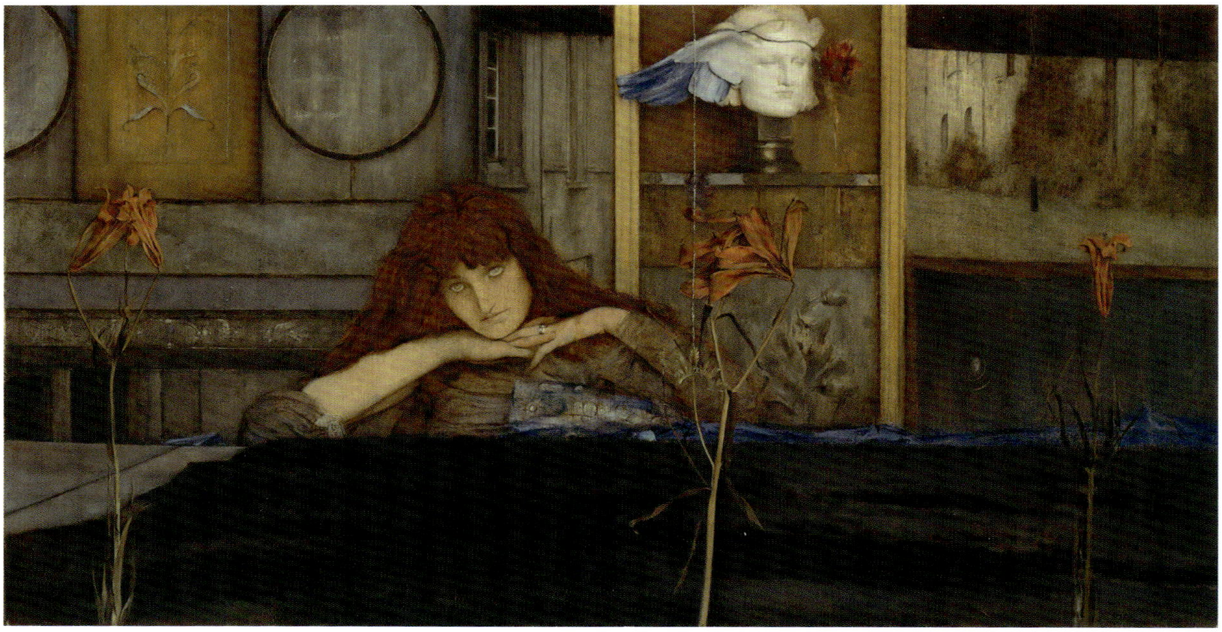

woman's neck – implies the horror and shame of physicality. It is a magnificently concentrated distillation of imagery.

Less urgent, but certainly more lavish, is Khnopff's oil painting of 1891, *I Lock My Door Upon Myself (Christina Georgina Rossetti)* (fig. 5.7), this title being the first line of the third stanza of the same poem. The painting was shown in both Brussels and London in 1892.[15] The figure here is a real young woman, a thinker or a poet rather than a spirit. Her chamber of the imagination is presided over by Hypnos, the god of sleep – there is a red poppy, for forgetfulness, next to him. Fading orange irises form a sort of screen between the main figure and the viewer, while the elegantly compartmentalised sections of the background suggest Japanese design and the work of Edward Burne-Jones, with whom Khnopff was on particularly good terms. Though without expressing the existential alarm of Rossetti's poem at the same high pitch as *Who Shall Deliver Me?*, this Symbolist masterpiece allows the mood of the poem to unfold and to find a new visual expression for the *fin de siècle*. It is as compelling as it is disturbing.

5.7 Fernand Khnopff, *I Lock My Door Upon Myself (Christina Georgina Rossetti)*, 1891, oil on canvas, 72.7 × 141 cm. Neue Pinakothek, Munich.

British Symbolism

Something of the same compartmentalising that Khnopff adopts in *I Lock My Door Upon Myself* can also be seen in Charles Ricketts's two-part illustration to 'An Echo from Willowwood', first published in the *Magazine of Art* in 1890 (see figs 4.19 and 4.20). Both poem and design are tributes to Dante Gabriel Rossetti, united in what we can recognise as an acutely self-conscious Art Nouveau style.[16] In Britain in the 1890s, the fracturing and regathering of Victorian idioms into new strains of modern art was evidently well able to make use of

5.8 Edward Robert Hughes, *'Oh what's that in the hollow…?'*, 1893, watercolour on paper, 63.2 × 93.3 cm. Royal Watercolour Society.

Christina Rossetti's verse. She provided, for some artists, an opportunity to take risks.

Edward Robert Hughes was the nephew of Arthur Hughes. He worked in a richly romanticised late Pre-Raphaelite style, and acted as studio assistant to Holman Hunt, helping most notably with the version of his *Light of the World* now in St Paul's Cathedral (Rossetti had been one of the models for the much earlier original version: fig. 2.13). In 1892 it seems Hughes had his head turned by the very different art of Khnopff, when he was able to admire *I Lock My Door Upon Myself (Christina Georgina Rossetti)* at the New Gallery on Regent Street. It was likely this experience that led him to emulate the Belgian the following year, by exhibiting a work with a quotation from Rossetti in place of a title (fig. 5.8):

> "Oh what's that in the hollow, so pale I quake to follow?"
> "Oh that's a thin dead body which waits the eternal term."[17]

These were lines from 'Amor Mundi', which had been illustrated by Frederick Sandys when first published in the *Shilling Magazine* in 1865 (fig. 4.1). While making nodding reference to Sandys, and to Burne-Jones's *Briar Rose* series, Hughes created an entirely different sort

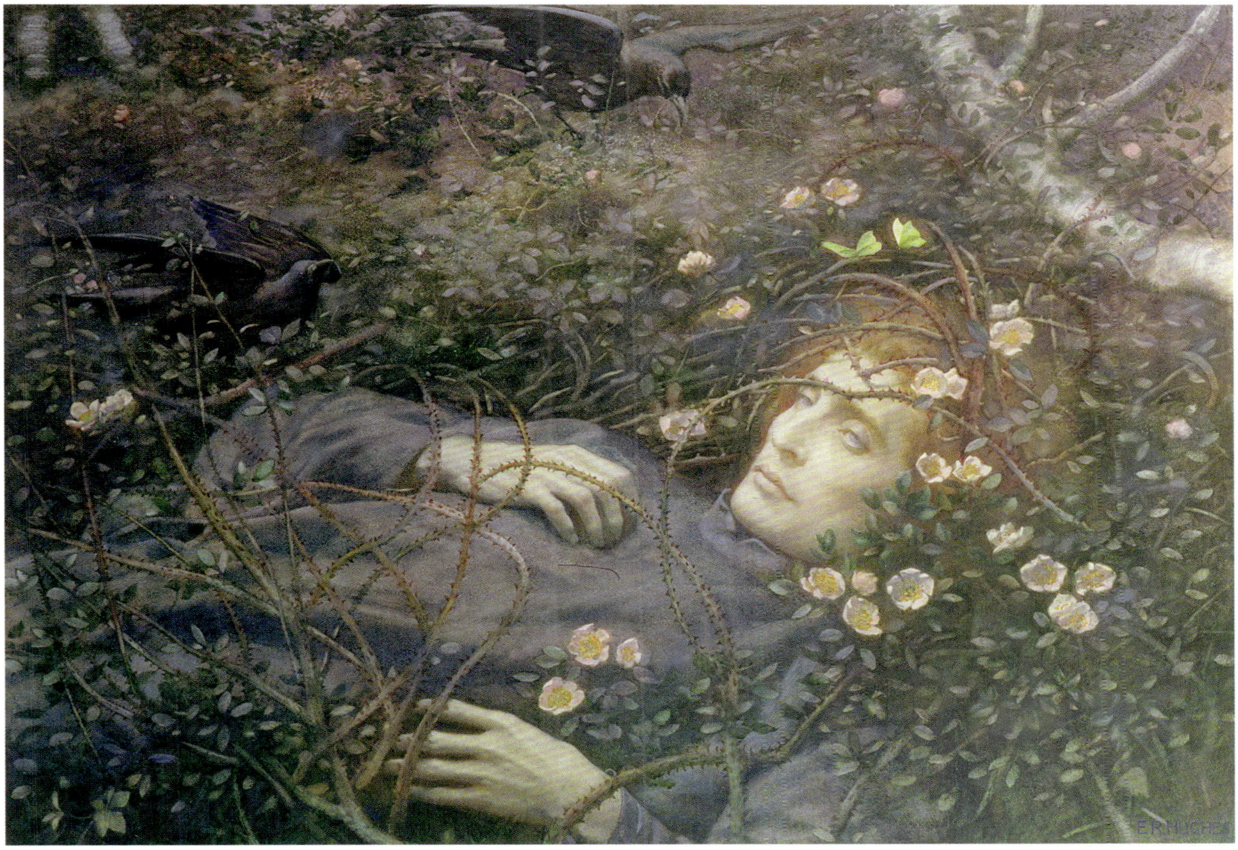

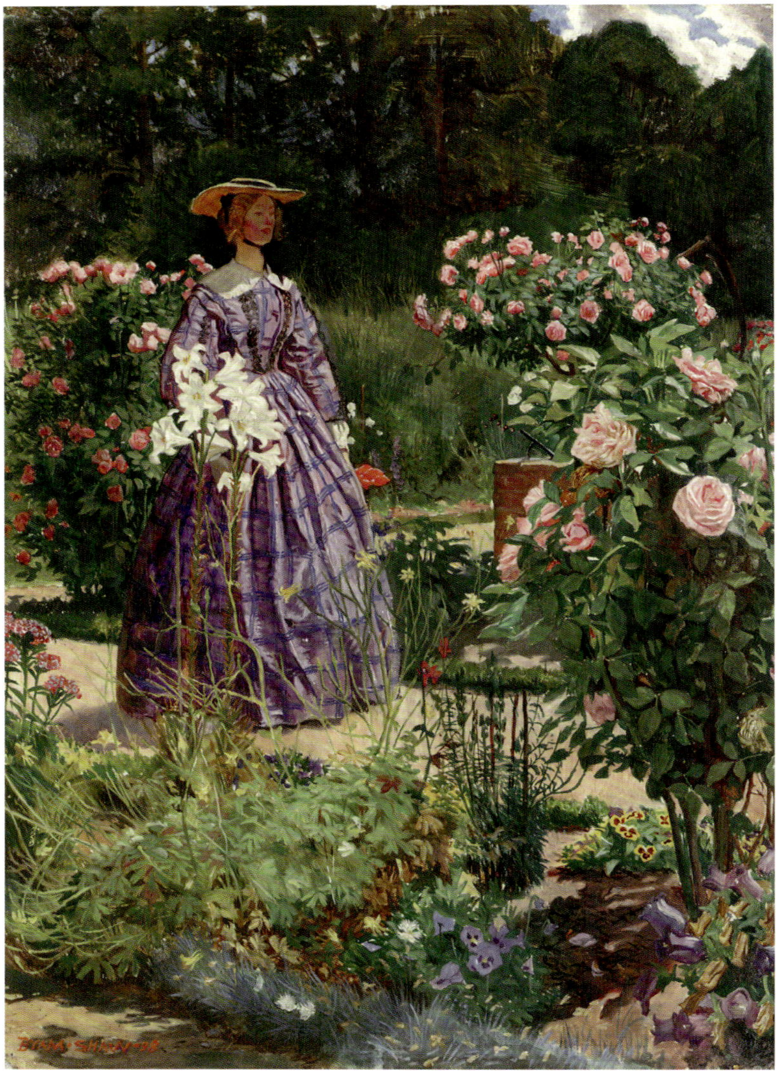

5.9 John Byam Shaw,
'While roses are so red, / While lilies are so white, / Shall a woman exalt her face / Because it gives delight?' (Beauty is Vain), 1898,
oil on panel, 40.5 × 29.5 cm.
Private collection.

of composition. The cruel revelation that meets the poem's pair of carefree lovers is isolated like the picture of a saint, or a still from a horror film of several decades later. The reviews of the picture dating from when it was shown at the Royal Society of Painters in Water Colours in 1893 reveal a disturbed audience, the *Athenaeum* complaining that, 'like the poem' on which it depended, Hughes's picture was 'a trifle morbid and hysterical'.[18] The suggestion was that an unhealthily nervous feminine sensibility had infected a man with otherwise impeccable Pre-Raphaelite credentials. Hughes nevertheless donated the picture to the Watercolour Society as his diploma work upon his election as a full member in 1895. A cynical suggestion would be that this choice was simply due to his not having been able to sell it in the wake of its reception two years previously: but equally Hughes

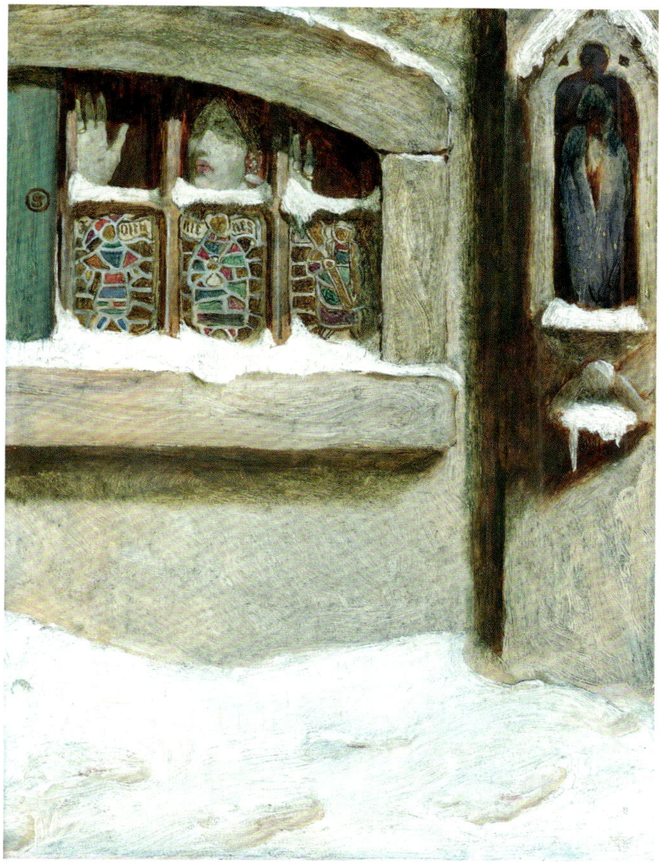

5.10 John Byam Shaw, *'Oh it was summer when I slept, / It's winter now I waken' (A Daughter of Eve)*, c.1899, oil on panel, 30.5 × 25.4 cm. Private collection.

may have been especially proud of this powerful and original image.

If the 1890s were a particularly fecund phase for painters mining the possibilities of Rossetti's poetry, then it is fitting that the decade ended with an exhibition at which an artist showed an entire suite of pictures based upon her verse. In 1899, Dowdeswell and Dowdeswell's on New Bond Street opened an exhibition by John Byam Shaw, a young artist who became a staple of their programme over the following years. *Thoughts Suggested by Some Passages from British Poets*, an exhibition of 'cabinet pictures', contained no fewer than eleven subjects taken from Rossetti.[19] Byam Shaw was a committed Christian: his next Dowdeswell's exhibition, in 1902, was *Sermons in Stones and Good in Everything: Suggested by the Book of Ecclesiastes*. As well as responding to the visual richness and symbolism in Rossetti's poetry, Byam Shaw was also primed to respond to her Christianity, sense of sin and preoccupation with the vanity of the world. Byam Shaw was furthermore an especially versatile reviver of early Pre-Raphaelite styles, and his 1899 Rossetti pictures offer a striking range of modes, summarising the variety of approaches to the poet explored since the 1860s.

Some of Byam Shaw's treatments illustrate Rossetti's themes literally, such as *Beauty is Vain* (fig. 5.9), in which a woman in a smart silk gown of the 1850s moves through a lush garden. Others manage to use a related literalness to create something eccentrically Symbolist, as in *Love, Strong as Death, is Dead* (the opening line of 'An End'), where a medieval couple prepare to bury a naked boy-Cupid who lies dead at their feet. At their best, Shaw's images are completely original: *Oh it was summer when I slept, It's winter now I waken* (lines from 'A Daughter of Eve': fig. 5.10) imagines a bloodless woman peering claustrophobically from the windows of a Pre-Raphaelite building onto a snowbound world. The quiet desperation of an isolated figure echoes Khnopff's *Who Shall Deliver Me?*, despite the ostensible gulf between the Christian Byam Shaw and the decadent Khnopff. Byam Shaw's 1899 cycle can perhaps finally be seen as an elaborate exercise preliminary to the creation of his minor masterpiece *Boer War 1900* (fig. 5.11), shown at the Academy in 1901 with the lines 'Oh last summer green things were greener, / Brambles fewer, the blue sky bluer' from 'A Bird Song', first published in the New York periodical *Scribner's Monthly* in 1873. A young widow in black and purple, bereaved by the South African war, stands on a stream bank, her sadness harshly offset by the profusion of

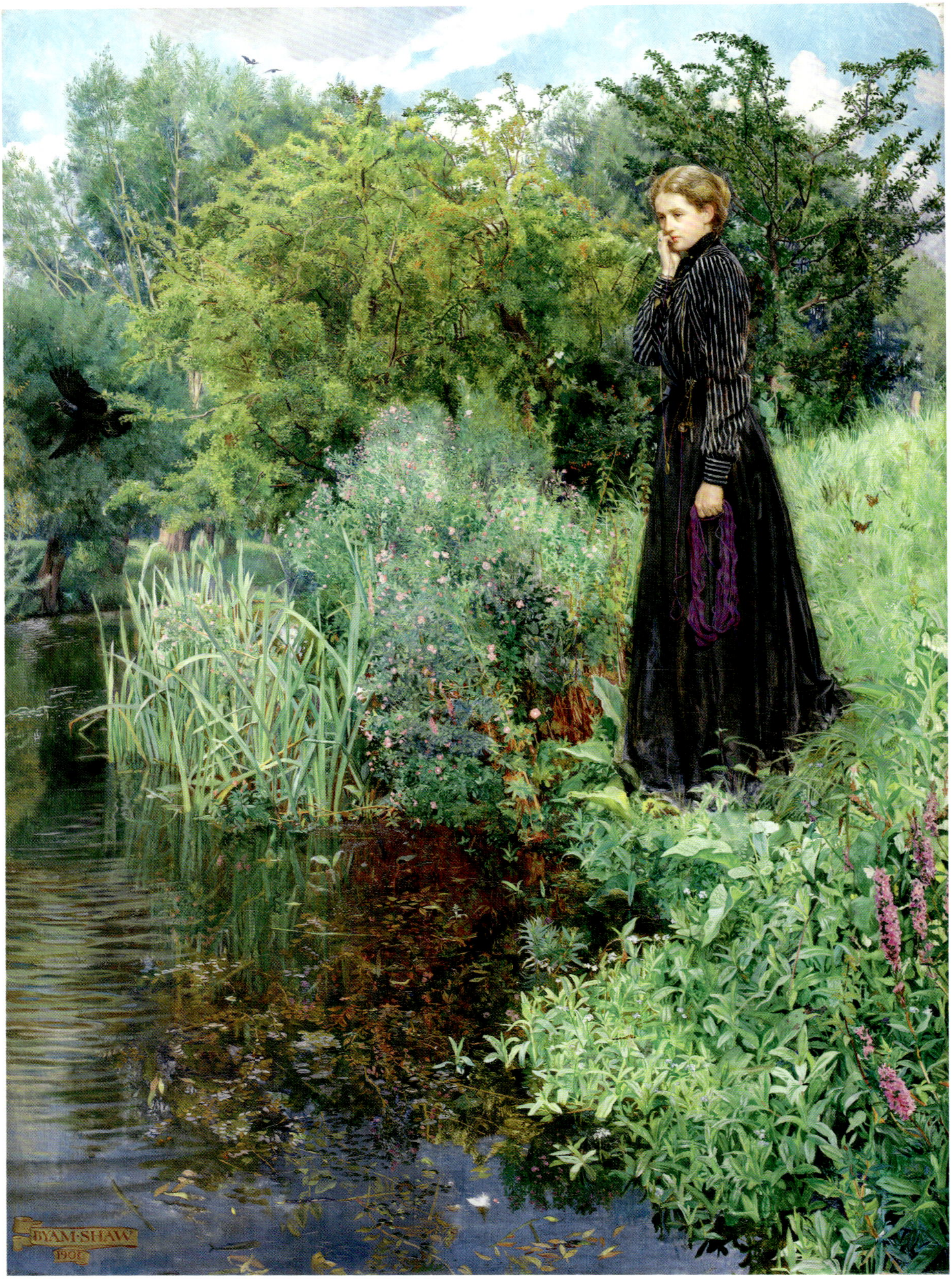
BYAM·SHAW
1901

5.11 John Byam Shaw, *Boer War 1900 ('Last Summer Things were Greener')*, 1901, oil on canvas, 101.8 × 76 cm. Birmingham Museum & Art Gallery.

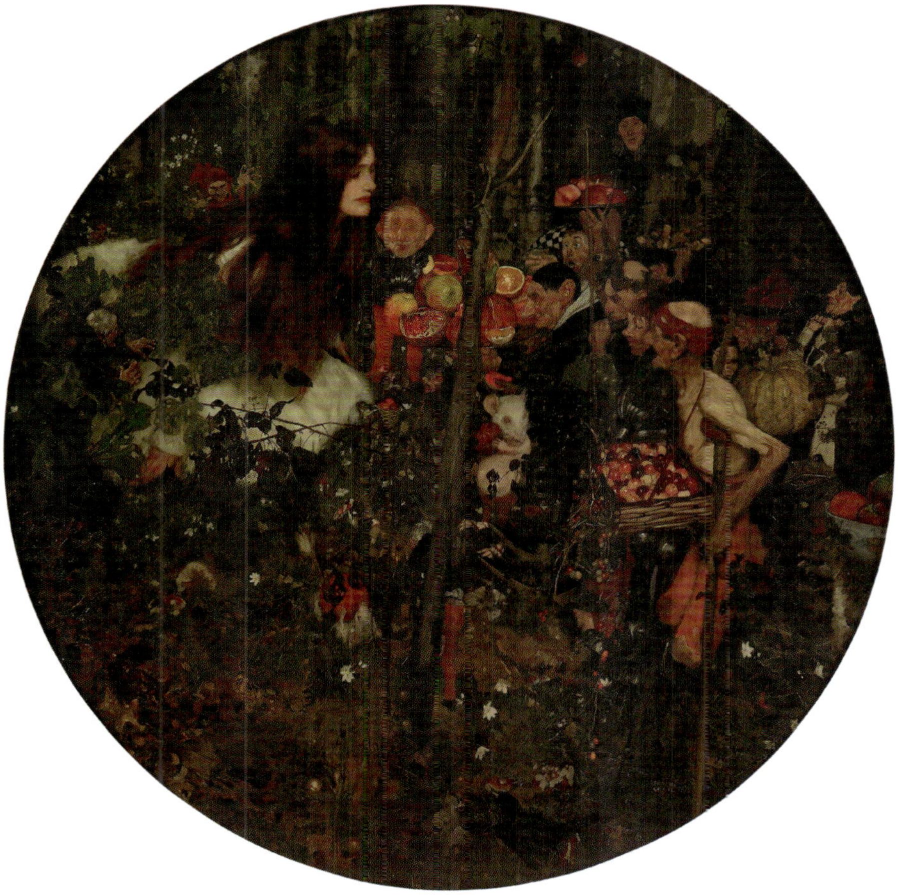

5.12 Frank Craig, *Goblin Market*, 1911, oil on canvas, 106 cm (diameter). Museum of New Zealand Te Papa Tongarewa.

life and growth of an early summer's day. The Rossettian tone is caught here without apparent effort, with a result both beautiful and tragic.

'Goblin Market' and the new century

One of Byam Shaw's 1899 Rossetti pictures took 'Goblin Market' as its subject. Unusually among the many artists who treated this most tempting of the poems, Byam Shaw showed Lizzie's successful resistance to the goblins in her quest to redeem her sister Laura. Lizzie is shown upright, 'white and golden' as the poem states, at the moment when the frustrated goblins abandon their temptation and upset their fruit. Byam Shaw's goblins appear initially entirely animal, but on closer inspection are appropriately twisted, indeterminate creatures. This voluptuous little painting forms part of a long sequence of 'Goblin Market' pictures and illustrations initiated by Laurence Housman's black-and-white cycle of 1893. The tradition gathered momentum during the Edwardian heyday of the colourfully illustrated children's book.

The incident most often represented is Laura's bargain with the goblins. The precedent was set by Dante Gabriel Rossetti's frontispiece for the original *Goblin Market and Other Poems* of 1862,

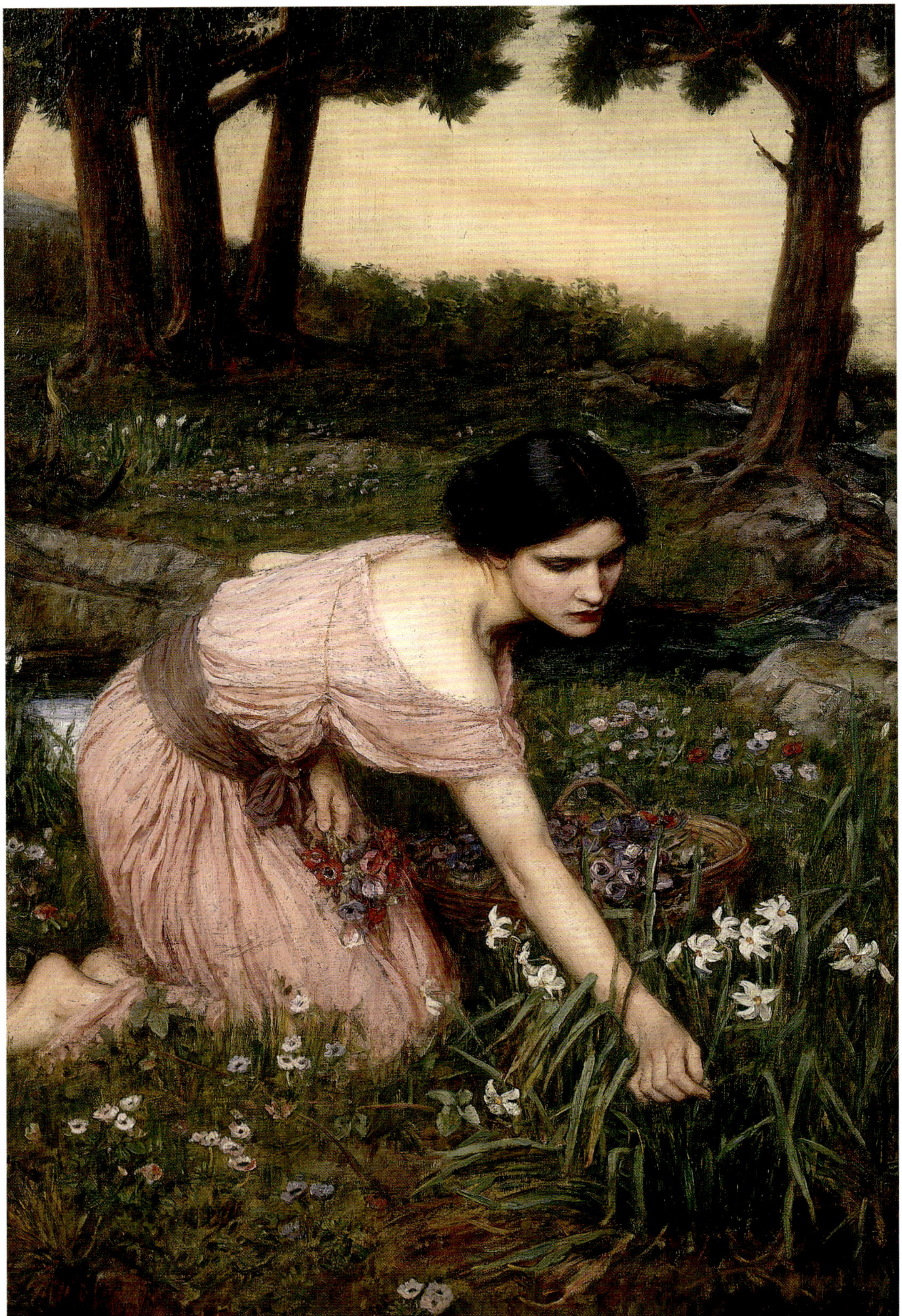

5.13 John William Waterhouse, *'Spring spread one green lap of flowers'*, 1910, oil on canvas, 106 × 77 cm. Private collection.

Buy from us with a Golden Curl (fig. 4.3). An especially ambitious example was shown by Frank Craig, a contemporary of Byam Shaw's, at the Academy in 1911 (fig. 5.12). Within a circular canvas, whose lens-like framing recalls perhaps the poem's original title, 'A Peep at the Goblins', Laura negotiates with the goblins. She is imagined as a svelte, darker-haired beauty in the mould of the women in the pictures of John William Waterhouse, who himself had used a tag from Rossetti as a title for a painting of a girl in a meadow at the previous year's Academy exhibition (fig. 5.13). Craig incorporates natural detail that reinforces the sinister theme of the poem, including nettles, brambles and deadly nightshade. Yet in common with most Edwardian painted representations of the theme, he diminishes the size of the goblins, so that they are much smaller than the human figure. Laura is shown allowing herself to be charmed by the little men who are, here, exactly that – eccentric micro-chaps who might have had roles in Richard Dadd's *The Fairy Feller's Master-Stroke* (1855–64). In Gabriel's inaugural conception, the goblins are comparable in bulk to Laura, and overtop her compositionally, suggesting the threat they will later pose to Lizzie. The iconography of fairyland has taken its toll upon Rossetti's goblins. The diminution of the scale and threat of the goblins can be seen in versions by Joseph Franklin Kershaw (1913–4) and Hilda Hechle (1916).

The checklist of Rossetti-inspired pictures following this chapter makes clear the growing fascination for 'Goblin Market' that was only to become stronger through the twentieth century, attracting illustrators and scholars of every stripe.[20] The poem is now on any self-respecting syllabus of Victorian literature. The checklist also makes plain another fundamental aspect in the history of the reception of Rossetti: the strong response of female readers and, in the case of our concern here, female artists. By the end of the Victorian period, after several decades of access to professional art education, women artists were making a substantial contribution to the annual art exhibitions. For instance, at the Royal Academy exhibition of 1900, 293 (approximately 22 per cent) of the 1,320 exhibitors were women. Yet of the fifteen artists listed below who exhibited a Rossetti-inspired work between 1900 and the 1930s, nine – 60 per cent – were women. In Rossetti, women artists of this generation were able to find dramas of the mind and body that evaded resolution in conventional romance, and an imagery that was both unworldly enough to hint at a different future and was yet emotionally urgent. Several of these women were obscure figures, to be sure, and their productions not guaranteed to be of the highest quality. But some of the names are more familiar. Alyce Thornycroft of the famous Victorian sculptural dynasty was the first woman known to have exhibited a Rossetti subject – a pencil drawing, *An Apple Gathering*, with a quotation from Rossetti's poem of that name at the Dudley Gallery watercolour exhibition of 1867. Eleanor Fortescue-Brickdale is now properly recognised as a major late or neo-Pre-Raphaelite: she exhibited a subject from 'A Royal Princess' at the Academy in 1911.

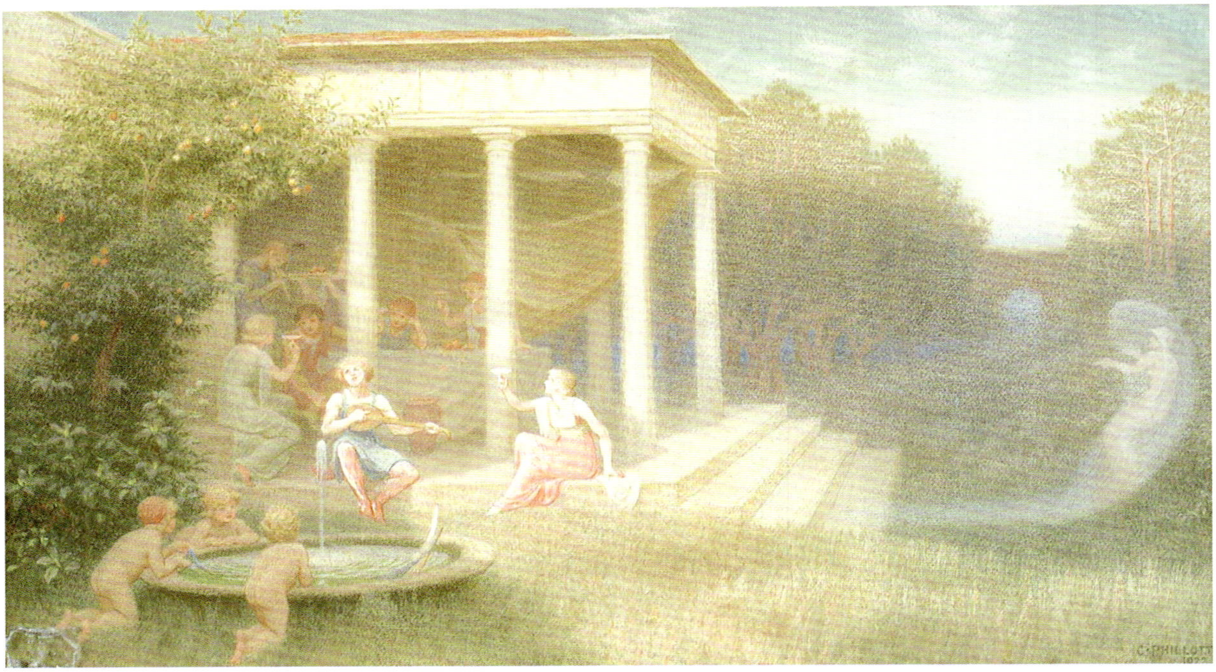

5.14 Constance Phillott,
The Ghost ('When I was dead my spirit turned / To seek the much frequented house'),
1922, oil on canvas,
29.2 × 53.3 cm.
Private collection.

As the study of the reception of Rossetti is continued, it must be hoped that more attention will be paid to responses such as Constance Phillott's picture *The Ghost,* which she created in 1922 at the age of eighty (fig. 5.14). She cites lines from 'At Home', where the writer imagines her spirit after death revisiting her home and observing the ongoing life of which she is no longer part. Phillott was a cousin of the designer William De Morgan, and her ghost subject may have been encouraged by the deep interest in spiritualism associated with De Morgan and his wife, the painter Evelyn De Morgan. As Susan Owens shows in Chapter Two, when discussing the portraits of Rossetti, no fixed formula was ever set for her representation. Equally, no clichés of visualising her poems have ever been established. Especially in the field of independent pictures, exhibited in parallel to her texts rather than in strict illustration of them, Rossetti's inward-looking and arresting verse offered endless scope for an artist to forge their own visions.

Checklist of works of art created in response to Christina Rossetti's poetry

This checklist gives basic details of independent works of art created between the 1860s and the 1930s that were inspired by Rossetti's poetry. It makes no claims to be exhaustive nor to fully document the works listed, which are treated as being distinct from commissioned illustrations (discussed in Chapter Four). Unless otherwise stated, the locations of the works are unknown.

Abbreviations:
Goblin Market and Other Poems (1862): *GM*

The Prince's Progress and Other Poems (1866): *PP*

Goblin Market, The Prince's Progress and Other Poems (1875), which included many additional poems: *GM & PP*

A Pageant and Other Poems (1881): *AP*

George R. Chapman (*fl.* 1863–1874)
Three Sisters Sang of Love Together
1863
oil on canvas
59.7 × 49.5 cm
Source: 'A Triad' (*GM*)

Dante Gabriel Rossetti (1828–1882)
Three Sang of Love Together (fig. 5.1)
c.1863–5
pencil on paper
45.1 × 32 cm
Source: 'A Triad' (*GM*)

Marcus Stone (1840–1921)
The Old Letters (fig. 5.4)
oil on canvas
71 × 92 cm
Private collection
First exhibited at the Royal Academy, 1865
Source: 'A Pause of Thought' (*GM*)

Arthur Hughes (1832–1915)
The Mower (fig. 5.2)
1865
oil on canvas
96.5 × 91.5 cm
Private collection
First exhibited at the Royal Academy, 1865
Source: 'Old and New Year Ditties (3)' (*GM*)

Arthur Hughes (1832–1915)
The Dove
1866
oil (support and dimensions unknown)
First exhibited at the French Gallery, 1866
Source: 'A Birthday' (*GM*)

Julia Margaret Cameron (1815–1879)
The Minstrel Group (fig. 5.3)
1866
albumen prints from wet collodion glass negative
The Victoria and Albert Museum, London holds several prints of this composition, two of which are inscribed: 'We sing a slow contented song / And knock at Paradise'.
Source: 'Advent' (*GM*)

Alyce Thornycroft (1844–1906)
An Apple Gathering
pencil on paper
Dimensions unknown
First exhibited at the Dudley Gallery, London (exhibition of watercolours), 1867
Source: 'An Apple Gathering' (*GM*)

Louisa Anne Beresford, Marchioness of Waterford (1818–1891)
Maiden-Song (fig. 4.9)
c.1868
watercolour on paper
18 × 13 cm
National Trust (Fenton House, London)
Source: 'Maiden-Song' (*PP*)

Frederic Shields (1833–1911)
A Royal Princess
1870
chalk drawing
First owned by Sir William Houldsworth
Source: 'A Royal Princess' (*PP*)

George Henry Boughton (1833–1905)
Two works with 'mottos' from Christina Rossetti's poems, 1872
Titles, medium, dimensions unknown

William Michael Rossetti's diary records that he visited Boughton's studio on 1 April 1872: 'Called by invitation to see Boughton's pictures for the R.A. – three subjects of human life in symbolic relation with birds, and among his most successful work, but ought to have more positiveness of truth and realisation. To two of them he has given mottos from Christina's poems'.[21] The paintings were probably *Springtime* and *The Coming of Winter* (both RA 1872) whose subjects were described in contemporary reviews as, respectively, a young woman amid orchard blossom and a young woman contemplating a dead bird in the snow.

Charles Lutwidge Dodgson (Lewis Carroll) (1832–1898)
The Birthday Wreath
1875
albumen print
15 × 8.7 cm
Princeton University Library
Source: 'A Birthday' (*GM*)

Frederick Morgan (1856–1927)
An Apple Gathering
oil on canvas
96.5 × 152.4 cm
Private collection
First exhibited at the Royal Academy, 1880
Source: 'A Year's Windfalls' (*PP*)

Edith Hipkins (*fl.* 1880–1884)
'He was born in the Spring, / And died before the harvesting'
Medium and dimensions unknown
First exhibited at the Society of Lady Artists, 1882
Source: 'An End' (*GM*)

Fernand Khnopff (1858–1921)
Who Shall Deliver Me? (Christina Georgina Rossetti) (fig. 5.6)
1890
coloured pencil on paper
22.4 × 13.4 cm
Barry Friedman, New York
First exhibited at the *Exposition d'oeuvres d'art*, Brussels, 1891
Source: 'Who Shall Deliver Me?' (*GM & PP*)

Fernand Khnopff (1858–1921)
I Lock My Door Upon Myself (Christina Georgina Rossetti) (fig. 5.7)
1891
oil on canvas
72.7 × 141 cm
Neue Pinakothek, Munich
First exhibited at *Les XX*, Brussels, 1892
Source: 'Who Shall Deliver Me?' (*GM & PP*)

Mary S. Pickett (*fl.* 1852–1909)
'Perhaps some angels read it as they move, / And cry to one another full of ruth, / "Her heart is breaking for a little love"'
watercolour on paper
Dimensions unknown
First exhibited at the Royal Academy, 1893
Source: 'L. E. L.' (*PP*)

Edward Robert Hughes (1851–1914)
'Oh what's that in the hollow...?' (fig 5.8)
1893
watercolour with bodycolour on paper
63.2 × 93.3 cm
Royal Watercolour Society
First exhibited at the Royal Society
of Painters in Water Colours, 1893
Source: 'Amor Mundi' (*GM & PP*)

Dorothea A. H. Drew (*fl.* 1896–1898)
'Does the road wind uphill all the way?'
Medium and dimensions unknown
First exhibited at the Society of
Lady Artists, 1896
Source: 'Up-Hill' (*GM*)

John Byam Shaw (1872–1919)
'While roses are so red, / While lilies are so white, / Shall a woman exalt her face / Because it gives delight?' (Beauty is Vain)
1896
pastel and watercolour
42.5 × 29.2 cm
London art market, 2013
Source: 'Beauty is Vain' (*PP*)

The following eleven works by Byam Shaw were included in his exhibition of cabinet pictures, *Thoughts Suggested by Some Passages from British Poets*, at Dowdeswell and Dowdeswell's Gallery, London, 1899:

John Byam Shaw (1872–1919)
The Prince's Progress
Medium and dimensions unknown
First exhibited at Dowdeswell's, 1899
(no. 2)
Source: 'The Prince's Progress' (*PP*)

John Byam Shaw (1872–1919)
'The Spring spreads one green lap of flowers / Which Autumn buries at the fall'
Medium and dimensions unknown
First exhibited at Dowdeswell's, 1899
(no. 4)
Source: 'Death-Watches' (*AP*)

John Byam Shaw (1872–1919)
'And all winds go sighing / For sweet things dying'
oil on board
40.6 × 30.5 cm
Portland, Maine art market, 2005
First exhibited at Dowdeswell's, 1899
(no. 11)
Source: 'A Dirge' (*GM & PP*)

John Byam Shaw (1872–1919)
Maude Clare
oil on board
22.5 × 20 cm
London art market, 2002
First exhibited at Dowdeswell's, 1899
(no. 12)
Source: 'Maude Clare' (*GM*)

John Byam Shaw (1872–1919)
'Oh it was summer when I slept, / It's winter now I waken' (fig. 5.10)
oil on panel
30.5 × 25.4 cm
London art market, 2013
First exhibited at Dowdeswell's, 1899
(no. 23)
Source: 'A Daughter of Eve' (*GM & PP*)

John Byam Shaw (1872–1919)
The Prince's Progress
Medium and dimensions unknown
First exhibited at Dowdeswell's, 1899
(no. 24)
Source: 'The Prince's Progress' (*PP*)

John Byam Shaw (1872–1919)
'While roses are so red, / While lilies are so white, / Shall a woman exalt her face / Because it gives delight?' (Beauty is Vain)
1898 (fig. 5.9)
oil on panel
40.5 × 29.5 cm
London art market, 2001
First exhibited at Dowdeswell's, 1899
(no. 30)
Source: 'Beauty is Vain' (*PP*)

John Byam Shaw (1872–1919)
'Love, strong as Death, is dead'
Medium and dimensions unknown
First exhibited at Dowdeswell's, 1899
(no. 31)
Reproduced in Malcolm Salaman, 'Lord Leverhulme's Pictures: His Modern Favourites', *Studio*, vol. 82, no. 341 (August 1921), p. 46
Source: 'An End' (*GM*)

John Byam Shaw (1872–1919)
Goblin Market
oil on panel
30.5 × 25.5 cm
First exhibited at Dowdeswell's, 1899
(no. 34)
Leyburn, North Yorks. art market, 2014
Source: 'Goblin Market' (*GM*)

John Byam Shaw (1872–1919)
Amor Mundi
oil on panel
35.6 × 25.4 cm
First exhibited at Dowdeswell's, 1899
(no. 35)
Source: 'Amor Mundi' (*GM & PP*)

John Byam Shaw (1872–1919)
'They praise my rustling show and never see my heart is breaking for a little love'
Medium and dimensions unknown
First exhibited at Dowdeswell's, 1899
(no. 38)
Reproduced in 'Some Pictures by Byam Shaw', *Studio*, vol. 16, no. 74 (May 1899), p. 264
Source: 'L. E. L.' (*PP*)

Hugh Goldwin Riviere (1869–1956)
The Lonely Life (fig. 5.15)
oil on canvas
165 × 99 cm
The Wilson, Cheltenham
First exhibited at the Royal Academy, 1899
Source: 'A Royal Princess' (*PP*)

The Hon. Mrs Walter James
(*née* Laura Gwenllian Rice) (1871–1952)
Goblin Market
oil on canvas
Dimensions unknown
First exhibited at the Royal Academy, 1900
Source: 'Goblin Market' (*GM*)

John Byam Shaw (1872–1919)
Boer War 1900 ('Last summer green things were greener')
(fig. 5.11)
oil on canvas
101.8 × 76 cm
Birmingham Museums Trust
First exhibited at the Royal Academy, 1901
Source: 'A Bird Song' (*GM & PP*)

Hilda Koe (*fl.* 1895–1901)
Goblin Market
oil on canvas
96.5 × 116.8 cm
First exhibited at the Royal Academy, 1901
Source: 'Goblin Market' (*GM*)

Amelia Bauerlë (1873–1916)
Laura and the Goblins
1901
etching
Dimensions unknown
Source: 'Goblin Market' (*GM*)

Archibald Wakley (1873–1906)
A Royal Princess ('But a vain shadow / If one considereth; / Vanity of vanities, / As the Preacher saith.')
pencil, watercolour and bodycolour heightened with gold
50.2 × 62.9 cm
First exhibited at the Royal Academy, 1903
Source: Although 'A Royal Princess' is the title of a poem by Rossetti published in *PP*, the lines beginning 'But a vain shadow' are quoted from 'Mother Country' (*GM & PP*)

Margaret Gere (1878–1965)
There's No Friend like a Sister in Calm or Stormy Weather
watercolour on paper
21.8 × 25.5 cm
Private collection
First exhibited at the New Gallery, 1903
Source: 'Goblin Market' (*GM*)

Margaret Rope (1882–1953)
Goblin Market
1905
painted, stained and leaded glass
41.3 × 41.3 cm
The Metropolitan Museum of Art, New York
Source: 'Goblin Market' (*GM*)

Margaret Rope (1882–1953)
Goblin Market
1905
painted, stained and leaded glass
Dimensions unknown
Private collection
Source: 'Goblin Market' (*GM*)

Catherine Ouless (1879–1961)
'Does the road wind uphill all the way?'
oil on canvas
Dimensions unknown
First exhibited at the Royal Academy, 1909
Source: 'Up-Hill' (*GM*)

John William Waterhouse (1849–1917)
'Spring spreads one green lap of flowers' (fig. 5.13)
oil on canvas
106 × 76.8 cm
Private collection
First exhibited at the Royal Academy, 1910
Source: 'Death-Watches' (*AP*)

Frank Craig (1874–1918)
Goblin Market (fig. 5.12)
oil on canvas
106 cm diameter (circular)
Museum of New Zealand, Te Papa Tongarewa
First exhibited at the Royal Academy, 1911
Source: 'Goblin Market' (*GM*)

Eleanor Fortescue-Brickdale (1872–1945)
'The dove that must not coo – eagle that must not soar'
watercolour
Dimensions unknown
First exhibited at the Leicester Galleries, 1911
Source: 'A Royal Princess' (*PP*)

Joseph Franklin Kershaw (1884–1917)
Goblin Market
1913–14
oil on canvas
127 × 76.2 cm
Private collection
Source: 'Goblin Market' (*GM*)

Hilda Hechle (1886–1939)
Goblin Market ('Buy from us with a golden curl')
watercolour
Dimensions unknown
First exhibited at the Royal Academy, 1916
Source: 'Goblin Market' (*GM*)

Constance Phillott (1842–1931)
The Ghost ('When I was dead, my spirit turned / To seek the much frequented house') (fig. 5.14)
1922
oil on canvas
29.2 × 53.3 cm
Private collection
Reproduced in A. M. W. Stirling, *Life's Little Day*, 1924
Source: 'At Home' (*GM*)

Gertrude Demain Hammond (1862–1952)
'Flowers preach to us if we will hear'
watercolour
Dimensions unknown
First exhibited at the Royal Institute of Painters in Watercolours, Centenary Exhibition, 1931
Source: '"Consider the Lilies of the Field"' (*GM*)

René Cloke (1905–1995)
Goblin Market
c.1920–1940
Medium and dimensions unknown
Private collection
Source: 'Goblin Market' (*GM*)

Primrose Harley (1908–1978)
Goblin Market
c.1930–1940
pen, ink and watercolour
29.8 × 20.3 cm
Source: 'Goblin Market' (*GM*)

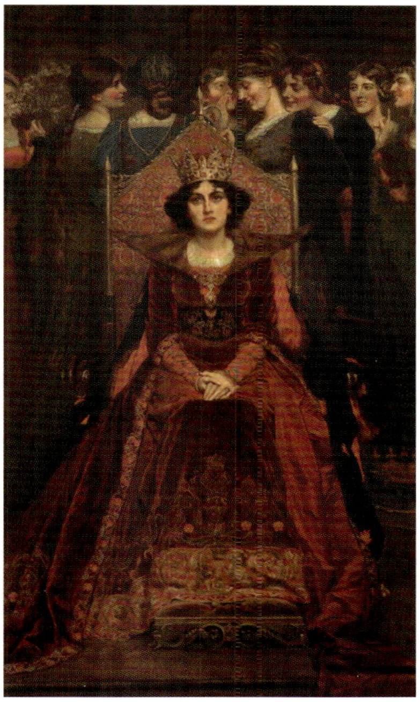

5.15 Hugh Goldwin Riviere, *The Lonely Life*, 1899, oil on canvas, 165 × 99 cm. The Wilson, Cheltenham.

Chronology TESSA KILGARRIFF

CGR (Christina Georgina Rossetti); **DGR** (Dante Gabriel Rossetti); **WMR** (William Michael Rossetti)

Christina Georgina Rossetti	Rossetti Family	Cultural Events
1830 5 December: Christina Georgina Rossetti born at 38 Charlotte Street (now Hallam Street), London. CGR has three older siblings: Maria Francesca (b. 1827), Dante Gabriel (b. 1828) and William Michael (b. 1829)		
1831	Gabriele Rossetti becomes professor of Italian at King's College London	
1832		Reform Bill passes
1833		Alfred Lord Tennyson publishes *The Lady of Shalott*
1835	Rossetti family moves to 50 Charlotte Street	
1838		The new National Gallery building opens on Trafalgar Square, with the Royal Academy sharing the premises
1839		First Anglo-Afghan War (1839–1842); 14 June: presentation of the first Chartist petition to the House of Commons (swiftly rejected)
1840		John Everett Millais enters the RA schools, aged eleven Publication of Charles Eastlake's translation of Goethe's *Theory of Colours*
1841		Launch of mass-circulation periodical *Punch* Sir Robert Peel leads Conservative majority government
1842 Writes first known poetry: stanzas for her mother's birthday		Launch of the *Illustrated London News*
1843		John Ruskin publishes *Modern Painters: Volume 1*
1844		Publication of Elizabeth Barrett Browning's *Poems*
1845 Dr Hare attends CGR's first health breakdown	William Michael Rossetti begins work at the Excise Office, aged sixteen	The Museums Act receives Royal Assent J. H. Newman converts to Roman Catholicism

Christina Georgina Rossetti	Rossetti Family	Cultural Events
1846		Repeal of the Corn Laws
1847 *Verses* privately printed		Publication of Emily Brontë's *Wuthering Heights*
1848 Introduced to James Collinson; they become engaged before the end of the year		Founding of the Pre-Raphaelite Brotherhood by William Holman Hunt, John Everett Millais, Dante Gabriel Rossetti, William Michael Rossetti, James Collinson, Frederic George Stephens and Thomas Woolner
1849	Dante Gabriel Rossetti exhibits *The Girlhood of Mary Virgin* at the Free Exhibition	
1850 James Collinson reverts to Catholicism; CGR ends their engagement	Publication of DGR's 'The Blessed Damozel'	January: publication of the first number of *The Germ*, the Pre-Raphaelite literary journal; Collinson resigns from the PRB Publication of Tennyson's *In Memoriam A.H.H.*
1851 Starts attending the North London School of Drawing and Modelling	Rossetti family moves to 38 Arlington Street; CGR and her mother open a day school	Ruskin's pamphlet on Pre-Raphaelitism published The Great Exhibition of the Works of Industry of All Nations opens at the Crystal Palace Publication of Henry Mayhew's *London Labour and the London Poor* Publication of Ruskin's *The Stones of Venice: Volume 1*
1852 Tutors the children of Swynfen Jervis in Italian at their home in Staffordshire, Darlaston Hall		Millais completes his painting *Ophelia* Death of the 1st Duke of Wellington
1853	CGR moves with her parents to Brunswick Terrace, Frome, Somerset to open a day school	
1854 CGR begins writing for John Francis Waller's *Imperial Dictionary of Universal Biography*; applies to undertake nursing in Crimea but is rejected	Rossetti family moves to 45 Upper Albany Street; 24 April: death of Gabriele Rossetti, the poet's father	Crystal Palace opens at Sydenham, after removal from Hyde Park William Holman Hunt exhibits *The Light of the World* and its counterpart *The Awakening Conscience* at the Royal Academy Britain enters the Crimean War

Christina Georgina Rossetti	Rossetti Family	Cultural Events
1855		Stamp Act passes, reducing the cost of newspapers
1856 Friendship with John Brett begins		Elizabeth Barrett Browning publishes *Aurora Leigh* Petition for Reform of the Married Women's Property Law presented
1857		Pre-Raphaelite Art Exhibition, Russell Square, London; Manchester Art Treasures Exhibition Publication of the Moxon & Co. edition of Tennyson's *Poems*, with illustrations by DGR, Millais, Holman Hunt and other artists Matrimonial Causes Act legalises divorce and provides protection for divorced women's property
1858		*English Woman's Journal* publishes first issue
1859 Begins working as a volunteer at St Mary Magdalene Penitentiary on Highgate Hill		National Portrait Gallery opens at first premises, 29 George Street, Westminster *All the Year Round* and *Macmillian's Magazine* publish first issues
1860	23 May: DGR marries Elizabeth Siddall; honeymoon in Paris	*Cornhill Magazine* publishes first issue
1861 Works on *Goblin Market and Other Poems*; travels in France with mother and WMR		
1862 Publication of *Goblin Market and Other Poems*, with illustrations by DGR (Macmillan & Co.)	11 February: death of Elizabeth Siddall, DGR's wife; DGR moves to Tudor House, Cheyne Walk	William Powell Frith exhibits *The Railway Station* at the Fine Arts Gallery
1863	Charles Lutwidge Dodgson photographs the Rossetti family at Cheyne Walk	
1864 For her health CGR spends winter in Hastings with her uncle Henry and cousin Henrietta Polydore	Rossetti family home renumbered to 166 Albany Street	Publication of J. H. Newman's *Apologia Pro Vita Sua*

Christina Georgina Rossetti	Rossetti Family	Cultural Events
1865 A second edition of *Goblin Market* is published by Macmillan & Co.; CGR travels in Europe		
1866 Publication of *The Prince's Progress and Other Poems*, with illustrations by DGR (Macmillan & Co.); Charles Bagot Cayley proposes marriage to CGR and is refused	September: DGR makes portrait of CGR in coloured chalks (fig. 2.25)	
1867	Aunt Margaret Polidori dies; CGR, her mother, Maria Francesca Rossetti, WMR and aunts Eliza and Charlotte move to 56 Euston Square	Royal Academy obtains a 999-year lease at its new home, Burlington House Second Reform Act
1869 Ill health continues		University of Oxford appoints Ruskin as Slade Professor of Art Suez Canal opens
1870 Publication of *Commonplace and Other Short Stories* (F. S. Ellis); poor sales of *Commonplace* disappoint Ellis and CGR cancels contract with him to publish *Sing-Song*	Publication of DGR's *Poems*	Franco-Prussian war begins in July; Married Women's Property Act passes, establishing limited protections for some separate property for married women, including the right to retain up to £200 of any earning or inheritance
1871 CGR spends time at Hampstead and Folkestone in attempt to revive poor health		October: Publication of 'The Fleshly School of Poetry' in *The Contemporary Review*: Robert Buchanan's article condemns the poetry of DGR and his circle December: DGR responds with 'The Stealthy School of Criticism' Publication of George Eliot's *Middlemarch* (appears in eight parts between 1871–2)
1872 Publication of *Sing-Song: A Nursery Rhyme Book*, with illustrations by Arthur Hughes (Routledge); diagnosed with Graves' disease	DGR suffers mental breakdown	
1873		Publication of Walter Pater's *Studies in the History of the Renaissance*

Christina Georgina Rossetti	Rossetti Family	Cultural Events
1874 Publication of *Speaking Likenesses*, with illustrations by Arthur Hughes (Macmillan & Co.) and of *Annus Domini* (James Parker)	WMR marries Lucy Madox Brown	Dissolution of Morris, Marshall, Faulkner & Co.
1875 Publication of *Goblin Market, Prince's Progress and Other Poems* (Macmillan & Co.)	30 September: Olivia (Olive) Rossetti born to WMR and Lucy Madox Brown Rossetti	Morris & Co. founded
1876 CGR moves with mother and aunts to 30 Torrington Square	24 November: death of Maria Francesca Rossetti	
1877 CGR attends ailing DGR at Cheyne Walk and Herne Bay with their mother	DGR completes portraits in coloured chalks of CGR and their mother at Herne Bay (figs 2.27–2.29)	Grosvenor Gallery holds first exhibition
1878		Whistler–Ruskin trial begins Exposition Universelle, Paris
1879 Publication of *Seek and Find: A Double Series of Short Studies of the Benedicite* (SPCK)		
1880 Publication of *Called to be Saints: The Minor Festivals Devotionally Studied*, with illustrations by 'T.S.' (SPCK) and of *A Pageant and Other Poems* (Macmillan & Co.)		
1882 CGR receives invitation from John Ingram to write a biography of Adelaide Proctor or Elizabeth Barrett Browning for Ingram's series *Eminent Women*; she declines EBB	9 April: death of Dante Gabriel Rossetti	Married Women's Property Act significantly increases the scope and protections for married women's acquisition and retention of property separate from their husbands
1883 Publication of *Letter and Spirit: Notes on the Commandments* (SPCK); petitions for antivivisection and minors' rights (until 1885)		Publication of Algernon Charles Swinburne's *A Century of Roundels*, dedicated to CGR
1885 Publication of *Time Flies: A Reading Diary* (SPCK)		Criminal Law Amendment Act raises the female age of consent from thirteen to sixteen

Christina Georgina Rossetti	Rossetti Family	Cultural Events
1886	8 April: death of Frances Rossetti	
1887 CGR sent to Torquay for her health		
1889		Trade Union agitation in London
1890 Publication of *Poems: New and Enlarged Edition* (Macmillan & Co.)		
1892 Publication of *The Face of the Deep: A Devotional Commentary on the Apocalypse* (SPCK); CGR has cancer surgery		Start of Gladstone's final premiership
1893 Publication of *Goblin Market*, with illustrations by Laurence Housman and *Verses* (SPCK); CGR's cancer returns		6 October: death of Ford Madox Brown
1894 29 December: death of Christina Georgina Rossetti	12 April: death of Lucy Madox Brown Rossetti	
1896 Publication of *New Poems*, edited by WMR (Macmillan & Co.)		13 August: death of John Everett Millais; 3 October: death of William Morris
1897 Publication of *Maude* (Bowden)		
1898 Publication of *Christina Rossetti: A Biographical and Critical Study* by Mackenzie Bell (Hurst & Blackett)		17 June: death of Edward Burne-Jones
1903 Publication of *Redeeming the Time* (SPCK)		
1904 Publication of *The Poetical Works of Christina Georgina Rossetti*, edited by WMR (Macmillan & Co.)		

Notes

Introduction

1 Jan Marsh, *Christina Rossetti: A Literary Biography* (London: Faber & Faber, 2012), p. 39.

2 Stuart Macdonald, *The History and Philosophy of Art Education* (London: University of London Press, 1970), p. 146. See also Matthew Potter, 'Fostering in the People the Purest Types of Beauty: Ford Madox Brown and Democratic Art Education', *Visual Culture in Britain*, vol. 15, no. 3 (2014), pp. 316–7.

3 William Bell Scott, *Autobiographical Notes*, 1, ed. W. Minto (London: Osgood, McIlvaine, 1892), p. 279.

4 The North London School of Drawing and Modelling was among the drawing schools set up for artisans to raise the standard of British design in the mid-nineteenth century. See Susan Owens, '"Straight lines are a national want": South Kensington and Art Education Reform' in *Art and Design For All: The Victoria and Albert Museum*, ed. Julius Bryant (London: V&A Publishing, 2011), pp. 75–81.

5 *The Letters of Christina Rossetti*, 1, ed. Antony H. Harrison (Charlottesville: University Press of Virginia, 1997–2004), p. 341.

6 Helen Rossetti Angeli, 'Aunt Christina: An Elusive Poet-Mystic', newspaper cutting dated 5 December 1930, in Private Collection: British Library, London, Loan MS 113, folder 6.

7 Mackenzie Bell, *Christina Rossetti: A Biographical and Critical Study* (London: Hurst and Blackett, 1898), pp. 70–71.

Chapter One

1 Anon., 'The Christina Rossetti Memorial, Sir Edward Burne-Jones's Last Work', *Magazine of Art* (December 1899), pp. 88–90; Colette M. Crossman, 'Art as Lived Religion: Edward Burne-Jones as Painter, Priest, Pilgrim, and Monk', PhD thesis (University of Maryland, 2007), pp. 211–20. The five-panelled painting was described as a reredos and showed 'Christ uttering the words of consecration of the eucharistic elements, and the four Evangelists as recorders of the event': *The Poetical Works of Christina Georgina Rossetti. With Memoir and Notes &c*, ed. William Michael Rossetti (London: Macmillan & Co., 1904), p. lix. The churches that Rossetti attended in Woburn Square (from 1876) and, earlier, in Albany Street (from 1843), shared the same dedication: Christ Church.

2 Mackenzie Bell, *Christina Rossetti: A Biographical and Critical Study* (London: Hurst and Blackett, 1898), pp. 142, 151.

3 Rossetti's use of the rooms of the house is explored by Diane D'Amico in 'The House of Christina Rossetti: Domestic and Poetic Spaces', *Journal of Pre-Raphaelite Studies*, no. 19 (Spring 2010), pp. 31–54. The house was built in the 1820s; the plaque was added around 1913.

4 Bell, *Christina Rossetti*, 1898, pp. 150–52. Rossetti admired the artist James Smetham on the same grounds of religious sympathy: Christina Rossetti, *The Letters of Christina Rossetti*, 2, ed. Antony H. Harrison (Charlottesville: University Press of Virginia, 1997–2004), p. 162. Her deathbed was placed directly below the Shields print: Bell, *Christina Rossetti*, 1898, p. 175.

5 The *Athenaeum* quoted in *The Autotype: A Decorative and Educational Art* (London: The Autotype Company, 1888), p. 25.

6 William Michael Rossetti, 'List of Works of Art framed or otherwise displayed in No.3 St. Edmund's Terrace ... 6 Decr. 1908', Rare Books & Special Collections, Library of the University of British Columbia, Vancouver, Angeli-Dennis collection, RBAC-ARC-1009-18-04.

7 W. M. Rossetti, 'List of Works of Art', 1908, no. 239.

8 W. M. Rossetti, 'List of Works of Art', 1908, no. 194; *Letters*, 1, 1997–2004, pp. 208–9, 219. Rossetti had herself made pencil illustrations to the poem: *Poetical Works*, 1904, p. 479. Also in this class of anthropomorphic humour were three comic studies of wombats given by Edward Burne-Jones to Christina: William Michael Rossetti, *Some Reminiscences*, 1 (London: Brown, Langham, 1906), p. 285.

9 When an engraving after the popular eighteenth-century rustic painter George Morland came into her hands around 1880, her first thought was to give it away: *Letters*, 4, 1997–2004, p. 418.

10 *Letters*, 3, 1997–2004, p. 106. In 1883 several pictures sent in for loan were not exhibited for want of space: *Whitechapel Fine Art Loan Exhibition*, exh. cat., St Jude's School House, London, 1883, p. 24.

11 Papers relating to Christina Rossetti's estate, National Archives, Kew, IR 59/163. Various books, objects, prints and photographs were subsequently sold at Sotheby's, 30 July–3 August 1895, 3rd day, lots 737–71.

12 Bell, *Christina Rossetti*, 1898, p. 145.

13 'Who Shall Deliver Me?', composed 1864.

14 Christina Rossetti, *Letter and Spirit: Notes on the Commandments* (London: SPCK, 1883), p. 104.

15 Christina Rossetti, *Seek and Find: A Double Series of Short Studies of the Benedicite* (London: SPCK, 1879), p. 14. On Rossetti's beatific vision, see also Esther T. Hu, 'Christina Rossetti, John Keble, and the Divine Gaze', *Victorian Poetry*, vol. 46, no. 2 (2008), pp. 175–89.

16 Christina Rossetti, *Called to be Saints: The Minor Festivals Devotionally Studied* (London: SPCK, 1881), p. 457: she glosses this typologically with two Old Testament passages, from Psalm 92 and Job 31:1 ('I made a covenant with mine eyes').

17 Rossetti herself owned one of these studies of Siddall (a drawing of her seated: W. M. Rossetti, 'List of Works of Art', 1908, no. 21, now in the Tate collection, N04628) as well as a couple of drawings by Siddall herself: William Michael Rossetti, *Selected Letters*, ed. Roger W. Peattie (University Park: Pennsylvania State University Press, 1990), p. 587.

18 *Letters*, 1, 1997–2004, p. 254. Anne Gilchrist was the widow of Alexander Gilchrist: she collaborated with the Rossetti brothers to complete her husband's pioneering biography of William Blake in 1863.

19 Christina Rossetti, *Time Flies: A Reading Diary* (London: SPCK, 1885), p. 111; cf. 'Later Life: A Double Sonnet of Sonnets', § 22 (first published 1881).

20 *Letters*, 1, 1997–2004, p. 110 (1857); Rossetti, *Times Flies*, 1885, pp. 4–5. Emma Mason's recent work returns to the theme of Rossetti's engagement with the natural world, from an ecological perspective: see her '"Whales and all that move in the waters": Christina Rossetti's ecology of grace' in Wendy Parkins (ed.), *Victorian Sustainability in Literature and Culture* (London: Routledge, 2018), pp. 69–84 and *Christina Rossetti: Poetry, Ecology, Faith* (Oxford: Oxford University Press, 2018).

21 H. C. Marillier, *Dante Gabriel Rossetti: An Illustrated Memorial of his Art and Life* (London: George Bell, 1899), p. 213.

22 D. G. Rossetti, *His Family-Letters: With a Memoir by William Michael Rossetti*, 1 (London: Ellis, 1895), p. 99; Lorraine Janzen Kooistra, *Christina Rossetti and Illustration: A Publishing History* (Athens: Ohio University Press, 2002), p. 280, n. 15.

23 W. M. Rossetti, 'List of Works of Art', 1908, nos. 56, 68.

24 Jan Marsh, *Christina Rossetti: A Literary Biography* (London: Faber & Faber, 2012), pp. 320–21. Maria Rossetti (1827–1876), the eldest of the Rossetti siblings, was an author and Anglican nun, joining the All Saints Sisters of the Poor (allied to All Saints, Margaret Street) in 1860, entering their convent in 1873 and becoming a full sister in 1875, the year before her early death. See Mary Arseneau, *Recovering*

Christina Rossetti (Basingstoke: Palgrave Macmillan, 2004), pp. 60–63.

25 Bell, *Christina Rossetti*, 1898, pp. 38, 50, 53; *Letters*, 1, 1997–2004, pp. 163, 165, 389; *Letters*, 2, 1997–2004, p. 206; *Letters*, 3, 1997–2004, p. 344; *Letters*, 4, 1997–2004, pp. 203, 258.

26 Bell, *Christina Rossetti*, 1898, p. 121; *Letters*, 3, 1997–2004, pp. 92, 98, 248. The affection for the pictures must have been coloured by the poet's liking of the model: they had spent a companionable summer together at Kelmscott Manor in 1873.

27 *Letters*, 3, 1997–2004, p. 92.

28 *The Correspondence of Dante Gabriel Rossetti*, 1, ed. William E. Fredeman (Cambridge: D. S. Brewer, 2002–15), p. 294 (8 November 1853). John Woolford has suggested Christina found her brother's imagery 'repressive and coercive' and sought strategies to evade it: 'The Advent of Christina Rossetti', *Review of English Studies*, vol. 62, no. 256 (2011), pp. 618–39.

29 *Letters*, 1, 1997–2004, p. 17.

30 William Holman Hunt, *Pre-Raphaelitism and the Pre-Raphaelite Brotherhood*, 1 (London: Macmillan & Co., 1905), pp. 158–60; Isobel Armstrong, 'The Pre-Raphaelites and Literature', in *The Cambridge Companion to the Pre-Raphaelites*, ed. Elizabeth Prettejohn (Cambridge: Cambridge University Press, 2012), p. 16; Elizabeth Ludlow, 'Christina Rossetti and the Pre-Raphaelites', in *The Oxford Handbook of the Oxford Movement*, eds Stewart J. Brown, Peter B. Nockles and James Pereiro (Oxford: Oxford University Press, 2017), pp. 427–40. For the larger problem of the tensions between religion and romanticism in Tractarian aesthetics, see Gregory H. Goodwin, 'Keble and Newman: Tractarian Aesthetics and the Romantic Tradition', *Victorian Studies*, vol. 30, no. 4 (1987), pp. 475–94.

31 *The Germ. Thoughts towards Nature in Poetry, Literature and Art. Being A Facsimile Reprint of the Literary Organ of the Pre-Raphaelite Brotherhood, published in 1850* (London: Elliot Stock, 1901), p. 117: this is the last stanza of three.

32 *Letters*, 1, 1997–2004, p. 32 (18 January 1850).

33 Ford Madox Brown, 'On the Mechanism of a Historical Picture', *The Germ*, p. 71.

34 Angela Thirlwell, *Into the Frame: The Four Loves of Ford Madox Brown* (London: Chatto & Windus, 2010), p. 112. See also *Letters*, 1, 1997–2004, p. 71; Marsh, *Christina Rossetti*, 2012, p. 128; Kooistra, *Christina Rossetti and Illustration*, 2002, pp. 23–24; Matthew Potter, 'Fostering in the People the Purest Types of Beauty: Ford Madox Brown and Democratic Art Education', *Visual Culture in Britain*, vol. 15, no. 3 (2014), pp. 313–33.

35 Ronald Parkinson, 'James Collinson', in *Pre-Raphaelite Papers*, ed. Leslie Parris (London: Tate Gallery, 1984), pp. 221–2, n. 32.

36 For the controversy, see Devon Fisher, *Roman Catholic Saints and Early Victorian Literature: Conservatism, Liberalism, and the Emergence of Secular Culture* (Farnham: Ashgate, 2012), pp. 89–98; for Collinson's picture, see Alastair Grieve, 'A Notice on Illustrations to Charles Kingsley's "The Saint's Tragedy"', *Burlington Magazine*, vol. 111 (1969), pp. 290–93 and D. M. R. Bentley, 'The Principal Pre-Raphaelite Pictures of James Collinson', *Victorian Review*, vol. 30, no. 1 (2004), pp. 21–43.

37 *Letters*, 1, 1997–2004, pp. 34, 40, 42; Marsh, *Christina Rossetti*, 2012, pp. 117–8.

38 William Rossetti assumed the poem was inspired by Collinson's painting (*Poetical Works*, 1904, p. 470); see also Marsh, *Christina Rossetti*, 2012, p. 137.

39 The poem claims that William Rossetti 'lops / His B.s', that is, he slashes at his Pre-Raphaelite Brothers in his role as art critic for *The Spectator* in which he had indeed made less than favourable remarks about Collinson.

40 *Poetical Works*, 1904, p. 479. The revised title is taken from *As You Like It*, II.i.

41 D. M. R. Bentley, 'A Possible Pictorial Inspiration for Christina Rossetti's "The Prince's Progress"', *Journal of Pre-Raphaelite Studies*, no. 9 (Fall 2000), pp. 51–4.

42 *Letters*, 1, 1997–2004, p. 145.

43 Ibid., pp. 72, 200. Rossetti showed more enthusiasm for other pictures by Millais, including his *The Proscribed Royalist, 1651* (1853): ibid., p. 72.

44 Linda K. Hughes, 'Inventing Poetry and Pictorialism in *Once a Week*: A Magazine of Visual Effects', *Victorian Poetry*, vol. 48, no. 1 (2010), pp. 60–63.

45 See Lorraine Janzen Kooistra, *Poetry, Pictures, and Popular Publishing: The Illustrated Gift Book and Victorian Visual Culture* (Athens: Ohio University Press, 2011), ch. 2. Rossetti owned – briefly – a copy of G. S. Layard's *Tennyson and his Pre-Raphaelite Illustrators*, published in the year of her death (lot 753 in Sotheby's 1895 sale, as in note 11).

46 Edmund Gosse, *Critical Kit-Kats* (London: Heinemann, 1900), p. 144; [John Ingram] Felix de Salamanca, *pseud.*, *The Philosophy of Handwriting* (London: Chatto & Windus, 1879), p. 119. For other early critiques of Rossetti that made such visual parallels to Pre-Raphaelite styles, see Edna Kotin Charles, *Christina Rossetti: Critical Perspectives, 1862–1982* (Selinsgrove, PA: Susquehanna University Press, 1985), pp. 42–3 and Antony H. Harrison, *Christina Rossetti in Context* (Brighton: Harvester, 1988), pp. 27–8.

47 *Letters*, 1, 1997–2004, p. 30; for the Holbeins, see Mary Louisa Boyle, *Biographical Catalogue of the Portraits at Longleat* (London: Elliot Stock, 1881), nos. 4, 10, 11, 24, 85, 93, 94, 157.

48 See Julian Treuherz, *Ford Madox Brown: Pre-Raphaelite Pioneer*, exh. cat. (Manchester: Manchester Art Gallery, 2011), no. 29 (1846).

49 *Letters*, 4, 1997–2004, p. 268 (1892); Mary Bennett, *Ford Madox Brown. A Catalogue Raisonné* (New Haven and London: Yale University Press, 2010), B.86. The portrait has recently been rediscovered and is published here for the first time. I am grateful to Alison Smith of the National Portrait Gallery, London, for facilitating this.

50 The significance of '*page 122*' at the end of the inscription is a puzzle: it does not match any of the printings of 'Christmas Eve' during William Michael Rossetti's lifetime. Possibly he became confused with the page numbering of 'A Christmas Carol: In the Bleak Mid-winter', which appears on p. 221 of the 1875 collection of his sister's works. As the original painting by Von Hess remained in Germany, Christina would have known the picture from an impression of the print inscribed by her brother.

51 Rossetti, *Time Flies*, 1885, p. 38. On Rossetti and Blake, see Bell, *Christina Rossetti*, 1898, pp. 308, 320–21.

52 *Letters*, 2, 1997–2004, p. 153; see also *Letters*, 1, 1997–2004, p. 403 for further caricatures sent to Rossetti and received with appreciation.

53 Rossetti, *Letter and Spirit*, 1883, p. 131: cf. *Seek and Find*, 1879, p. 244: 'All the world over, visible things typify things invisible'. An exception to Rossetti's antipathy to the picturesque – such as I am arguing for – was her admiration of Whistler's *Wapping* at the Royal Academy in 1864 (*Letters*, 1, 1997–2004, p. 200). I have left Ruskin out of my discussion, but on Rossetti's engagement with some of his ideas, see Serena Trowbridge, *Christina Rossetti's Gothic* (London: Bloomsbury Academic, 2015), ch. 3.

54 Rossetti, *Time Flies*, 1885, p. 35. The nearest things to a sculpture that Rossetti appears to have possessed were a decorative paperweight in the form of a spaniel, made and given by a family

friend (*Letters*, 1, 1997–2004, pp. 45–6), and a Minton vase with applied modelled creatures including a snake and toads (a gift from Gabriel, now in the Museum of London: see D'Amico, 'The House of Christina Rossetti', 2010).

55 *Letters*, 3, 1997–2004, pp. 164–5; Frederic Shields, *The Life and Letters of Frederic Shields*, ed. Ernestine Mills (London: Longmans, Green & Co., 1912), pp. 247–8; Marsh, *Christina Rossetti*, 2012, pp. 478–9, 516–7. Earlier, in her short story 'Hero', collected in *Commonplace and Other Short Stories* (London: Ellis, 1870), fairies appear as teachers of harsh moral truths.

56 Rossetti, *Time Flies*, 1885, p. 71; Bell, *Christina Rossetti*, 1898, p. 61.

57 Among key work is: Mary Arseneau, 'Symbol and Sacrament: The Incarnational Aesthetic of Christina Rossetti', PhD dissertation (University of Western Ontario, 1991); Robert M. Kachur, 'Repositioning the Female Christian Reader: Christina Rossetti as Tractarian Hermeneut in "The Face of the Deep"', *Victorian Poetry*, vol. 35, no. 2 (1997), pp. 193–214; Diane D'Amico, *Christina Rossetti: Faith, Gender, and Time* (Baton Rouge: Louisiana State University Press, 1999); Emma Mason, '"A Sort of Aesthetico-Catholic revival": Christina Rossetti and the London Ritualist Scene', *Outsiders Looking In: The Rossettis Then and Now*, eds David Clifford and Laurence Roussillon (London: Anthem Press, 2004), pp. 115–30; Diane D'Amico and David A. Kent, 'Rossetti and the Tractarians', *Victorian Poetry*, vol. 44, no. 1 (2006), pp. 93–104; Dinah Roe, *Christina Rossetti's Faithful Imagination: The Devotional Poetry and Prose* (Basingstoke: Palgrave Macmillan, 2006), ch. 1; Karen Dieleman, *Religious Imaginaries: The Liturgical and Poetic Practices of Elizabeth Barrett Browning, Christina Rossetti, and Adelaide Procter* (Athens: Ohio University Press, 2012), ch. 3.

58 See Emma Mason, 'Christina Rossetti and the Doctrine of Reserve', *Journal of Victorian Culture*, vol. 7, iss. 2 (2002), pp. 196–219.

59 Marsh, *Christina Rossetti*, 2012, p. 52.

60 Henry William Burrows, *The Half-Century of Christ Church, Albany Street, St. Pancras* (London: Skeffington, 1887). Dodsworth 'went over' to Rome in 1850.

61 *Maude: Prose & Verse by Christina Rossetti*, ed. William Michael Rossetti (Chicago: Stone, 1897), pp. 47–8, 67–8. The poem quoted here was not included in the first London edition of *Maude* (Bowden, 1897) for copyright reasons; it appears in the *Complete Poems* as 'St. Andrew's Church'.

62 The expression is William Michael Rossetti's: *Maude*, 1897a, p. 4.

63 Christ Church was changed and decorated in the late 1860s by the High Church movement's favourite architect, William Butterfield, after which Rossetti felt it had been 'improved' (*Letters*, 1, 1997–2004, p. 419). In 1853, Gabriel Rossetti had written to his sister that the church's appearance was 'very poor' (D. G. Rossetti, *Family-Letters*, 2, 1895, p. 121): he contributed a design for a Morris & Co. window of *The Sermon on the Mount* that formed part of the new decorative scheme. Dieleman, *Religious Imaginaries*, 2012, pp. 121–4 emphasises Christina Rossetti's interest in such decorative features as there were. It is worth noting that the changes of the 1860s at Christ Church were prompted by the desire to open up the church's seating to all, ending the system of renting pews that had restricted the congregation to the better-heeled, a decision in sympathy with Rossetti's own opinions: Burrows, *Half-Century of Christ Church*, 1887, pp. 47–8; Mary Arseneau, 'Pews, Periodicals and Politics: The Rossetti Women as High Church Controversialists' in *Outsiders Looking In: The Rossettis Then and Now*, ed. David Clifford and Laurence Roussillon (London: Anthem Press, 2004), pp. 97–113.

64 Harrison, *Christina Rossetti in Context*, 1988, pp. 87–8. One of Rossetti's favoured Tractarian authors, Isaac Williams, warned against 'the proud and curious eye / Of connoisseur' in beautiful ancient churches: *The Cathedral* (Oxford: Parker, 1839), p. 19.

65 See David Hilliard, 'Unenglish and Unmanly: Anglo-Catholicism and Homosexuality', *Victorian Studies*, vol. 25, no. 2 (1982), pp. 181–210; Mary Arseneau, *Recovering Christina Rossetti: Female Community and Incarnational Poetics* (Basingstoke: Palgrave Macmillan, 2004).

66 Collected in *Commonplace* (1870), pp. 145–63.

67 *The Face of the Deep: A Devotional Commentary on the Apocalypse* (London: SPCK, 1892), p. 99; Mason, 'Christina Rossetti and the Doctrine of Reserve', 2002, pp. 210–11.

68 For a survey, see John Manning, *The Emblem* (London: Reaktion, 2002).

69 Diane D'Amico, 'Christina Rossetti's *Christian Year*: Comfort for "the weary heart"', *Victorian Newsletter*, vol. 72 (1987), pp. 36–42; Kooistra, *Christina Rossetti and Illustration*, 2002, pp. 29–38. Keble himself defended abstruse symbolism, allegory and 'emblems' (understood as symbolism working between elements of scripture and between scripture and the world) as theologically sound: *On the Mysticism Attributed to the Early Fathers of the Church: Tracts for the Times*, no. 89 (London: Rivington, 1841). Rossetti added similar drawings to at least three further books by authors other than herself that were evidently of special significance to her: Isaac Williams's *The Altar* (published 1847), her father Gabriele's *L'Arpa evangelica* (Genoa, 1852) and her sister Maria's *A Shadow of Dante* (1871): see *Poetical Works*, 1904, p. 471; Kooistra, *Christina Rossetti and Illustration*, 2002, pp. 28, 277, n. 9.

70 *Poetical Works*, 1904, p. 464.

71 Ibid., pp. 465–6.

72 Ibid., p. 460. In addition to *Verses* and *Goblin Market*, Rossetti also added illustrations to a copy of *Seek and Find*.

73 Chapman's painting was sold to Leathart late in 1863 and was still in the family collection when lent to the exhibition of *Paintings and Drawings from the Leathart Collection* held at the Laing Art Gallery in Newcastle in 1968 (no. 32); it is presently untraced. See D. G. Rossetti, *Family-Letters*, 2, 1895, p. 185; William Michael Rossetti in the *Art Journal*, 1896, p. 132; Bell, *Christina Rossetti*, 1898, p. 213; W. M. Rossetti, *Selected Letters*, 1990, p. 192, n. 6; Kooistra, *Christina Rossetti and Illustration*, 2002, p. 83.

74 Christina Rossetti, *Speaking Likenesses* (London: Macmillan & Co., 1874), pp. 77–9.

75 *Letters*, 2, 1997–2004, pp. 30–31.

76 *Letters*, 2, 1997–2004, p. 109; Gisela Hönnighausen, 'Emblematic Tendencies in the Works of Christina Rossetti', *Victorian Poetry*, vol. 10, no. 1 (1972), pp. 1–15; Kooistra, *Christina Rossetti and Illustration*, 2002, pp. 149–61.

77 *Letters*, 1, 1997–2004, p. 436; early musical settings of Rossetti's words are listed by Maura Ives, *Christina Rossetti: A Descriptive Bibliography* (New Castle, DE: Oak Knoll Press, 2011), pp. 249–94.

78 Susan Conley, '"Poet's Right": Christina Rossetti as Anti-Muse and the Legacy of the "Poetess"', *Victorian Poetry*, vol. 32, nos 3–4 (1994), pp. 365–86.

Chapter Two

1 *The Letters of Christina Rossetti*, 1, ed. Antony H. Harrison (Charlottesville: University Press of Virginia, 1997–2004), p. 55.

2 William Michael Rossetti, *Some Reminiscences*, 1 (London: Brown, Langham, 1906), pp. 3 and 12–13.
3 William Bell Scott made an etching from this earlier watercolour, which he illustrated in his *Autobiographical Notes*, 1, ed. W. Minto (London: Osgood, McIlvaine, 1892), facing p. 248.
4 See the entry 'Pistrucci, Filippo', *Treccani* website, accessed June 2018, available at www.treccani.it/enciclopedia/filippo-pistrucci_%28Dizionario-Biografico%29/.
5 William Michael Rossetti, 'Memoir', in *The Poetical Works of Christina Georgina Rossetti. With Memoir and Notes &c*, ed. William Michael Rossetti (London: Macmillan & Co., 1904), pp. lx–lxi. As this watercolour shows, Rossetti's eyes were originally blue: see also the Brett portrait of 1857 (fig. 2.20). According to William, 'Her eyes were originally a blueish-grey (portraits show this); but in adult years they might rather be called a greyish hazel, or a richly hazelled grey, and towards the close they may have told out to most persons as being a warm brown, of dark tint' (ibid., p. lix).
6 Rossetti, *Poetical Works*, 1904, p. lxi.
7 Scott, *Autobiographical Notes*, 1, 1892, p. 247.
8 Christina Rossetti, *Maude: A Story for Girls*, ed. William Michael Rossetti (London: Bowden, 1897), pp. 6–7.
9 Rossetti, *Poetical Works*, 1904, p. lxi.
10 This information was presumably given by Golde Moeller, the Heimanns' daughter, when she presented the drawing to the V&A in 1928. I am grateful to Ruth Hibbard at the V&A for her kind help.
11 Rossetti, *Letters*, 1, 1997–2004, p. 7.
12 Jan Marsh, *Christina Rossetti: A Literary Biography* (London: Faber & Faber, 2012), p. 112.
13 Rossetti, *Poetical Works*, p. lxi.
14 Ibid.
15 *The Correspondence of Dante Gabriel Rossetti*, 1, ed. William E. Fredeman (Cambridge: D. S. Brewer, 2002–15), p. 66.
16 Ibid.
17 Rossetti, *Letters*, 1, 1997–2004, p. 17.
18 Ibid., p. 72.
19 Ibid., pp. 62, 80 and 88.
20 Ronald Parkinson, 'James Collinson', in *Pre-Raphaelite Papers*, ed. Leslie Parris (London: Tate Gallery, 1984), p. 64.
21 D. G. Rossetti, *Correspondence*, 1, 2002–15, pp. 75–6.
22 Marsh, *Christina Rossetti*, 2012, p. 5; W. M. Rossetti, *Some Reminiscences*, 1, 1906, p. 20.
23 Marsh, *Christina Rossetti*, 2012, p. 90.
24 Rossetti, *Poetical Works*, 1904, p. lxii.
25 Here quoted from Rossetti, *Letters*, 1, 1997–2004, p. 15.
26 Ibid., p. 14.
27 William Michael Rossetti, *Praeraphaelite Diaries and Letters* (London: Hurst and Blackett, 1900), p. 235.
28 Gabriel also made a nude study for the figure of the Virgin: Virginia Surtees, *The Paintings and Drawings of Dante Gabriel Rossetti 1828–1882: A Catalogue Raisonné* (Oxford: Clarendon Press, 1971), cat. 44B. This was probably executed at the Maddox Street life class he attended at this time: Jan Marsh, *Dante Gabriel Rossetti: Painter and Poet* (London: Weidenfeld & Nicolson, 1999), pp. 36–37.
29 W. M. Rossetti, *Praeraphaelite Diaries*, 1900, pp. 268, 271 and 290.
30 Rossetti, *Poetical Works*, 1904, p. lxii.
31 There is some disagreement about the date of this picture. Ronald Parkinson dates it to 1849 or 1850 (Parkinson 1984, p. 70). Allen Staley, however, has posited a later date for the picture, *c*.1855, which would rule out Christina's involvement: Allen Staley, *The Pre-Raphaelite Landscape* (New Haven and London: Yale University Press, 2001), p. 103.
32 This is suggested by Marsh, *Christina Rossetti*, 2012, p. 118.
33 Rossetti, *Letters*, 1, 1997–2004, p. 42.
34 Elizabeth Prettejohn makes this point in *The Art of the Pre-Raphaelites* (London: Tate Publishing, 2000), p. 73.
35 Hunt to Edward Clodd, 11 January 1893, quoted in Edward Clodd, *Memories* (London: Chapman and Hall, 1916), p. 198. See also Judith Bronkhurst, *William Holman Hunt: A Catalogue Raisonné*, 1 (New Haven and London: Yale University Press, 2006), p. 153.
36 Hunt to J. L. Tupper, 20 June 1878, quoted in Bronkhurst, *William Holman Hunt*, 1, 2006, p. 153.
37 William Holman Hunt, *Pre-Raphaelitism and the Pre-Raphaelite Brotherhood*, 1 (London: Macmillan & Co., 1905), p. 307; and Clodd, *Memories*, 1916, pp. 197–8. See also Bronkhurst, *William Holman Hunt*, 1, 2006, p. 153.
38 Tate N01394.
39 See Rossetti, *Letters*, 1, 1997–2004, p. 71 and Marsh, *Christina Rossetti*, 2012, p. 128
40 Ford Madox Hueffer, *Ford Madox Brown: A Record of his Life and Work* (London: Longmans, Green & Co., 1896), p. 81.
41 Rossetti, *Letters*, 4, 1997–2004, p. 366. Christina, writing in early January 1894, was presumably responding to a request for information in connection with *Dante Gabriel Rossetti*, a book Stephens published that year.
42 Hueffer, *Ford Madox Brown*, 1896, p. 81; Stephens, writing in 1898, is quoted in *The Diary of Ford Madox Brown*, ed. Virginia Surtees (New Haven and London: Yale University Press, 1981), p. 83, n. 35.
43 Quoted in *Dante Gabriel Rossetti*, ed. Julian Treuherz, Elizabeth Prettejohn and Edwin Becker, exh. cat. (Liverpool: Walker Art Gallery, 2003), cat. 52, p. 164.
44 William includes *Hesterna Rosa* in his list of representations of Christina, writing: 'I think it is clear that this face is drawn from Christina, whom it resembles well' (Rossetti, *Poetical Works*, 1904, p. lxii).
45 Ibid.
46 *The Family Letters of Christina Georgina Rossetti*, ed. William Michael Rossetti (London: Brown, Langham, 1908), p. 21.
47 D. G. Rossetti, *Correspondence*, 1, 2002–15, p. 197.
48 Rossetti, *Poetical Works*, 1904, p. lxiii.
49 Rossetti, *Letters*, 1, 1997–2004, p. 230.
50 In the mid-1880s, Scott produced a portfolio of six etchings illustrating various scenes from his mural. There is a set in the British Museum (1912,0802.109.1-6) although, as William remarks, Christina's features are not recognisable in the print (Rossetti, *Poetical Works*, 1904, p. lxiv).
51 Quoted in David Cordingly, '"The Stonebreaker": An Examination of the Landscape in a Painting by John Brett', *Burlington Magazine*, vol. 124 (1982), p. 141.
52 Christiana Payne and Ann Sumner, *Objects of Affection: Pre-Raphaelite Portraits by John Brett*, exh. cat. (Birmingham: Barber Institute of Fine Arts, University of Birmingham, 2010), pp. 12–13 and *passim*.
53 I should like to thank Annabel Warne and Paul Denny of the Wild Meat Company, Lorna Evans of the RSPB and Hein van Grouw, Senior Curator, Bird Group, at the Natural History Museum for their help in identifying the feather.
54 It is not certain that the small inky blot between 'Rossetti' and 'Mickleham 1857' in the inscription was intended to be a question mark; it could be interpreted as a colon.
55 The social situation surrounding the relationship between Brett and Rossetti is set out in detail by Mike Hickox in 'John Brett and the Rossettis', *Journal of Pre-Raphaelite Studies*, vol. 5 (Spring 1985), pp. 105–10 and by Marsh, *Christina Rossetti*, 2012, pp. 202–8.
56 Rossetti, *Letters*, 1, 1997–2004, p. 109. Brett was at that time giving drawing lessons to Laura Epps and her sisters.
57 W. M. Rossetti, *Praeraphaelite Diaries and Letters*, 1908, p. 54.
58 Rossetti, *Poetical Works*, 1904, p. 481.

59 Although the markings of the left and right sides of the feather are both consistent with those found on a bronze turkey tail feather, the two halves are coloured slightly differently. It is possible that Brett spliced together two separate feathers as a symbol of union; but it is more likely, perhaps, that he had simply not finished painting the right-hand side when he abandoned the picture. I am grateful to Hein van Grouw for sharing his thoughts on this issue.
60 Violet Hunt, *The Wife of Rossetti: Her Life and Death* (London: John Lane and Bodley Head, 1932), p. 272.
61 Rossetti, *Letters*, 2, 1997–2004, p. 74.
62 Rossetti, *Poetical Works*, 1904, p. 483. William writes that the 'combined *Poems*' she inscribed was published in 1895, which must be a typographical slip, probably either for 1875 or 1890 (see Chapter Four of this book). '"No, Thank You, John"' was first published in *Goblin Market and Other Poems* in 1862.
63 Rossetti, *Letters*, 1, 1997–2004, p. 163.
64 Ibid., p. 165.
65 Rossetti, *Poetical Works*, 1904, p. lxiii.
66 Rossetti, *Letters*, 1, 1997–2004, p. 188.
67 William's 1904 list includes, as no. 22, 'Three carte-de-visite photographs taken (if I remember rightly) soon before Christina started on her Norman trip of 1861. These, again, are extremely good, rendering very well the subdued dignity and elegant (though not fashionable) quietude of her aspect. Two of the figures are standing – the third is seated, bonneted' (*Poetical Works*, 1904, p. lxiii). I would suggest that William was not remembering rightly, and that the photographs he describes here are actually from the 1863 sitting recorded in Christina's letters, which does not appear on his list.
68 Rossetti, *Letters*, 1, 1997–2004, pp. 188–9.
69 Ibid., pp. 190 and 193.
70 Ibid., p. 239.
71 In July 1863 the painter George Chapman approached Gabriel about asking Christina to sit for him, but there is no further mention of the project (D. G. Rossetti, *Correspondence*, 3, 2002–15, p. 66).
72 Ibid., p. 79.
73 *Lewis Carroll's Diaries: The Private Journals of Charles Lutwidge Dodgson (Lewis Carroll)*, 4, ed. Edward Wakeling (Luton: Lewis Carroll Society, 1993–2007), pp. 243–4.
74 Ibid., p. 251, n. 288.
75 Rossetti, *Poetical Works*, 1904, p. lxiv.
76 Letter to Amelia Heimann in D. G. Rossetti, *Correspondence*, 3, 2002–15, p. 474.
77 W. M. Rossetti, *Some Reminiscences*, 2, 1906, p. 311.
78 Marsh, *Christina Rossetti*, 2012, pp. 359–61; Rossetti, *Letters*, 1, 1997–2004, p. 283.
79 'On a Portrait' (Sonnet XXVII) in Charles Bagot Cayley, *Poems and Translations* (London: Brain, 1880), p. 63.
80 On 30 September 1866, Gabriel wrote that he intended to have photographs taken of the drawing: D. G. Rossetti, *Correspondence*, 3, 2002–15, p. 474.
81 Rossetti, *Letters*, 1, 1997–2004, p. 363.
82 Mackenzie Bell, *Christina Rossetti: A Biographical and Critical Study* (London: Hurst and Blackett, 1898), p. 149.
83 Rossetti, *Letters*, 1, 1997–2004, p. 274.
84 Julian Cox and Colin Ford, *Julia Margaret Cameron: The Complete Photographs* (London: Thames & Hudson, 2003), pp. 5, 24.
85 Quoted in Marsh, *Christina Rossetti*, 2012, p. 445.
86 D. G. Rossetti, *Correspondence*, 7, 2002–15, p. 410.
87 Ibid.
88 Ibid., pp. 423 and 425.
89 Ibid., p. 435.
90 Christina self-deprecatingly referred to the full-face photograph (fig. 2.31) as 'the idiot': Bell, *Christina Rossetti*, 1898, p. 53 and Rossetti, *Poetical Works*, 1904, p. lxv.
91 William Michael Rossetti, *Rossetti Papers 1862 to 1870: A Compilation* (London: Sands, 1903), p. 227.
92 Rossetti, *Letters*, 4, 1997–2004, p. 258.
93 On the 'Hall of Fame' see Nicholas Tromans, *The Art of G. F. Watts* (London: Paul Holberton Publishing, 2017), pp. 70–79.
94 W. M. Rossetti, *The Family Letters*, 1908, p. 216.
95 Virginia Woolf, '"I am Christina Rossetti"', *The Common Reader: Second Series* (London: Hogarth Press, 1932), p. 237. This essay was first published on 6 December 1930 in *Nation & Athenaeum*.
96 Ibid., p. 240.

Chapter Three

1 The title of this chapter refers to the poem 'Come and See' (1859) by Elizabeth Rundle Charles, which Christina Rossetti transcribed in her copy of *The Christian Year*. John Keble, *Occasional Papers and Reviews* (Oxford: Parker, 1877), p. xiii. On Tractarianism and its relationship to the Oxford Movement, see Owen Chadwick, *The Spirit of the Oxford Movement: Tractarian Essays* (Cambridge: Cambridge University Press, 1992).
2 Mackenzie Bell, *Christina Rossetti: A Biographical and Critical Study* (London: Hurst and Blackett, 1898), p. 335.
3 For a detailed explanation of the Tractarian doctrine of reserve and of its use in poetry, see G. B. Tennyson, *Victorian Devotional Poetry: The Tractarian Mode* (Cambridge, MA: Harvard University Press, 1981). See also Emma Mason, 'Christina Rossetti and the Doctrine of Reserve', *Journal of Victorian Culture*, vol. 7, iss. 2 (2002), pp. 196–219.
4 Christina Rossetti, *The Face of the Deep: A Devotional Commentary on the Apocalypse* (London: SPCK, 1892), p. 432.
5 For essential reading on the subject of Christina Rossetti's drawings, see: Diane D'Amico, 'Christina Rossetti's *Christian Year*: Comfort for "the weary heart"', *Victorian Newsletter*, vol. 72 (1987), pp. 36–42; Mary Arseneau, '"May My Great Love Avail Me": Christina Rossetti and Dante', in *The Culture of Christina Rossetti: Female Poetics and Victorian Contexts*, ed. Mary Arseneau, Antony H. Harrison and Lorraine Janzen Kooistra (Athens: Ohio University Press, 1999), pp. 22–45; and Lorraine Janzen Kooistra, *Christina Rossetti and Illustration: A Publishing History* (Athens: Ohio University Press, 2002), pp. 21–55.
6 Christina Rossetti, *The Poetical Works of Christina Georgina Rossetti. With Memoir and Notes &c*, ed. William Michael Rossetti (London: Macmillan & Co., 1904), p. 464.
7 This period saw the publication of the Pre-Raphaelite illustrated journal, *The Germ*. Rossetti's poems were published in the journal, and she was closely involved in its preparation. See Alexis Easley, 'Gender and the Politics of Literary Fame: Christina Rossetti and "The Germ"', *Critical Survey*, vol. 13, no. 2 (2001), pp. 61–77.
8 Rossetti, *Poetical Works*, 1904, p. 464.
9 *The Correspondence of Dante Gabriel Rossetti*, 1, ed. William E. Fredeman (Cambridge: D. S. Brewer, 2002–15), p. 197.
10 Quoted in Angela Thirlwell, *Into The Frame: The Four Loves of Ford Madox Brown* (London: Chatto & Windus, 2010), p. 112.
11 Christina Rossetti, *The Letters of Christina Rossetti*, 1, ed. Antony H. Harrison (Charlottesville: University Press of Virginia, 1997–2004), p. 71.
12 William Michael Rossetti, *Some Reminiscences*, 1 (London: Brown, Langham, 1906), p. 39. William, Maria and Frances Rossetti all sought work outside the home in order to support the family.
13 For a discussion of the network of government-run schools that did admit women in the period, see Susan Owens,

'"Straight Lines Are A National Want"', in *Art and Design For Life: The Victoria and Albert Museum*, ed. Julius Bryant (London: V&A Publishing, 2011), pp. 75–81.
14 William Powell Frith, *My Autobiography and Reminiscences*, 2 (London: Bentley, 1887–88), p. 323.
15 Frances Rossetti to D. G. Rossetti, 23 July 1853, quoted in Kooistra, *Christina Rossetti and Illustration*, 2002, p. 26.
16 D. G. Rossetti, *Correspondence*, 1, 2002–15, p. 285.
17 Ibid., p. 294.
18 Rossetti, *Letters*, 1, 1997–2004, p. 62, n. 1.
19 Ibid., p. 71.
20 Kooistra, *Christina Rossetti and Illustration*, 2002, p. 28.
21 Rossetti, *Poetical Works*, 1904, p. 471.
22 See pp. 119–22 of the 1852 volume.
23 Rossetti, *Poetical Works*, 1904, p. 184.
24 D. G. Rossetti, *Correspondence*, 1, 2002–15, p. 285.
25 The authors of this volume are very grateful for the assistance of Giuseppe Albano, Mary Arseneau, Lorraine Janzen Kooistra, Jan Marsh, Susan Plowden, Linda Schofield and Angela Thirlwell in seeking to locate Rossetti's illustrated books.
26 Kirstie Blair, *Form and Faith in Victorian Poetry and Religion* (Oxford: Oxford University Press, 2012), p. 40.
27 Samantha Matthews, 'Marketplaces', in *The Oxford Handbook of Victorian Poetry*, ed. Matthew Bevis (Oxford: Oxford University Press, 2013), p. 664.
28 John Keble, 'Advertisement' to *The Christian Year* (Oxford: Parker, 1837), p. vi.
29 Keble, 'Advertisement', 1837, pp. v–vi.
30 John Henry Newman, 'John Keble' (1846) quoted in Blair, *Form and Faith in Victorian Poetry and Religion*, 2012, p. 40.
31 Rossetti's copy of *The Christian Year* is on loan to the British Library from a private collection. I am grateful for permission to examine it for the purposes of this essay.
32 D'Amico, 'Christina Rossetti's Christian Year', 1987, p. 36.
33 Arseneau, '"May My Great Love Avail Me"', 1999, p. 31. Arseneau's chapter reproduces Rossetti's pencil drawings for chapters 3 and 4 of Maria Rossetti's *A Shadow of Dante* (1871). The illustrations closely resemble those for *The Christian Year* in both subject and technique.
34 Emma Mason, *Christina Rossetti: Poetry, Ecology, Faith* (Oxford: Oxford University Press, 2018), p. 161. Rossetti writes that in its depiction of 'the descending soul and the arising body rushing together in an indissoluble embrace', Blake's illustration 'stands alone in expressing the rapture of that reunion': *Time Flies: A Reading Diary* (London: SPCK, 1885), p. 88.
35 For the most authoritative discussion of Tractarian poetics and their relationship to Rossetti's work, see Tennyson, *Victorian Devotional Poetry*, 1981.
36 Rossetti, *The Face of the Deep*, 1892, p. 267.
37 Ibid., p. 116.
38 John Ruskin, *Modern Painters*, 1 (London: Smith, Elder, 1848), p. 417. The passage from which this extract is taken is considered a formative influence on the Pre-Raphaelite Brotherhood.
39 Rossetti, *Poetical Works*, 1904, p. 460.
40 D'Amico, 'Christina Rossetti's *Christian Year*', 1987, p. 39.
41 Kooistra, *Christina Rossetti and Illustration*, 2002, p. 31.
42 Rossetti, *The Face of the Deep*, 1892, p. 195.
43 'Septuagesima'. This poem originally appeared in *Time Flies* and was given its title on its publication in Christina Rossetti, *Verses* (London: SPCK, 1893).
44 D'Amico, 'Christina Rossetti's *Christian Year*', 1987, p. 38.
45 D'Amico notes that this posture also suggests that the figure is straining to hear heavenly sounds, while Kooistra identifies her as a possible sitter for the portrait painted by the central figure.
46 Rossetti, *Time Flies*, 1885, p. 277.
47 Ibid., p. 277.
48 Matthew 25:1–13.
49 Genesis 25:19–34.
50 Rossetti, *Time Flies*, 1885, p. 153.
51 Exodus 24.
52 Revelation 14:4. Keble's note credits Jeremy Taylor's *Holy Living* (1650) as a source for this idea.
53 Christina Rossetti, *Sing-Song: A Nursery Rhyme Book* (London: Routledge, 1872), p. 130.
54 Rossetti, *The Face of the Deep*, 1892, p. 312. Rossetti quotes Genesis 30:1: these words are spoken by Rachel, who is unable to conceive.
55 Rossetti, *Sing-Song*, 1872, p. 4. Rossetti's composition also bears some resemblance to Heinrich von Hess's 'Christmas Eve', discussed by Nicholas Tromans in Chapter One (fig. 1.12).
56 Rossetti, *Letters*, 1, 1997–2004, p. 375. For more on this collaboration, see Kooistra, *Christina Rossetti and Illustration*, 2002, pp. 11–12, 121–5.
57 Kooistra, *Christina Rossetti and Illustration*, 2002, p. 102.
58 Rossetti, *Times Flies*, 1885, p. 128.
59 See Mason, *Christina Rossetti: Poetry, Ecology, Faith*, 2018, for an illuminating exploration of the relationship of Rossetti's faith to the natural world.
60 W. M. Rossetti quoted in ibid., p. 123.
61 Richard Maxwell, 'Walter Scott, Historical Fiction, and the Genesis of the Victorian Illustrated Book', in *The Victorian Illustrated Book*, ed. Richard Maxwell (Charlottesville: University Press of Virginia, 2002), p. 1.
62 Four of Charles's five stanzas begin with 'Master, where abidest Thou?' (John 1:38). Later in the same chapter, Philip tells Nathaniel to 'Come and see' Christ for himself (1:46). 'Come and See' also has darker biblical connotations, which Rossetti explores in *The Face of the Deep*, 1892 (see pp. 193–205).
63 Elizabeth Rundle Charles, 'Come and See', in *The Three Wakings: With Hymns and Songs* (London: Nisbet, 1859), *l*. 40. First published anonymously.
64 John Keble, 'Morning', *The Christian Year*, 1837.
65 John Keble, *Lectures on Poetry 1832–1841*, 1, trans. Edward Kershaw Francis (Oxford: Clarendon Press, 1912), p. 257.

Chapter Four

1 William Michael Rossetti, *Bibliography of the Works of Dante Gabriel Rossetti*, 1 (London: Ellis, 1905), p. 5; William E. Fredeman, *Pre-Raphaelitism: A Bibliocritical Study* (Cambridge, MA: Harvard University Press, 1965), p. 92. In later years D. G. Rossetti would attempt to destroy any of these booklets that he came across, but – as with Christina's early printings – several copies survived in the library and archive of his brother William Michael and in other collections.
2 'Notes', in Christina Rossetti, *New Poems*, ed. William Michael Rossetti (London: Macmillan & Co., 1896), p. 394.
3 Maura Ives, *Christina Rossetti: A Descriptive Bibliography* (New Castle, DE: Oak Knoll Press, 2011), A.1, p. 29. The dimensions of the card are 15.4 × 9.5 cm. It is dated 27 April 1842 (Frances Rossetti's birthday).
4 Ives, *Christina Rossetti*, 2011, A 2, pp. 31–2. The page size is a mere 11.9 × 5.5 cm. Copies in various paper wrappers (as issued) and in the original uncut sheets are recorded; as might be expected, a good many of the former have the author's or other family presentation inscriptions.
5 Christina Rossetti, *Verses* (Hammersmith: Eragny Press, 1906).
6 Fredeman, *Pre-Raphaelitism*, 1965, p. 242. Only the first two numbers bore the title *The Germ*; from no. 3 it was changed to *Art and Nature*.
7 Ives, *Christina Rossetti*, 2011, C 3–4, pp. 233–4.

8 Ibid., C.5–9, p. 234.
9 D. G. Rossetti to William Allingham, 23 January 1855, in *The Correspondence of Dante Gabriel Rossetti*, 2, ed. William E. Fredeman (Cambridge: D. S. Brewer, 2002–15), p. 7.
10 Ives, *Christina Rossetti*, 2011, C.19, p. 235.
11 Ibid., C.44, p. 237; Betty Elzea, *Frederick Sandys 1829–1904: A Catalogue Raisonné*, (Woodbridge: Antique Collectors' Club, 2001), 2.B.67, pp. 221–3.
12 *The Letters of Christina Rossetti*, 1, ed. Antony H. Harrison (Charlottesville: University Press of Virginia, 1997–2004), p. 240.
13 Ives, *Christina Rossetti*, 2011, C.51. p. 237; Elzea, *Frederick Sandys*, 2001, 2.B.87, p. 228.
14 The many versions of Sandys's *Proud Maisie* are described in Elzea, *Frederick Sandys*, 2001, 2.A.111–21, pp. 193–6.
15 Lona Mosk Packer (ed.), *The Rossetti-Macmillan Letters* (Berkeley: University of California Press, 1963), p. 6.
16 Ives, *Christina Rossetti*, 2011, A.3, pp. 34–6. Announcements appeared in *The Times*, 30 November 1861, and again on 7 December 1861.
17 Rossetti, *Letters*, 1, 1997–2004, p. 153.
18 The frontispiece illustration for *Goblin Market* (1862 and later editions) is signed with the initials *MMF* for Morris, Marshall and Faulkner, the original partners in 'The Firm'. This led to the mistaken notion that the woodblock had been cut by Morris himself. It was only later that Morris cut a few blocks after Burne-Jones's designs for their ultimately abortive *Cupid and Psyche* project.
19 The sofa, although photographed at the time, no longer seems to exist. Rossetti's design drawing has annotations with measurements and notes concerning construction details initialled by William Morris (Birmingham City Museum and Art Gallery, Inv. No. 1904P471). Another sofa that Rossetti designed for his own use (which in this case does survive in the Fitzwilliam Museum, Cambridge), whilst more conventional in form, shows an almost equal disregard for comfort that is surprising considering the artist's known propensity for informal lounging.
20 Packer, *The Rossetti-Macmillan Letters*, 1963, p. 40.
21 Ibid., p. 2.
22 The Portfolio Society was a small gathering of, mostly, women writers; they wrote contributions on a monthly theme and circulated them for mutual criticism, rather in the manner of the Cyclographic Club, the similar informal organisation – though visually based and male in membership – in which D. G. Rossetti had participated in the immediate pre-Pre-Raphaelite period in the 1840s.
23 'The Fairy Prince Who Arrived Too Late', *Macmillan's Magazine*, no. 8, May 1863, p. 36.
24 Ives, *Christina Rossetti*, 2011, A.5, pp. 43–5.
25 Virginia Surtees, *The Paintings and Drawings of Dante Gabriel Rossetti (1828–1882): A Catalogue Raisonné* (Oxford: Clarendon Press, 1971), no. 143 (its present location is the Metropolitan Museum, New York).
26 Ibid., nos 185, 185 *a–l*, 186, 186 *a–h*.
27 The sketch is in the collection of the National Trust (Belton House); the finished drawing, at one time in the collection of the watercolour expert Martin Hardie, also belongs to the National Trust (Fenton House).
28 Gleeson White, 'Children's Books and their Illustrators', *The Studio: Special Winter Number* (1897–8), p. 42.
29 Wilde's dictum is quoted in Vincent O'Sullivan, *Aspects of Wilde* (London: Constable, 1936), p. 217.
30 See Stephen Calloway, 'The Book Beautiful', in *The Cult of Beauty: The Aesthetic Movement 1860–1900*, ed. Stephen Calloway and Lynn Federle Orr, exh. cat. (London: V&A, 2011), pp. 252–5.
31 Quoted in Packer, *The Rossetti-Macmillan Letters*, 1963, p. 72.
32 William Michael Rossetti, *Rossetti Papers 1862 to 1870: A Compilation* (London: Sands, 1903), p. 489.
33 Rossetti to F. S. Ellis, 25 February 1870: *Letters*, 1, 1997–2004, p. 342.
34 Murray was Ellis's choice. Alice Boyd was suggested by Gabriel and William Bell Scott: Christina wrote to Ellis on 7 March 1870 that 'she would probably do them with more fun and zest than Murray though perhaps not so artistically': *Letters*, 1, 1997–2004, pp. 343–4.
35 Ives, *Christina Rossetti*, 2011, A.8, pp. 50–52.
36 D. G. Rossetti to Swinburne, 29 November 1871: D. G. Rossetti, *Correspondence*, 5, 2002–15, pp. 198–9.
37 Presumably meaning plain cloth without ornament.
38 Ives, *Christina Rossetti*, 2011, A.10, pp. 59–60.
39 *Letters*, 1, 1997–2004, pp. 418–9.
40 An important cause of change in Christina's appearance was her gradual decline into ill health and in particular the onset of Graves' disease (see Chapter Two).
41 Ives, *Christina Rossetti*, 2011, A.11, pp. 62–5.
42 Rossetti to Macmillan, 27 August 1875: *Letters*, 2, 1997–2004, p. 54.
43 W. M. Rossetti, *Rossetti Papers*, 1903, p. 236.
44 Rossetti, *Letters*, 2, 1997–2004, p. 269.
45 Ives, *Christina Rossetti*, 2011, A.15, pp. 81–3.
46 As with others of her works, Roberts Brothers of Boston issued an edition of *A Pageant* solely for the American market; it appeared in the same year as the English edition, but with the erroneous title *The Pageant*. This enterprising New England firm enthusiastically took up several English writers around this time (securing Oscar Wilde's *Poems* the following year was a great coup), but their editions generally appeared without the distinctive designs of the originals and, whilst occasionally significant textually, they are conventional and uniformly uninteresting from an aesthetic point of view. Roberts Brothers did at least publish with the agreement of English authors and their publishers; many writers, Swinburne included, suffered at the hands of less scrupulous American firms who simply pirated their texts.
47 Rossetti to Macmillan, 3 June 1890: *Letters*, 4, 1997–2004, p. 204.
48 Ives, *Christina Rossetti*, 2011, A.22, pp. 104–8.
49 Macmillan's 'Edition Book' lists impressions in October and December 1890, February and August 1891, December 1892, July 1894, April 1895, February 1896, December 1897, May 1899 and March 1901 (Ives, *Christina Rossetti*, 2011, pp. 107–8).
50 *Magazine of Art*, September 1890, p. 385: Ives, *Christina Rossetti*, 2011, C.133, pp. 244–5.
51 Rossetti to Spielmann, 27 August 1888: *Letters*, 4, 1997–2004, p. 87.
52 Ricketts to Cecil French, 12 July 1915, in Charles Ricketts, *Self-Portrait, taken from the letters and journals of Charles Ricketts, R.A.*, ed. T. Sturge Moore and Cecil Lewis (London: Peter Davies, 1939), p. 379.
53 One of the great treasures of the collection formed by Charles Ricketts and his partner Charles Shannon was Rossetti's ink drawing *Mary Magdalene at the Door of Simon the Pharisee* (1858): later it was bequeathed to the Fitzwilliam Museum, Cambridge (inv. no. 2151).
54 Rossetti to Spielmann, 1890: *Letters*, 4, 1997–2004, p. 212.
55 *Magazine of Art*, July 1894, p. 304; Ives, *Christina Rossetti*, 2011, C.138, p. 245.
56 Quoted in Simon Nowell-Smith (ed.), *Letters to Macmillan* (London: Macmillan & Co., 1967), p. 238–9. See also Rodney Engen, *Laurence Housman* (Stroud: Catalpa Press, 1983), pp. 49–51.
57 Nowell-Smith, *Letters to Macmillan*, 1967, p. 239.
58 Ibid., p. 240.

59 Rossetti, *Letters*, 4, p. 306, n. 2.

60 From Morris's commissioning letter to Harrison, August 1908: quoted in Lorraine Janzen Kooistra, *Christina Rossetti and Illustration: A Publishing History* (Athens: Ohio University Press, 2002), p. 233.

61 Evelyn Waugh's study of D. G. Rossetti published that year is often cited as an important marker of the Victorian Revival. But it should be remembered that in the period between Christina's death in 1894 and 1928, W. M. Rossetti's memoirs (containing much about Christina) as well as his editions of her poems and her family letters had all appeared.

62 *Playboy Magazine*, vol. 20, no. 9, September 1973, pp. 115–9.

63 See, *inter alia*, Kooistra, *Christina Rossetti and Illustration* 2002, pp. 74–5 and 240–44, and Jan Marsh, *Christina Rossetti: A Literary Biography* (London: Faber & Faber, 2012), pp. 232–8 and 259–64.

Chapter Five

1 Our title refers to Rossetti's sonnet 'The P.R.B.' (1853). *The George Eliot Letters*, 4, ed. Gordon S. Haight (London and New Haven: Yale University Press, 1954–78), pp. 55–6; Henry James, *The Golden Bowl*, 1 (New York: Scribner's, 1909), p. x.

2 See Susan Owens, 'Literature and the Aesthetic Movement', in *The Cult of Beauty: The Aesthetic Movement 1860–1900*, ed. Stephen Calloway and Lynn Federle Orr, exh. cat. (London: V&A, 2011), pp. 40–51.

3 Paintings inspired by Christina Rossetti's poems have previously been studied by Lorraine Janzen Kooistra in *Christina Rossetti and Illustration: A Publishing History* (Athens: Ohio University Press, 2002), pp. 254–61. Research by Hilary Underwood has now roughly doubled the number known: see the checklist at the end of this chapter. We cannot accept as proven Andrew Wilton's intriguing suggestion that William Blake Richmond's *The Watchers* (1876) was inspired by Rossetti, as her poem of that name was not published until 1896 (although composed as early as 1850): see Andrew Wilton, 'Symbolism in Britain', in *The Age of Rossetti, Burne-Jones and Watts: Symbolism in Britain 1860–1910*, exh. cat., ed. Andrew Wilton and Robert Upstone (London: Tate, 1997), p. 22. Although poem and painting have some elements in common, it is perhaps more likely that they share a common source.

4 Mackenzie Bell, *Christina Rossetti: A Biographical and Critical Study* (London: Hurst and Blackett, 1898), p. 213.

5 The date of this drawing is uncertain. Virginia Surtees suggests c.1865 in *The Paintings and Drawings of Dante Gabriel Rossetti (1828–1882): A Catalogue Raisonné* (Oxford: Clarendon Press, 1971), no. 184. It is however possible that it was produced nearer the time of the poem's composition in 1856, or around 1863 when Chapman was painting *Three Sisters Sang of Love Together*.

6 *The Correspondence of Dante Gabriel Rossetti*, 3, ed. William E. Fredeman (Cambridge: D. S. Brewer, 2002–15), p. 372.

7 Jerome McGann, 'Double Works', *The Rossetti Archive*, accessed June 2018, www.rossettiarchive.org/racs/doubleworks.rac.html.

8 Among the images within 'A Birthday' is a richly decorated dais, carved with 'doves and pomegranates'.

9 Christina Rossetti, *The Letters of Christina Rossetti*, 1, ed. Antony H. Harrison (Charlottesville: University Press of Virginia, 1997–2004), p. 118.

10 Julian Cox and Colin Ford, *Julia Margaret Cameron: The Complete Photographs* (London: Thames & Hudson, 2003), p. 31, no. 1099.

11 Roger Taylor and Edward Wakeling, *Lewis Carroll Photographer. The Princeton University Library Albums* (Princeton, NJ: Princeton University Press, 2002), HH: 9, p. 220 ('The Birthday Wreath', 13 July 1875).

12 See Van Gogh's letters to his brother, 26 August and 3 November 1876, nos 89 and 96 in Leo Jansen, Hans Luijten and Nienke Bakker (eds), *Vincent van Gogh – The Letters*, online archive, Van Gogh Museum & Huygens ING, 2009, accessed June 2018, vangoghletters.org. There is disagreement over precisely which painting of Boughton's Van Gogh had seen. For a full treatment of the problem see Ronald de Leeuw, 'George Henry Boughton and the "beautiful picture" in Van Gogh's 1876 sermon', *Van Gogh Museum Journal* (1995), pp. 48–61; and for more on Boughton see Luke Hermann, 'Van Gogh's favourite English artist: George Boughton (1833–1905)', *British Art Journal*, vol. 6, no. 3 (Winter 2005), pp. 37–40.

13 *The Diary of W. M. Rossetti, 1870–1873*, ed. Odette Bornand (Oxford: Clarendon Press, 1977), p. 184.

14 The date of 1890 for this work has been taken from Patrick Derom (ed.), *Symbolist Works 6* (Brussels: Patrick Derom Gallery, 2005), p. 14.

15 When shown at the New Gallery in 1892, *I Lock My Door Upon Myself* was understood to have no title, only the motto from Rossetti; the picture was hung above G. F. Watts's *Sic Transit* (1891–2): see M. Phipps Jackson, 'Current Art: The New Gallery', *Magazine of Art*, vol. 15 (1892), p. 290. *Who Shall Deliver Me?* was also shown at the New Gallery in 1892 and its first owner was British. On Khnopff and Britain, see Laurent Busine, 'From Edward Burne-Jones to Fernand Khnopff', in *Burne-Jones (1833–1898). Dessins du Fitzwilliam Museum de Cambridge*, ed. Jane Munro, exh. cat. (Nantes: Musée des Beaux-Arts, 1992), pp. 59–68.

16 See Linda K. Hughes, 'Prefiguring Future Pasts: Imagined Histories in Victorian Poetic-Graphic Texts, 1860–1910', in Anna Maria Jones and Rebecca N. Mitchell (eds), *Drawing on the Victorians: The Palimpsest of Victorian and Neo-Victorian Graphic Texts* (Athens: Ohio University Press, 2016), p. 228.

17 See Victoria Osborne, 'A British Symbolist in Pre-Raphaelite Circles: Edward Robert Hughes RWS (1851–1914)', MPhil thesis (University of Birmingham, 2009), p. 75.

18 Ibid., p. 80.

19 Six of these pictures joined an exhibition (using the same title as the London exhibition) the next year at the Art Institute of Chicago, all lent by R. Hall McCormick. Byam Shaw made his first appearances at the Royal Academy in 1893–5 with subjects from D. G. Rossetti.

20 Omitted from the list is Amy Sawyer's *Goblin Market* (Sotheby's, London, 10 October 1985, lot 300), which despite the title has nothing to do with Rossetti.

21 W. M. Rossetti, *Diary*, 1977, p. 184.

Bibliography

Manuscript Material

Christina Rossetti, illustrated manuscript of *Sing-Song: A Nursery Rhyme Book* (1868/70)
British Library, London, Ashley MS 1371

Christina Rossetti's annotated and hand-illustrated copy of John Keble's *The Christian Year* (1837)
Private Collection: British Library, London, Loan MS 113

Papers relating to Christina Rossetti's estate
National Archives, Kew, IR 59/163

William Michael Rossetti, 'List of Works of Art framed or otherwise displayed in No.3 St. Edmund's Terrace ... 6 Decr. 1908'
Library of the University of British Columbia, Vancouver, Angeli-Dennis collection, RBAC-ARC-1009-18-04

Printed Texts

Anon. 'The Christina Rossetti Memorial, Sir Edward Burne-Jones's Last Work', pp. 88–90. *Magazine of Art*, vol. 22, December 1899.

Anon. 'Some pictures by Byam Shaw', pp. 259–65. *Studio*, vol. 16, no. 74, May 1899a.

Armstrong, Isobel. 'The Pre-Raphaelites and Literature', pp. 15–31. *The Cambridge Companion to the Pre-Raphaelites*, ed. Elizabeth Prettejohn. Cambridge: Cambridge University Press, 2012.

Armstrong, Isobel. *Victorian Poetry: Poetry, Poetics and Politics*. London: Routledge, 1993.

Arseneau, Mary. 'Incarnation and Interpretation: Christina Rossetti, the Oxford Movement, and "Goblin Market"', pp. 79–93. *Victorian Poetry*, vol. 31, no. 1, 1993.

Arseneau, Mary. '"May My Great Love Avail Me": Christina Rossetti and Dante', pp. 22–45. *The Culture of Christina Rossetti*, ed. Mary Arseneau, Antony H. Harrison and Lorraine Janzen Kooistra. Athens: Ohio University Press, 1999.

Arseneau, Mary. 'Pews, Periodicals and Politics: The Rossetti Women as High Church Controversialists', pp. 97–113. *Outsiders Looking In: The Rossettis Then and Now*, eds David Clifford and Laurence Roussillon. London: Anthem Press, 2004.

Arseneau, Mary. *Recovering Christina Rossetti: Female Community and Incarnational Poetics*. Basingstoke: Palgrave Macmillan, 2004.

Arseneau, Mary. 'Symbol and Sacrament: The Incarnational Aesthetic of Christina Rossetti.' PhD dissertation, University of Western Ontario, 1991.

Arseneau, Mary, Antony H. Harrison and Lorraine Janzen Kooistra, eds. *The Culture of Christina Rossetti: Female Poetics and Victorian Contexts*. Athens: Ohio University Press, 1999.

Battiscombe, Georgina. *Christina Rossetti: A Divided Life*. London: Constable, 1981.

Bell, Mackenzie. *Christina Rossetti: A Biographical and Critical Study*. London: Hurst and Blackett, 1898.

Bennett, Mary. *Ford Madox Brown: A Catalogue Raisonné*, 2 vols. New Haven and London: Yale University Press, 2010.

Bentley, D. M. R. 'A Possible Pictorial Inspiration for Christina Rossetti's "The Prince's Progress"', pp. 51–54. *Journal of Pre-Raphaelite Studies*, no. 9, Fall 2000.

Bentley, D. M. R. 'The Principal Pre-Raphaelite Pictures of James Collinson', pp. 21–43. *Victorian Review*, vol. 30, no. 1, 2004.

Blair, Kirstie. *Form and Faith in Victorian Poetry and Religion*. Oxford: Oxford University Press, 2012.

Boyle, Mary Louisa. *Biographical Catalogue of the Portraits at Longleat*. London: Elliot Stock, 1881.

Bronkhurst, Judith. *William Holman Hunt: A Catalogue Raisonné*, 2 vols. New Haven and London: Yale University Press, 2006.

Brown, Ford Madox. *The Diary of Ford Madox Brown*, ed. Virginia Surtees. New Haven and London: Yale University Press, 1981.

Brown, Ford Madox. 'On the Mechanism of a Historical Picture', pp. 71–3. *The Germ: Thoughts Towards Nature in Poetry, Literature and Art Being A Facsimile Reprint of the Literary Organ of the Pre-Raphaelite Brotherhood, Published in 1850*. London: Elliot Stock, 1901.

Burrows, Henry William. *The Half-Century of Christ Church, Albany Street, St. Pancras*. London: Skeffington, 1887.

Busine, Laurent. 'From Edward Burne-Jones to Fernand Khnopff', pp. 59–68. *Burne-Jones (1833–1898). Dessins du Fitzwilliam Museum de Cambridge*, ed. Jane Munro, exh. cat. Nantes: Musée des Beaux-Arts, 1992.

Calloway, Stephen. 'The Book Beautiful', pp. 252–5. *The Cult of Beauty: The Aesthetic Movement 1860–1900*, eds Stephen Calloway and Lynn Federle Orr, exh. cat. London: V&A, 2011.

Cayley, Charles Bagot. *Poems and Translations*. London: Brain, 1880.

Chadwick, Owen. *The Spirit of the Oxford Movement: Tractarian Essays*. Cambridge: Cambridge University Press, 1992.

Chapman, Alison. *The Afterlife of Christina Rossetti*. Basingstoke: Palgrave Macmillan, 2000.

Chapman, Alison and Joanna Meacock. *A Rossetti Family Chronology*. Basingstoke: Palgrave Macmillan, 2007.

Charles, Edna Kotin. *Christina Rossetti: Critical Perspectives, 1862–1982*. Selinsgrove, PA: Susquehanna University Press, 1985.

Charles, Elizabeth Rundle. *The Three Wakings: With Hymns and Songs*. London: Nisbet, 1859.

Chatterjee, Ronjaunee. 'Precarious Lives: Christina Rossetti and the Form of Likeness', pp. 745–62. *Victorian Literature and Culture*, vol. 45, no. 4, 2017.

Christian, John, ed. *The Last Romantics: The Romantic Tradition in British Art. Burne-Jones to Stanley Spencer*, exh. cat. London: Barbican Art Gallery, 1989.

Clifford, David and Laurence Roussillon, eds. *Outsiders Looking In: The Rossettis Then and Now*. London: Anthem Press, 2004.

Clodd, Edward. *Memories*. London: Chapman and Hall, 1916.

Cole, Rex Vicat. *The Art and Life of Byam Shaw*. London: Seeley, Service & Co., 1932.

Conley, Susan. '"Poet's Right": Christina Rossetti as Anti-Muse and the Legacy of the "Poetess"', pp. 365–86. *Victorian Poetry*, vol. 32, nos 3–4, 1994.

Cordingly, David. '"The Stonebreaker": An Examination of the Landscape in a Painting by John Brett', pp. 141–5. *Burlington Magazine*, vol. 124, 1982.

Cox, Julian and Colin Ford. *Julia Margaret Cameron: The Complete Photographs*. London: Thames & Hudson, 2003.

Crossman, Colette M. 'Art as Lived Religion: Edward Burne-Jones as Painter, Priest, Pilgrim, and Monk.' PhD dissertation, University of Maryland, 2007.

Crump, Rebecca W. *Christina Rossetti: A Reference Guide*. Boston, MA: G. K. Hall, 1976.

D'Amico, Diane. 'Christina Rossetti's *Christian Year*: Comfort for "the weary heart"', pp. 36–42. *Victorian Newsletter*, vol. 72, 1987.

D'Amico, Diane. *Christina Rossetti: Faith, Gender, and Time*. Baton Rouge, LA: Louisiana State University Press, 1999.

D'Amico, Diane. 'The House of Christina Rossetti: Domestic and Poetic Spaces', pp. 31–54. *Journal of Pre-Raphaelite Studies*, no. 19, Spring 2010.

D'Amico, Diane and David A. Kent. 'Rossetti and the Tractarians', pp. 93–104. *Victorian Poetry*, vol. 44, no. 1, 2006.

Derom, Patrick, ed. *Symbolist Works 6*. Brussels: Patrick Derom Gallery, 2005.

Despotopoulou, Anna. 'Nowhere or Somewhere? (Dis)Locating Gender and Class Boundaries in Christina Rossetti's "Speaking Likenesses"', pp. 414–34. *Review of English Studies*, vol. 61, no. 250, 2010.

Dieleman, Karen. *Religious Imaginaries: The Liturgical and Poetic Practices of Elizabeth Barrett Browning, Christina Rossetti, and Adelaide Procter*. Athens: Ohio University Press, 2012.

[Dodgson, Charles Lutwidge] Lewis Carroll, *pseud. Lewis Carroll's Diaries: The Private Journals of Charles Lutwidge Dodgson (Lewis Carroll)*, ed. Edward Wakeling, 10 vols Luton: Lewis Carroll Society, 1993–2007.

Easley, Alexis. 'Gender and the Politics of Literary Fame: Christina Rossetti and "The Germ"', pp. 61–77. *Critical Survey*, vol. 13, no. 2, 2001.

Eliot, George. *The George Eliot Letters*, ed. Gordon S. Haight, 9 vols. New Haven and London: Yale University Press, 1954–78.

Elzea, Betty. *Frederick Sandys 1829–1904: A Catalogue Raisonné*. Woodbridge: Antique Collectors' Club, 2001.

Engen, Rodney. *Laurence Housman*. Stroud: Catalpa Press, 1983.

Fisher, Devon. *Roman Catholic Saints and Early Victorian Literature: Conservatism, Liberalism, and the Emergence of Secular Culture*. Farnham: Ashgate, 2012.

Fredeman, William E. *Pre-Raphaelitism A Bibliocritical Study*. Cambridge, MA: Harvard University Press, 1965.

Frith, William Powell. *My Autobiography and Reminiscences*, 3 vols. London: Bentley, 1887–88.

The Germ: Thoughts Towards Nature in Poetry, Literature and Art Being A Facsimile Reprint of the Literary Organ of the Pre-Raphaelite Brotherhood, Published in 1850. London: Elliot Stock, 1901.

Goldberg, Gail Lynn. 'Dante Gabriel Rossetti's "Revising Hand": His Illustrations for Christina Rossetti's Poems', pp. 145–59. *Victorian Poetry*, vol. 20, nos 3–4, 1982.

Goodwin, Gregory H. 'Keble and Newman: Tractarian Aesthetics and the Romantic Tradition', pp. 475–94. *Victorian Studies*, vol. 30, no. 4, 1987.

Gosse, Edmund. 'Christina Rossetti', pp. 135–62. *Critical Kit-Kats*. London: Heinemann, 1900.

Grieve, Alastair. 'A Notice on Illustrations to Charles Kingsley's "The Saint's Tragedy"', pp. 290–93. *Burlington Magazine*, vol. 111, 1969.

Hares-Stryker, Carolyn. '"Slight Channels": Arthur Hughes and the Illustration of Children's Books', pp. 91–118. *Haunted Texts: Studies in Pre-Raphaelitism in Honour of William E. Fredeman*, ed. David Latham. Toronto: University of Toronto Press, 2003.

Harrison, Antony H. *Christina Rossetti in Context*. Brighton: Harvester, 1988.

Harrison, Antony H. *Victorian Poets and the Politics of Culture: Discourse and Ideology*. Charlottesville: University Press of Virginia, 1998.

Hermann, Luke. 'Van Gogh's favourite English artist: George Boughton (1833–1905)', pp. 37–40. *British Art Journal*, vol. 6, no. 3, 2005.

Hickox, M. S. H. 'John Brett and the Rossettis', pp. 105–10. *Journal of Pre-Raphaelite Studies*, vol. 5, Spring 1985.

Hilliard, David. 'Unenglish and Unmanly: Anglo-Catholicism and Homosexuality', pp. 181–210. *Victorian Studies*, vol. 25, no. 2, 1982.

Hönnighausen, Gisela. 'Emblematic Tendencies in the Works of Christina Rossetti', pp. 1–15. *Victorian Poetry*, vol. 10, no. 1, 1972.

Hu, Esther T. 'Christina Rossetti, John Keble, and the Divine Gaze', pp. 175–89. *Victorian Poetry*, vol. 46, no. 2, 2008.

Hueffer, Ford M. *Ford Madox Brown: A Record of his Life and Work*. London: Longmans, Green & Co., 1896.

Hughes, Linda K. 'Inventing Poetry and Pictorialism in *Once a Week*: A Magazine of Visual Effects', pp. 41–72. *Victorian Poetry*, vol. 48, no. 1, 2010.

Hughes, Linda K. 'Prefiguring Future Pasts: Imagined Histories in Victorian Poetic-Graphic Texts, 1860–1910', pp. 207–36. *Drawing on the Victorians: The Palimpsest of Victorian and Neo-Victorian Graphic Texts*, eds Anna Maria Jones and Rebecca N. Mitchell. Athens: Ohio University Press, 2016.

Hunt, Violet. *The Wife of Rossetti: Her Life and Death*. London: John Lane and Bodley Head, 1932.

Hunt, William Holman. *Pre-Raphaelitism and the Pre-Raphaelite Brotherhood*, 2 vols. London: Macmillan & Co., 1905

[Ingram, John] Don Felix de Salamanca, *pseud. The Philosophy of Handwriting*. London: Chatto & Windus, 1879.

Ives, Maura. *Christina Rossetti: A Descriptive Bibliography*. New Castle, DE: Oak Knoll Press, 2011.

Jackson, M. Phipps. 'Current Art: The New Gallery', pp. 289–95. *Magazine of Art*, vol. 15, 1892.

James, Henry. *The Golden Bowl*, 2 vols. New York: Scribner's, 1909.

Jansen, Leo, Hans Luijten and Nienke Bakker, eds. *Vincent van Gogh – The Letters*. Van Gogh Museum & Huygens ING, vangoghletters.org, 2009.

Jones, Kathleen. *Learning Not To Be First: The Life of Christina Rossetti*. Adlestrop: Windrush Press, 1991.

Kachur, Robert M. 'Repositioning the Female Christian Reader: Christina Rossetti as Tractarian Hermeneut in "The Face of the Deep"', pp. 193–214. *Victorian Poetry*, vol. 35, no. 2, 1997.

Kaston, Andrea J. 'Speaking Pictures: The Fantastic World of Christina Rossetti and Arthur Hughes', pp. 305–28. *Journal of Narrative Technique*, vol. 28, no. 3, 1998.

Keble, John. *The Christian Year* [1827], 16th edn. Oxford: Parker, 1837.

Keble, John. *Lectures on Poetry 1832–1841*, trans. Edward Kershaw Francis, 2 vols. Oxford: Clarendon Press, 1912.

Keble, John. *Occasional Papers and Reviews*. Oxford: Parker, 1877.

Keble, John. *On the Mysticism Attributed to the Early Fathers of the Church: Tracts for the Times*, no. 89. London: Rivington, 1841.

Kent, David A., ed. *The Achievement of Christina Rossetti*. Ithaca, NY: Cornell University Press, 1987.

Knoepflmacher, U. C. 'Avenging Alice: Christina Rossetti and Lewis Carroll', pp. 299–328. *Nineteenth-Century Literature*, vol. 41, no. 3, 1986.

Kooistra, Lorraine Janzen. 'Christina Rossetti (1830–1894)', pp. 164–82. *The Cambridge Companion to the Pre-Raphaelites*, ed. Elizabeth Prettejohn. Cambridge: Cambridge University Press, 2012.

Kooistra, Lorraine Janzen. *Christina Rossetti and Illustration: A Publishing History*. Athens: Ohio University Press, 2002.

Kooistra, Lorraine Janzen. 'Copyright and Control: Christina Rossetti and her Publishers', pp. 61–75. *Outsiders Looking In: The Rossettis Then and Now*, eds David Clifford and Laurence Roussillon. London: Anthem Press, 2004.

Kooistra, Lorraine Janzen. *Poetry, Pictures, and Popular Publishing: The Illustrated Gift Book and Victorian Visual Culture*. Athens: Ohio University Press, 2011.

de Leeuw, Ronald. 'George Henry Boughton and the "beautiful picture" in Van Gogh's 1876 sermon', pp. 48–61. *Van Gogh Museum Journal*, 1995.

Ludlow, Elizabeth. *Christina Rossetti and the Bible: Waiting with the Saints*. London: Bloomsbury, 2014.

Ludlow, Elizabeth. 'Christina Rossetti and the Pre-Raphaelites', pp. 427–40. *The Oxford Handbook of the Oxford Movement*, ed. Stewart J. Brown, Peter B. Nockles and James Pereiro. Oxford: Oxford University Press, 2017.

Macdonald, Stuart. *The History and Philosophy of Art Education*. London: University of London Press, 1970.

Manning, John. *The Emblem*. London: Reaktion, 2002.

Marillier, H. C. *Dante Gabriel Rossetti: An Illustrated Memorial of his Art and Life*. London: George Bell, 1899.

Marsh, Jan. *Christina Rossetti: A Literary Biography* [1994]. London: Faber & Faber, 2012.

Marsh, Jan. *Dante Gabriel Rossetti: Painter and Poet*. London: Weidenfeld & Nicolson, 1999.

Marsh, Jan. *The Pre-Raphaelite Sisterhood*. London: St Martin's Press, 1985.

Mason, Emma. '"A Sort of Aesthetico-Catholic revival": Christina Rossetti and the London Ritualist Scene', pp. 115–30. *Outsiders Looking In: The Rossettis Then and Now*, eds David Clifford and Laurence Roussillon. London: Anthem Press, 2004.

Mason, Emma. 'Christina Rossetti and the Doctrine of Reserve', pp. 196–219. *Journal of Victorian Culture*, vol. 7, iss. 2, 2002.

Mason, Emma. *Christina Rossetti: Poetry, Ecology, Faith*. Oxford: Oxford University Press, 2018.

Mason, Emma. '"Whales and all that move in the waters": Christina Rossetti's Ecology of Grace', pp. 69–84. *Victorian Sustainability in Literature and Culture*, ed. Wendy Parkins. London: Routledge, 2018.

Matthews, Samantha. 'Marketplaces', pp. 655–72. *The Oxford Handbook of Victorian Poetry*, ed. Matthew Bevis. Oxford: Oxford University Press, 2013.

Maxwell, Richard. 'Walter Scott, Historical Fiction, and the Genesis of the Victorian Illustrated Book', pp. 1–51. *The Victorian Illustrated Book*, ed. Richard Maxwell. Charlottesville: University Press of Virginia, 2002.

[National Institution] *The Exhibition of the National Institution of Fine Arts*. exh. cat. London: Portland Gallery, 1852.

Newman, Helen D. *James Collinson (aka 'The Dormouse')*. Foulsham: Reuben Books, 2016.

Newman, John Henry. 'John Keble' [1846], pp. 421–53. *Essays Critical and Historical*, vol. 2. London: Pickering, 1871.

Newman, John Henry. *Thoughts on the Ministerial Commission: Tracts for the Times*, no. 1. London: Rivington, 1833.

Nowell-Smith, Simon, ed. *Letters to Macmillan*. London: Macmillan & Co., 1967.

Oakley, Maroussia. *The Book and Periodical Illustrations of Arthur Hughes*. New Castle, DE: Oak Knoll Press, 2016.

Osborne, Victoria. 'A British Symbolist in Pre-Raphaelite Circles: Edward Robert Hughes RWS (1851–1914).' MPhil thesis, University of Birmingham, 2009.

O'Sullivan, Vincent. *Aspects of Wilde*. London: Constable, 1936.

Owens, Susan. 'Literature and the Aesthetic Movement', pp. 40–59. *The Cult of Beauty: The Aesthetic Movement 1860–1900*, eds Stephen Calloway and Lynn Federle Orr, exh. cat. London: V&A, 2011.

Owens, Susan. '"Straight Lines Are A National Want": South Kensington and Art Education Reform', pp. 75–81. *Art and Design for All: The Victoria and Albert Museum*, ed. Julius Bryant. London: V&A, 2011.

Packer, Lona Mosk, ed. *The Rossetti-Macmillan Letters*. Berkeley and Los Angeles: University of California Press, 1963.

Parkinson, Ronald. 'James Collinson', pp. 61–75. *Pre-Raphaelite Papers*, ed. Leslie Parris. London: Tate Gallery, 1984.

Payne, Christiana and Ann Sumner. *Objects of Affection: Pre-Raphaelite Portraits by John Brett*, exh. cat. Birmingham: Barber Institute of Fine Arts, University of Birmingham, 2010.

Peterson, Linda H. 'Christina Rossetti', pp. 422–38. *The Cambridge Companion to English Poets*, ed. Claude Rawson. Cambridge: Cambridge University Press, 2011.

Potter, Matthew. 'Fostering in the People the Purest Types of Beauty: Ford Madox Brown and Democratic Art Education', pp. 313–33. *Visual Culture in Britain*, vol. 15, no. 3, 2014.

The Pre-Raphaelites. exh. cat. London: Tate Gallery, 1984.

Prettejohn, Elizabeth. *The Art of the Pre-Raphaelites*. London: Tate, 2000.

Prettejohn, Elizabeth, ed. *The Cambridge Companion to the Pre-Raphaelites*. Cambridge: Cambridge University Press, 2012.

Proctor, Ellen A. *A Brief Memoir of Christina G. Rossetti*. London: SPCK, 1895.

Ricketts, Charles. *Self-Portrait, taken from the letters and journals of Charles Ricketts, R.A.*, ed. T. Sturge Moore and Cecil Lewis. London: Peter Davies, 1939.

Roberts, Leonard. *Arthur Hughes: His Life and Works: A Catalogue Raisonné*. Woodbridge: Antique Collectors' Club, 1997.

Roe, Dinah. *Christina Rossetti's Faithful Imagination: The Devotional Poetry and Prose*. Basingstoke: Palgrave Macmillan, 2006.

Roe, Dinah. *The Rossettis in Wonderland: A Victorian Family History*. London: Haus, 2011.

Rossetti, Christina. *Annus Domini; a prayer for each day of the year, founded on a text of Holy Scripture*. Oxford: James Parker, 1874.

Rossetti, Christina. *Called to be Saints: The Minor Festivals Devotionally Studied*. London: SPCK, 1881.

Rossetti, Christina. *Commonplace, and Other Short Stories*. London: Ellis, 1870.

Rossetti, Christina. *The Complete Poems* [2001], ed. R. W. Crump with notes and introduction by Betty S. Flowers. London: Penguin, 2005.

Rossetti, Christina. *The Face of the Deep: A Devotional Commentary on the Apocalypse*. London: SPCK, 1892.

Rossetti, Christina. 'The Fairy Prince Who Arrived Too Late', p. 36. *Macmillan's Magazine*, no. 8, May 1863.

Rossetti, Christina. *The Family Letters of Christina Georgina Rossetti*, ed. William Michael Rossetti. London: Brown, Langham, 1908.

Rossetti, Christina. *Goblin Market and Other Poems*. London: Macmillan & Co., 1862.

Rossetti, Christina. *Goblin Market, The Prince's Progress and other Poems*. London: Macmillan & Co., 1875.

Rossetti, Christina. *Letter and Spirit: Notes on the Commandments*. London: SPCK, 1883.

Rossetti, Christina. *The Letters of Christina Rossetti*, ed. Antony H. Harrison, 4 vols. Charlottesville: University Press of Virginia, 1997–2004.

Rossetti, Christina. *Maude: A Story for Girls*, ed. William Michael Rossetti. London: Bowden, 1897.

Rossetti, Christina. *Maude: Prose and Verse*, ed. William Michael Rossetti. Chicago, IL: Stone, 1897a.

Rossetti, Christina. *New Poems*, ed. William Michael Rossetti. London: Macmillan & Co., 1896.

Rossetti, Christina. *A Pageant and Other Poems*. London: Macmillan & Co., 1881.

Rossetti, Christina. *Poems: New and Enlarged Edition*. London: Macmillan & Co., 1890.

Rossetti, Christina. *The Poetical Works of Christina Georgina Rossetti. With Memoir and Notes &c*, ed. William Michael Rossetti. London: Macmillan & Co., 1904.

Rossetti, Christina. *The Prince's Progress and Other Poems*. London: Macmillan & Co., 1866.

Rossetti, Christina. *Seek and Find: A Double Series of Short Studies of the Benedicite*. London: SPCK, 1879.

Rossetti, Christina. *Selected Prose*, eds David A. Kent and P. G. Stanwood. Basingstoke: Macmillan & Co., 1998.

Rossetti, Christina. *Sing-Song: A Nursery Rhyme Book*. London: Routledge, 1872.

Rossetti, Christina. *Speaking Likenesses*. London: Macmillan & Co., 1874.

Rossetti, Christina. *Time Flies: A Reading Diary*. London: SPCK, 1885.

Rossetti, Christina. *Verses*. London: privately printed, 1847.

Rossetti, Christina. *Verses*. London: SPCK, 1893 (post-dated 1894).

Rossetti, Christina. *Verses* [1847]. Hammersmith: Eragny Press, 1906.

Rossetti, Dante Gabriel. *The Correspondence of Dante Gabriel Rossetti*, ed. William E. Fredeman, 10 vols. Cambridge: D. S. Brewer, 2002–15.

Rossetti, Dante Gabriel. *His Family-Letters: With a Memoir by William Michael Rossetti*, 2 vols. London: Ellis, 1895.

Rossetti, Gabriele. *A Versified Autobiography*, ed. William Michael Rossetti. London: Sands, 1901.

Rossetti, William Michael, ed. *Bibliography of the Works of Dante Gabriel Rossetti.* London: Ellis, 1905.

Rossetti, William Michael. *The Diary of W. M. Rossetti, 1870–1873*, ed. Odette Bornand. Oxford: Clarendon Press, 1977.

Rossetti, William Michael, ed. *The Family Letters of Christina Georgina Rossetti: With some Supplementary Letters and Appendices.* London: Brown, Langham, 1908.

Rossetti, William Michael, ed. *Præraphaelite Diaries and Letters.* London: Hurst and Blackett, 1900.

Rossetti, William Michael, ed. *Rossetti Papers 1862 to 1870: A Compilation.* London: Sands, 1903.

Rossetti, William Michael. *Selected Letters*, ed. Roger W. Peattie. University Park: Pennsylvania State University Press, 1990.

Rossetti, William Michael. *Some Reminiscences*, 2 vols. London: Brown, Langham, 1906.

Rota, Bertram. *Catalogue No.180: Books from the Libraries of Christina, Dante Gabriel and William Michael Rossetti*, with an introduction by William E. Fredeman. London: Rota, 1973.

Ruskin, John. *Modern Painters*, vol. 1 [1843], 4th edn. London: Smith, Elder & Co., 1848.

Salaman, Malcolm C. 'Lord Leverhulme's Pictures: His Modern Favourites', pp. 45–57. *The Studio*, vol. 82, no. 341, August 1921.

Scott, William Bell. *Autobiographical Notes*, ed. W. Minto, 2 vols. London: James R. Osgood, McIlvaine & Co., 1892.

Shields, Frederic. *The Life and Letters of Frederic Shields*, ed. Ernestine Mills. London: Longmans, Green & Co., 1912.

Staley, Allen. *The Pre-Raphaelite Landscape*, 2nd edn. New Haven and London: Yale University Press, 2001.

Stirling, A. M. W. *Life's Little Day: Some Tales and Other Reminiscences.* London: Thornton Butterworth, 1924.

Surtees, Virginia. *The Paintings and Drawings of Dante Gabriel Rossetti (1828–1882): A Catalogue Raisonné.* Oxford: Clarendon Press, 1971.

Taylor, Roger and Edward Wakeling. *Lewis Carroll Photographer. The Princeton University Library Albums.* Princeton, NJ: Princeton University Press, 2002.

Tennyson, G. B. *Victorian Devotional Poetry: The Tractarian Mode.* Cambridge, MA: Harvard University Press, 1981.

Thirlwell, Angela. *Into the Frame: The Four Loves of Ford Madox Brown.* London: Chatto & Windus, 2010.

Thirlwell, Angela. *William and Lucy: The Other Rossettis.* New Haven and London: Yale University Press, 2003.

Treuherz, Julian. *Ford Madox Brown: Pre-Raphaelite Pioneer*, exh. cat. Manchester: Manchester Art Gallery, 2011.

Treuherz, Julian, Elizabeth Prettejohn and Edwin Becker. *Dante Gabriel Rossetti*, exh. cat. Liverpool: Walker Art Gallery; London: Thames & Hudson, 2003.

Tromans, Nicholas. *The Art of G. F. Watts.* London: Paul Holberton Publishing, 2017.

Trowbridge, Serena. *Christina Rossetti's Gothic.* London: Bloomsbury Academic, 2015.

Waller, John O. 'Christ's Second Coming: Christina Rossetti and the Premillenarianist William Dodsworth', pp. 465–82. *Bulletin of the New York Public Library*, vol. 73, 1969.

Weintraub, Stanley. *Four Rossettis: A Victorian Biography.* London: W. H. Allen, 1978.

White, Gleeson. 'Children's Books and their Illustrators.' *The Studio: Special Winter Number.* London: The Studio, 1897–1898.

Williams, Isaac. *The Cathedral, or the Catholic and Apostolic Church in England.* Oxford: Parker, 1839.

Wilton, Andrew. 'Symbolism in Britain', pp. 11–33. *The Age of Rossetti, Burne-Jones and Watts: Symbolism in Britain 1860–1910*, ed. Andrew Wilton and Robert Upstone, exh. cat. London: Tate Gallery, 1997.

Woolf, Virginia. '"I am Christina Rossetti"' [1930], pp. 237–44. *The Common Reader: Second Series.* London: Hogarth Press, 1932.

Woolford, John. 'The Advent of Christina Rossetti', pp. 618–39. *Review of English Studies*, vol. 62, no. 256, 2011.

Sources of Epigraphs

Chapter One
'Two Enigmas (II)'

Chapter Two
'In an Artist's Studio'

Chapter Three
from *The Face of the Deep*

Chapter Four
'Goblin Market'

Chapter Five
'Twilight Calm'

Index

Page numbers in *italic* refer to the illustrations

Picture Credits

© AF Fotografie/Alamy Stock Photo (fig. 1.15)
© 2018 Andrew G. Prior (fig. 1.1)
© Ashmolean Museum, University of Oxford WA.PA.77.4011 Ashmolean Pissarro Collection (fig. 4.28)
© Ashmolean Museum, University of Oxford WA1977.77 (fig. 2.3)
© Archival Playboy Magazine material, 1973 by Playboy, used with permission, all rights reserved (fig. 4.32)
© Barry Friedman, New York (fig. 5.6)
© Birmingham Museums Trust (figs 1.10, 1.16, 2.18, 4.6, 4.8, 5.11)
© bpk-Bildagentur/Neue Pinakothek, Munich (fig. 5.7)
© Bonhams 1793 Ltd (fig. 5.14)
© British Library Board. All Rights Reserved / Bridgeman Images (figs 1.3, 1.6, 1.21, 2.32, 3.20, 3.22)
© The Cheltenham Trust and Cheltenham Borough Council / Bridgeman Images (fig. 5.15)
© 2018 Christie's Images Limited (fig. 5.1)
© 2014 Christie's Images Limited (fig. 5.4)
© 2013 Christie's Images Limited (figs 2.1, 5.10)
© 2004 Christie's Images Limited (figs 2.28, 4.24)
© 1998 Christie's Images Limited (fig. 5.9)
© Collection of Stephen Calloway (figs 1.19, 2.16, 2.33, 3.21, 3.23, 4.1, 4.2, 4.3, 4.4, 4.5, 4.7, 4.10, 4.11, 4.12, 4.13, 4.14, 4.15, 4.16, 4.17, 4.18, 4.21, 4.22, 4.23, 4.27, 4.29, 4.30, 4.31)
© Delaware Art Museum, Wilmington, USA / Samuel and Mary R. Bancroft Memorial / Bridgeman Images (fig. 1.8)
© Fitzwilliam Museum, Cambridge (fig. 2.26)
© Hilary Paynter (fig. 4.33)
© Harry Ransom Center, The University of Texas at Austin (figs 1.7, 1.18)
© Illustrated London News Ltd/Mary Evans (fig. 0.4)
© Johannesburg Art Gallery, South Africa / Bridgeman Images (fig. 1.9)
© John Bolton (fig. 4.35)
© The Leicester Galleries (fig. 2.27, 4.19)
© By Kind Permission of the Warden and Fellows of Keble College, Oxford / Bridgeman Images (fig. 2.13)
© National Portrait Gallery, London (figs 0.2, 1.4, 2.23, 2.29, 2.30, 2.31, 3.1)
© National Trust / Fenton House (fig. 4.9)
© National Trust / Sophia Farley and Claire Reeves (fig. 2.15)
© National Trust Images/Derrick E. Witty (fig. 2.22)
© Manchester Art Gallery, UK / Bridgeman Images (fig 1.5)
© Mark Samuels Lasner Collection, University of Delaware Library (fig 0.5)
© Mark Samuels Lasner Collection, University of Delaware Library/ Image provided by Amber Kehoe (fig. 2.24)
© Martin Ware (fig. 4.34)
© Museum of New Zealand Te Papa Tongarewa, Wellington, New Zealand / Purchased 1912 by Public Subscription / Bridgeman Images (fig. 5.12)
© Punch Magazine Cartoon Archive www.punch.co.uk (fig. 1.13)
© Private Collection (figs 0.1, 1.2, 1.11, 2.6, 2.8, 2.20, 2.25, 3.4, 3.25, 4.25, 4.26, 5.2)
© Royal Museums of Fine Arts of Belgium, Brussels / Archives of Contemporary Art in Belgium (fig. 5.5)
© Sotheby's (figs 1.2, 5.13)
© 2018 Tate, London (figs 2.7, 2.10, 2.11, 2.14)
© The Trustees of the British Museum (figs 1.12, 2.5)
© Trustees of the Royal Watercolour Society, London, UK / Bridgeman Images (fig. 5.8)
© The Cleveland Museum of Art (fig. 0.3)
© Unknown collection; Photograph National Portrait Gallery, London (fig. 2.9)
© Victoria and Albert Museum, London (figs 2.4, 2.21, 5.3)
© Watts Gallery Trust (figs 2.2, 2.17, 4.20)
© William Morris Gallery, London Borough of Waltham Forest (2.19)
Private Collection. Photographs British Library Board (figs 1.17, 3.2, 3.3, 3.5, 3.6, 3.7, 3.8, 3.9, 3.10, 3.11, 3.12, 3.13, 3.14, 3.15, 3.16, 3.17, 3.18, 3.19, 3.24, 3.26, 3.27, 3.28). Please contact Watts Gallery Trust in writing with information regarding the copyright of this item.
Public Domain – Metropolitan Museum of Art, New York (figs 1.14, 1.20)
Public Domain – Yale Center for British Art, Paul Mellon Collection (fig. 2.12)

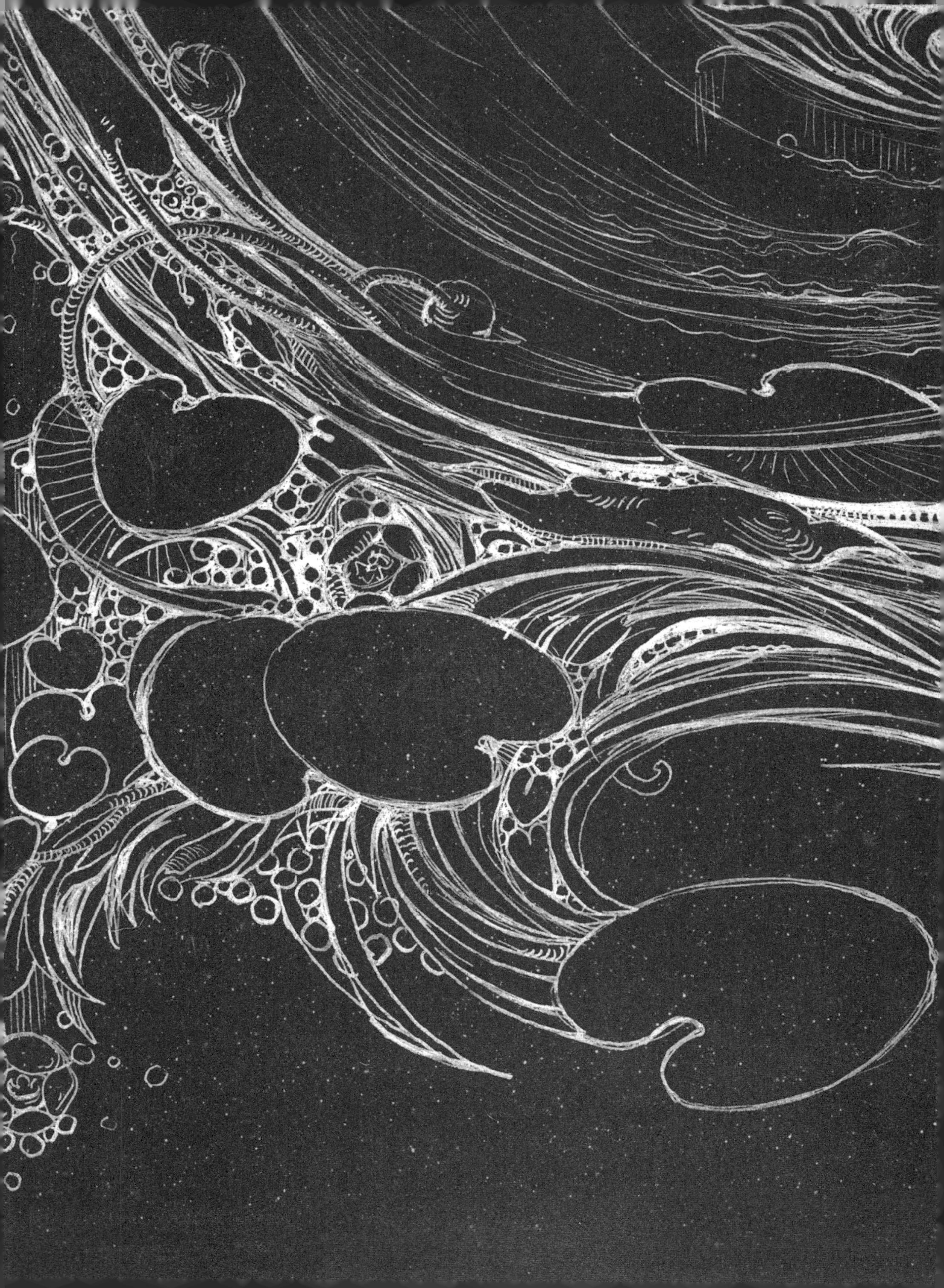